EFFECTIVE INTERNATIONAL JOINT VENTURE MANAGEMENT

EFFECTIVE INTERNATIONAL JOINT VENTURE MANAGEMENT

Practical Legal Insights
for
Successful Organization
and
Implementation

Ronald Charles Wolf

M.E. Sharpe
Armonk, New York
London, England

Library of Congress Cataloging-in-Publication Data

Wolf, Ronald Charles.
    Effective international joint venture management : practical legal insights for
successful organization and implementation / Ronald Charles Wolf.
        p. cm.
    Includes bibliographical references and index.
    ISBN 0-7656-0547-3 (hc : alk. paper)
    1. Joint ventures—Law and legislation. 2. Joint ventures—Management. I. Title.

K1309.W649 2000
346′.0682—dc21   99-055641

Printed in the United States of America

The paper used in this publication meets the minimum requirements of
American National Standard for Information Sciences
Permanence of Paper for Printed Library Materials,
ANSI Z 39.48-1984.

BM (c)   10   9   8   7   6   5   4   3   2   1

TABLE OF CONTENTS

EFFECTIVE INTERNATIONAL JOINT VENTURE MANAGEMENT

INTRODUCTION

PART ONE

0.1 THE NATURE OF THE INTERNATIONAL JOINT VENTURE: THEORY, PRACTICE, AND POWER

This reference book is a survey of the practical steps and the intellectual choices that must be made in forming an international joint venture. It also offers many recommendations as to its successful management, so that it works, with satisfaction to its partners, no matter what their capital participation.

The advice is from a lawyer, a consultant to companies wanting to establish joint ventures in countries far from their home office. Pragmatic solutions are given to the complex economic and legal relationships present in the average international joint venture. A further step is taken.

For the most part, the practice of international joint ventures has been experience improving on prior knowledge. The book seeks to unify the practice and theory of international joint ventures into language accessible to its participants. It strives for plain words.

Legal instruments define rights and obligations. They also conceal power. In the commercial world, power struggles are supported or impeded by legal instruments. It is imperative, consequently, to understand initially the basic outline of the international joint venture as reflected in written material. This will provide a helpful, continual background for the entire book. The documentary core contains the following:

3

- the letter of intent, which is the general economic vision of the proposed transaction
- the joint venture agreement, which is the constitution between the parties
- the shareholders' agreement, which is a bill of rights, a declaration of shareholder privileges
- the articles of incorporation, which are as the rules of a parliament, the guidelines of how business is conducted internally
- various ancillary agreements such as technology licenses or distribution contracts

With these instruments, a joint venture can be properly created. There can be many more. Nevertheless, the average joint venture will fit into the preceding mold as one lengthy instrument can contain many purposes. Documents are the instruments of lawyering. The preceding list could also serve for a domestic joint venture, between companies from the same jurisdiction. What causes an international joint venture to be a separate field?

Without intending to create an exhaustive list, some relevant topics are as follows:

- absentee ownership
- the frequent presence of a minority ownership
- shareholder rights without special legislative protection from foreign laws
- lack of legal and accounting transparency due to local laws
- unfamiliar legal forms for companies
- regulation of foreign investment
- limits to foreign capital participation
- lack of familiarity with the legal system
- difficulty in judicial enforcement of legal rights due to ownership from diverse legal systems
- cultural and language differences

International joint ventures are thus business and legal concerns that do business in another country. An understanding requires an exploration into many fields (economics, law, accounting, finance), and of course each of these major areas has further logical subdivisions. The common link is human behavior.

It should be no surprise, therefore, to find the economic origins of international joint ventures in the necessity to collaborate to gain profit, which at the same time is the principal cause for friction. With time, conflict often replaces cooperation. If the joint venture is successful, a majority partner may try to force the minority partner out of the venture. When this is not possible, attempts are made to dominate and determine the major decisions to be made without regard to the interests of minority owners. If the joint venture is a failure, or struggling along, then each partner seeks to extract the utmost benefit with the minimum investment and effort.

This is the economic background, but the practice of an international joint venture is also the realization of power and its curtailment. An international joint venture with no functional sanctions quickly becomes disorganized, a platform for antagonism. The theory of an international joint venture must recognize this empirical fact and protect all interests against the abuse of power. The underlying thesis of our exposition is law and economics but also the regulation of power. If properly harnessed, collaboration will be fomented. The practice of international joint ventures is a lesson in the cult of power and its artful use.

Our subject material is essentially concerned with the *everyman international joint venture,* the vast majority of commercial international joint ventures, with a moderate amount of capital, established in various parts of the world, by medium and small enterprises. A great deal of attention in the text is addressed to this pervasive, mercantile venture.

The everyman international joint venture is an overseas version of the domestic, closely held corporation, sometimes called the close corporation, where there is an identity of personages between ownership and management, a small organization, the lack of a market for the shares as they are not quoted on any public stock exchange, a shared economic vision, restrictions on the sale of equity interests to others, and, of course, cultural differences.

In spite of their moderate financial resources, the everyman international joint ventures are not the occasional economic event. On the contrary, they are the galleons of global mercantilism. In number, they vastly outweigh the mega mergers or newsmaking transnational acquisitions. They usually do not make economic headlines, but the cumulative economic consequences are considerable, introducing new products, employing people, creating a trained cadre of executives, and establishing the necessary infrastructures. Without them, the frontiers of international trade would have hardly changed.

As individual explorers once discovered new and strange spice markets, executives from diverse capitals are encountering one another at trade fairs or professional congresses. Ideas are exchanged, which frequently lead to the desire to form a company, pool capital, and share other resources to take advantage of a perceived economic opportunity, a market not yet explored. The principles and practices enunciated in this book are addressed to these international joint ventures yet to be formed and to furnish the international manager with theory and practical knowledge not easily available.

Our review will be directed toward all international joint ventures but the predominance of the everyman international joint venture will command substantial attention. Nevertheless, the analysis made and the practical suggestions given are applicable to all international joint ventures, including those established by multinationals and normally forming part of a global strategy for penetration of world markets. Defenses against the manipulations of an unscrupulous majority owner, agreed restrictions on budgets or capital augments, limitations on salaries to key executives are issues equally applicable to the global, mega international joint ventures as well as to their modest counterparts.

Ultimately, this textbook seeks to be a useful companion and corrective influence to experience.

0.1.1 DEFINITION OF AN INTERNATIONAL JOINT VENTURE

Repeated references have been made to the term *international joint ventures*. A joint venture, whether international or domestic, is not another term for a *joint adventure,* in spite of its grammatical affinity. The latter is an expression revealing its historical origins when collaboration on an overseas commercial enterprise was formulated primarily through a contract. Nor is an international joint venture another name for an incorporated partnership. In the legal classification of companies, an incorporated partnership is usually confined to a profession, such as a group of physicians, that is permitted to incorporate for many purposes except limiting professional liability. As will become evident with further analysis and descriptive material, a joint venture can be achieved through various methods and adopt multiple forms. But we do need at least a tentative definition, no matter how imperfect, to begin our study.

The expression *joint venture* in this text refers to a particular form of doing business by one party in a jurisdiction, either foreign or domestic, by means of a stable, permanent legal entity with another party, for a term, usually indefinite, with economic independence and a lawful commercial purpose.

An international joint venture arises when the joint venture is doing business in a jurisdiction that is not the country of origin of at least one of the parties. When all the parties are citizens of the country, we then have a domestic joint venture. It is not hard to imagine exceptions to the common sense of this definition that make it inapplicable. Such is the nature of the law. However, it is probably how most business professionals would describe the situation. The key words are *stability,* a *legal form,* a *partner,* a *term,* an *economic independence,* and a *lawful object.* Time and time again, we will refer to and analyze this combination of concepts.

The use of the word *lawful* might seem out of place, but it is intended to exclude from our consideration cartels, monopolies, business trusts formed for anticompetitive purposes, holding companies structured to indirectly influence and control markets, in short, a wide variety of legal forms whose ultimate object, if transparent, would be considered *unlawful.* Our sole concern is with the typical commercial international joint venture formed for multiple legitimate purposes such as encountering new markets, improving efficiency, complementing skills, or diversifying the product line.

The term *international joint venture* is specific as it refers to the material to be studied; it is also a generality because the material investigated covers a wide variety of circumstances. International joint ventures have been an area of specialization primarily developed in the collaboration that exists between entrepreneurs and lawyers; it has grown up from commercial origins, practical necessities, resolutions to problems devised by managers and lawyers; it has been less theory and more reality. Not being held initially within any theoretical framework, the international joint venture has been adapted to confront an immense diversity of factual situations. As material to be studied, it has had almost an underground existence, finding reflection in documents that are filed away in the offices of the companies and their lawyers. This book seeks, among other objectives, to extract from these files, full of practical experience, the recurring topics and documentation that justify a treatment of the topic of international joint ventures.

The term *international joint venture* also contains a perspective. To an individual, any country other than his own is a foreign jurisdiction. A U.S. corporation purchasing a Swedish corporation is doing business, according to the U.S. corporation, in a foreign jurisdiction. Were the Swedish corporation the purchasing entity in the United States, its conclusion would be the same except in reverse. Consequently, we may ask ourselves: are there repeated problems and legal answers that can be made about international joint ventures without reference to any jurisdiction? A problem dependent on merely a point of view would seem to annul any generalizations. In fact, it is actually the displacement of one commercial entity to a foreign jurisdiction that forms the basis of so many of the unique problems inherent in international joint ventures.

Consequently, this is one of the other objectives that this book pursues, to put before the reader ownership and management issues that occur frequently in international joint ventures because of being in a foreign jurisdiction, with different laws, a different business culture, but to which experience has provided valid solutions. It is not merely a point of view. It is being elsewhere that confers on the international joint venture its distinctive problems and eventually the nature of the material needed to be studied.

Naturally, there are limits to generalizations. We can reasonably expect that countries exist, such as in Asia, where the laws are so different that the legal experience derived from common law, for example, the UK or United States, or civil law countries, such as France or Spain, has little relevance. But the common law and civil law countries represent a substantial part of the industrial world and these systems of law have had worldwide influence. The principles to be enunciated, therefore, will find extensive global application and usefulness. This book does not draw on an assumed body of international commercial law. That there are moral codes of behavior that affect merchants from all over the world is no doubt part of the human condition. However, no attempt is made to encounter such typical patterns. This book is concerned with ideas and principles that rest in part on the usual laws of common law and civil law countries, but also in developing an analysis and raising for discussion problems that arise from the collaboration between people. Practical suggestions are made that will indicate possible legal solutions adapted to the local jurisdiction.

As we are going to investigate fundamental principles and investigate the structures of international joint ventures, we must always be cognizant that there are many areas of commercial activity, such as accounting, taxation, or concentrations of companies, where specialized knowledge is necessary. The application of such knowledge and its relevance to the fundamentals of international joint ventures are similar to an automobile code. There are the fundamentals of driving, that is, the basics of forming an international joint venture, and then there are special rules to be applied in certain circumstances such as driving on a highway or driving on a dirt road. In this book, we are concerned with the basic rules, although, of course, at times, it will be necessary to make reference or call attention to particular laws in the form of a red alert if the road becomes twisting.

0.1.2 SYNONYMS FOR AN INTERNATIONAL JOINT VENTURE

As international joint ventures form part of the stream of international commerce, many phrases are used with variable meanings in an attempt to capture in a few words some of the ideas associated with these words. Before illustrating some of the synonyms used, it is necessary to remind the reader that a joint venture as used throughout this book is not equal to a joint adventure, or joint partnership, or any other common pursuit of a commercial objective, that is only expressed through the form of a contract.

This was the early, historical origins of the modern day joint venture, but it has significantly outgrown its origins both as to complexity and adaptability to different legal forms. Today, the term *joint adventure* is an oddity of grammar, hardly used. A *joint partnership* is a vague expression for the true partnership. Although created by contract, it is properly designated a *partnership*.

Presently, the designation *international joint venture* encompasses a wide variety of concepts usually contained in expressions used by others such as

- co-partnering arrangements
- cross-border cooperation
- cross-border mergers
- international acquisitions
- international cooperation
- international mergers
- joint adventure
- joint partnership
- mergers and acquisitions (M&A)
- strategic alliances

Clearly, a great deal of alternate and variable terminology exists in the literature. These are helpful, verbal shortcuts. When such phrases are used, they are normally intended to describe a particular form of an international joint venture or include the international joint venture as one way of doing business among various options. Other times, these terms do not mean an international joint venture, but a different approach to engaging in international commerce such as technology licensing, franchising, or even a distribution contract.

Thus, the terms *strategic alliance* and *international cooperation,* as well as similar nomenclature, are fruitful in calling attention to the various methods of operating a business abroad and in revealing the broad scope of legal alliances possible, in highlighting the myriad techniques entrepreneurs have developed through trial and experience. Such descriptions are often contained in technical literature that describe a wide variety of related, important topics such as financing, valuation of assets, taxes, and human resources issues, all significant components of a successful international joint venture. With such a wide diversity of designations, there is naturally a difficulty in choosing a term that finds universal acceptance. However, in this book, *international joint venture,* supported by the definition already given, will prove to be more precise, yet elastic, in conformity with judicial decisions, and corresponds to commercial reality.

With these preliminary remarks, we can now consider the formal structure of this book, which will be in accordance with the following topical outline, although in some instances, more than one chapter is necessary for a particular subject, such as formation or documentation.

0.1.3 WHY COMPANIES CHOOSE INTERNATIONAL JOINT VENTURES FOR DOING BUSINESS

When thinking of the best way to do business abroad, there is a variety of legal possibilities. There are distribution contracts, agency relationships, franchises, and, of course, the various licenses regarding patents, copyrights, trade secrets, and know-how. This list is by no means complete. Yet, as a manner for initiating business in a foreign jurisdiction, the popularity of international joint ventures suggests that there are valid economic reasons for choosing this vehicle. We will explore the various advantages that frequently impel a company to elect to do business abroad through a joint venture company.

0.1.4 FORMATION

The formation process involves an analysis of two different processes. Initially, there must be chosen the method by which a joint venture relationship will be created. This can be done by acquisition of an equity interest, such as purchasing a share(s) in an existing company. It can also be done by forming a company; or establishing a relationship by contract, which is quite common in unincorporated joint ventures. However, the method does not tell us the final legal form of the joint venture. A company can be formed, but what will be the legal form of the company? It can be a share corporation; or a private limited liability company; or a partnership. There are many alternatives. Consequently, the formation process requires an investigation into what is the most appropriate method and what is the most appropriate legal form. They are separate thoughts, involving different analytical elements, and will require separate discussion.

0.1.5 CAPITAL STRUCTURE AND NEGOTIATIONS

The theory of how an international joint venture is constructed will prepare us for determining if the capital structure of the projected joint venture assists in achieving the commercial objectives without compromising shareholder rights. This will require an understanding of the relationship between capital and corporate control; accounting implications; minimum percentages necessary to obtain veto rights; alternatives to capital contributions; and some aspects regarding debt.

There is a general review as to negotiations. In our presentation, negotiations make more sense after the basic economic facts have been understood, not before. A financial and commercial investigation of the target company or potential partner should precede earnest discussion. With this knowledge and the decision to form a joint venture taken, we will then need to examine the indispensable documentation.

0.1.6 DOCUMENTATION, INCLUDING THE SHAREHOLDERS' AGREEMENT

The study of the international joint venture is an examination of multiple documentation, another objective of this book. Naturally, the commitment to paper of the commercial purpose must find expression in legal documents. The international joint venture is substantially dependent on multiple documents for the elements involved are diverse, varied, many merely commercial, such as ancillary supply contracts; others, an expression of ownership, such as dividend rights; others relevant to management, such as annual budgets or capital expenditures.

Of critical relevancy is the appreciation that the typical international joint venture is reliant on joint venture documentation complementary to the articles of the company. Out of a basic list of dozens of important issues to ownership and management, the vast majority must be secured through documentation in addition to the basic articles of the joint venture company. Corporate executives responsible for originating and implementing international joint ventures thus need to have a solid understanding of the essential legal documents, their function, what ownership and managerial issues have critical relevance, in what documents these rights can be protected, and why one document may be more appropriate than another.

The source of ownership power and management control is derived from a variety of legal documents, simple in their concept and purpose. Our investigation will audit these essential conceptual tools corporate management needs to comprehend, so as to protect rights and to acquire authority. One legal document may be more appropriate for ownership rights, another for management functions. More importantly, some rights are more firmly consecrated in one legal document or source than in another. Not all origins of power are equal in duration or immune from being diminished.

Of major importance to successful documentation will be the shareholders' agreement, which permits minority rights to be secured and which permits an item-by-item discussion and resolution of multiple commercial facets of the international joint venture. Material that cannot be easily transposed to the company articles, such as budget limitations, salaries, capital expenditures, hiring of key personnel, can find adequate expression in the shareholders' agreement. This agreement is one of the paramount legal instruments used to customize an international joint venture. It is consequently useful and beneficial to have a general understanding of the advantages of this instrument so crucial to management objectives.

0.1.7 DUE DILIGENCE PROCEDURES

When an international joint venture is formed through the purchase of an interest in an existing company, a recurring uncertainty is a proper identification of what is being bought, the status of the entity that owns the assets and a determination of the economic and legal culture of the site of the joint venture. Contained in this simple description is a range of information to be garnered that can be truly staggering depending on the entities involved, the complexity of the joint venture, what has been negotiated, and the laws of the foreign jurisdiction in question.

Do the financial statements accurately reflect the accounts of the seller? What will happen to the business during the interim period between signing the contract and the purchase? What shares are outstanding? Are there financial instruments that confer the right to a conversion into equity? What is the management structure? Personnel history? There is probably no limit to the legitimate questions a potential partner or buyer can raise concerning a purchase.

In view of the substantial depth of material that could be determined, traditional questions have been developed that form part of due diligence procedures, a phrase meaning to indicate the steps a potential partner or buyer will take to ensure his investment is predicated on facts correctly represented to him as well. The material to be obtained can be voluminous and one of the other objectives of this book will be to indicate the essential material needed for the most elementary joint venture.

0.1.8 THE PROTECTION OF OWNERSHIP RIGHTS, INCLUDING MANAGEMENT FUNCTIONS

One of our stated objectives is to encounter the repetitive, vital ownership rights and management issues that are part of international joint ventures. In addition to the right product in the right market, the success of any international joint venture will be usually the happy combination of two elements: ownership rights and management power. It is this dual axis of ownership and management that is both the motive for the international joint venture and its ultimate success, the same axis as profit and efficiency. There cannot be management without ownership; but there cannot be profit when there is mismanagement. The proper expression and protection of ownership rights and management functions ensures the prosperity of the international joint venture. These are not static concepts.

What rights are needed to ensure distribution of dividends? How can one owner prevent another owner from driving it out of the company by increased calls for augments of capital? How can one partner ensure he will have authority over the distribution division of the international joint venture? Or the financial department? How can the majority rule of the board of directors on vital management issues be curtailed by the minority partner? These are typical questions for which standard solutions have been devised through experience.

A further objective of this book has to be the protection of the minority interest, for management by a minority interest is not common. But the minority interest does not have to seek to have management domination; it will be satisfactory if it can participate in management, or perhaps have control over one managerial area. It is possible to have a minimal ownership interest and substantial management authority. Management rights are separate from ownership rights and their exercise does not have to be linked in direct proportion to traditional ownership. Majority ownership does not compel majority management control. Minority ownership does not have to obligate taking a minority role in management. Minority interests can have absolute management control.

Shareholder rights normally confer managerial functions that are a consequence of ownership. But management is a separate legal concept from ownership and this study will demonstrate how ample management rights can be secured even though derived only from ownership, which is in the minority. This presentation is important because many international joint ventures are formed in which one entity or more holds only a minority ownership interest. International joint ventures do not mean all parties have the same amount of ownership. However, many minority owners expect to have a responsible participation in the management of the joint venture. If management rights are not to be dependent on simple calculations of ownership, a knowledge of how this can be achieved becomes paramount.

In those international joint ventures in which there is an unequal division of ownership, it is critical for the minority owner to have protection from the sheer mathematical force of a superior vote. Having a majority should not reasonably mean the right to control or manage the international joint venture without interference. A difference of 2 percent (51/49) should not logically confer absolute power. It is a legal conclusion which often contradicts the economics of joint venture.

International joint ventures will succeed when the various partners are obligated to seek solutions to any differences. When there is a majority/minority division of equity, the containment of majority voting power by several legal techniques produces compromise. A successful international joint venture thus means management power by all parties. Not just one. Management power does not have to be a consequence of capital voting strength. This conclusion can be reached by the parties understanding what minority rights need to be protected, negotiating a sensible compromise on these rights, and ensuring their presence in the proper document.

0.1.9 DISPUTE RESOLUTION AND TERMINATION

Dissension is a common occurrence in an international joint venture and many of the techniques described in this book are intended to reduce conflict, support collaboration, and ensure to the greatest extent possible that the common, shared commercial experience will be fruitful.

An additional objective, therefore, is to present suggestions as to peaceful forms of resolving differences between international joint venture partners and what legal concepts are available to this end. Litigation only becomes the province of lawyers when all avenues of reconciliation have been exhausted. Too often, management does not have the proper mechanisms created within the joint venture for informally resolving situations of conflict. If one side becomes stubborn, the other side has no available procedures to appeal to, other than a court of law or arbitration. Most international joint venture documents either detail what law will be applicable in the event of conflict or else recite how arbitration will be initiated and before whom. There are other alternatives, which might be called *informal corporate dispute procedures,* that permit the parties to air their differences and hear the opinions of others. Very often, conflict at a lower platform of the hierarchy, at the subsidiary level, for example, is considered a tempest in a teapot by a remote board of directors.

Naturally, strife will not always find a compromise in a relaxed, boardroom atmosphere. There are many alternatives to dispute resolution that range from the simple presentation of differences to a board of directors to recourse to third parties. There are the possibilities of conciliation, mediation, and adjudication, all with their specific characteristics and appropriate use. When all extra-judicial solutions have failed, or if they do not exist, arbitration or litigation must be considered. Going to court is not simply drafting pleadings. The outcome of litigation will be influenced substantially by the law regulating the transaction and where the litigation will take place. These issues can be conditioned by the joint venture documentation. However, dispute is not the only reason that may cause an international joint venture to end.

It may happen that the joint venture does not obtain the results foreseen or external events intervene, such as nationalization or privatization. This causes the parties, or one of them, to invoke a reason for terminating the joint venture. In this context, termination implies a previously agreed-on course of action that permits one or more parties to receive back their capital investment or a part of it and effectively withdraw from the joint venture. It is a voluntary course of action resulting in the collaboration ceasing.

However, there will be situations in which termination is not voluntary but arising because of a contract right. One party may believe there has been a breach of the joint venture agreement and withdraws from the joint venture, causing it to dissolve. Or there may be a deadlock that results in an inability of the board of directors to proceed on a day-to-day operational basis because no decisions can be made. For every "yes," there is a corresponding "no." The joint venture agreement may have foreseen this situation and details how termination will be regulated.

Termination of the international joint venture raises many questions, ranging from what constitutes a reason for termination to the procedures to be followed, their consequences, and the rights and obligations of the participants toward each other and the joint venture company. Termination is thus not merely "bringing a matter to a conclusion." It often creates "material for the future." As many as possible of these problems should be foreseen in the joint venture documentation.

0.1.10 THE CLOSING PROCESS

The joint venture documentation creates a series of circumstances that indicates the sequence of steps leading to the formation of the international joint venture. These events proceed according to fairly standard procedures and there is a summary of the usual agendum indicated in Chapter Ten. This will provide to the corporate manager an overall view of the mechanics of forming an international joint venture.

0.1.11 SUMMARY

The major linear objectives of this book are, accordingly, an analysis, by broad headings:

- formation
- capital structure
- documentation
- due diligence procedures
- protection of minority interests
- dispute resolution and termination
- the closing

There are also broad objectives to be heeded. As business entities are dynamic organizations, classifications assist in understanding, but there is always considerable interrelation. What is needed during this era, which is witnessing a profusion of international joint venture formation, is a general understanding by management of how such joint ventures are created, the recurring difficult management and ownership questions, the safeguards that need to be constructed to protect minority rights, the investigatory procedures to ensure that the representations of the forthcoming partner are correct, and a general appreciation of the vital issues international joint ventures raise so that, even before counsel is retained, all parties are aware of a number of unresolved problems that need to be further discussed.

The appropriateness of this book, when considering the various contributions already made by other writers, lies in its approach to a consolidation of international joint venture legal theory and a realistic description of the practice of forming an international joint venture. The formation of an international joint venture has largely been an art, almost a trade, the province of a specialized group of professionals. A substantial revelation of this craft should permit management to better understand and control more effectively any international joint venture undertaken. There is an urgency for a multidisciplinary, pragmatic approach with an emphasis on plain text writing and an avoidance of legal jargon.

For corporate managers, it is the international joint venture that will be the chosen legal vehicle used to form an alliance in another jurisdiction. It is the international joint venture that is inevitably chosen as the legal shelter or vehicle required for international alliances and cooperation as it contains the commercial flexibility needed for such endeavors. It is the international joint venture that includes the multiple legal alternatives such as mergers, acquisitions, establishment of subsidiaries, contractual arrangements designated consortiums, and all the heterogeneous forms of such legal structures that have made it the preferred form for companies engaging in alliances with other foreign entities. The alliance is the result; the international joint venture is the form.

Why management so frequently makes this choice forms one of the themes of Chapter One.

PART TWO

0.2 TERMINOLOGY

Various commercial and legal concepts require a formulation of a definition, no matter how imperfect. This can be reasonably done only after some discussion and analysis. Certain critical ideas, such as an *international joint venture,* have already been defined, but without further commentary, its significance will be lost. Therefore, we will reserve for Chapter Three a more detailed and hopefully profitable review of the meaning of a domestic and an international joint venture. For the moment, we need to clarify frequently used words whose precise meaning in a context is merely descriptive of a situation.

0.2.1 FOREIGN INVESTOR, HOME JURISDICTION, FOREIGN JURISDICTION, HOST COUNTRY, AND NATIONAL OR LOCAL INVESTOR

In our discussions, the corporate entity or individual making an investment out of its jurisdiction, what is colloquially called "abroad," is denominated the "foreign investor" and the foreign partner the "national investor" or "local investor." Thus, "Chicago Oil" is a foreign investor, from the home jurisdiction of Illinois, when it forms a subsidiary abroad in Kenya, the foreign jurisdiction, with Kenya Petroleum Corp., the national investor. Kenya is also the host country because it is extending as a protection to the foreign investor its laws and governmental institutions. These descriptions represent the viewpoint of the host country. Chicago Oil is the foreign investor because it comes from another country to do business in Kenya. Consequently, the reader contemplating an investment overseas, or in another jurisdiction, is the "foreign investor."

0.2.2 VENTURE PARTY, PARTNERS, AND OWNERS

How to describe the participants in a joint venture can be verbally awkward. One common expression is *venture party,* singular, and *venture parties,* plural. These are common words to lawyers, but normally require explanation to others. Other writers simply use *foreign investor* and *national investor.* Business people usually say *partners* or *owners.* This is a perfectly good description. *Partners* or *owners* means the entities, individuals or companies, having equity interests in the joint venture company. *Partners* in this use is its commercial vernacular sense, meaning cooperation by individual or corporate entities. It avoids having to set forth with legal precision the actual capital participation and under what form.

Lawyers shy away from this usage because the word *partners* conveys, and rightly so, a specific legal form known as a *partnership,* with its own set of rules. However, it is how managers see their foreign investment, a partnership with another entity, partnership of course in the informal, nonlegal sense of doing business with someone.

Owners is an even vaguer term because it conveys no information as to the nature of the entity, neither its legal form nor the nature of the ownership interest. Nevertheless, similar to the word *partners,* its usage is so ingrained that it facilitates reading if we follow the custom. Consequently, this usage is also utilized in this book, and if ever a legal partnership is intended, it will be evident, or if it is necessary to know how an ownership interest is acquired, this will also be explained.

0.2.3 OPERATING COMPANY, LOCAL COMPANY, OBJECT CORPORATION, TARGET CORPORATION, JOINT VENTURE VEHICLE, OR JOINT VENTURE FORM

The operating company, local company, object corporation, target corporation, target company, joint venture vehicle, or joint venture form means the legal structure chosen by the foreigner and the national for their common commercial efforts in the host country. All that is intended is to indicate that there exists a common legal structure utilized by a foreign and national partner or sought—targeted—by one or both. The variety of words is to assist ease of reading.

Finally, an observation about consistency. Sometimes the word *agreement* is used. Other times, *contract* is used. No difference is intended. Frequently, *share corporation, corporation,* or *company* is written. Again, no significant difference is intended. The terms *articles of incorporation, corporate articles, articles of association,* and *company articles* are interchangeable.

There are surely other examples of imprecise language in this book, but then what is being sought is to convey information. Often language is not used with precision in commerce. The emphasis throughout has been to approximate writing to the vernacular. This book might be thought of as a series of legal guideposts for the corporate manager, indicating the main roads to be traveled.

When accuracy in defining or examining a particular legal structure or concept is needed, it will be used with rigor. We are now prepared to examine the international joint venture in more detail.

1

THE COMMERCIAL ASPECTS
OF THE INTERNATIONAL JOINT VENTURE

PART ONE

1.1 WHY COMPANIES ESTABLISH THEMSELVES IN FOREIGN MARKETS

The management of a company is a dynamic process that requires constant vigilance if growth is to be maintained. However, sustaining growth, or at least consolidating it, may require an enterprise to secure this objective in a distant, foreign jurisdiction. On the other hand, growth means expansion, but this may not be probable in the home market. Growth requires new markets and the home market may be saturated. In other circumstances, with other firms, for growth to continue, the product image must be maintained. A company with sales overseas may find for various reasons that its product image is being damaged and it must exercise more direct control in the various jurisdictions where the product circulates. Not infrequently, a corporation possesses expertise in a particular technology that cannot be licensed. It is an art, a trade secret. The most effective way of transferring the technology to a foreign enterprise is to form a company: one contributes the knowledge, the other capital.

At other times, a manufacturer wishes to ensure a continuous supply of raw materials or semifinished goods. One effective manner is for purchaser and supplier to be partners in an export company in the foreign jurisdiction. Frequently, separate entities may possess different skills that are needed to develop a product. A simple way for this to occur is through a company jointly owned by the various parties. Occasionally, the business of a firm by its nature impels it to go abroad. It is not possible to build dams forever in your home jurisdiction. Varied and many, with a sensible basis, are the reasons for establishing a presence in a foreign market. Some of the more frequent ones will be considered at length.

1.1.1 RIVALRY

The average economic pattern of a company is its formation, a period of struggle and implantation, followed by a period of growth and stabilization provided there is a market for its product or services. A period of mature solid progress is registered. Quite commonly, after a time, a period of stagnation sets in. There is neither further development nor necessarily a decline. A status quo is achieved. Competition from other companies encroaches on the market. The pressure of retaining a customer base is constant. As there is invariably a certain attrition to an existing level of patronage, management rightly concerns itself with new markets and different clients. The problem of losing customers is compensated by obtaining others. Whereas for many enterprises, expansion is possible in their domestic market, for others, this is not a viable alternative. Usually, there are too many similar products or services. It is natural that sooner or later, the board of directors considers the possibility of establishing a presence in a foreign jurisdiction. Relief from normal, healthy competition may require a geographical dislocation.

Such a new economic area may be simply another outlet in the same town, another city, or a different state or province. Often, however, the natural choice is another country, what is often called a *foreign market,* an option forced by necessity and imagination because of product saturation in the traditional home market. Management searches for new markets as merchant ships once plowed awesome oceans in hopes of discovering new ports. Domestic expansion is no longer confined to the same culture and nearby geographical regions.

Establishing a company abroad is becoming more and more common, less an adventurous undertaking, as globalization of commerce and telecommunications reduces world trade to understandable and understood dimensions. Establishing a company presence in a foreign country may be the only solution for sustained growth. The constant activity of mergers, acquisitions, and establishment of subsidiaries all over the world confirms the importance of this diffuse corporate need.

But finding new markets because of home market competition is not the only reason for going abroad with the company product. Without doubt, there is often a convergence of motives that initiates the launch of a company into other distinct commercial regions, even those where there are substantial differences in language and culture.

1.1.2 NEW ECONOMIC ZONES AS FUTURE MARKETS

A company may wish to enter another distant economic zone because it may believe it is the market of the future with expansionary forces, strong consumer demand, and subject to less marked economic cycles. A typical example is the expanding European Union, now fifteen countries, with more applicants from the former Soviet sphere, and its single currency: the Euro. Economic blocs, such as the European Union, the various South American trade zones, or NAFTA, may provide a growth alternative to the national market, perhaps the United States, or Canada, when its economic cycle is in a recession trough. Management may have the opinion that the European Union, or any other economic bloc, represents a market of such dimensions that a company presence is a form of economic insurance.

Often, international economic zones are at different stages, and when one economic region is in a mild recession, another is in a strong expansion. The theory behind investing in diverse equities as a form of capital insurance holds true for different national economies. Operating in a "basket" of commercial zones is equally a form of expansion guaranty. Being present in an emerging economy may ensure continued growth for traditional company products while new ones are being developed. If at one time establishing a company in Brazil seemed hazardous, such managerial temerity would be frowned on today.

1.1.3 MARKETING REASONS

Corporate management entrusted with marketing often has good reasons for deciding to establish a company in another, distant locality. Typical motivations are geographical necessities for a more efficient distribution system, particularly in countries with a common economic zone such as the European Union or the United States; this may mean creating an independent distribution system in alliance with national distributors; or being present to lend technical support to distributors; or even stepping into a commercial void left by a bankrupt distributor or one that has terminated the distributorship.

Irregular price structures in different geographical areas inevitably create end user or consumer dissatisfaction that is aggravated as national frontiers disappear and markets become integrated. Product sales in foreign countries engender their own, but different problems. Distributors, agents, and other middlemen may have a different philosophy from the manufacturer. Their concern is perhaps with cash turnover and rapid sales with little regard for creating a loyal customer base. Large discount houses and other operators have their own methods with no loyalty to any brand name. The laws concerning parallel importing in the European Union permit a Spanish importer to obtain his goods from a Belgian subsidiary of a U.S. manufacturer and resell them in Spain. Regardless of the price structure in Belgium, the U.S. management cannot impose any resale price conditions on the purchase nor refuse to sell.

It is not unusual to find in a foreign jurisdiction, as it is in a domestic market, a wide range of prices for the same product. However, in a national market, a manufacturer can simultaneously protect its price structure and image by selling through company-approved outlets that adhere to quality standards and customer satisfaction. This attitude is then reflected in a price structure not imposed by the manufacturer, but a result of a method of doing business. Control over foreign agents and distributors is not very efficient. Distance makes reasonable supervision of such activities difficult and costly. The product may be distributed in uneven patterns, at times too much quantity, at other times a shortage. Being present in a foreign jurisdiction thus permits a manufacturer to uphold quality in different jurisdictions that in turn avoids the need for wanton, frenetic price cutting to regain or retain a market that often leads to a degradation of the product image to the consumer.

1.1.4 PRODUCT IMAGE AND TECHNICAL ASSISTANCE

Again, a company's existence in a foreign market may be chosen because the company product may be well-known abroad, but the circumstances of after-sales assistance are destroying the product's image. In the foreign jurisdiction, the manufacturing company may have no permanent presence. It may use an agent, or distributor or a sales representative responsible for various countries. Consumer or retail contacts are sporadic. There is no stable corporate entity that responds to consumer questions or complaints. Technical assistance is poor in quality. Parts are not kept in stock. Customers begin to switch to other brands.

Governmental regulations, such as in the pharmaceutical industry, may be ignored by local representatives with unfavorable publicity for the exporter/manufacturer. If the product is being manufactured in a foreign country under a license, the licensor has only sporadic, infrequent control over quality issues. The local representative may be engaging in competitive practices that are contrary to the local laws and that the authorities may impute to the exporter. The traditional commercial contracts of agency or distribution require a vigilant supervision not easily performed by a distant company where knowledge of the local language and culture may be limited.

1.1.5 NEW PRODUCTS, NEW IDEAS, AND TECHNOLOGY TRANSFER

Inventiveness is a natural condition of the human mind and new products or new methods of manufacture are being constantly developed. The licensing of technology is a specialty in law and commerce. The traditional pattern is licensor and licensee. However, there are a variety of circumstances in which a license is not the most suitable avenue for exploration of technology. The technology may be in an incipient stage and two or more parties from different countries are required to collaborate and produce a successful product. The technology may not be capable of being reduced to writing. It is a craft that needs to be taught. The teacher of such knowledge will feel more secure in obtaining financial results if there is an equity participation in the manufacturing venture with a local partner. There will be situations where the possessor of a technology wishes to control and supervise its manufacture but does not have sufficient knowledge of foreign local markets to exploit its potential. A partner from the foreign jurisdiction is a sensible solution.

New product lines may be needed. A simple method of acquiring a new product is to purchase the corporate owner of the product, which may be a company in another jurisdiction. The astronomical activity in the acquisition field and formation of subsidiaries worldwide is substantially documented by even a casual reading of any major financial newspaper. Behind this activity is the relentless search by companies for new products, which means acquiring other companies.

However, acquiring companies do not confine themselves to obtaining only new products, distinct from their traditional product lines. The development of one product line may become more visionary by entering into a complementary business activity. A mobile telephone manufacturer from Finland may decide to acquire a software company in England that has created a special program for sending and receiving faxes by mobile telephones. The Finnish company may reasonably conclude that it wishes to ensure future development of such an important component of its product. Thus, acquisitions are made to obtain new products or products complementary to the principal activity of the acquirer.

1.1.6 MISCELLANEOUS REASONS: FROM RESOURCES TO CAPITAL

A wide variety of ad hoc reasons exists to explain why management goes abroad. They are so varied and even haphazard in origin that they do not warrant separate, detailed treatment. For example, two executives meet at an industrial fair in Beijing and decide to do business together. The board of directors of one company decides the corporation must diversify and someone knows of a company for sale in France. Or, perhaps, an enterprise has excess cash reserves and it decides to diversify. The fastest route is to purchase an equity interest in another company.

In order to win a government bid in a foreign country, the bidder must form a local operating company with a subsidiary owned by the foreign government. The local law may prohibit the foreign investor from having a majority position.

A manufacturer becomes concerned it will lose access to needed resources. Competitors are beginning to drive up the price. A solution is to form a company with the producer of the resource.

Some countries facilitate the formation of companies with foreign capital participation by offering loans at low interest rates or an exemption from taxes for a determined period of time. The package is extremely attractive and so foreign capital flows in and companies are formed. The host country obtains the needed commercial expertise its local population lacks.

For all the reasons just mentioned, and without question many more, a business entity decides it is going to do business abroad and the most common form is the international joint venture. However, it is logical to first consider an apparent paradox. A company wishes to do business abroad. Why are partners needed? Why choose an international joint venture?

PART TWO

1.2 WHY CHOOSE AN INTERNATIONAL JOINT VENTURE AS A FORM FOR DOING BUSINESS?

Once such a decision has been made by key management to do business in a foreign jurisdiction, a difficult option presents itself. Should our company establish a 100 percent owned subsidiary or form an alliance with a local entity? On the one hand, there is the understandable belief that the representation and control of the company in a foreign jurisdiction is best done through complete administrative dominion. Frequently, this is the chosen method with multinationals having operations all over the world and particularly so as experience is gained in various countries through years of trial and error. Nevertheless there are strong compelling reasons for forming local alliances for all business entities, no matter the magnitude or previous knowledge of the company.

Forming an association does not necessarily mean losing management control. These are different (although complex) issues as we will see later. But such problems do not detract from the compelling reasons to forge a local affiliation. There are many arguments in favor of forming an association, in particular a joint venture, with another national group. Although some of the reasons are valid for a 100 percent owned subsidiary, the accumulation of all reasons favors the use of a joint venture. The reasons may be summarized succinctly:

From the viewpoint of the foreign investor

- avoiding regional trade barriers
- capital flexibility
- return on capital, interest reductions, and tax exemptions
- organizational needs
- natural resources
- human resources
- cultural aptitude, knowledge of local business and moral customs
- complementary knowledge creates economies of goods and services
- consolidation of markets
- easy withdrawal
- diversification
- risk reduction
- host country requires formation of an international joint venture

From the viewpoint of the national investor

- modernization
- realization of capital gains
- avoidance of multiple, fractional interests because of inheritance

1.2.1 REGIONAL TRADE BARRIERS

Globalization of commerce has meant international flows of capital and goods. In contradiction with this development has been the rise of agreements between countries forming among themselves trading blocs with discriminatory tariffs against goods or services coming from nonparticipating countries. Transnational commerce has increased but so has the appearance of economic zones with customs discrimination. In some cases, the commercial association is becoming a legal union on its way to a complete federation. The primary example is the European Union (EU). Other less integrated economic unions, but ones that nevertheless have common tariffs between themselves and different ones for the nonparticipants, exist all over the world. This clearly puts exporters in other countries at a serious disadvantage.

The only effective way for a company wishing to do business in these economic blocs is by forming a joint venture with a company whose head office is in a member country. Since the creation of these integrated trade zones, many companies from the United States and Europe have set up joint ventures outside their own countries. Instead of exports, the emphasis switches to producing the goods locally. The practice of technology licensing only diminishes and the licensor now establishes a joint venture with a local partner. Quality is controlled, proper marketing assured, and technical assistance is guaranteed.

1.2.2 CAPITAL FLEXIBILITY: INCREASING AND DECREASING THE JOINT VENTURE CAPITAL

Doing business abroad through a joint venture, or other commercial form, permits the separation of the home corporate structure from the local structure. This may confer considerable financial advantages to the foreign investor. Doing business in another jurisdiction through a local company reduces the currency risks associated with a foreign investment. If a U.S. company does business in the European Union, it can either export dollars to finance its commercial operations or it can form a company in the EU, borrow substantial local funds, and need not concern itself if the local currency—the Euro—should devalue against the dollar. On the other hand, should the Euro appreciate against the dollar since the inception of the investment, dividends declared and remitted back to the United States will represent a currency gain.

Moreover, forming an international joint venture with a local partner achieves additional capital objectives. It reduces the amount of a strong currency the foreign investor has to utilize. Less capital is locked into the joint venture, thus permitting the foreign investor to gain needed experience in doing business in another jurisdiction with different laws, commercial customs, and cultural ways. A joint venture also creates an experimental phase or a capital escape valve dependent on the commercial progress or lack of it.

A subsidiary formed between a foreign investor and a national investor permits limiting the capital investment of the foreign investor but does not necessarily preclude the foreign investor from having a legal right to increase its capital investment should there be solid commercial success. This can be done by the parties agreeing that the capital of the subsidiary will be augmented in accordance with additional equity participation rights granted to the foreign investor. The investing corporation would like to have a 100 percent owned subsidiary, but it realistically judges it needs more familiarity with the local foreign market. The parties may negotiate a contractual provision whereby the capital of the local subsidiary is augmented in harmony with predetermined objectives or watersheds: gross sales, net profit, or volume turnover as an illustration. This is an increasing equity joint venture. There exists, of course, the corollary, a decreasing joint venture.

In a decreasing joint venture, the foreign investor has a *put* to compel the local partner to buy out all or a part of the foreign investor's stake. This might be dependent on issues of nationalization, loss of government contracts, enactment of unfavorable investment laws, or change in share ownership of the national investor, to name a few reasons. Understanding these general legal ideas permits the corporate financial department to tailor its foreign investment very carefully. With a local partner, our foreign investor may take a dual stance and arrange a flexible equity investment: if the business venture goes well, the investment can be increased. If there appear unforeseen economic factors, the investment can be liquidated on an agreed-on basis, for example, purchase of the shares of the foreign investor at their par value or net asset value. The standards to be chosen vary considerably.

1.2.3 RETURN ON CAPITAL, INTEREST REDUCTIONS, AND TAX EXEMPTIONS

The classic managerial problem of securing a fair return on capital invested for a reasonable length of time is conveniently solved through the legal form of an international joint venture. Less capital invested by having a local partner with local marketing experience should permit years of trial and error to be bypassed and the corporate purpose to be realized quickly. The period of trial and error is substantially reduced with an experienced, local partner. Having to discuss marketing and business strategy with another economic entity, such as the national partner, requires the parties to substantiate their ideas; a local partner will not want to see an investment dissipated by advice not sensible in the local business environment. An international joint venture thus affords an opportunity to invest less on a new venture, provide for further injections of capital if events run well, and benefit from local, accurate orientation.

An attractive return on capital is also accelerated if the foreign government has a strong policy of favoring foreign investment. It permits the use of local funds without recourse to a local bank. The funds may be lent at a very favorable rate of interest. The host government may have an aggressive policy of attracting foreign capital. Interest payments may be waived for a specified period of time as well as there being given a tax holiday. If there is no problem with retained earnings, capital needs can be quickly accumulated with no associated debt service cost. This affects favorably all the financial ratios.

1.2.4 ORGANIZATIONAL FLEXIBILITY

Monolithic corporate entities establishing a solely owned company in a foreign jurisdiction are necessarily subject to, and affected by, their own multiple by-law restrictions, formal management guidelines, a need for shareholder general assemblies, and most importantly from the viewpoint of doing business abroad, management policies perhaps unharmonious with local business practices. Wholly owned subsidiaries of multinationals are naturally copies of the home office organization. This can be disadvantageous.

Requiring a local manager to constantly report or request to home-office management various local financial expenditures, personnel requirements, expansion plans, or new product development and wait for approval from the home office is time-consuming and inefficient. Communications between a distant subsidiary and the home office are difficult not because of technical communication problems, which today hardly exist, but because there is not a common economic or social reference. The ultimate authority of a London board of directors simply cannot have firsthand knowledge of the day-to-day economic realities of a subsidiary in Ecuador. It is possible, but not probable.

On the other hand, ameliorating the situation by conferring a general power of attorney to a local manager and thereby making it possible to bind the entire group is not an attractive alternative to the London board of directors. Managing an active subsidiary with many employees in a foreign jurisdiction but whose general director is a foreigner to the nationals may be interpreted as a vote of "no confidence" toward local citizens. Moreover, we have no reason to believe a Londoner sent to Ecuador as general manager of a 100 percent owned subsidiary is going to have any more understanding of the local economic climate than our London board of directors. Of course, the London company could employ a national of Ecuador to be the subsidiary manager. But this is not always a practical solution, due to the corporate culture of the foreign investor.

If we are not dealing with blue-chip multinationals with years of overseas experience, but rather modest capital companies with imaginative direction, there is an understandable reluctance to turn over a new venture to an "outsider" who is an employee with no prior responsibilities with the corporate organization. Between these two extremes, total reliance on the home office and complete independence of the subsidiary, there exists a compromise.

A well-chosen national partner for a local subsidiary is an ideal choice, the necessary hybrid method, the perfect interlocutor between the foreign investor and the national economy. Having a national partner with capital invested dilutes the fears normally associated with outsider management, someone strange to the team, because in this case the outsider has capital invested and this should mean a commitment to a common goal. As we will see, having a national partner does not mean relinquishing control over a substantial equity investment. Management controls can be established easily through various legal documents. A foreign subsidiary with a national partner therefore resolves two troublesome issues for corporate investors: creating a suitable foreign structure and obtaining experienced local personnel. This latter category is quite properly considered an important material acquisition.

Moreover, a local subsidiary, with a local partner, and management responsibilities well defined by the local corporate structure, confers multiple advantages. The risk of negligent management is limited to the local corporate assets. The general director may be an employee of the foreign partner, in our case, the English company, but his lack of local commercial customs is complemented by the national partner and other national managers. Accordingly, establishing a subsidiary with a local entity not only reduces unexpected liability exposure but permits tailoring the corporate structure, the bureaucratic form, in accordance with local necessities, which can range from a two-employee office to a staff of three hundred people.

Whereas the foreign corporate investor may have a base of thousands of shareholders, this does not prevent the foreign investor from forming a local, national limited liability company in another jurisdiction with a foreign partner but along simpler management lines, yet still with the necessary controls, checks, and balances. The limited liability company so formed can have a modest capital and a simple corporate structure, perhaps one general manager who represents the subsidiary before third parties, although this authority is delegated authority, emanating from the board of directors of the subsidiary.

The highly intricate corporate structure of a typical multinational thus can be shed for a simple, linear chain of command in another jurisdiction. As an additional bonus, this is probably more in accordance with the way the national companies do business and more familiar to national banks and other important third parties with whom the subsidiary must deal on a daily basis. Local government officials normally look to one individual with whom to deal and do not appreciate being informed their request is being considered by a distant board of directors.

Market knowledge is gained through experience and presence, and many corporate joint ventures fail because qualified, well-meaning foreign personnel simply do not understand the local business rules, often not articulated, submerged in a foreign language, concealed behind cultural barriers not immediately surmounted. When we begin to consider some of the other reasons listed subsequently, we will see how quickly the force of economic logic favors forming a joint venture when doing business in a foreign jurisdiction.

1.2.5 NATURAL RESOURCES

A great deal of joint venture activity takes place between companies from industrialized countries and companies from the so-called emerging, or third world, or developing countries. A very common motive is that the foreign group needs the raw materials of the host country. The manufacturer of furniture needs trees; the processor of tea needs plantations; the wholesale florist needs fields of flowers; the producer of cars needs labor.

Many of these joint ventures involve a mixture of private and public capital. In a small economy with a strong centralized government, the access to the raw material may require the foreign company to take a minority position in a jointly owned subsidiary so that the benefits of the commercial exploration of the natural resource find their way back into the local economy. Oil and mining companies are well-known examples. All along the West African coast are many operating foreign oil development companies; some search for petroleum, others furnish the bore drivers. However, in many instances, these foreign entities are obligated to transact their business in joint ventures, in which the national or host country takes an equity stake, ranging from a minority to a majority position. The resource need not be so globally important as petroleum.

The cosmetic industry uses sardine oil as a vital, important ingredient. Forming a joint venture with a local sardine supplier in a Mediterranean country ensures a much needed raw material and, more importantly, secures it on quality terms. From the catch to the extraction, our cosmetic manufacturer can have certainty that the final product will be in the state of quality it requires.

An airline company with government capital may form a subsidiary with a catering company to ensure the quality and price of food served on its routes. The resources in this example may be access to a reasonably priced agricultural economy and labor market, but the sales price to the airline company is cost plus a specified margin. The prepared food is served on worldwide routes with quality and price ensured.

Between natural resources and human resources there is a fine line, and probably only in the most basic of industries can the division be made with any economic sense.

1.2.6 HUMAN RESOURCES

One of the great discoveries of the present epoch has not been sighting new lands but the encounter with talented people from different parts of the world. With software developers from India, electronics engineers from Mexico, mold designers from Portugal, skilled personnel are needed in international economic endeavors and the surest way to utilize their expertise is to work with them through a local subsidiary. The international auditing firms, which must draw on countless skills and highly developed professional qualifications, have found that only by admitting local partners, by setting up joint ventures with national professionals, has it been possible to sustain steady, qualified growth. But the necessity for acquiring proficient local professional skill is also present in any industry or service. The skill of a national crane operator is as necessary to an international consortium as the expertise of a national lawyer. With the service sector of commerce beginning to obtain ascendancy over the basic production industries in many countries, the quest for skilled, human resources required for a foreign presence has fomented the formation of joint ventures. However, an integral part of human resources is the human cultural element. They cannot be separated. Consequently, closely associated with technical skills, and forming part of human resources, is what might be called *cultural aptitude,* which is usually associated with local, national personnel.

1.2.7 CULTURAL APTITUDE, KNOWLEDGE OF LOCAL BUSINESS, AND MORAL CUSTOMS

Even in very familiar cultures, such as England or France, there are ways of doing business that enhance success or at least make it initially more possible. There is always the language barrier. Consumers, suppliers, wholesalers, government officials, the public in general, whatever its function before the company, naturally feel more confident when speaking their own language because there are no doubts as to comprehension. What is said or written in the native language is understood with all its subtlety. This makes dealing with people and marketing more effective. Imported ideas from another culture sometimes clash with unfortunate results.

For those of us who have lived abroad there is also another more elusive element besides language: behavior. Every country, every culture, every geographical unit of similar people with a common history have accepted and prohibited rules of conduct that may be totally unknown or not understood by a foreigner. Aggressive marketing behavior may be frowned on or even considered in such bad taste that there is a backlash against the company product totally disproportionate to the advertising campaign in question. Advertising announcements that disparage another product in an indirect comical fashion, although acceptable in one country, may be totally shocking in another. Only persons intimately familiar with any given culture will possess this knowledge beforehand, before the results cannot be undone. Appearing without an appointment at the door of a government official may mean the end of the company in that culture. Failing to use the correct title when speaking, particularly a title indicating an educational qualification such as "Engineer X" or "Dr. Y" (when dealing with university graduates) may cause a social affront that is difficult to later surmount, even if the person offended knows no offense was intended. Certain cultural codes are so ingrained that no excuse will ameliorate the deleterious effects from ignoring prescribed rules of conduct.

Besides language and personal conduct, business cannot be done unless the commercial structure of the country is understood and this is simply not knowledge acquired from one day to the next nor gathered quickly by a marketing study or a consultant's report. Of course, such reports are helpful, useful, a necessary complement, but difficult decisions require in-depth knowledge, and the latter is only possible with accumulated experience. The proper and well-chosen partner, in the commercial sense, ensures that local practices are followed, such as requiring programmed payments for apartment developments in construction before the units are complete. This practice may be quite common in a country where there is a shortage of housing and the consumer wishes to ensure his residential needs even in the planning. A similar demand in the country of the foreign investor might be seen as evidence of a possible fraud. Not knowing this increases credit or cash requirements for the builder unnecessarily.

A prudent, experienced local partner avoids ruining what was a potentially sound investment and commercial operation.

1.2.8 COMPLEMENTARY KNOWLEDGE CREATES ECONOMIES OF GOODS AND SERVICES

It may happen that a U.S. company and, perhaps, an Italian company form a joint venture in Italy with each group participating in the capital. These partners may be substantially *cash heavy* multinationals with no need for capital assistance from anyone. Yet they join forces through a common subsidiary. Why? The U.S. company may possess substantial know-how in the construction of a plant for manufacturing a specific plastic product and the Italian company may possess substantial knowledge for transforming the product, refining it, if such be the case, seeing the intermediate production process through to its end. Joint efforts result in a transformed product ready for sale. Each group contributes what it does best with the economies it has perfected. Although the total is larger than the sum of its parts, the expenses are not.

There are many other examples. Joint ventures between a manufacturer and a distributor in a foreign country are quite common. The manufacturer may be responsible for the technical support, the importing of its own product, whereas the distributor is responsible for the sales and advertising. All of these activities in a jointly owned subsidiary are delegated to the partners possessing the particular skills in the relevant area.

At times a mammoth building construction or complex enterprise requires a temporary alliance of multiple skills, such as the erection of a dam. These skills may be bound contractually in the consortium contract wherein each party sets forth its rights and obligations.

Research and development, marketing, purchasing, and selling are all areas where cooperation is possible, complementary services are united. Many of these forms of collaboration have received special legislative attention from competition authorities so as to better define the rules affecting such activities.

1.2.9 CONSOLIDATION OF MARKETS

One of the reasons for the ever present threat of the application of competition law principles to international joint ventures is that many alliances are often created by horizontal or vertical consolidation, which tends to reduce competition or enhance an incipient dominant position. Consequently, the corporate manager when considering one of the typical situations hereinafter described has to consult with counsel to ensure that what seems like a perfect commercial marriage is not infringing on competition law principles.

The more simple and less legally threatening joint venture occurs when a foreign manufacturer operating in the host country forms a subsidiary with a local distributor to retail the product in question. This is a vertical joint venture downwards, an attempt to control commercial success by owning interests at the crucial stages of manufacturing and retailing. Such vertical joint ventures may tend to eliminate competition. Although the participants feel this is quite fair and even logical, complex rules have been evolved by national competition authorities as to when or when not such a vertical merger will be permitted. When not allowed, they are described as *vertical restraints* on trade. But they often are permitted, particularly when those involved are not substantial market players. When allowed, such vertical alliances make a lot of business sense since they concentrate in the hands of management the multiple facets of shifting products from the manufacturing locale to a retail outlet.

Of course, the vertical joint venture may be *upwards* when a large retail discount house joins forces with a manufacturer through a common-owned subsidiary. Here the legal act is from a less primary activity upwards from the retail chain to the manufacturing site and such a joint venture is referred to by practitioners as a vertical joint venture upwards.

Besides vertical joint ventures, there are also horizontal joint ventures, involving two or more participants active in the same industry. Three manufacturers of sound equipment may decide to form a joint subsidiary. Such a horizontal joint venture tends to result more quickly in the creation of a dominant position in a particular industry, which domination may be forbidden by the local competition authorities. Horizontal mergers tend to be more frowned on by governmental authorities, more prone to sanctions since primary industries tend to be involved and this results in strangulating competition.

However, often there are no legal obstacles for a variety of reasons. The simplest may be that the participants have a small fraction of the market; or that there are many competitors and the market structure is unlikely to be affected; or even that the horizontal merger may bring benefits to the consumer.

In summary, vertical and horizontal joint ventures may infringe on national competition laws. But for the everyman international joint venture, the modest market share involved will render any competition laws inapplicable.

1.2.10 WITHDRAWAL SIMPLIFIED

One difficulty existing in establishing a 100 percent owned subsidiary is wanting to withdraw from it, an event provoked by a multitude of reasons ranging from bankruptcy to a desire to sell for capital gains due to an immensely profitable operation. But a company cannot withdraw easily from a foreign jurisdiction, although its partners can sell their interests. Withdrawal of a company in legal language normally requires a formal dissolution and then a liquidation, costly and complex legal procedures. How far simpler if you have a partner who is willing to purchase your interest. Even in an insolvent situation, it may still be possible to make a distress sale to your partner. Should the interest being sold be a profitable one, a partner avoids the necessity for looking for a buyer. Consequently, having more than one partner in a subsidiary, operating in an international joint venture, facilitates withdrawal from the jurisdiction in question.

Selling a 100 percent owned subsidiary requires encountering a buyer with more significant financial recourses than required for a partial equity interest. It also usually means a different management style enters with new key personnel. This is often seen as a threat by the existing labor force, even if none is intended. However, the sale of a block of shares in a joint venture implies a more moderate disruption.

Having partners in an unsuccessful venture, or one that is bringing below-average returns, permits withdrawing as a matter of fact, if not legally. The disinterested partner simply allows the other partners to manage the company with the minimum of vigilance needed. Other than potential liability problems, there is not much to be feared. And if we are dealing with a legal form that insulates the owners from the debts of the entity, even a possible liability threat becomes remote.

1.2.11 RISK REDUCTION

Complementary skills and knowledge of local customs have already been cited. Additionally, starting up a wholly owned business in a foreign jurisdiction entails various uncertainties and even competent, skilled interlocutors do not eliminate situations of misunderstanding entirely. It is not simply possible for an outsider to come into another business culture and make the correct assessment of the economic climate. There are so many factors to be considered. There are questions of obtaining credit, foreign investment rules, civil and commercial law codes, laws buried that are suddenly resurrected, union considerations, exchange-rate fluctuations, zoning and safety orders, import and export decrees, taxation, restrictions on hiring foreign personnel: the list is lengthy. Having a local partner is a prudent approach to becoming integrated into the local business and legal milieu and avoiding costly mistakes.

1.2.12 REQUIREMENTS FOR INTERNATIONAL JOINT VENTURE BY HOST COUNTRIES

Many international joint ventures are formed because it is the only way to be considered as a candidate for a specific task. A company wishing to participate in a construction bid may be obligated by the local law to have a local partner. In these cases, there has not been a conscious choice, but of course compliance with the law. The formation of a joint venture has been thrust on the candidate if it wishes to have its proposal reviewed.

Other times, the laws of the particular jurisdiction may not permit foreign capital to own more than a specific percentage of the equity of a company. This is not confined only to sensitive commercial areas, such as banking or telecommunications. It may be an investment policy of the foreign government that fears domination of its general commerce by nonnationals.

1.2.13 DIVERSIFICATION

Frequently, references are made that an international joint venture is one method of diversifying, and there have been corporate epochs when any company with excess cash preferred the adventure of diversification to earning bank interest. It surely may happen that a corporation decides to do just that and the investment object presented happens to be an equity interest in a foreign corporation. An acquisition, which also constitutes a method for forming a joint venture, is a form of diversification. However, this motive for entering into an international joint venture has probably been overstressed. It perhaps happens more frequently in national joint ventures, between companies from the same jurisdiction or federation, such as the United States, where a common business and social culture facilitates a passive, nonmanagerial participation. However, an international joint venture originating solely for reasons of cash diversity is substantially uncommon.

1.2.14 MODERNIZATION

So far we have been viewing joint ventures from the optic of the exporting, industrialized, capital-sufficient multinational entity or company. But large local corporations and small, local family companies also have their reasons for wanting to enter into a joint venture.

The most obvious reason to enter into a joint venture is the need for modernization. This can be true of a significant commercial local group as well as a *niche* industry, operated by a family, such as a porcelain or bottle manufacturer. By modernization may be meant everything from equipment to accounting standards, necessitating installation of computer hardware and complex software, ranging from inventory control to human resource management. Often, the local group only wants to modernize its structure and/or have access to particular markets. It does not want to sell its entire capital interest. A convenient solution for the local entity is the right foreign partner.

1.2.15 REALIZATION OF CAPITAL GAINS

With local companies that are family-owned, there is a tendency for the original management to prolong its tenure. Suddenly, there is a realization that one day there will be no one left to continue the business. Perhaps the obvious heirs have turned their efforts to professions or other interests. Under these circumstances, it is usual for the family group to seek to sell its interest and obtain the concomitant capital gains for the decades of work. It may be a controlling interest or a minority interest. This often depends on the degree of involvement the family management has had and sentimental reasons associated with the business. Such a situation is a classic case of when a minority interest may be initially put up for sale but an increasing equity position can be obtained by the buyer.

1.2.16 AVOIDANCE OF MULTIPLE FRACTIONAL INTERESTS BECAUSE OF INHERITANCE

A variation of the controlling-family pattern is when there has been no foresight as to the frailty of human life. The founder leaves her interests to her descendants and they do the same. In a short span of two generations, there may be various owners each having modest equity interests. It is impossible to form an effective, dedicated management team. The only sensible solution is for at least a majority of the capital to be sold, although as an investment, the value of the sale will be increased if all the interests can be purchased. A further variant is when on inheritance, the heirs of an estate cannot agree as to a division of their various interests and the decision is made to turn assets into cash, which produces a quantity that can be easily divided. In both situations, sometimes not all the owners sell and only a percentage of the capital is purchased. The result is, of course, an international joint venture.

PART THREE

1.3 THE CHARACTERISTICS OF AN INTERNATIONAL JOINT VENTURE

Once a decision is made to form an international joint venture, a bewildering array of legal possibilities may be presented to management. Words commonly used in boardrooms, such as *international alliances, cross-border mergers, transnational corporations,* must now begin to have a more precise meaning so that choices can be made. This requires a methodology. Two objectives are paramount in the ensuing discussion:

- the special characteristics of an international joint venture
- a practical classification

A U.S. company purchases a license for making audio equipment from a South Korean manufacturer but they also sign an agreement to establish a partnership with each other for countries in which neither licensor nor licensee have manufacturing outlets at the time of the license agreement. A

Spanish and Canadian corporation form a subsidiary in Florida State to develop software in Spanish for a particular computer application. An English group purchases a majority position in a French discount retailer. A South African mining company and an Italian equipment manufacturer form a consortium to explore a mine in Mozambique.

All of these commercial arrangements are joint ventures and are denominated international joint ventures because they involve entities from different countries. The same set of facts involving legal entities from the same jurisdiction, or the same country, would be considered a domestic joint venture. Why, then, should international joint ventures be considered a separate field of study? Why does the difference in national origins of the parties confer any special characteristics on their collaboration? International joint ventures and domestic joint ventures clearly have much in common. There is considerable overlapping of material as to legal principles and documentation. The corporate executive specialized in domestic acquisitions or mergers when asked to switch her attention to the international sphere would naturally think the same principles are going to be applicable. The difference is one of degree and it is difficult to know when this difference becomes a qualitative one.

In fact, the only significant differences between them, the only substantive distinctions between domestic and international joint ventures, are the problems they raise, the issues to be considered, the emphasis on rights to be protected, and the possible solutions to a wide variety of disputes. In other words, domestic and international joint ventures have similar, if not identical, legal structures, but they are operating in a different environment that is total, specifically a foreign culture with its laws and customs.

A domestic joint venture will not have to consider topics such as foreign exchange control, repatriation of dividends, or limits on equity participation or control because it is in the hands of nonnationals. But it would be unfair to focus on material specifically directed toward foreigners. That would make the distinctions too rudimentary. They are more subtle.

Companies doing business with each other from different countries often do so for different reasons than applicable to a domestic joint venture. Purely local joint ventures can be motivated by cost efficiency resulting from a merger or access to excess capital on the balance sheet of a company by a corporate raid. These are not the dominant reasons for forming an international joint venture. Rather, international joint ventures are launched on a collaborative basis: to enter into new markets; new technology is wanted; there is a need for foreign capital; for modern management; for implanting a presence in a particular country; for protecting the public image of a trademark; for pooling resources; for acquiring skills not possessed; or because it was the only way to qualify for a bid. This is patently not an exhaustive list. All of these reasons also can be the motive for a domestic joint venture. But even with a substantial identity of reasons between domestic and international joint ventures, the latter are inserted in a qualitative, different fact situation.

There are the problems that doing business far from the home office creates. The international joint venture creates more examples of absentee ownership and management. The foreign partners are there with a capital presence but an infrequent physical appearance. Being absent requires more concern with controls on local management. The form of the joint venture company may not lend itself to a hierarchical form of management and there is reliance on a local manager, which can be beneficial but also prejudicial.

Acquisitions of participations in a foreign company require substantial investigation into the financial and legal situation of the target company. The jurisdiction in question, with its different commercial customs and laws, does not permit the acquirer the luxury of assuming anything. Public information may be in short supply. Substantial due diligence procedures, the formal name for a company investigation, are seen as obligatory by specialists in this field. This is because the credit information may be scarce. Local banks may welcome a joint venture to rescue an otherwise ailing company and a silent conspiracy against transparency reigns. Nor may there even be another alternative. In a small country, there are not that many players, which makes another acquisition worthwhile. One target company may be the only possibility, and there is a tendency to make do with the acquisition and see if the problems cannot be resolved later.

Moreover, conflict and dispute resolution create preoccupations different from domestic joint ventures as the participants do not have the same experience with the local law. There may be reluctance in subjecting disputes to the national tribunal. Besides the appropriate tribunal, there is also the question of the law to be applied. A domestic joint venture between English companies in England will not be concerned with the law of the contract, which will surely be English law. And this is eminently satisfactory to the parties. This may not be the case in a joint venture in Angola between a Belgian company and an Irish corporation operating an oil platform. What will be the applicable tribunal and law?

Furthermore, the possible sale of an interest in an international joint venture must be considered in a different perspective than in a domestic joint venture. Expropriation and nationalization are dramatic occurrences, but not necessarily that frequent with global trends toward privatization.

Rather, cultural differences that heighten the possibility of conflict and the need for sale are more realistic concerns. Local partners may not want sales without their permission. Restrictions are imposed on the transfer of shares. If a public entity is the other partner, it may have a right of preference calculated on the market value of the shares. How does one obtain such a valuation? What if there is no agreement on the valuation? The markets for equity participations in an international joint venture are not as vast as they are in one jurisdiction with identity of culture and commercial experience.

Even the appraisal of the economics of forming an international joint venture becomes more difficult than a domestic joint venture. The standards of financial analysis, published commercial information, industry standards may be incomplete or absent. The traditional financial tools, such as financial ratios or comparable industry figures, may not be of any significant use.

All this might seem not to warrant any division of joint ventures into two separate fields of study. It could be argued that the only difference between domestic and international joint ventures is a matter of degree of emphasis but not any material distinctions. There is much truth to this assertion. Nevertheless, cooperation between entities from different countries does mean a different system of law, different legal forms for companies, different accounting standards, different management styles, different systems of resolving disputes. All of this translates into business and legal caution that spills over into elaborate documentation affecting the rights and duties of the participants.

From this difference in emphasis, there has developed an industry of professionals devoted to international joint ventures. These experienced experts have created the field of international joint ventures, which is an emphasis on the problems raised in doing business abroad and documents that are a consequence of such preoccupations.

Some system of classification is needed. Although much of the future material discussed will be useful for any joint venture, it is intended to assist in a greater understanding of international joint ventures due to the focus on the various problems. Our immediate focus will be on two aspects: methods for forming a joint venture and the final form of the joint venture. They are two independent processes, an observation not often made.

1.3.1 DIVERSITY OF LEGAL METHODS

From a commercial viewpoint, ask an entrepreneur what an international joint venture is and he will probably reply: "doing business out of my country with a foreigner." This is a fair description and satisfies eminently an initial inquiry. Some writers define an international joint venture as simply doing business with another entity in another jurisdiction whose laws and language are different from yours. This accurately describes a cultural fact while emphasizing the commonality between domestic joint ventures and international joint ventures. Going beyond a cultural description, we find that joint ventures present unusual factors.

There is no one method for creating a joint venture, and the possibilities are even greater with an international joint venture since there are so many different legal systems. There are significant variations even as to the most internationally utilized forms. In one country, it may be possible to form a corporation with three shareholders, whereas in another, five will be necessary. One jurisdiction recognizes a closely held corporation, whereas in another, this legal form can be only approximated. Export of legal concepts is not always possible, and it is hazardous to assume that legal concepts that have the same name in various jurisdictions, although with the necessary appropriate translation, for example, "Inc.," "S.A.," "S.A.R.L." (all corporations), are identical in legal principles. There are surely substantial similarities but the differences may be critical for a particular problem.

If there is no one sure route, no one certain method for entering into a joint venture, this obviously brings various theoretical problems. Why not simply make a list of legal methods, or even forms, for an international encyclopedia that can be consulted? It's possible. But although much would be learned about the laws of different jurisdictions, little would be gathered about forming an international joint venture.

The reason is that the kernel of a joint venture is the collaboration between two or more entities from different countries. What creates the joint venture is the motive of collaboration. The presence of different partners united in the pursuit of profit erects a constellation of issues that must find expression and resolution through documentation. This an encyclopedic list cannot do, as it will be dependent on an enormous variety of facts, as we will eventually see, and will lack the particulars of any commercial transaction.

However, just wanting to work together does not justify calling such cooperation a joint venture, whether domestic or international. Entities can ally their efforts in an informal manner. Having a sales representative in another country would not be usually considered a joint venture. More elements are necessary. Cooperation to become meaningful and permit long-term planning will require a solid legal foundation. Intent and form must become welded. The step toward a stable, formal legal structure lies in legal history, basically the formation of *joint adventures* to explore the commercial opportunities offered by trade in the Orient. English and Dutch merchants were early users of commercial *joint adventures.*

When the commercial need for doing business abroad arose, with the necessity for substantial amounts of capital, investors naturally elected traditional legal forms with well-known legal characteristics. Entrepreneurs being asked to collaborate in a foreign country with substantial expenditures of capital thought of doing this through written forms of collaboration, and the easiest was the contract form, a recorded understanding of the financial adventures each participant was undertaking. Eventually, when overseas trade passed from the "one ship" gamble to long-term barter and the need for capital resources, legal forms of companies, with a traditional known body of laws and judicial history, became the choice. Legal conservatism was the preferred route to the joint venture company. The early, simpler method of contract, an ad hoc approach, eventually was replaced by the method of forming a share company. But forming a company is not the only method to create a joint venture.

Joint ventures are often consummated after the fact. There is an operating company and one partner wants to sell his equity share. This means that a foreign company wanting to take a position in the seller's company can only do so by purchasing his interest. The result, an international joint venture if the interest purchased has any significance, requires a number of legal alterations to the target company to safeguard the interests of the substantial, but perhaps new minority partner.

Besides creating a joint venture through the methods of contract, formation, and acquisition, there are other categories with specific characteristics, so that if we wish to have a complete understanding of the various methods and create a reasonable classification, we will need to analyze more legal arrangements. International joint ventures have developed through use of traditional legal methods of acquiring interests and forming binding collaboration. However, "traditional" often has its roots in earlier "innovative" ideas. Thus the dynamic, fluid aspect of commercial law is always present. With the wide variety of available legal materials, it should be clear there is no one sole method to constructing an international joint venture.

Nevertheless, we should be hesitant in describing as a joint venture a method that is not erected on a form that is intended to have a reasonable duration nor creates any common ownership. The method of appointing a distributor does not lead to the formation of a joint venture. Traditionally, principal and distributor are legally independent, not partners in any common legal form such as a corporation, and are not responsible for the debts of one another. The distributor may represent hundreds of principals. Thus, collaboration is not synonymous with commercial relationships. Collaboration to signify a joint venture requires two or more entities working through a commonly owned legal form, a topic we will develop in more detail in Chapter Two.

1.3.2 DIVERSITY OF LEGAL FORMS

There is also no typical legal form of a joint venture. There are corporations, private limited liability companies, partnerships, business trusts, general and limited partnerships, and even this enumeration is just a reasonable part of the legal possibilities without even considering the substantial variations to the most typical legal forms in the multiple jurisdictions of the world. Consequently, the study of international joint ventures presents a body of law in which the form is more dependent on the underlying purpose of the participants. Intent being very subjective, it is difficult to force the classification of joint ventures into predetermined molds. Variety and innovation thus often accompany the creation of an international joint venture.

However, this flexibility has one limiting factor. The possible final legal form of a joint venture can be only a legal form recognized by the law and this in turn reduces the selection to the usual legal forms of companies known to entrepreneurs and lawyers and selected even more by familiarity and prior experience. Consequently, although there is considerable variation in the methods utilized to form a joint venture, the final form chosen tends to be that popular in the laws of the jurisdiction and that is more easily understood by the foreign investor. This favors a confluence toward the traditional legal models utilized in the national or foreign jurisdiction with common elements of characterization, e.g., the share corporation.

1.3.3 CONVERGENCE OF LEGAL METHODS AND LEGAL FORMS

The distinction between legal methods and the final legal form of a joint venture has its exceptions. There are methods that are also the final legal form and a distinction cannot be made between method and form. One method for creating a joint venture is by forming a partnership. But a partnership is also the final legal form. The drafting of a partnership contract results in the partnership contract.

One can purchase an interest in a company. This is a method that is separate from the form of the targeted company. Commonly, interests are purchased in companies that have one legal form and the partners after the acquisition may decide to change the legal form of the company. This is normal where there is a substantial input of new capital. An interest in a small family partnership becomes integrated into the network of a multinational and is converted into a share corporation. Here there is a difference between method and form. The parties initially proceeded by making an acquisition, but decided to change the final form of the joint venture vehicle into a share corporation.

Besides partnerships, consortiums and mergers present the same exceptions. As we will come to understand when discussed later, the formation of a consortium cannot separate method from form as the method, a detailed execution of a contract, is also the final form. Normally, mergers present the same pattern. Two companies merge, the method, and only one survives in its original form. It is not obligatory to be so, but it is very rare to be otherwise. Later, we will examine these ideas in more detail.

1.3.4 INTERNATIONAL JOINT VENTURES RAISE SPECIFIC PROBLEMS OF DOCUMENTATION

As previously indicated, the differences between domestic joint ventures, involving entities from the same jurisdiction, and international joint ventures reside not in different legal precepts, but in legal, property, and management issues, and problems habitual to international operations. Because of this preoccupation, there has developed a legal sphere of specialization associated with international joint ventures that focuses on ownership and managerial topics that must be clarified through substantial legal documents. One of our primary concerns will be consequently to organize the voluminous legal documents that often accompany an international joint venture into a sensible pattern whose reason the corporate executive understands.

However, our task is not to detail the multiple legal clauses and counsel their drafting. This will be avoided entirely. Our principal concentration will be on the purpose of the documents, the material for which the corporate executive may have a particular interest, and practical advice on how to ensure ownership rights and management functions are protected and implemented. International joint ventures have been traditionally accompanied by voluminous legal documents. Nevertheless, it would create poor preparation if one plunged into an analysis of documentation without first giving more explanations as to the characteristic of an international joint venture.

Joint ventures fall into two large divisions: contractual and equity.

1.3.5 Contractual joint ventures, also known as the unincorporated joint venture

The fundamental cleavage within joint ventures is that they fall into two general broad categories: contractual joint ventures, often denominated the unincorporated joint venture, and equity joint ventures. Other terminology is sometimes *contract-based* and *separate-entity-based*. This distinction is basic to the practice of joint ventures, but even national laws erroneously characterize their own laws. A law directed at the contractual joint venture may be denominated, for example, "Regulation of Joint Ventures." Although this legislative ambiguity might seem a minor deviation from purism, it does have importance for the corporate executive who goes abroad to exchange ideas with her counsel. Exactly what sort of joint venture is intended? The right questions will reveal whether the law in question defines the joint venture being contemplated as contractual or equity or sui generis to the jurisdiction.

A consortium is the most familiar legal example of the contractual joint venture. Frequently and correctly in legislation, the contractual joint venture is referred to as an *unincorporated joint venture* to contrast it with those legal forms in which there is a stated corporate capital requiring in some jurisdictions proof that it has been deposited in a bank and that the corporation is formed with the minimum capital.

The contractual joint venture is normally established for a specific object, such as constructing a dam, and customarily has a limited existence in time, although there are no legal impediments to the parties extending their relationship. The contractual joint venture finds its written existence in a detailed contract that defines who will do and contribute what. There are no articles of incorporation nor bylaws, nor general assembly meetings. Rules must be created by contract as to how authority will be delegated, to whom, and how meetings will be organized. This form of organization derives its complexity only from what is drafted, not what is normally imposed by a legislative source such as a corporation law or general partnership statute. The unincorporated joint venture is historically closer in form and spirit to the original English joint adventure contracts.

Contractual joint ventures are dependent on an alliance with other entities whose rights and obligations are entirely derived from an operating contract between all participants. There is no fixed capital. A management board must be created to run the organization, but there is not the same statutory division of authority between management and ownership. The terms of the dissolution and its consequences must be determined beforehand, for a contractual joint venture by definition does not last indefinitely. Each participant is responsible for the acts of the other acting in the name of the contract joint venture.

1.3.6 Contractual joint venture definition

Earlier in the Introduction, we formulated a tentative definition of an international joint venture:

> The expression *joint venture* in this text refers to a particular form of doing business by one party in a jurisdiction, either foreign or domestic, by means of a stable, permanent legal entity with another party, for a term, usually indefinite, with economic independence and a lawful commercial purpose. . . . The key words are stability, a legal form, a partner, a term, an economic independence, and a lawful object.

The joint venture is our genus. International joint venture is our species.

A workable definition of a contractual joint venture, which first must satisfy the generic definition, identifies the following complementary elements:

> Contractual joint ventures are temporary commercial alliances for a specific period between two or more parties where the rights and obligations of the parties are expressed usually in a written document and where the individual partners are responsible personally for the acts of the others. There is no permanent legal form nor a statutory capital but instead an elaborate system of contractual obligations, normally including cash contributions.

In other words, in a contractual joint venture, the total is only composed of parts temporarily working together, but each part is legally treated as if it were the whole. Being temporary contractual arrangements, there are less problems raised with property rights or management rights, as these are predefined in the basic contract. The element of collaborating for a specific period reduces the tendency for conflicts between partners.

1.3.7 Partnership: contractual or equity joint venture?

The traditional partnership, whereby various parties sign partnership articles, appears to be a contractual joint venture, since the embodiment of the collaboration is through an elaborate contract. On the other hand, most partnerships are intended to last for an indefinite term; they are not usually created for a specific purpose, such as a erecting a bridge; the partnership can be dissolved by the withdrawal and is dissolved by the death of a partner. A partnership can accommodate a large number of persons as partners, whereas a contract is better confined to a small aggregation of entities or individuals. But for every reason given why a partnership is a contractual joint venture, we can evoke reasons why it is more similar to an equity joint venture, particularly in its long-term duration and its commitment to a permanent relationship.

The partnership is an early form of legal association with substantial legal history and reported cases. It is a typical legal form in that due to its substantial heritage, most lawyers and judges are in agreement as to what is a partnership. Contracts present an enormous variety of factual situations and every contract is probably unique. Most lawyers would consider a partnership an equity joint venture. It is a hybrid but will be classified in this book as an equity form of association.

1.3.8 EQUITY JOINT VENTURES

Common understanding and usage usually associates a joint venture with an equity joint venture. The word *equity* is not a legal expression normally used in corporate law discussions. To a lawyer, *equity* means *what is just* and finds its application in procedural issues or trust law. However, in common day business language, *equity* means *an investment, ownership interests,* or *rights attaching to ownership,* and of course lawyers in discussions with clients know this and will also use the expression *equity interest* or *equity participation* because such usage is well-established, understood by all parties, and perfectly acceptable. Lawyers in legal writing or when addressing judicial authorities refer not to *equity interests* but *capital* interests or *capital* rights because to a lawyer equity in a business setting means how much capital was contributed to an organization that confers certain rights on an investor. Thus, equity joint ventures are those in which capital has been invested or locked into a legal entity and the contributors of this investment obtain rights of ownership normally evidenced by shares or other forms of ownership, such as a recorded partnership interest. Lawyers may use the expression *equity joint ventures* when they wish to distinguish such a joint venture from noncapital structures, that is, the contractual joint venture.

Equity joint ventures constitute the vast majority of joint ventures established in other countries. Often, reference is made in literature to *joint ventures* with no distinction being made as to what is the nature of the joint venture. But we can be almost sure it is the equity joint venture. It is the equity joint venture that has created an enormous body of laws and documents relating to this form of doing business. It is the equity joint venture that will herein receive extensive consideration as it is the type of joint venture the average company will make. The equity joint venture is the most common joint venture utilized by companies when structuring alliances. It is the equity joint venture that is meant in this book when the term *joint venture* is used, unless, of course, the text clearly indicates something else is intended, as when we discuss various possible contractual joint ventures.

1.3.9 Equity joint venture definition

To facilitate reading, we will repeat once again the generic definition of an international joint venture:

> The expression *joint venture* in this text refers to a particular form of doing business by one party in a jurisdiction, either foreign or domestic, by means of a stable, permanent legal entity with another party, for a term, usually indefinite, with economic independence and a lawful commercial purpose. . . . The key words are stability, a legal form, a partner, a term, an economic independence, and a lawful object.

Our refinement for an equity joint venture requires only one further element: the quantification of the capital.

1.3.10 Particular legal issues may alter general definition

Unfortunately, attempting to define conclusively a joint venture is further complicated because what is a joint venture is often determined by the specific legal problem being considered or even the entity seeking to encounter a definition. This is one of the impediments to an ease of comprehension with law problems. So often an understanding is dependent on the specific facts. There are few universal definitions, perhaps none. This is very pertinent under competition law in which the words *joint venture* may have a more broad meaning than in national legislation in which the term is used to perhaps differentiate between joint ventures that do not imply the creation of a third corporate entity, such as a consortium, and those joint ventures that do, such as the formation of a commonly owned subsidiary.

Under competition law principles, a joint venture may be classified as to what is its declared objective: to control markets making it an illegal cooperation or whether it is one of the many other ways companies have participations in one another's capital. Additionally, to escape being classified as an illegal cooperation, local national laws may have elaborate standards to separate permitted joint ventures from those considered prejudicial.

When the participants in a joint venture are not dominant market players, these legal concerns ordinarily will not be relevant. Naturally, local counsel must be sought for advice.

1.3.11 MANAGEMENT RIGHTS AS PROPERTY RIGHTS

We are used to separating management rights from property rights. You own something and then you manage it. In fact, one could reasonably argue that managing an asset is more important than owning it. This is not a new idea. The impact of the managerial revolution has been eloquently documented in many books. A review of any financial journal indicates the voluminous public-share companies whose owners, the shareholders, do not even know the names of the principal operating officers. One cannot be seriously considered an owner when one owns a share in a corporation for one week and then sells the share to acquire another share, another ownership package of rights. This is confusing investment with ownership.

But the entrenched doctrine that ownership confers automatically substantial rights is hard to dislodge and unfortunately this attitude is often carried over into situations in which it has no place. Worse, it creates havoc with the alliance, for in the end, a minority partner may find it has no say in important issues, which eventually leads to conflict. Imagine a Canadian corporation forms a limited liability company in Portugal and it owns 49 percent of the capital. The articles of incorporation do not address any issues pertaining to minority rights. A 49 percent ownership is a minority interest. If the capital of the company is Canadian $10,000,000, our Canadian corporation has invested Canadian $4,900,000. A general assembly can be called and the difference of 2 percent in the hands of a local partner means the local partner can elect the entire board of directors whose loyalty is to the local partner. Can this 49 percent ownership be seriously considered as *owning* anything? It is an investment and nothing more. But it is not what the Canadian corporation intended. Of course, attentive, experienced counsel for our Canadian corporation would not let this happen.

Throughout our considerations, there will be many instances in which the all important issue of management rights is reviewed and discussed from many points of view. It is hoped that there will emerge one of the fundamental propositions underlying joint ventures: there is no effective ownership without concurrent management rights.

1.3.12 SUMMARY OF CHARACTERISTICS OF EQUITY JOINT VENTURES

As the overwhelming majority of international joint ventures are equity joint ventures and will accordingly occupy most of our analysis, it is productive to review their salient features in more detail. An equity joint venture, whether domestic or international, should contain at least the following characteristics:

A stable formal relationship between two or more parties, what lawyers call a structural alliance. Acquiring a 40 percent share interest in a corporation is clearly an equity joint venture as the purchase becomes affected by multiple legal principles affecting ownership and company law.

A relationship whose duration is reasonably protracted. There is no magical number to insert but rather judgmental decisions must be made. Does the entity created have a bona fide existence? Are we dealing with an economic organization other people would consider to be permanent and stable, not from the point of view of financial health, but rather of purpose, with an intention of doing business in the community for an undetermined period?

An economic and legal independence where the joint venture is not merely another operating division, branch of the home office, or totally dominated by it. If Montreal Wax Canada forms a corporation in Italy between Montreal Wax Canada and Montreal Wax England, but owns one hundred (100) percent of Montreal Wax England, denominating it Milan Wax Italy will not conceal the legal realities: Montreal Wax Canada is simply doing business under another name. Technically, there exists a joint venture because there are two corporate entities owning a subsidiary. However, by knowing the details of the share structure of all the corporations, we realize there is only one partner, one owner: Montreal Wax Canada and this is not a joint venture.

A reasonable capital contribution. If one party owns only 1 percent of a subsidiary and the other 99 percent is in the possession of another party without any curtailment of ownership or managerial rights, this cannot be seriously considered a joint venture. It is a legal and economic masquerade that national courts and administrative agencies treat rather quickly as being a mere appendage of another, more dominating economic entity, belonging usually to the 99 percent partner. A joint venture normally implies a reasonable contribution of capital by all parties. It is the common fact situation of a significant majority of international joint ventures. Obviously, there are many situations in which one partner only subscribes to a small amount of the capital, perhaps even symbolic, but for other reasons, may have a substantial influence in the management of the joint venture. These are special circumstances, affiliated with corporations having many subsidiaries in different countries, and attempting through the boards of directors to exercise a central control. They do not constitute the average joint venture elements.

The commercial purpose of the joint venture should not be to control or coordinate market activity. This latter requirement probably appears a strange element, particularly when oftentimes joint ventures are inspired precisely because this is what the interlocutors desire. Why else form the joint venture, one might ask? However, competition law problems arise as soon as coordination of market activity is seen or suspected. For our analysis, we are not going to review subtle issues of how market activity may or may not be controlled. These are themes belonging to competition law discussions. We are concerned with bona fide joint ventures between entities who wish to do business together and not control any market. Of course, commercial success is desired and foreseen. The law does not nor could it condemn such a vision. But achieving commercial success is different from creating arrangements whose boardroom origin is to control a market, steady prices, even force out competition. Our concern and analysis will concentrate primarily on how successful alliances are forged between different commercial entities.

Managerial participation by all parties is an important factor. If one partner owns 49 percent of a subsidiary but there are no curtailments of the normal rights pertaining to a majority 51 percent interest, all the 49 percent owner has done is to furnish capital. Under these circumstances, it is a capital investment and nothing more. The money could have been furnished by a bank! How minority and majority interests should be balanced so as to ensure participation by all significant partners will occupy a substantial part of our academic analysis of equity joint ventures throughout this book.

PART FOUR

1.4 FOREIGN REGULATION OF INTERNATIONAL JOINT VENTURES

In Chapter Two, we will consider in particular the formation process of the international joint venture. However, there are many jurisdictions in which the formation of a joint venture is regulated for a variety of reasons. To form a company, it is necessary to make a capital contribution. If one of the partners is a foreigner (to the host country), then its capital contribution may be imported in one form, for example, U.S. dollars, and then converted into the currency of the country, for example, Spanish pesetas. Although there has been a substantial liberalization of capital movements throughout the world, there are still many jurisdictions that require the foreign participant to obtain a license for the import from the relevant national authorities. Such a license should be sufficient to permit the repatriation of profits to the home offices of the foreign owner, whose profits will be a purchase of dollars on the official exchange market by the use of pesetas.

But the foreign investment laws may be more sweeping in scope. They may require the entire project to be submitted to the licensing authorities to determine if the proposed joint venture makes commercial sense. The host country may not want the joint venture company, partially owned by a foreigner, to have any material access to loans in local currency, on the theory that this is depriving nationally owned companies as there are just so many bank loans available.

Furthermore, the licensing authorities may believe that their own nationals lack the necessary sophistication or just plain knowledge in dealing with foreign entities and in order to prevent predatory behavior by the foreign partner on the local, the complete proposed joint venture is submitted for review, approval, and, if granted, a license is issued.

Clearly, there are countless variations to such laws and this text is not a review of the foreign investment laws of different jurisdictions. It is a requirement that management must be aware may exist. Foreign investment regulation is a legal concern of joint venture law whose interpretation is the responsibility of local counsel.

2

THE INTERNATIONAL JOINT VENTURE: METHOD

PART ONE

2.1 VARIOUS METHODS AND POSSIBLE COMMERCIAL ALLIANCES

The formation of a joint venture is not a unitary process. It is composed of many components and possible choices to be made. Among other possibilities, a joint venture is created by an acquisition, or the establishment of a subsidiary, or the execution of a contract. But this statement is not revelatory. To understand the joint venture agendum, it is necessary to make an important distinction. There is a difference between method and form and this division pervades the formation of the international joint venture.

As a simple example, method is whether we create a joint venture by acquisition or establishing a subsidiary. The carpenter must decide if he will construct a bureau (subsidiary). Or, perhaps, he will only repair, buying a bureau and making do with the basic structure (acquisition). This is method. But how will the bureau appear? How many drawers? Simple or fancy style? After the acquisition, we can create a share corporation or an unincorporated joint venture.

Our analogy can be carried further. What is the consequence of having one or more drawers? Do more drawers mean more practical or too bulky? In legal terms, once we have chosen the method, whether we will purchase or start from the beginning, we still have another decision to make. We must decide whether the joint venture form, or shelter, will be a share corporation, a limited partnership, or other form recognized by the law. We may accept the legal form represented by our purchase or we may introduce change. It frequently happens that an acquisition is made of a quota interest in a private limited liability company (acquisition is thus the method). After closing, the company purchased is transformed into a share corporation (the final form of the joint venture shelter).

Once the joint venture shelter is chosen, there follow legal consequences that affect a significant variety of issues affecting ownership and management. To mention only two, our choice of legal form will determine whether there is limited liability for the partners as well as instructing us what type of management will be possible, a board of directors or other social organ. From the final joint venture form will be derived the characteristics of the joint venture company that, as they differ according to their legal classification, require management to make an election. When is one form to be preferred over another? This is a pertinent inquiry that we will investigate and attempt to answer. Resuming, we have the following:

- method, which leads to
- form, which confers
- characteristics on the joint venture,
- which obligate management to choose the most appropriate form

The most familiar examples of method leading to an equity joint venture form are

- acquisitions
- subsidiaries

Acquisitions and the formation of subsidiaries are the most common methods of creating a joint venture and are clearly methods that do not, could not, determine the final form. This is a decision that will have to be taken by the clients with the aid of their counsel. The parties agree to form a company (method). Will it be a share corporation or private limited liability company (form)? A company purchases a 55 percent interest in a private limited liability company. Will the acquired company retain its legal form or be changed to a share corporation?

These most common methods permit a clear distinction between method and form. However, in some cases, the method and form converge; the method chosen determines the final form. Another legal step is not necessary. Method and form are not distinguishable. Although this is surely not an exhaustive list, we can affirm that method and form unite in four types of popular joint venture forms:

1. mergers
2. partnerships
3. unincorporated joint ventures
4. management contracts

Partnerships, unincorporated joint ventures (consortiums), and management agreements are all contracts. However, we have classified these separately for ease of discussion as they represent popular forms of a joint venture.

With these four forms of international joint ventures, method and form cannot be separated out easily, at least, not as a practical matter. The corporate manager when dealing with mergers is going to mostly encounter fact situations when two or more share corporations are united, one share corporation survives, one share corporation does not survive. The method, the merger, results in nothing more to be done. Once completed, the surviving share corporation continues. This is what is meant by saying "method and form have converged." In a partnership, the method chosen—the execution of an elaborate contract—creates the form known as a general or limited partnership.

There is a subsidiary question that we will not explore. It represents another dimension of analysis. What ultimate form the joint venture shelter takes does not have to condition how the ownership interest of any party will be represented. Two share corporations decide to form a limited liability company in Belgium. The method is the establishment of a subsidiary and the joint venture form is the limited liability company. But prior to the formation of the limited liability company, one of the future partners might decide to assign its interests in the forthcoming joint venture vehicle to a limited partnership.

Thus, the Belgian limited liability company will have as partners a share corporation and a limited partnership. This decision, what will be the legal form of the partners of a joint venture, is not a topic relevant to our discussions throughout this book. This is because the information to make this choice is highly dependent on a wide variety of facts affecting corporate taxation, consolidated reports, foreign tax credits, group organization, and even issues of identity: the extent to which a partner wishes to be known as being present in a joint venture. It is a question we will not explore, since it is heavily influenced by factors from which generalities are not easily formulated and does not affect the basic principles of creating joint ventures.

We may construct an outline as follows:

Methods for forming an international joint venture

(a) method that is separate from form
    1. acquisitions
    2. subsidiary formation
(b) where method and form converge
    3. mergers
    4. partnerships
    5. unincorporated joint ventures
    6. management agreements

In our discussion of methods, we will want to discern those features of a method that confer advantages or disadvantages, why one method may be preferable to another, and then of course what are the relevant characteristics of the more popular joint venture forms. This will be necessary in order to make a selection as to what is the more suitable joint venture form for any specific collaboration.

Consequently, our point of departure for further understanding is naturally an inquiry into method as this is the first choice that will be made when forming an international joint venture. Nevertheless, there is a close legal approximation between joint venture law and contract law and one genus is not always more simple than the other. Complex contracts can easily appear to be joint ventures. Joint venture law and contract law are thus neighbors at times without a clear, easily defined line of demarcation. The distinction is made more difficult as contracts often accompany a joint venture.

One easily slips into thinking a complex contractual relationship must be a joint venture or something akin to it due to the inordinate amount of legal drafting and negotiations forming part of a particular contract process, particularly if the contract calls for royalties based on net income. This obviously requires the right to verify the accounts of the licensee and so a contract right becomes enforced by having the power to investigate the financial statements of the licensee. The operations of one business unit become involved in the operations of another business unit. This is not, however, a joint venture.

Separating out the method and characteristics of a joint venture from the constellation of numerous contracts accompanying it requires a clear perception. It is difficult to encounter a joint venture that does not have a multitude of independent contracts associated with the venture. Consequently, some fundamental knowledge is needed to recognize such typical contracts and their legal characteristics and to understand better their function. In the formation of an international joint venture, all easily becomes blended into an unending mound of papers unless their purpose is well understood.

For the corporate executive, it is simultaneously necessary to see distinctly the various legal relationships but understand their reciprocal design, to understand the basic method and not be confused by multiple legal documents. The primary, fundamental joint venture documents must take precedence in establishing the indispensable rights of owners. Any complementary contracts will not usually enhance the rights of owners and management.

Moreover, many traditional forms of doing business are loosely characterized as being a *joint venture*. It is common to hear of the franchise relationship or distributorships being characterized as *joint ventures*. They clearly are not, and for purposes of focusing attention on the true characteristics of a joint venture our ensuing review includes typical contractual relationships that may form part of a joint venture but are independent of it.

Consequently, a simple explanation of the principal characteristics of common contractual alliances should assist in understanding how such legal relationships are kin to joint ventures, where they differ, and what part they play in the total complex process of establishing a joint venture. There is the joint venture and there are the various contracts.

What is a joint venture and what is merely an elaborate contractual relationship must be distinguished. We therefore will consider various contracts and transactions akin to joint ventures and explain why they are not joint ventures in this chapter.

The following list deals with the more popular contracts that may appear to be joint ventures but are not:

Contracts and transactions that have joint venture aspects

1. Licensing of patents, trademarks, trade secrets, know-how
2. Turn-key contracts
3. Franchising
4. Distributorships and agency contracts

5. Sale of assets or a division
6. Branches

PART TWO

2.2 A MERCHANT'S VIEWPOINT

In this Chapter Two and Chapter Three, we will review in detail many aspects of the different legal methods for forming a joint venture and various characteristics of dissimilar company forms. This is not a survey of all possible differences recognized by the law. It is a selected exposition. In both cases, when describing method and form, what have been chosen are those characteristics that are of greater importance to the entrepreneur class. Most businessmen are rightly concerned about limited liability, whether one legal form confers it and another does not. But there are elements of legal forms that have minor interest for the corporate executive. A corporation can be created only by complying with the statutory requirements. On the other hand, a partnership may be inferred by law based on the acts of the parties and their conduct. Although this distinction is important to lawyers, businessmen generally are not overly interested in these theoretical divergences unless they are themselves involved in litigation in which such facts are at issue. Palpably this is not one of the subjects of this book. Consequently, the choices for discussion are based on those basic topics often raised during meetings regarding the formation of an international joint venture.

We will now consider the essentials of some selected methods before passing to a more detailed review of various facets of each method.

2.2.1 ACQUISITIONS

An acquisition is clearly a method and not a form as we can purchase an interest in any legal structure, be it a share corporation, a private limited liability company, or a limited partnership. Acquisitions of contractual positions, such as in a consortium, are referred to as assignments, the purchaser being the assignee and the seller the assignor. To state we are making an acquisition as a way of proceeding to engaging in a joint venture does not reveal what the ultimate joint venture shelter will be.

An acquisition can be for the totality of the equity interests of another entity or only a part of its equity. Nothing is immutable. The legal form of what has been purchased can usually be modified into another legal form. Thus, a limited partnership can purchase the entirely equity interests of a private limited liability company and convert it to a share corporation.

Although the legal concept of an acquisition is elementary—an interest is sold and purchased—the visualization of the sale can become complex. A share certificate is the physical representation of an interest in a share corporation. But there are many legal forms that have no physical representation of ownership other than through a contract. When confronted with the possibility of an acquisition, therefore, one critical issue for the corporate manager to consider is: How will the ownership of the interest purchased be documented? For shares, it is a physical delivery. For partnerships, a more complex step is required, namely, alteration of the articles of partnership and filing the amendment at the relevant conservatory. For the moment, we will defer further analysis of such differences, and other aspects of acquisitions, other than to emphasize that acquisitions are simple in theory but not necessarily so in practice, a topic related in detail in Part Five of this chapter.

2.2.2 SUBSIDIARY FORMATION

Probably the most frequent method of forming an equity joint venture is by the creation of a local subsidiary, whose legal outlines, capital structure, and managerial aspects are negotiated between the parties. Forming a subsidiary means establishing a new company. The word *subsidiary* means it is owned by other entities, the partners. The word *subsidiary* indicates other entities are utilizing a separate legal form to do business. When someone says "a subsidiary will be formed," this is equivalent to saying "a company is going to be established." However, we are not informed as to what will be the legal nature, or characteristics, of the company. It is a way, a method, of proceeding. This is a very clear demonstration of the two-step mental process in forming a joint venture. It may make very good business sense to start up a company with another entity. However, once that step is decided, the future partners have to decide on the form of the joint venture vehicle: share corporation, partnership, consortium.

Acquisitions and subsidiary formation constitute the kernel of equity joint ventures. Each has its advantages and disadvantages, which we will explore when discussing criteria for choosing one form over another in Chapter Three.

2.2.3 MERGERS

Megamergers often make newspaper headlines. Although it is helpful to understand this method, it is not the usual method for forming a joint venture. Most mergers have very different objectives from the origins of the average joint venture. The underlying motif of a joint venture is collaboration. Mergers are frequently hostile in origin vis-à-vis the target company, and instead of collaboration, what is achieved is survivorship of the stronger. What is wanted are assets, not cooperation; economies through size; more clients through complementary services; market conquest by global networks. This is not the usual fact pattern of the everyman joint venture. To omit any discussion of mergers might seem an oversight, a lapse. However, the average company seeking a joint venture in another jurisdiction is highly unlikely to use a merger as a method of constructing an international joint venture.

There are two typical forms of merger. There is merger by incorporation and merger by fusion. In some jurisdictions, there is also recognized as a merger a situation in which one corporation acquires all the shares of another corporation and the acquired corporation transfers all its assets to the acquiring corporation. The acquired corporation thus becomes a corporate shell, with no assets, a ghost on a corporate registry.

In merger by incorporation, one company or more disappears into another. Survival Corp. and Not Surviving Corp. decide to merge. There is held the necessary general assembly; on approval, various legal procedures are required, including a public notice to creditors. Only one company will survive, obviously Survival Corp., and this corporation will most likely have its capital increased with an issuance of shares to the former shareholders of the now extinct Not Surviving Corp.

In merger by fusion, two companies or more disappear to form a third company. Continuing with the same nomenclature, Survival Corp. and Not Surviving Corp. may both transfer all their assets to another company called Third Corp. The transferring corporations then go through dissolution and liquidation procedures, as all assets have been transferred to Third Corp., and both are eventually extinguished. These latter two examples are the common methods of engaging in a merger. Although in theory, other legal forms of companies could engage in mergers, the great majority of mergers are confined to share corporations and it is the corporate merger the manager is most likely to encounter.

Mergers are frequently a result of a hostile takeover and occur within a particular jurisdiction between companies of that jurisdiction where the entities have a common business background and there do not exist substantial differences of national identity or culture. As a voluntary process, not involving a hostile takeover, being a consensual procedure desired by all parties, it is not a procedure that is lightly to be undertaken for once a corporation is legally expired it cannot be resurrected.

Merger is a method that rarely is utilized in forming an international joint venture. So drastic are the consequences to one of the corporations, so intricate are the accounting aspects, so unknown the consumer reaction, it is difficult to imagine why such a method would ordinarily be chosen in a foreign jurisdiction. Newspapers frequently refer to *mergers and acquisitions* (M&A) as if they were one activity, one set of legal facts, one having to exist with the other. This, of course, is obviously incorrect. They are two distinct processes.

2.2.4 PARTNERSHIPS

The word *partners,* or a *partnership,* is frequently used to mean entities are working together, without specifying the form, and even in this book, such nontechnical usage is employed. It is a simple way of expressing the idea of collaboration. However, in the law, a partnership has a specific meaning.

A partnership is formed by contract. It is an equity joint venture because it is formed with a capital by a contribution of assets by the individual partners. It indicates an agreement of persons, individuals, or corporations to form an organization in which each is the agent of the other. Every partner can bind the totality of partners unless the articles of partnership establish special rules. Even so, this may have a dubious effect with the public, dependent on the jurisdiction. There is no limited liability in a partnership. All partners are responsible for the acts of the other partners in the name of the partnership.

Withdrawal of a partnership is the inherent right of every partner, which act causes the partnership to dissolve.

Normally, the participants to a partnership foresee a duration and collaboration for an indefinite period. When the parties do not foresee an alliance of indefinite duration, as when the principal object is to complete a specific task, it is common to do this through an unincorporated joint venture.

2.2.5 UNINCORPORATED JOINT VENTURES ALSO DENOMINATED CONSORTIUMS

When heard or read for the first time, the expression *joint venture* conveys no precise meaning. Even if the context seems to make such content clear— "I am looking forward to our corporation doing a joint venture together with you in Poland . . . ,"—it is not a meaningful statement other than a possible trip to a distant land with new restaurants. It is impossible to know what is intended. The essential clarification needed is the basic division of joint ventures: Does our future partner want to form a commonly owned company or is something else conceived? Often, what is intended is a consortium, the classic unincorporated joint venture, a temporary alliance of entities to achieve a common purpose.

The key characteristics that inform us we are dealing with an unincorporated joint venture will be the absence of a stated capital; the requirement that there be a contract that defines the rights and obligations of each party; who is responsible for what financial contribution; each participant has unlimited liability for the acts of the others; and ownership is evidenced by the indication of the partners in the contract.

The unincorporated joint venture shares many legal characteristics in common with the partnership except that the unincorporated joint venture contract contains a substantial difference. Whereas the partnership is normally of unlimited duration, the unincorporated joint venture agreement is limited in duration and has a specific object. The unincorporated joint venture is temporary. It is finite. It is intended to end. There is a specific task to be completed after which the parties intend to disband their association.

A consortium is accredited as a satisfactory way of doing business for short periods. Its existence is temporary, in that a specific task is confronted by multiple parties with a view toward completing the job within a specific time frame. This form is often thrust on the participants because of public bidding requirements. A foreign construction company is obligated to associate itself with a local entity by the conditions of the public tender.

Building a petrochemical complex, constructing a tunnel, and erecting a barrage are all traditional examples of situations in which entities from different countries may work together to achieve a common goal. It is precisely the temporal aspect of a consortium that may be its principal attraction. The parties do not want to have a permanent nor prolonged ongoing commercial relationship. Naturally, consortiums are a way of parties working together, gaining a shared experience, and they may lead to other permanent forms of doing business jointly in the future in a common corporate structure.

2.2.6 MANAGEMENT CONTRACTS

The frontier line between contractual joint ventures and contractual relationships appears to be the management contract, in which there is a close cooperation between the parties and a sharing in the profits. However, as in so many descriptions of legal issues, there is a rampant confusion in terminology. There are three distinct types of contracts bearing the name of *management* contracts or agreements but three distinct services are being rendered and only one assimilates many of the features of a contractual joint venture.

1. management services of a partner in a joint venture or joint venture administration contract
2. management services by a third party of the assets of another or profit-sharing management contract
3. consulting or outsourcing services for a specific task or management consultancy agreement

2.2.6.1 JOINT VENTURE ADMINISTRATION CONTRACT

Contracts affecting management are quite common as complementary to joint ventures, in which one party, besides being a partner and making a capital contribution, also executes an agreement between itself and the operating company. Thus, Brazil Co. forms a subsidiary with Argentine Inc., denominated Brazil-Argentine Corp., but in the joint venture agreement, Brazil Co. has specific tasks affecting the management of Brazil-Argentine Corp.: to supervise the accounting department, to be responsible for personnel selection, to conduct marketing studies, to supervise research and development; or any other operational facet.

Such a legal situation is extremely frequent in the creation of joint ventures. A division of operational functions between joint venture partners is sensible, prudent in many aspects, and some joint venture agreements may contain a separate management contract between the joint venture company and one of the partners; or the division of managerial tasks is reflected in clauses in one or more of the documents forming part of the joint venture. The precise technique used depends on many factors and of course the complexity and magnitude of the joint venture.

This relationship is designated a *joint venture administration contract* for its purpose is an assumption of responsibility by one partner to administer, partially or totally, various phases of company operations; it is the type often associated with joint ventures in which one partner may assume specific administrative tasks within the structure of the joint venture. There is no need for stressing any joint venture aspect of this contract since the parties are, in fact, involved in a joint venture and the joint venture administration contract is an ancillary contract.

2.2.6.2 PROFIT-SHARING MANAGEMENT CONTRACT

There is the contract whereby one party, not in a joint venture with another entity, turns over, for reasons we will see shortly, many aspects of management to another entity. A typical example is a management contract involving hotels in which often the operator of the hotel lends its international name to a building but does not own or even lease the premises. The manager of the asset, through the prestige associated with its name, its highly developed marketing and client-referral system, attracts clients to the premises. It is this management contract that incorporates many features of joint ventures into a contractual form. It is the legal frontier between an unincorporated joint venture and a mere contract, albeit complex.

The contract contains many elements common to a joint venture in that there is profit sharing, delegation of powers, use of a common name and purpose. This arrangement is denominated *a profit-sharing management contract* for that is one of its distinguishing, unusual features, combining the efforts of management with results but no common ownership.

The profit-sharing management contract exists therefore when the only operative legal contract between the parties is a management contract and neither party is a partner with the other in a company or other legal entity, but there is a close legal involvement of the parties in running the business and in obtaining profitable results. Such a contract bears many of the problems of joint ventures. Nevertheless, the source of profit-sharing management contracts is not within a joint venture, not an allocation of responsibilities between partners, but the secondment of a third party to the premises of another.

2.2.6.3 MANAGEMENT CONSULTANCY AGREEMENT

Then there are those *consultancy agreements*, often also called *management consultancy agreements,* or *outsourcing agreements*, in which a third party assumes the obligation to provide services to a business, which the business could perform, but does not wish to employ personnel, for example, preparing shareholder reports and other glossy publications destined to the public. The expression *outsourcing* in this example is verbally accurate.

It can be seen now how profit-sharing management contracts, involving operational aspects of another entity's commerce, are substantially different from other contracts also commonly denoted *management consultancy agreements.* The outsourcing is done for a fee, with no intention of a participation in profits, nor is there even a joint effort toward a common corporate goal. What is contracted is one segment of the total corporate activities.

Typical examples include management contracts for installing and supervising hardware and software applications for inventory control; managing a bookkeeping department for smaller companies; running a transportation service for a chain of supermarkets. Such activities differ considerably from the hotel management contracts, as such *outsourcing* does not involve any sharing in profits, or fees on gross sales, or representing the owner of the business to the public or advertising the premises as being a "Great Eastern" hotel; nor do such contracts, although entitled *management* contracts, imply operational involvement by one partner in a common business structure, contracts that we have designated *joint venture administration* contracts.

PART THREE

2.3 TECHNOLOGY LICENSING: ROUTES OF COLLISION AND AVOIDANCE WITH THE JOINT VENTURE

Besides management contracts, there are a variety of other legal relations that may be integral parts of a joint venture. Separate from the legal issues pertaining to joint ventures, yet constituting often one of the key elements in the totality of documents accompanying the formation of a joint venture, many such contracts assume a primordial importance. In fact, the joint venture may have been constituted for the sole purpose of exploiting a contractual right, for example, a patent. Patent Owner Corp. forms a subsidiary with Corp. Learning and the joint venture receives a license to utilize the patent belonging to one of the partners, in this case Patent Owner Corp. In this way, the subsidiary will have direct access to the expertise of the patent owner, one of its partners, and the patent owner, by being a partner, has a privileged position from which to ensure the quality of the product manufactured. The concession of technology is often best exploited by forming a subsidiary between the licensor and licensee.

This is because a rigid separation between company law and contract law is not possible. They are not self-contained legal departments. There is a constant interaction between contract rights and ownership rights. Legal rights associated with ownership in the joint venture may collide with the obligations undertaken in contracts associated with the joint venture. In addition to possible confrontation between a contract and rights derived from the joint venture, it is also necessary to realize how, also, contractual rights may be avoided by joint venture acts, steps taken in contravening contractual clauses.

Thus, when we have a joint venture with associated contracts, there exist routes of collision and routes of avoidance, an area we will explore. Presently, further comments are necessary regarding technology licenses as they constitute a segment of much of the activity surrounding joint ventures and have been one of the material incentives to such formation. Consequently, an understanding of this area will enhance our comprehension of those joint ventures in which they have a predominant role before examining the routes of collision and avoidance.

2.3.1 LICENSING OF TECHNOLOGY: PATENTS, COPYRIGHT, TRADEMARKS, TRADE SECRETS, AND KNOW-HOW

The licensing of technology constitutes an important specialization in the law and receives considerable attention in many jurisdictions. Vital technical information is often licensed by one party to a joint venture to the operating company. It may be that this is the only way the operating company can have access to the technology. A manufacturing outlet established in South Korea with a French developer of computer chips must obtain a license for the chip technology to the joint venture subsidiary; otherwise the technology will become part of the public domain, lose its protection, and thus be available to anyone who can gain access, such as key employees of the joint venture.

There is a wide variety of legal rights that fall within the description of technology licenses. There are the traditional patents, a monopoly granted by the law to make, use, or sell an invention. There are trademarks, which are symbols, words, and designs combined together to impart a difference to the goods and distinguish such goods from other competitors.

However, legally, technology is not confined to only written, agency-approved applications reflected in designs. In the law, technology is whatever has novelty, is not known to others, has not been divulged to others other than under contractual conditions, and is consistent with public order and morals. Trade secrets, know-how only reflected in a sequence of events, customer lists, quality control procedures, packing methods, and training techniques are considered as worthy of protection as patents, trademarks, and designs. Thus, the law confers protection to a wide variety of human effort on which there can be extracted some commercial value and which can be summarized as industrial or commercial processes not of common knowledge and not easily obtained by third parties.

Besides what is denominated *technology* are a wide range of rights protected under the legal designation of *copyright*. Copyright for many decades was associated with the written word. What was written had to be protected before it was spoken; otherwise it became part of the public domain. With the growth of technology, traditional copyright categories such as books became extended to films and music, and, today, software programs are now acknowledged to fall within the traditional category of copyrights.

Consequently, technology licenses transfer any manifestation of knowledge that is within the particular knowledge of an entity, not revealed except under contractual conditions, many times protected by deposits, such as with the patent or copyright office but not always (trade secrets cannot be written and then deposited anywhere), and that receives a monopolistic exploration for a specified statutory period.

2.3.2 WHY TECHNOLOGY LICENSES ARE OFTEN ASSOCIATED WITH JOINT VENTURES

Technology licenses are sold separately and constitute a division of general contract law. Their frequent association with joint ventures is a result of being a convenient method for obtaining income. Besides just straight licensing, with no further involvement between licensor and licensee, oftentimes the licensor has a dual position. The most frequent example is when a technology license may be granted by one party to a subsidiary in which the licensor has an equity position along with a national partner. Partner and licensor are the same entity although with different rights, rights that may collide with attitudes assumed by the licensee. This dual position, licensor and partner, may be undertaken for a number of reasons:

- To earn royalty income is the most common motive asserted for the existence of technology transfers and probably the one that most readily comes to the mind of the reader. However, in a joint venture, one party may prefer to grant a license on favorable terms, for example, a joint venture to package spray wax, in which the alleged assertion of "technology receives royalty" is not in truth the prime incentive. Royalty income permits the licensor to receive a fixed income and not be dependent on dividend income. Dividends may not be declared. Royalties have to be paid.

- The royalty income may also be taxed at a more favorable rate. Thus, technology licenses for often very simple products, for products one wonders why a license is even needed, are frequently sought for income and tax reasons having nothing to do with the need for the technology. All the more reason why the associated risks described in what follows must receive consideration. Eventually, the licensee discovers the true inducement, or feigns ignorance in order to launch the joint venture with hopes of acquiring knowledge and earning income, and later attempts to avoid the consequences of the license.

- To furnish technical assistance to the subsidiary is another frequent motive for the association of technology licenses with joint ventures. If a subsidiary is selling or manufacturing complex equipment, for example, audio parts, it is going to need technical assistance and of course if one of the partners has been chosen because of its expertise, it is expected that the chosen partner will also be a licensor.

- To gain access to other markets and be present wherever there are consumers. Classic examples are beverage companies. However, it is not practical to set up one hundred percent owned subsidiaries. The manufacturer may take a small percentage of the equity and should, for the reasons noted in what follows. In this case, the salient legal feature is the technology license superimposed on a joint venture. This permits quality control and, if the joint venture is properly structured, management participation in the subsidiary.

- To purchase an equity interest instead of investing cash. Many laws allow, as a part of the capital of a company, cash or its *equivalence in kind,* meaning a substitute of value. Technology licenses fulfill this criterion and thus are often associated with joint ventures. Contributing technology as part of the capital avoids any tax consequences to the furnisher of the technology as contributing capital is not earning income. When there are assurances of future dividends or other income in a joint venture, this method is often utilized.

- To have access to a reasonable cost-basis labor market. When a manufacturing subsidiary is set up with another partner, and when the joint venture is assembled to take advantage of the labor market, it is often considered good public relations to have a local partner to deal with labor and governmental entities. This avoids the conflict of *we* and *they.* However, it also means that the local partner does not have the same convergence of interests as his foreign partner and with the onus of a technology license encumbering the subsidiary, the partner may feel the same exploitation as the laborer. Under these circumstances, foreign management participation becomes important to ensure compliance with the terms of the license.

2.3.3 TECHNOLOGY LICENSES AND JOINT VENTURES: LEGAL PRECAUTIONS

For every reason why a technology license may be appropriate, there are always reasons to consider that affect negatively the granting of such licenses or jeopardize its clauses. These risks are considered in what follows. In view of these hazards, any contract of technology forming part of a joint venture must be supported by additional clauses in the other legal documents forming part of the joint venture. There must be constructed additional complementary defenses. What are needed are clauses that address typical contract-avoidance behavior, and such protective clauses can be inserted in the shareholders' agreement (this is the agreement that binds the shareholders who are partners in the joint venture) or in other joint venture legal documents, such as the articles of the joint venture company. In subsequent chapters, we will consider the contents of the appropriate documents.

The reasons for various clauses are straightforward, if not apparent. The management of the joint venture company licensee may be dominated by the local partner; if management becomes discontented with the technology license, the license is not honored or grudgingly so. To enforce a contract right by the licensor against the licensee requires court action and various proofs. What is more effective is actual power within the company structure by one of the parties, which can fiscalize the commercial behavior of the licensee, the joint venture company, and even influence it so as to ensure substantial compliance.

With this in mind, far more safe, far more prudent are cautionary clauses in agreements between shareholders that can be implemented through the board of directors. This avoids court action. We will see that with a shareholders' agreement, for example, a licensor can have a direct route to the decision-making organ of the licensee. Preventing repudiation of a license is more effective and substantially less costly than seeking to enforce a licensing agreement.

What, then, are the concerns a licensor should have when executing a technology license and the parties are also involved in a joint venture and what additional means can be taken that permit the licensor to prohibit violation of the license agreement?

2.3.4 THE RISK OF COMPETITION

Obviously, furnishing knowledge to a party means you are making that party a potential competitor. Therefore, we want to reduce the risk that our joint venture subsidiary will become a competitor to the licensor when the license expires. This realistic fear must be sanctioned not only in the appropriate license, where it would find natural expression, but also in other joint venture documents such as the shareholders' agreement. When the license terminates, if the licensor still retains an equity position in the joint venture subsidiary, there exists an avenue of persuasion and action that reduces the possibility of a posterior violation of the license terms. With a properly drafted shareholders' agreement containing a provision allowing all partners veto rights in certain topics, we can be sure that after the foreseen expiration of the license agreement, the former licensee will not easily set in motion acts construed to be prohibited competition.

2.3.5 LOSS OF EXPANSION IN MARKET

Dependent on the equity participation and the terms of the license, the licensor-owner may not bear the fruits of a natural development of the market, particularly if the licensor-owner is a minority owner in the joint venture. Any collateral commercial possibilities will be seized on by the majority owner and instead of expansion through the licensee—the joint venture subsidiary—the other partner may set up a separate company to explore the market in question. This then relates to the object of the joint venture. What do the articles of incorporation say? The ideal solution to a forthcoming problem in this joint venture is better solved in the articles of incorporation than in a shareholders' agreement. This is because, generally, partners in a company cannot form other companies to compete. Therefore, the broader the expressed corporate purpose of the joint venture subsidiary, the more effectively is competition from a partner in a collateral field prevented.

Unfortunately, some jurisdictions insist on very limited object clauses. It may be prohibited to recite the purpose of the corporation is for *any and all commerce.* It must be specific: manufacture of test tubes; manufacture and selling of carburetors. The legal scope is confined within articulated limits. In such a case, our licensor-owner must fall back on a clause in the joint venture agreement or a separate shareholders' agreement where entry by the joint venture company or any of its partners into new ventures must be accompanied by a similar right being afforded to all the partners.

2.3.6 LOSS OF QUALITY CONTROL

If the licensor does not have a significant equity position, its managerial rights may normally be modest in the joint venture. This means the licensor loses control over manufacture, marketing, and after-sales service assistance. This raises issues of quality of the product and possibly product liability if there are injuries from a defective product manufactured under the brand name of the licensor, for example, "Good Boy Tires."

When the licensor holds a modest ownership interest, when perhaps the licensor is more interested in receiving royalty income, without general managerial responsibility being assigned to the licensor within the manufacturing joint venture company, there is no practical manner of ensuring quality control. Although the terms of the license may require quality standards, how are they enforced by a distant licensor? Unless the licensor has a quality control engineer working on the premises of the joint venture, the administrative burden of periodically sending someone abroad for inspections has few significant consequences.

The execution of a joint venture administration contract resolves these problems. It is not even necessary that the terms of the contract be a substantial source of fees for the licensor. It is a direct method for fiscalizing and ensuring quality control. Another alternative is for the shareholders' agreement to assign to the licensor-partner direct responsibility over the relevant department. These are simple complementary means to lend direct support to the technology license.

2.3.7 LICENSE TERMINATION, CONSEQUENCES, AND AVOIDANCE

We are used to hearing expressions such as "The license has terminated" or "On termination . . . " or even "With termination. . . ." What does the expression *termination* mean? In the context of a joint venture, where a trade secret for creating and exploiting mailing lists has been conveyed, what exactly is being terminated? The contract? Knowledge? But how do you eliminate knowledge or prevent its circulation?

What can be licensed has many properties. There is manual art, how you make something. There is know-how, how you blend the pieces together. There are trade secrets, which may be unusual applications of common knowledge. These are the difficult areas of knowledge that cannot easily find expression in documents deposited in a patent office, for once published, a minimum alteration of the application divulged will produce the same results. In other words, state of the art, manual expertise, trade secrets, marketing strategies, and proven display winners are simple examples of knowledge that can be licensed, but once the license is terminated, control over its future use is nearly impossible.

Avoidance of license requirements for such material is difficult to control unless the licensor has a presence in the ownership of the licensed company and there exists a vehicle for impeding intended breaches of the license agreement after its termination. Even with a minimum equity position, a right to elect a member of the board of directors, which can be a right attached to a special class of shares, can give the former licensor the needed mechanism to control posttermination avoidance of the license by insisting that the joint venture honor its contractual obligations. In later sections, we will review in detail how special managerial rights can be incorporated into various joint venture documents.

PART FOUR

2.4 TURN-KEY CONTRACTS

Once we leave the specialization of technology licenses and begin to consider other contractual arrangements often associated with a joint venture, the dividing line between a joint venture and a contract exists but requires careful analysis.

Turn-key contracts are construction contracts, but normally comprise one entity acting as a general contractor without any interference from the eventual owner of the premises. A turn-key typically involves the construction of a highly technical industrial complex. However, it may entail elements that interact with a joint venture, specifically, the possibility of management and ownership coinciding in the same legal structure that will own the factory.

In the classic turn-key contract, one party constructs a normally complicated engineering facility and after ensuring it is mechanically operational "turns the key" to the plant over to the other contracting party, that is, the owner. The owner of the industrial complex may finance the construction but does not want the supervisory complications that arise with a multitude of subcontracts, obtaining a variety of specialized equipment, and requisitioning the necessary personnel. Up to this point, we are confronting the usual construction contract with the additional requirement of putting the plant into operation and ensuring it is functioning as it should. There even may be a continuing fee for the know-how conceded, in which event the turn-key contract also assumes aspects of a technology license.

However, what if the owner of the plant wants the builder to maintain the equipment? Or manage it? Or manage the plant and export the final product? Or do all of the previous and resell the product through a commonly owned subsidiary? This last scenario is quite likely if the product in question involves a basic raw material being extracted in a country with a relatively simple industrial base and in which the owner, or part owner, is a public entity.

The affinity of a turn-key contract to a joint venture is thus apparent. It certainly becomes a joint venture when the party responsible for the construction has an equity position in the owner of the complex. And, of course, having had a brief review of management contracts, we can understand how, besides building the complex, a party may pass from being the builder to the manager through a profit-sharing management contract.

Thus, in a turn-key contract we may have

- a one-time turn-key contract that ends on completion of the plant fully functioning
- continuing royalty fees, and the turn-key contract now assumes elements of a technology license
- a potential joint venture if the provider of the technology and builder of the plant is also a partner in the owner of the plant
- a possible management joint venture administration contract or even a profit-sharing management contract

2.4.1 FRANCHISING

Franchising does not involve the establishment of a joint venture, notwithstanding appearances to the contrary. Its inclusion in our discussion is to ensure that the concept is correctly understood and not confused with a joint venture. For all the apparent homogenous aspect of a French retailer and a Spanish retailer selling the same goods from the same manufacturer, it is not a joint venture between the manufacturer and the individual retailers.

Franchising may be described as a standardized system of doing business that involves a transfer of know-how: the creation of a uniform image of the product, the transfer of decoration standards, display aspects, marketing knowledge, pricing, and advertising. Franchises, of course, involve a uniform appearance. There are utilized similar service marks and logos, designs that identify the product. There are granted rights for a period of time to utilize all external identification of the product with the consumer. Frequently, there is given help in choosing the right location for the outlet, merchandising techniques, display patterns, and even training manuals for personnel.

If we designate the seller of this know-how, the franchiser, then the recipient is the franchisee. The franchisee pays a fixed fee or a fee on gross turnover. Normally, however, the franchisee must also purchase the goods from the franchiser. Consequently, besides a transfer of know-how, we are also dealing with a distributorship. The franchiser is the principal and the franchisee is the distributor. The franchise contract may combine both legal concepts into one document or there may be two contracts.

Between the parties, there is no joint venture. However, to the public, on the contrary, it appears there is a joint venture or even the conviction that they are dealing with the principal with outlets throughout various parts of the country. The franchise contract is a separate legal concept that may incorporate other legal instruments but does not contain the essential characteristics of a joint venture. Why?

The franchiser does not have an equity position in the operating company of the franchisee. There is no ongoing participation in the management of the retailing company. The retailer pursues its own commercial objectives subject, however, to not engaging in any acts damaging to the image of the service mark. One party is not an agent for the other. The profits of the franchise may be subject to a royalty payment in favor of the franchiser, but the franchisee does not participate in the net income of the franchiser.

A reading of a typical franchise contract reveals the elaborate drafting constructed to ensure there is no joint venture and the franchisee cannot speak in the name of the franchiser. For all the aspects that appear to be common, this is only a result of deliberate marketing policies. The franchiser and the franchisee wish the public to believe there is a close alliance, a profound legal involvement between the local, operating national and the foreign manufacturer. It is not, however, a joint venture, just as the traditional distribution contract or agency agreement does not merit such a classification.

2.4.2 DISTRIBUTORSHIPS, AGENCY CONTRACTS, AND SALES REPRESENTATION

Although we often see a sign that states Corp. Distributor is an "Authorized distributor or agent of Corp. Manufacturer," there does not exist ordinarily any of the elements of a joint venture. Of course, a manufacturer may have an equity position in a distribution and that surely is a joint venture. But in the absence of joint ownership in a legal entity, the relationship of principal (the entity selling the goods) and distributor is only contractual. An entity can be an authorized or even exclusive distributor. The conditions of this exclusivity normally prohibit the appointment of another distributor in a specified territory. Exclusive distribution contracts are often subject to special legislation as in the European Union.

The essentials of the distribution contract are one party sells to another, the distributor, goods or services. The distributor is an independent contractor. The sale passes ownership of the goods to the buyer, what lawyers call *title*. Title confers all rights of ownership and the hallmark of a distribution contract is that there is a transfer of title from one party to another. This might not seem significant, but from title, at least with goods, are associated all economic advantages and disadvantages, including, of course, the right to resell.

Thus, Manufacturer Paris sells perfume to Distributor New York. Distributor New York defaults on payment but there is still perfume stock at the warehouse. If Manufacturer Paris can find it, he cannot take it because it belongs to Distributor New York. Manufacturer Paris must first obtain a court sentence that Distributor New York owns it. They also owe a debt.

From this simple concept flows a number of other legal ideas. The distributor is not a representative of the seller, usually a manufacturer. The distributor cannot bind the seller; the distributor is an independent party, not part of the organization of the seller; any assertions the distributor makes about the goods are his responsibility, unless contained in literature authorized by the seller. The legal relations the distributor establishes with other parties have nothing to do with the seller. The distributor sets the price, terms, and conditions of the sale. Not surprisingly, sellers often want to control resale prices to keep prices uniform; this restriction is forbidden in a great majority of jurisdictions. The seller can make suggestions but not impose obligations. The distributor must make an investment and normally carry stock. The passage of title means a sale and a sale requires payment or a promise to do same. When the distributor resells the goods, the risk of payment is with the distributor, not the manufacturer of the goods.

This is not the case with agency agreements. In an agency agreement, title never passes. The agent is not an independent contractor because the key to an agency agreement is "If." "If the goods are sold, if payment is received . . . then you (the agent) will receive a commission." Not otherwise.

In fact, often goods are not even stored and the agent merely has some samples or illustrative brochures. The agent is a mere extension of the owner of the goods, or the principal as he is denominated in the law. Goods sold by the agent require the principal, the manufacturer, to sign the contract before there is a valid sale. Title to the goods remains with the principal until time of delivery. It is possible to have an "authorized agent" relationship but the significance of this legally is dubious. Normally, there are many authorized agents within proximity of each other.

If there is a default in payment by the purchaser, it is not the agent who must pay but the purchaser. The agent did not sell anything as title to the goods was never with the agent, who was a mere conduit of information and nothing more. Consequently, it is the principal who will determine the price and under what conditions the goods will be sold. The agent never buys the goods of the principal. He makes no investment except his time, which is normally paid on a commission basis.

There are countless variations on different types of distribution contracts and agency agreements with important distinctions. But the essence of such arrangements can be reduced: In distribution contracts, title passes; in agency agreements, it does not.

Presently, with increased ease of communications and capital flows, these contracts have acquired a substantial relevance in international joint ventures as the parties involved rely on these contracts for the success of the joint venture, particularly with distributorship contracts. Often a manufacturing joint venture can succeed only if one of the parties ensures a steady supply of a raw material or parts through a distribution contract. Such contracts can establish exclusive relationships and have been legislated on by antitrust authorities such as the European Union Commission, which is responsible for detecting antitrust behavior in the European Union. Consequently, joint ventures involving distribution contracts must be carefully reviewed by counsel to ensure there are no anticompetition rules being breached in a particular jurisdiction.

As distribution and agency contracts are totally independent of joint ventures, their frequent association with joint ventures makes them important relevant legal instruments. When the manufacturer does not have an equity interest in the joint venture, the normal problems that arise are those associated with any contract, but it often occurs that the manufacturer does have an equity interest in the joint venture. The manufacturer derives a benefit as it is a form of monitoring the activities of the distribution company, which is the joint venture. The other partners derive an advantage in securing a source of goods. This creates the background for a typical problem of distributorships associated with joint ventures.

While the principal is a partner, the flow of goods is guaranteed. What if the partner-manufacturer sells his interest to a third party? Perhaps the manufacturer is disappointed with sales results; worse, is unable to collaborate with the other partners for various reasons. An event may have occurred that leaves the manufacturer in an unfriendly state of mind. Once free from the joint venture, the manufacturer may wish to sever the contractual distributorship with the ex-partner. Such a possible fact situation must be foreseen in the joint venture documents in that any alleged breach of duties between the partners cannot affect the contract of distributorship. The two concepts must be kept separate. Collaboration in a joint venture should not affect the principal-distributor relationship.

However, there may be cross-default clauses. This means that a clause has been inserted into the shareholders' agreement that causes another contract to be terminated, in our case, the distributor contract, if there is a default under any obligations contained in the shareholders' agreement. This is a legal weapon the partner-principal has if one of the partners refuses to adhere to the terms of the shareholders' agreement: The distributorship will be terminated unless the shareholders' agreement is fully honored.

Finally, another frequent form of selling the goods of another party is through a sales representation, which is less formal than an agency agreement. The sales representative, however, normally has a wide range of goods to sell, even of the same category, belonging to various manufacturers. For what is sold, there is paid a commission. The sales representative works for his own account. Title to the goods is with the manufacturer. Any contracts of purchase must be sent to the manufacturer for approval.

The typical sales representation is a contract that can be terminated by the supplier at will and is an ill-defined, ambiguous legal category. Such contracts do not have a substantial association with joint ventures. They do not have a stable enough environment to motivate forming a joint venture. A sales representation is a vague expression devoid of any legal substance.

Consequently, when two parties are going to form a joint venture and one of the parties will also be a supplier, the corporate manager must elect one of the traditional forms of supply, bearing in mind their practical distinctions and their consequences. The distributorship contract will confer the most rights.

2.4.3 SALE OF ASSETS OR A DIVISION

Purchasing assets is an alternative to purchasing shares. Company Buyer wanting to take over the business of Company Target can either purchase all the shares of Company Target or buy all, or some, of its assets. The different methods raise different legal considerations. Asset acquisitions occur frequently as an alternative to share acquisitions and various considerations, usually taxation, dictate one method over another. Company Buyer in our example clearly has not entered into a joint venture with Company Target. But assets can be sold to be used in a joint venture.

Assets or a conglomeration of assets forming an economically related unit, such as a division, are sold between companies. This frequently permits simplifying a business organization for management purposes and allowing others to produce the product with total commitment. The association with joint ventures occurs when one of the partners in a joint venture sells assets it possesses in another company to the joint venture.

This might occur when a corporation with a varied product line or activities wishes to separate out a sector and collaborate with another in such a sector. Perhaps a manufacturer of radios that also added a television division now wishes to sell this division to an operating company it forms with a software developer specialized in Internet matters and the subsidiary will attempt to merge the expertise into marketing television sets with accessories, permitting Internet access.

A sale of assets creates serious issues of valuation for the seller and the buyer and is not a common occurrence in the establishment of joint ventures. The sale of assets as an isolated contract of sale bears no affinity to a joint venture. When it is part of a joint venture, when the seller is also a partner in the purchasing company, there are troublesome issues relating to values to be given to and the quality of the assets transferred. We might even suppose a sale of assets is made to a joint venture company for accounting reasons: Sell the asset at a high cost and use the values as a means of purchasing an equity interest in a joint venture company.

Moreover, the sale of a division or multiple assets must be distinguished from the contribution of specified assets, in lieu of cash, to the capital of a joint venture company. This is a frequent occurrence and one of the more usual methods of creating a joint venture without a cash outlay. This is in contrast to the infrequent sale of assets by a partner to the joint venture company of which he owns an equity interest.

2.4.4 BRANCHES

There has been left to the last a short reference to branches because this legal form has nothing to do with international joint ventures. However, as sometimes references are made to this form of doing business, it is necessary to explain the legal design of a branch.

A branch is a transplant of a company to another jurisdiction. Corporation Commerce Belgium opens a branch in Spain. In Spain, the office will have on its door "Corporation Commerce Belgium." The reader will observe that a reference has been made to a "transplant" and not a "partial transplant." In legal theory, a branch is the cloning of a legal entity elsewhere. It is entirely reproduced. To register a branch in a jurisdiction, it is normal that the local law require the entire articles of the mother corporation, in our case Corporation Commerce Belgium, be translated and published in a local name with the indication of the local representative.

It is true that many jurisdictions permit legal entities that wish to open a branch to allocate a capital to the branch. This allocation of capital is an accounting device to ensure the local authorities that the branch will have a certain financial capacity. Otherwise, unscrupulous entrepreneurs could form corporations in jurisdictions that demand little in terms of capital security or few legal safeguards, and then register the branch in a more serious jurisdiction. Once a branch is established, in legal theory, the entire assets of the corporate investor are exposed to a creditor. Corporation Commerce Belgium is fully present; its entire assets have to respond to claimants, in Belgium or in Spain.

Consequently, a branch cannot be a joint venture. Only one entity is involved. There may be intercompany transactions, but they are all between the same company. For this reason, it is well established in antitrust law that the acts of the branch are the acts of the main principal offices, of the mother corporation, not just its branch. The home office is precluded from arguing that the acts of the branch cannot be attributed to it because the branch has economic independence and perhaps even financial autonomy.

This all may be true. The main office may have little knowledge as to what the branch is doing. However, as valid as this reasoning is economically, this is contrary to legal theory. Such an argument has been many times declared an invalid defense, a poor legal apology. A branch is just one more tentacle of the legal creature. For these reasons, branches as a legal form of creating a joint venture must be excluded from consideration in our analysis. It is legally impossible to have a joint venture with yourself. It would be a legal farce although possibly an economic reality.

This short survey reveals the characteristics of the usual ways of forming a joint venture and contracts associated with a joint venture. Having knowledge of the species does not ensure the choosing the right variety and it is this very difficult process we will now examine: how to determine what legal method is the one most suitable to the proposed joint venture.

PART FIVE

2.5 VARIOUS METHODS FOR FORMING INTERNATIONAL JOINT VENTURES

Our concern is with six basic alternatives that commercial experience indicates to be presently the common methods eventually leading to a joint venture. A summary has been made of their advantages and disadvantages. This is then followed in Part Six by a table that focuses more on topics of interest to managers. The order of alternatives is not by popularity but rather from noncontractual fixed legal structures with ownership interests to the contractual form. Consortiums, a contractual form of joint ventures, are far more popular than mergers, but they are indicated farther down the list. The purpose of this discussion is to illustrate various practical consequences of one method over another. The alternatives are

- acquisition
- subsidiary
- mergers
- partnerships
- consortium
- management contract

2.5.1 ADVANTAGES OF ACQUISITION AS A METHOD

An acquisition can be an exercise of legal simplicity. Purchasing a share can be realized by a deed of sale drawn by a lawyer, an endorsement of shares, or, in many jurisdictions, going to a notary who drafts the deed of purchase and sale.

The salient feature of an acquisition is that a legal form already exists. A joint venture vehicle is available for use. There is a company, an economic unit, a going concern. For the moment, it does not matter the form. The advantages to the method of an acquisition lie in the factual reality of a company already functioning. It's there. There are no approvals to be obtained, nor licenses. Forming a company is often a tedious, lengthy legal process requiring myriad documents to be published and filed.

With an acquisition, there are no legal articles of incorporation to create, which, if constructed from the beginning, usually involve a lengthy negotiating procedure. Most foreign partners purchasing an interest in an existing company require some changes to the corporate charter, but there is a tendency not to make too many requests. This is realistic as such a solicitation involves a lot of legal bureaucracy for the existing company: a general assembly, publications, and registrations. The willingness of the seller to make legal alterations to the target company or not being so disposed is like shifting sand. It changes and varies daily dependent on what is being discussed.

Another clear advantage to an acquisition is the prior history of the corporation being acquired, in part or whole. The annual gross sales are known. Calculations can be more securely made on an assumed return of capital. The market has been tested. Consumer habits are known. There is less commercial risk. There may be virtually none if we are dealing with an acquisition because of a retiring family ownership. The only calculation required is a valuation of the company.

A further benefit comes with purchasing into an existing economic unit. What is being purchased is a going concern and, except for some key personnel, there is no need to go through a lengthy selection and employment process. This reasoning can be extended to all aspects of an economic unity. With buildings, supply contracts, market contacts, technical assistance, the acquiring party loses no time with mounting the essentials. It is hoped that they are already in place.

Additionally, there may be less involvement by executives after the formation of the joint venture. Starting up a company requires an initial, total commitment by the participants. The added value, the potential capital gains, is often a result of going through the laborious, difficult choices that must be made in the early stages of a new enterprise. A financially healthy going concern may require only modest monitoring. With the high degree of corporate organization so much a feature of present economic life, the degree of engagement on a day-to-day basis is substantially reduced. The needed daily involvement of a major South Korean automobile manufacturer in a joint venture factory in Spain may be moderate. Monthly profit-and-loss statements, along with other current accounting material, coupled with periodic visits, may reveal all that is necessary. This would not be the case if we were starting from the beginning.

Moreover, the acquisition of a partial equity interest permits the investor to adopt a "wait and watch" approach. If the joint venture proves successful, the investment can be increased. Thus, unlike forming a company, an acquisition can be a step-by-step process, the avoidance of a total, financial commitment.

Withdrawing from the investment is a substantial inducement to an acquisition as there is an economic history that induced the buyer originally and that therefore may also interest others in the future. Selling a company under distress, with no prior economic record of results, is normally a protracted procedure. The sale of a share(s) in a going concern, even in a company whose financial condition is suspect, is usually possible as there are investors who will buy a share, or an equity interest, because they believe they can correct the errors of present management or they can bring new markets and they will make use of the existing facilities and personnel. A failed start-up company is not an attractive sales package.

Few investors would go through the trouble of establishing a joint venture with the idea of selling out within the near term. On the other hand, an acquisition does not involve the same commitment, at least not when the participant is taking a minority position and the main contribution of the new partner is capital. An acquisition for a minority partner is more of an experiment. For the partner in a start-up venture, there is a long process from study and research, negotiation and formation that normally leads to a longer "wait and see" attitude.

2.5.2 DISADVANTAGES OF ACQUISITION AS A METHOD

Nevertheless, purchasing an interest in a local corporation does have many drawbacks. There is a considerable hurdle to purchasing an interest in a going economic unit. What exactly is being purchased? What is the economic situation of the company? Have any facts occurred that may lead to a major lawsuit, as yet not initiated? How does our foreign investor know that the representations made about the accounts, the legal affirmations as to the assets of the company, are as they are being claimed? Any consequential acquisition requires the execution of a legal document that confers on the purchaser, prior to the purchase, broad investigatory powers. This investigation has received the formal name of *due diligence procedures* and it is a process that is a common feature of international joint features. Its importance is underlined by the extensive discussion in Chapter Seven.

Due diligence procedures may be met with some resistance, if not by the sellers, then by personnel who will be subjected to countless questions. Due diligence procedures require probing into all aspects of the corporate life, examining accounts, raising interrogations with employees, even having discussions with third parties, such as financial institutions and major suppliers.

A further significant drawback to purchasing an equity interest is there exists a corporate structure whose details may not conform to the interests of the new, entering partner. The corporate charter may call for an odd number of members of a board of directors when an even number is desirable, so as to prevent the concept of a *majority vote.* What is wanted is consensual management, but in an acquisition, existing management structures are difficult to modify. There may be only one class of shares and, for purposes of election of members to the board, it is convenient to have different classes of shares, in which each class has the right to nominate a specified number of directors. Such changes may be refused.

In addition, the company may have a stated capital not at all reflecting its financial strength. In some jurisdictions, companies traditionally have been started with modest initial capital in order to avoid tying up money for a venture that may not succeed. Growth is not reflected in any augments of capital so as not to attract the attention of the tax authorities. The shares of such a low-capital company may have considerable worth. How does a U.S. corporation justify to its shareholders a purchase of a share for U.S.$1,000,000 when the capital of the company is U.S.$5,000? There is a legitimate explanation, but it is long, tedious, and invariably implies to the board of directors of the purchaser, whose approval is necessary, "something is funny. That's not how we do business. "

Moreover, proposed legal amendments to an existing corporate charter, although perfectly possible, are often not accepted. There is fear that once changes are introduced, the consequences will not be known. Why make changes for purposes of a foreign entity? There is the foreign way of doing business and the local way. When the joint venture is seen with some reluctance by the nationals, wanting to effectuate changes motivates the nationals in the opposite direction. We have been doing business by ourselves for a long time; why do we need others? This is particularly true in family corporations. The proposed joint venture either comes to a halt or the foreign investor, a purchasing English corporation, for example, not understanding the tardy reaction to much needed statutory changes, desists.

The undesirability of the existing corporate structure normally increases in harmony with the enlargement in the amount of the investment. This has particular relevance for management aspects. When the investment is significant, the purchasing party expects to perform managerial functions. However, an acquisition often is an obstacle to effective management when the object corporation has a management structure not in conformity with the traditional stock corporation.

There exist in many jurisdictions private limited liability companies in which the ownership is reflected in *parts* recorded in a Commercial Conservatory. The management may be conferred by the articles of the company on the partners, not on a board of managers. When for legal purposes, as recorded in the local Spanish Commercial Conservatory, Sr. Gomez, an individual, is the *legal manager,* the one responsible by law for the proper administration of Gomez Ltd., how can the company thereafter be run by a board of directors?

Although in legal theory, Sr. Gomez could pass a power of attorney to a *group* of individuals, this is not satisfactory to either Sr. Gomez or the *group.* Sr. Gomez loses effective control but is legally responsible, being the legal manager. On the other hand, the *group* has practical managerial functions that can be revoked at any time by canceling the power of attorney. Its management functions are subject to the pleasure or ire of Sr. Gomez. It is thus not the ideal situation for either Sr. Gomez or the ad hoc board of management.

Even assuming legal dissatisfaction with the existing corporate structure can be minimized, the entire managerial aspects of the object corporation make the joint venture clumsy and awkward to administer. Thus, managerial aspects may be completely out of harmony with the legal realities, obligating substantial alterations to the legal structure that are not easy to achieve.

Finally, a going concern has personnel and assets. Whereas this avoids having to engage in a recruitment process, often human resources exceeds what the incoming management believes is necessary. Reduction of staff is not possible in many jurisdictions. In others, termination is only possible with payment of elevated amounts of indemnities. Assets may be hopelessly inadequate, but their disposal improbable. In short, an existing economic unit reflects other visions, other ideas, and a new participant will see quickly the need for multiple changes, which cannot be implemented in a brief period.

2.5.3 SUMMARY OF ADVANTAGES AND DISADVANTAGES OF THE METHOD OF ACQUISITION

As the comparison of the benefits and drawbacks in an acquisition involves many elements, a summary may be helpful. The advantages to a purchase of an interest in a corporate or other entity can be linearly summarized as follows:

- avoidance of multiple legal formation requirements and approvals
- simpler legal formalities to obtain ownership representing the equity interest

- the articles of incorporation are already drafted and this reduces lengthy discussions to altering only significant provisions
- there is a known economic history
- there is no need to search for personnel or purchase assets; these are present as part of the ongoing economic unit
- there is less executive involvement by the buyer after the purchase
- it is more probable to have management functions superior to mathematical aspects of ownership
- an increase in investment if results are positive is simply made by purchasing more shares
- a withdrawal from jurisdiction is facilitated by sale of shares and there is no need for the dissolution of the joint venture company

The disadvantages are as follows:

- the necessity for considerable due diligence procedures
- an existing legal structure that is not satisfactory but difficult to change
- a management form not suitable to substantial investments; change is only possible with the complete alteration of the legal form
- accounting difficulties when purchases are made in low-capital companies
- normally existing personnel exceed the requirements of the new partner but reduction of personnel is possible, if at all, only at a substantial cost

Naturally, each joint venture may warrant more emphasis on one aspect than on another. Sometimes an acquisition must be accepted on its terms. There is an interest for sale. It's a good business opportunity and no one wants legal niceties to stand in the way of the acquisition. Everyone takes the approach that any legal changes needed later will be implemented. Obviously, expediency often takes precedence over the ideal and when the joint venture is proceeding well with good economic expectations the parties will often be willing subsequent to the purchase to make the necessary alterations.

One technique is not to create a stressful atmosphere prior to the acquisition but secure a simple exchange of letters that the parties agree sometime in the future to discuss necessary alterations to the corporate structure. Such a good-will attitude is usually honored if not too much time is allowed to pass.

2.5.4 ADVANTAGES OF METHOD OF FORMING A SUBSIDIARY

As all potential partners are involved from the beginning, subsidiary formation obligates a consensual process and normally all parties reach a conclusion at the preformation stages when conflicting interests become resolved by compromise or the concession of special rights to one partner. All parties start with a clean slate. There is no corporate baggage that must be carried forth. Personnel requirements and capital assets are determined in accordance with the budget plans of the partners. The object of the subsidiary can be confined to a commercial area clearly delineated, or the opposite goal may be selected and a broad zone of commercial activity enunciated. Competition law principles may impose the requirement of a narrow corporate purpose.

Forming a subsidiary confers a substantial benefit in the form of a company tailored to the purposes of the participants. Corporate articles do not have to be altered, always a bureaucratic legal procedure in many jurisdictions. The formation of a subsidiary permits adopting articles in harmony with the terms of the joint venture. There is no attitude of "having to live" with articles of incorporation not entirely satisfactory. In contrast to a purchase of shares, which means buying into an existing economic unit, personnel requirements are established at the very beginning when subsidiary formation is chosen. Subsidiary formation permits a tailored, perfect legal fit.

At times, it is very difficult to determine whether a joint venture should be structured through a purchase of an interest in an existing company or the formation of a subsidiary. The notable advantage of forming a subsidiary is its ultimate, final equitable design. It can reflect the various legal and economic interests of all parties with considerable rapport. In the negotiation stage, there can be created a legal blueprint that reflects all the underlying reasons for the joint venture. A subsidiary displays a harmony between ownership and management. All parts beneficially contribute to the whole. The amount of capital bears a reasonable relationship to voting power; management rights are protected by the necessary shareholders' agreement; the articles of incorporation can provide for a special class of shares to protect minority interests.

A further considerable advantage is the absence of any due diligence procedures. Of course, forming a joint venture company with a partner requires having knowledge of the partner. But this does not imply prolonged, protracted due diligence procedures. It may be a partner with whom there has been some prior commercial experience, such as a distributor. Even without profound commercial knowledge of the future partner, the commercial risks are contained. There can be no creditors against a company not yet formed, nor the possibility of lawsuits.

2.5.5 DISADVANTAGES OF THE METHOD OF FORMING A SUBSIDIARY

The formation of a closely held company means starting with no prior results, and if the venture proves to be fruitless, it is difficult to convince third parties they can make a success of it. Another salient, striking disadvantage to establishing a subsidiary is that as all parties are beginning with a blank paper, each party has lines and paragraphs it wishes to see sanctified. Clearly, the more complex the joint venture, the more details have to be harmonized. Forming a company requires every detail to be discussed: capital, class of shares, corporate object, management structure, annual budgets, dividend policies, preparing the annual budget, identifying the capital needs; the list can be extended considerably.

Then there are the governmental approvals. When an acquisition is made, the target company should have all its operational licenses. Starting up a company requires compliance with all applicable legislative requirements, which can be numerous. An industrial joint venture will obligate satisfying zoning, safety, environmental and a host of "green" laws beyond the usual licenses relating to the industry in question, for example, pharmaceutical or chemical.

A subsidiary means personnel have to be employed. There is not an existing, seasoned staff. Many joint ventures are commenced without knowing if there exists an experienced labor pool. Even if one exists, it has to be selected and employed on current price conditions, which are usually higher than with personnel already employed, such as found in an acquisition.

Besides employees, there is the whole range of collateral activities that are so important to a successful operation: suppliers, bankers, premises, equipment. Everything has to be coordinated. Although this can have certain benefits, such as being current, it is a time-consuming activity.

Finally, but still meaningful, is the absence of an actual commercial experience. In an acquisition, there is a known history. In the formation of a subsidiary, no matter how experienced the partners, there is still an element of mercantile adventure in uncharted commercial waters.

2.5.6 SUMMARY OF ADVANTAGES AND DISADVANTAGES OF METHOD OF FORMING A SUBSIDIARY

Although the list of disadvantages of forming a subsidiary seems lengthy, in fact, the ability to customize a subsidiary to the interests of all the participants confers on a subsidiary an enormous utility for which existing disadvantages are assumed with patience. A partial list of itemized advantages is as follows:

- constructing a joint venture that reflects the objectives and intentions of all participants and is therefore a harmonious legal structure
- there are no needed alterations to existing legal documents or the corporate structure
- due diligence procedures are avoided
- there are no unnecessary corporate components, such as excess personnel or useless assets
- the corporate purpose can be broad or specific

Disadvantages may be summarized as follows:

- everyone has specific issues he or she wishes incorporated into the joint venture, at times conflicting with the other partners; finding the right compromise may not be simple and require prolonged negotiations
- government and other regulatory bodies must be solicited for approvals on a wide variety of items
- there are no personnel nor other services; the subsidiary must be created from the base
- there is no prior history; perhaps, the joint venture idea is not well conceived

On balance, establishing a joint venture with another party and having the opportunity to discuss all aspects from the beginning have much to commend as a preferred form for doing business. There is avoided making do with legal structures that are not satisfactory because of the perceived economic opportunities. What seems to be borne out by actual experience is that acquisitions are the result of hearing about interests up for sale, whereas subsidiary formation comes from meetings or dealing between commercial enterprises over a period of time. These comments are of course empirical generalities.

2.5.7 ADVANTAGES OF THE METHOD OF MERGER

Mergers, as described previously, have a technical meaning in the law. It is a word that indicates a sequences of events, the extinguishing of one entity by being absorbed by another entity or two entities go through the same process, forming a third. Regarding international joint ventures, the advantages of a merger are in a substantial corporate reorganization. All of this may be accomplished without any tax consequences since Corp. A and Corp. B now become Corp. A & B. The sum cannot be quantitatively greater than its parts, only qualitatively, which is precisely the reason for the merger.

Domestic mergers, those between entities from the same jurisdiction or same federation, as in the United States, are frequent enough. One of the great attractions of mergers is when one group may "acquire" another group and no cash payments are made; shares of the acquiring corporation may be given to the shareholders of the acquired corporation. Such a procedure raises many tax questions that require careful planning, but in spite of its complexity, mergers are a much used method when the parties are from the same jurisdiction or federation. A further motivation to mergers is access to the cash resources of the acquired company, also a frequent objective of hostile takeovers.

Oftentimes, companies from the same jurisdiction merge to pool complementary skills that mutually enhance the client base of each company, e.g., an Internet company and a manufacturer of CDs merge.

However, despite considerable reference to mergers and joint ventures as if they were one and the same, there is a legal ravine between the two concepts. Domestic mergers should not be confused with joint ventures. Many of the megamergers capturing business comment are concerned with hostile takeovers, analyzing the methods by which one group buys out another, raising for discussion what rights the former shareholders will have in the acquiring corporation, whether the takeover will be tax-free for all shareholders or what creative legal methods are employed to legitimately avoid onerous tax burdens. Substantially more goals could be enumerated, but none of them is concerned with joint ventures, the latter being a cooperative, fraternal legal relationship sought out voluntarily by various parties. The use of mergers as a method to form a joint venture is not frequent although it can surely have its logic.

Thus, with the European Union becoming more harmonized in its tax and financial laws, cross-country mergers are taking place between companies such as Berne Chocolate Swiss Tablets Corp. and Berne Chocolate Italy Tablets Corp. This permits putting operations under one managerial umbrella, consolidating reports, utilizing tax credits and losses more effectively with consolidated reports being accepted in the tax structures of the many jurisdictions. Again, Japan Watch Manufacturer Inc. (JWM) may have a subsidiary distributor Netherlands Watch Inc. and a merger is effectuated so that the distributor disappears and JWM establishes itself in The Netherlands. The reasons could be quite varied. However, a merger between companies from different cultures, not belonging to the same federation, is not a procedure normally followed for international joint ventures. The reasons should be obvious enough. The legal disappearance of a company is not a step to be taken lightly. What then are the advantages to a merger from the point of view of international joint ventures?

It is hard to enumerate any except those relevant to group reorganizations when multiple subsidiaries are involved and the disappearance of some of these legal entities is exactly what the parties want. A merger is therefore best understood as an alternative to dissolution and liquidation. It is less threatening to employees and creditors. Instead of the employer disappearing, another one is assuming the contractual obligations, the employees, the bank debts. Merger as an alternative to liquidation and dissolution thus presents itself in a more favorable posture.

However, the appropriateness of this form may be infrequently encountered but not in the traditional manner. We might imagine a U.S. hotel operator making a successful bid for a number of hotel units in an Eastern European country that are being privatized. If the hotel units are owned separately by different local corporations, the U.S. hotel operator might consider merging all the separate hotel corporations into one and then the U.S. operator might be the sole shareholder of the surviving corporation. This would be a horizontal *holding* structure in which one company now owns shares in various entities.

There are also many instances of vertical holding structures in which there is a long chain of shareholding starting in one country and spreading out vertically: Delaware Corp. owns Portugal Corp., which owns Spain Corp., and so on. Management decides to eliminate some of the intermediate corporations by merging them by incorporation so to centralize management and accounting control.

Nevertheless, the vast majority of international joint ventures involving entities from different continents or diverse jurisdictions with different legal characteristics are not derived from mergers but rather from parties seeking one another to construct a harmonious commercial entity.

2.5.8 DISADVANTAGES OF THE METHOD OF MERGER

Besides the severe legal alterations, a merger implies a wide range of problems that need to be resolved. Valuation of assets is paramount, as one group of shareholders is exchanging its assets for other assets. Management and personnel transfers to a new entity clearly are going to create anxieties of employment, tenure, and retirement benefits. There is also the modification of the corporate image before the public. Two trademarks may become one or a hyphened combination of the two, but it is not certain if decades of product image may not disappear without a clear marketing reason in spite of all the solid legal and financial reasons for the merger.

A merger requires shareholder approval or consent by the owners of the legal structure involved. Management cannot extinguish property rights without obtaining agreement from the owners of those property rights. It is not easy to imagine a board of directors securing consent to extinguish itself to be incorporated into a corporation in another part of the world. Furthermore, in most jurisdictions, mergers require substantial statutory compliance with procedures to be followed to notify creditors and all shareholders. If we are dealing with large corporations, the distant legal requirements are serious obstacles due to language problems and comprehension of what is required; if we are dealing with modest capital entities, the cost is not balanced by any significant advantages. There are so many other ways of achieving the same goal.

Certainly, domestic mergers have their reason and justification and these are evidenced by the substantial amount of activity in this area. For corporate managers who are going abroad for the first time, who must advise their board of directors how to proceed, there is little reason to utilize this method. That the occasional motive may appear cannot be denied, but searching for it is not productive. There seems little reason to compare the advantages and disadvantages to this method as they are sparse and tenuous.

2.5.9 ADVANTAGES OF THE METHOD OF FORMING A PARTNERSHIP

A partnership is formed by executing articles of partnership, which is a contract between the partners whereby they agree to be associates. A partnership, as a method, is therefore not any more complex or more simple than the drafting of any contract. However, although a partnership is the second of our classifications that represent a deviation from the method-form cleavage, it is far more prevalent and more chosen as a joint venture form. The method of creating a partnership, by contractual articles, also creates the final form. There is nothing further to be done. No one would create a partnership and then convert it into a share corporation. The corporation could be formed from the beginning.

If an interest is being purchased in a partnership, the method is then one of acquisition and in these circumstances method and form are different.

However, it is the rare joint venture that is established by purchasing an interest in a partnership unless we are dealing with professional groups. The reason will be better understood after reading Chapter Three. Essentially, the characteristics of a partnership include unlimited liability for all as all partners are responsible for the debts of the partnership and its temporary nature. Any alteration in the composition of the partnership, such as death of a partner, causes an automatic dissolution of the partnership. Most businessmen would not risk unlimited liability in a foreign jurisdiction.

Probably most partnerships are established from the beginning and thus the steps associated with forming a company find their equivalence in the establishment of a partnership. All the advantages associated with forming a company are true for a partnership. We can thus rephrase them within the context of creating articles of partnership:

- The articles of partnership will be specific to the purpose of the partnership.
- There are no needed alterations to the partnership agreement.
- Due diligence procedures are not required.
- The assets and liabilities of the partnership are acquired as needed.
- The purpose of the partnership can be broad or specific.

2.5.10 DISADVANTAGES OF THE METHOD OF FORMING A PARTNERSHIP

The disadvantages of establishing a partnership as a method are those of forming a subsidiary:

- The drafting of the articles of partnership will require prolonged negotiations.
- Approval for the formation of the partnership may require a government license.
- There are no personnel nor assets. The partnership is created from the base.
- The partnership is a new entity. There is no prior commercial experience to determine if the commercial object is viable.

Due to the restricted use of partnerships in forming international joint ventures as they create unlimited liability, there is no practical utility in comparing their advantages and disadvantages. In any event, the same inferences can be made based on the comparisons made with acquisitions and subsidiaries.

2.5.11 ADVANTAGES AND DISADVANTAGES OF THE METHOD OF FORMING AN UNINCORPORATED JOINT VENTURE

All the methods described earlier fall within the category of equity joint ventures. Even a partnership, which is formed by a contract, is considered an equity joint venture because of the various features it has in common with other legal structures such as the share corporation or the private limited liability company. These common features include a capital fund. The parties foresee a stable relationship over an indefinite time. There is not a concrete project to be completed but rather a coordinated activity to enter into the stream of commerce with a specific product or service. The purpose may be even less precise than it should. Business is commenced with one objective, which is modified quickly in view of unexpected market conditions. This is one of the emblems of equity investments, flexibility in view of the changing conditions over a period of time.

However, the unincorporated joint venture is the second of our classifications where method and form converge. Very often, this method is imposed on the participants by the foreign government. A bid will not be accepted unless one of the associates is a local entity. The foreign constructor has no choice other than to form an unincorporated joint venture.

A further prominent reason for choosing the consortium as a method-form lies in its limited duration. It is not intended to endure indefinitely. However, a better appreciation of the benefits of this legal form will be gained in Chapter Three where the characteristics of the various forms are discussed.

2.5.12 PROFIT-SHARING MANAGEMENT CONTRACT: ADVANTAGES AND DISADVANTAGES AS A METHOD

The last of our possible joint ventures—the profit-sharing management contract—being used only for niche industries, does not warrant an extensive treatment. Rather, the significant aspects of this method-form will be summarized now due to its limited application.

Running a business requires mental resources and physical assets. Oftentimes, the same entity does not possess both, at least initially. The profit-sharing management contracts offer a method for doing business in which one party has no capital risk although there is an abdication of future profits. A traditional industry to which this concept applies is the hotel industry because ownership of the hotel installations often has its origins in access to capital but not necessarily hotel expertise. Consequently, many of the world-famous hotel chains are managed by one corporate group and the underlying asset, in this case the building, is owned by a local group, who has furnished the assets, built the hotel, decorated the hotel, but lacks, for the moment, the knowledge to run it or has no recourse to a database of clients and travel agencies. It is even frequent procedure for the owners of the premises and the operator to sign a contract before the hotel is built so that the specifications of the hotel, its appearance, décor, and location are in accordance with the tourist standards expected of the hotel chain; but ownership and operations belong to different groups.

There is executed a profit-sharing management contract. For a percentage of the gross income, or fixed fee, an experienced hotel group takes over the management and, with personnel furnished by the owners of the physical asset, administers the hotel in accordance with quality standards. The operator may install temporarily some of the key personnel to ensure a proper initiation of activity, which is always the critical period. Many of these contracts have a natural term or can be terminated with notice, so once the local group obtains sufficient operational knowledge or believes tourist income is assured, the management contract may be terminated in accordance with the appropriate clause. Consequently, the managers lose the benefits of a now ongoing business but have received a solid return for their time.

A particular aspect of hotel management contracts, which betrays their close affinity to a joint venture, is the involvement of one entity in managing the assets of another entity. The issues normally the subject of draftsmanship include the operation of the hotel, who will be responsible for what sector, what authority management will have, what expenses the managers may incur, when the owners are obliged to make capital expenditures, limitations on expenditures by the managers, when fees will be paid, all these an incomplete list. Even so, such a list reveals many of the typical problems facing partners in a joint venture.

The conspicuous disadvantage to a profit-sharing management contract is that it is usually temporary in nature with a foreseen expiration date. There is no guarantee therefore that the efforts of the manager are going to be prolonged. If the business can be learned by the owner, the management contract is not renewed. The hotel adopts a different name.

The industries in which such contracts are utilized are specialty sectors, not the usual commercial areas. Consequently, the average manager is unlikely to have to consider the advantages or not of a profit-sharing management contract because when such an opportunity arises, it is probably only the profit-sharing management contract that will make any commercial sense.

Part Six

2.6 Time, simplicity, cost, and management objectives

The brief, earlier summary does not attempt to review the many other items that can influence the choice of any one method. This will be done in the tables found later in Part Six. An effort has been made to list the more frequent relevant material the corporate manager should review. However, even the tables are a shortened version of the multiple considerations that enter into the decision-making process. The tables are intended as a general reference, a quick survey to assist understanding in the early stages of selection. In fact, sometimes there is no alternative. An opportunity is presented that must be accepted in the method and form in which it is offered.

Other times, management may have freedom to choose. To be able to decide what is the most appropriate method for the particular facts requires a standard by which comparisons can be made. Unfortunately, there are no standardized tables that list the advantages and disadvantages of each method, and then compare them with all other legal methods. This is because each international joint venture is fact-specific, the weight to be given to any item variable and dependent on the participants and their objectives.

Nevertheless, the various legal methods leading to an international joint venture should not obscure the underlying commercial realities. Forming companies, purchasing shares, executing contracts and other legal acts involve personnel, boardroom discussions, strategies, trips to other countries, legal advice, and, of course, expense. When searching for the decisive element that suggests a particular method over another, when considering a method by which to proceed, a comparison should also be made with the practical consequences in mind. We cannot make a selection based only on the theoretical legal advantages. By the time we have completed our legal survey on a particular proposition, the potential acquisition is gone, the equity ownership having been bought by a third party.

Consequently, the various methods have several patent commercial consequences. Time is a crucial factor to most corporate executives. Some methods are more complicated then others. Complexity and time often accompany one another in direct relationship. This may be unavoidable. There is no way of unraveling complexities quickly. Cost is a more elusive element. Complexity may involve more disbursements, but this is because the advisors are attempting to avoid future problems. Seen in this light, the present cost, even if high, may be cost-effective later. There may be no cost if the future is free from problems. A clumsy method with no thought of consequences, no matter how simple and quick, is an expensive method. Later, there will be uncertainties and issues to unravel that will cause a significant disbursement. If there exists no simple alternative to forming a joint venture, the complexity should not be ignored but dealt with in the proper manner: obtaining expert advice.

Perhaps the most important practical element is what method most closely achieves management objectives. Acquiring a company with too many personnel and a diversity of product lines no one wants is leading to an international joint venture without clear management purpose. Thus, amongst all the various methods, the element of management objectives should assume a primordial importance. The method that most closely approximates the reasons management has for entering into an international joint venture is the method that will prove to be the most beneficial and therefore the least costly, even if initially greater disbursements are expended.

The tables compiled are intended to give to the corporate manager a quick reference for various topics dependent on the method chosen. It is a systematic outline of each method in contrast with the earlier discursive treatment, which was a basic introduction to the consequences of the more popular available methods.

They are tables based on experience and hardly can be called anything but "empirical." The topics listed are those encountered in international joint ventures but surely not exhaustive. Every joint venture brings its unique set of facts. The functions of the tables are to synthesize succinctly the consequences of the usual available methods and rapidly convey the outstanding advantage, disadvantage, or neutrality of each method. The first item listed in each table is *management objectives* because irrespective of the latter considerations, such a consideration is the first to be considered by the corporate executive. Each table will review the following elements, how they are affected by the different methods, and which usually accompany international joint ventures.

The tables reveal what has been the experience of practitioners of international joint ventures. In most cases, our conclusion is that forming a subsidiary is the simplest method and confers the most advantages for it should result in a business entity in which the rights and duties of all parties are in equilibrium. Management objectives can be defined succinctly. The management style can be customized. Expensive, costly due diligence procedures are avoided. Of course, the dynamics of commerce do not always permit the parties the freedom of making a choice. How the opportunity is presented may be the only election possible. For this reason, the tables consider the following elements for the six major methods of forming an international joint venture:

1. Management objectives
2. Management structure
3. Due diligence procedures
4. Confidentiality agreement/procedures
5. Accounting complexities
6. Alterations to target company legal structure
7. Company formation
8. Shareholder approval
9. Organizational meetings
10. Investment license
11. Governmental notices or approvals
12. Necessity to obtain licenses and permits
13. Going concern
14. Creditor claims/litigation
15. Personnel
16. Tax on transaction
17. Specific tax implications
18. Formalities of transaction
19. Necessity to acquire assets
20. Necessity to acquire contracts
21. Necessity to acquire leases
22. Patents, technology licenses, and copyrights
23. Flexibility in payment
24. Flexibility in financing
25. Closing
26. Summary

TABLE 2.1   Acquisition

By acquisition, we mean the purchase of a significant interest, although it may be a minority, in a legal entity, such as the purchase of shares, quotas, or partnership interest. This is a method frequently utilized by moderate capitalized companies as well as multinationals.

1. Management objectives

Acquiring an interest in an operating company means having to accept the current economic and market objectives of the acquired company. Ordinarily, this is not as customized as the acquiring managers would want. It is normally difficult to alter the general economic and legal outlines of an existing company; for this reason, acquisitions tend to provoke conflict more readily than, for example, forming a subsidiary. An acquisition is not readily tailored to a specific management objective. Substantial time will be spent negotiating alterations to the company articles of incorporation.

2. Management structure

An acquisition is unlikely to result in any substantial change to the way the management of the company is organized. The passage of time in companies naturally tends to create vested interests by employees in the organization. There will be resistance to making any changes. Consequently, the managerial structure resulting from an acquisition tends to foment conflict.

3. Due diligence procedures

The acquired company normally has a substantial economic history, which means creditors and always the possibility of litigation. Due diligence procedures therefore must be undertaken, which is time-consuming and costly. An acquisition as a method of forming a joint venture requires considerably more caution, which translates into due diligence procedures as to the legal, financial, and economic aspects of the target company.

4. Confidentiality agreement/procedures

The necessity of due diligence procedures means the execution of a confidentiality agreement and procedures to enforce it. This naturally lengthens the investigatory procedures. Although the method of forming a new company may also involve an exchange of information, and hence require a confidentiality agreement, forming a company is normally preceded by a period of commercial relationships between the parties. Due diligence procedures in an acquisition of necessity must delve into all major aspects of the target company.

5. Accounting complexities

The purchase of an equity interest does not involve any special accounting complexities.

6. Alterations to target company legal structure

They will probably be necessary and these always involve protracted negotiations and compromises reached.

7. Company formation

There is a considerable advantage in an acquisition as it avoids the drafting aspects and decision making associated with forming a company and they can be considerable. These range from practical considerations such as capital structure and shareholder rights to legal requirements of drafting articles, publishing them, and making registrations.

8. Shareholder approval

If there are transfer restrictions in the articles of the company, and there usually are, the buyer may have to go through protracted procedures to obtain approval from the shareholders of the target company.

9. Organizational meetings

An acquisition will require changes in management, which means new nominations to the board of directors. It is the same procedure when forming a company except for one important difference, which usually leads to conflict: there is a change of management at the top.

10. Investment license

A license to import capital to make the purchase may be necessary.

11. Governmental notices or approvals

As approvals have been obtained previously by the target company, they usually are not necessary unless there are antitrust considerations.

12. Necessity to obtain licenses and permits

The operating company should have them. As a method, an acquisition thus confers a substantial benefit by avoiding a myriad of preformation requirements and petitioning for licenses.

13. Going concern

This is a decided advantage since one does not purchase an interest in a company unless there is the strong expectation of profit.

14. Creditor claims/litigation

A purchaser is buying into a going concern, which means there are going to be creditors and probably litigation, and these create the need for thorough due diligence procedures. However, no amount of due diligence procedures will avoid the unexpected, unforeseen lawsuit. Thus, acquisitions always contain this latent danger.

15. Personnel

Except for key personnel of the purchaser, the operating company should have the necessary staff. However, as we are dealing with international joint ventures, the employment laws will probably have special features that prevent reduction of staff and there will be accrued employee benefits. Acquisitions tend to result in an excess of personnel.

16. Tax on transaction

There may be stamp duties or transfer fees on the purchase, but these are not normally a deterrent to the sale.

17. Specific tax implications

We are not discussing the general tax characteristics of the joint venture vehicle but if the method of acquisition creates any special taxes. There may be a capital gains tax owed by the seller, which is passed on to the buyer in the sales price.

(continued)

TABLE 2.1 *(continued)*

18. Formalities of transaction

The purchase of shares or other equity interests is normally simple. There are not many formalities involved. In some jurisdictions, an endorsement on the shares is sufficient. In others, there may be a deed of sale.

19. Necessity to acquire assets

The operating company should have the assets needed, which is thus an advantage.

20. Necessity to acquire contracts

Same as the preceding.

21. Necessity to acquire leases

Same as the preceding.

22. Patents, technology licenses, and copyrights

Same as the preceding.

23. Flexibility in payment

Flexibility is dependent on the sellers. Normally it is just cash or its equivalence. If the seller is leaving the acquired company, he may require a contract for personal services to stay on as an interim manager or even as a form of further payment. But flexibility of payment is normally absent in an acquisition.

24. Flexibility in financing

An acquisition usually means less flexibility in financing unless there is a 100 percent buyout, which means we are not dealing with a joint venture. If other partners exist, they are not going to consent readily to any financing that creates charges or encumbrances on their interests.

25. Closing

In an acquisition, there are multiple steps that must be completed before the final transaction can take place and even then there are probably provisions for postclosing adjustments to the price dependent on a final verification of the accounts or the performance of the company.

26. Summary

An acquisition as a method of forming a joint venture will not be any less complex than when forming a company, but a great deal more of prudence and investigation is necessary as there exists a going economic concern. Problems may not be transparent. They may even be concealed.

There will not be the same freedom of erecting the corporate structure that is a perfect fit for all the partners as in forming a company. Often in international acquisitions, the buyer has to adjust to a management style that is not the natural organizational style of the purchaser. Management objectives are likely to be less specific.

Due procedures and compliance with transfer restrictions are time-consuming. The material advantage to an acquisition is not having to construct and furnish the house from the very beginning. If the buyer can secure multiple warranties and covenants from the seller who is a solvent, reputable concern, an acquisition can be made very quickly, and after the acquisition there can be conducted the necessary verifications and due diligence procedures. This only occurs in those situations in which the acquisition is seen as very favorable and there is no time to be lost.

TABLE 2.2   Subsidiary

By forming a subsidiary, we are referring to two or more entities deciding to establish a company between them. For our purposes, the final legal form of the subsidiary is irrelevant. As a method, subsidiary formation is utilized by companies of all sizes.

1. Management objectives

Establishing a subsidiary affords the best opportunity to reflect the managerial objectives of all parties. The parties can make the commercial purposes broad or narrow, dependent on the corporate strategy of each participant. Jurisdictional requirements may be imposed by antitrust considerations, which invariably means a narrow corporate purpose. However, subsidiary formation is to construct a joint venture vehicle that reflects the commercial vision of the participants. Subsidiary formation thus tends to be more harmonious in results. There are no expectations perhaps fomented by the sellers as in an acquisition.

2. Management structure

With formation of a company, the parties will create a management structure in accordance with the size and dimension of the company. Therefore, there should not be inadequate management structures in place, which often happens in an acquisition. More importantly, the method of management will reflect the philosophies of the partners.

3. Due diligence procedures

None is needed, a significant, decided advantage.

4. Confidentiality agreement/procedures

The exchange of confidential information will be minimal. When technology is being contributed, the confidentiality of such knowledge is no greater than in a licensing of technology. The problem is not in the method but what is being divulged. Secrecy therefore must be contractually established.

5. Accounting complexities

There are none.

6. Alterations to target company legal structure

None needed, as the stellar feature of forming a subsidiary is creating the precise legal structure the parties desire.

(continued)

TABLE 2.2 *(continued)*

7. Company formation

This can be time-consuming. Articles of incorporation have to be drafted and this normally involves multiple discussions. Many choices have to be made, ranging from capital structure to creating the entire corporate structure with all the appropriate rights and obligations.

8. Shareholder approval

None is needed.

9. Organizational meetings

A first board of directors and other offices need to be nominated. It is not any more time-consuming than having to make substitutions to the board of directors in an acquisition, although since no one is being removed, there should not be encountered any hostility resulting from the composition.

10. Investment license

The capital contribution, as with a capital acquisition, may require local approval.

11. Governmental notices or approvals

These may be needed as a new company is being formed. They may involve considerable time.

12. Necessity to obtain licenses and permits

Same as the preceding.

13. Going concern

The subsidiary is starting from the beginning with all this implies. It is normally a significant cost-incurring step, ranging from asset purchases to personnel selection.

14. Creditor claims/litigation

There are none to anticipate. This is a decided advantage.

15. Personnel

They must be hired but this brings an advantage since only necessary personnel will be employed.

16. Tax on transaction

There should not be any, although in some jurisdictions, there is a tax on the capital of the company to be formed. Such a tax is not normally a deterrent.

17. Specific tax implications

Forming a subsidiary does not imply any special tax features. However, as it is possible to contribute to capital assets other than cash, the use of goods, such as equipment, has to be evaluated and this raises accounting implications in the jurisdiction of the foreign investor. In the case of consolidated reports, Foreign Investor Inc. contributing machinery for a value of $1 million when its depreciated value is $0.5 million has accounting and hence tax consequences in the jurisdiction of Foreign Investor Inc.

18. Formalities of transaction

They will be more than in an acquisition. In most European countries, the formation of a company whereby ownership will be evidenced requires conferences with the local public notary and proof of the capacity of the parties. This, in turn, may require the parties, particularly if they are companies, to secure multiple documents from their state of incorporation and have them translated into the language of the locality.

19. Necessity to acquire assets

They must be bought.

20. Necessity to acquire contracts

If necessary, they must be acquired. Consequently, in subsidiary formation as a method, they must be well-planned and well-negotiated if they are crucial, key contracts.

21. Necessity to acquire leases

Same as the preceding.

22. Patents, technology licenses, and copyrights

Same as the preceding.

23. Flexibility in payment

There is the most flexibility in this method since it is common for one party to contribute to capital many rights other than cash such as assets, contracts, technology, even services. On the contrary, in an acquisition, the seller wants cash. Subsidiary formation affords corporate finance substantial flexibility in what will be used as a capital contribution.

24. Flexibility in financing

Subsidiary formation normally permits greater financial engineering because even prior to the establishment of the company, approval in principle can be secured from a local bank for its financing needs. If all partners need to give guarantees, this can be achieved. In an acquisition, the buyer must procure his own financing. The remaining partners are not normally involved.

25. Closing

Closing formalities are substantially reduced when compared to an acquisition. The prime reason is the absence of due diligence procedures. There is nothing to confirm. There are no warranties, no conditions a seller must fulfill. However, there are some formal procedures, such as signing the necessary documents before a notary or filing same in a commercial conservatory.

(continued)

TABLE 2.2 *(continued)*

26. Summary

Forming a subsidiary is a method that confers on the participants the most advantages. Although it is necessary to start from the beginning and obtain many approvals, the company established should reflect closely the management aspirations of the participants. Company establishment tends to be conducted in a less frenzied atmosphere than acquisitions. The participants have studied the market and exchanged many ideas. There is a tendency to gradually drift toward a common middle ground on issues. When forming a subsidiary, parties working together to form the company generally create a cooperative milieu, a working spirit of driving toward the final objective: the formation of a company evidencing the individual characteristics of all the partners.

The absence of due diligence procedures reduces considerably the steps to a closing.

TABLE 2.3   Merger

A merger is an awkward legal method to utilize on the road to an international joint venture. A merger occurs when one corporation absorbs another; or two corporations dissolve and form a third corporation, transferring their assets to this latter corporation. Another form of merger occurs when one company acquires all the shares of another company and the acquirer has conveyed to it all the assets of the acquired company. As not all situations can be anticipated, it is helpful to have an understanding of this method, if for no other reason than mergers often make headlines although those mergers have little to do with joint ventures. The mergers in newspaper headlines are predatory mergers, the absorption and elimination of an entire corporate structure and share ownership. For international joint ventures, there is a modest alteration to this general scheme. The process will be the same except the parties intend to continue with previous owners and management to some degree in the surviving corporation. The most common form of mergers for international joint ventures is by absorption, the first example indicated.

1. Management objectives

A merger creates the most problems concerning management objectives and will surely raise antitrust considerations if the companies involved have substantial market shares. As there is only one surviving corporation, an amalgamation of two previous corporate activities into one necessitates a considerable adjustment between the corporate purposes; between the markets being pursued; and, the most difficult question of all, between the human resources from different organizations.

2. Management structure

In a merger, the harmonizing of the two different management structures will produce without doubt tension and resignations. These are frequently written about and the success rate of joint ventures from mergers is not good.

3. Due diligence procedures

A merger necessitates a thorough legal and financial examination of the company to be absorbed. It requires the most complete due diligence procedures the parties can muster. Of necessity, this is a protracted process.

4. Confidentiality agreement/procedures

Any merger between two successful corporations with strong economic performance will require two due diligence procedures, one for each company, the acquirer and the acquired, which means a considerable exchange of confidential information and related procedures. Much time will be spent in these procedures.

5. Accounting complexities

Multiple complex accounting aspects characterize the merger method. Two accounting systems have to be blended, and before this can be done, there are the recurring problems of what accounting standards are being used, valuation of assets, a correct summary of assets and liabilities, human resource details, undisclosed information, control procedures, to list only some of the most obvious. Obtaining this information requires substantial efforts and is time-consuming.

6. Alterations to target company legal structure

As one company, the acquired, will be dissolved, there will be often present serious legal complications requiring extensive legal reviews and consultations between counsel for the involved companies.

7. Company formation

Planning a merger will require substantial expertise in law, accounting, taxation, and corporate finance. It is a complex process that leads to the merger.

8. Shareholder approval

Mergers require shareholder approval. This necessitates detailed legal procedures.

9. Organizational meetings

This would not be any more complex than in an acquisition or subsidiary formation. However, as frequently there is a clean sweep made of management from the acquired company, there is the possibility of considerable backlash from retained personnel.

10. Investment license

This would not be required since we are dealing with existing companies that presumably already have the necessary licenses. However, there are surely jurisdictions in which any alterations to capital structure that has a presence of foreign capital require further approval from the licensing authorities.

11. Governmental notices or approvals

Mergers do not necessarily require governmental notices or approvals unless they are of such a magnitude that causes security and exchange laws or antitrust considerations to be applicable. Should this be the case, the approvals then involve complex procedures and the furnishing of much information to governmental authorities. The everyman international joint venture formed by this method is unlikely to cross the monetary or other thresholds causing such laws to be effective.

12. Necessity to obtain licenses and permits

A merger extinguishes one corporation. Therefore, it is necessary to obtain all necessary licenses if the surviving corporation does not already possess them. It is not likely a merger would be effected if such procurement were an onerous task.

13. Going concern

One of the principal advantages of a merger is that there is acquired a going concern and hopefully an enlarged client base.

(continued)

TABLE 2.3 *(continued)*

14. Creditor claims/litigation

The succeeding corporation also succeeds to all of the liabilities of the acquired corporation as well as any undisclosed litigation. Normally, this can be uncovered by due diligence procedures but not always. A merger therefore requires detailed due diligence procedures and there is always an associated risk of undisclosed liabilities.

15. Personnel

Most mergers create a surplus of personnel, resulting in an obligatory reduction or else living with an inefficient management structure.

16. Tax on transaction

Although it is a substantially complex procedure, it is possible to have a tax-free merger.

17. Specific tax implications

There may be considerable tax consequences depending on what the previous and continuing shareholders receive when the merger is complete.

18. Formalities of transaction

The statutory requirements for effectuating a merger are considerable and in most jurisdictions require extensive formalities, public notices, shareholder approval, publications, resolutions, and registrations with various official entities.

19. Necessity to acquire assets

There should not be any necessity to acquire assets.

20. Necessity to acquire contracts

Same as the preceding.

21. Necessity to acquire leases

Same as the preceding.

22. Patents, technology licenses, and copyrights

Same as the preceding.

23. Flexibility in payment

There is considerable flexibility in structuring a merger if tax considerations do not constitute an obstacle. The flexibility possible is often countered by other accounting complexities, for example, in a payment by cash and shares of the acquirer, valuations would have to be made.

24. Flexibility in financing

The presence of bank loans and other lenders may constitute a serious obstacle and necessitate their permission. Mergers are often a triggering reason in a bank loan clause to have the debts mature immediately.

25. Closing

In a merger, closing procedures will be complex.

26. Summary

The only advantage accompanying a merger is that the surviving corporation presumably acquires the assets and the markets desired by the parties. Beyond this, the complexities are considerable, requiring much expert advice, time periods are protracted, and the expense is usually substantial. Of course, all of these can be of minor importance if the merger brings considerable market power and profits. Mergers are not normally a frequent feature of international joint ventures. International mergers are usually confined to the key players in niche markets, typical examples being the chemical, banking, or petroleum industry. Domestic mergers are more frequent and present different characteristics. They are often the result of a hostile takeover or the enlargement of corporate activity into various complementary markets and invariably involve leaders in a particular industry and considerable sums. In short, not the average international joint venture.

TABLE 2.4   Partnership

With partnerships, method and form converge. The method of creating a partnership precludes another final form. Consequently, many of the reasons why a partnership might be chosen have to do with its legal aspects, which are developed and discussed in Chapter Three.

For our analysis, partnership as a method is intended to be by the method of formation. A purchase of a partnership interest would be by the method of acquisition, and this is infrequent.

A partnership is a contractual relationship between persons or companies. Although it is created by a contract, it is nevertheless classified as an equity joint venture as there are a capital contribution, a formalized agreement between partners for an indefinite time, a centralized management, unlimited liability of the partners, publication of the agreement in an official government gazette, and finally registration at the appropriate commercial conservatory. Although a partnership is terminable on the death of one of the partners, the agreement is for an indefinite term. All partners have access to the capital fund and all general partners speak for the partnership. It is common to see as a name for a partnership "Jones, Smith & Jones Co.," but this designation is misleading for in fact there is no "Co." There is only an agglomeration of individuals trading under a collective name.

Limited partnerships, where there is one general partner, and the other partners only have responsibility to the extent of their contribution, are not a common feature of international joint ventures. A limited partner cannot partake in the management of a limited partnership. Its function as a method of forming an international joint venture is too rare to merit inclusion in our discussion of a partnership.

1. Management objectives

As a partnership is based on a contract, it can be made quite specific as to its purpose.

2. Management structure

Usually, a partnership has no formal management structure other than a managing partner as all partners can speak for the partnership. However, the larger the partnership, the more the managing partner may become a board of managers. Usually in partnerships with commercial operations in diverse jurisdictions, such as the auditing firms, each country will have its reporting or managing partner. Nevertheless, the management hierarchy is substantially less complex than that of a multinational corporation in the average partnership.

(continued)

Table 2.4 *(continued)*

3. Due diligence procedures

In ordinary circumstances, none should be necessary.

4. Confidentiality agreement/procedures

Same as the preceding.

5. Accounting complexities

There should not be any.

6. Alterations to target company legal structure

None should be necessary since the partnership is created from the beginning.

7. Company formation

Articles of partnership must be drafted and thus, similar to the articles of corporation, much care must be taken to ensure the articles reflect the interests of all parties. However, a partnership usually does not have the internal complexity of a share corporation.

8. Shareholder approval

None is required since we are discussing the formation of a partnership.

9. Organizational meetings

There are no special requirements. The nomination of a general manager would be by agreement amongst the general partners.

10. Investment license

If a foreign jurisdiction requires any license for forming companies, it will also require the same for a partnership.

11. Governmental notices or approvals

They may be necessary as often partnerships are formed in a service sector specifically regulated, such as accounting or the law.

12. Necessity to obtain licenses and permits

Same as the preceding.

13. Going concern

There is none.

14. Creditor claims/litigation

There are none.

15. Personnel

They have to be hired.

16. Tax on transaction

There are no particular taxes.

17. Specific tax implications

The method of a partnership does not create any significant tax consequences. However, the legal form of a partnership is one of the principal reasons for its use. Profits and losses are passed through directly to the individual partners. There is no two-tier taxation. The various implications of this will be discussed more thoroughly in Chapter Three.

18. Formalities of transaction

In various jurisdictions, the partnership is created by going to a public official such as a public notary and signing the articles of partnership before the notary. Thereafter, the articles are published and registered.

19. Necessity to acquire assets

The partnership has to purchase all necessary assets.

20. Necessity to acquire contracts

Same as the preceding.

21. Necessity to acquire leases

Same as the preceding.

22. Patents, technology licenses, and copyrights

Same as the preceding.

23. Flexibility in payment

Moderate. Normally, cash is paid in as initial capital, although it is certainly possible to contribute another form of asset that has a monetary value, such as machinery.

24. Flexibility in financing

The flexibility is limited since any loans or other forms of financing would require the approval of all the partners as they would all be liable.

25. Closing

The closing procedure for a partnership or a transfer of interest requires the signing of the partnership agreement usually executed before a public official. In jurisdictions such as the United States, this can be done in the offices of counsel although registration of the agreement at a public office is still necessary.

26. Summary

The partnership as a method for forming a joint venture is relatively simple. However, it is not often used for the average joint venture due to the legal characteristics resulting from this form. Its main disadvantage lies in its unlimited liability for the partners. Consequently, as a method for establishing a joint venture, partnerships are normally confined to professional partnerships, such as auditors, accountants, lawyers, medical doctors, engineers, in other words, professional groups. It is rare for commercial companies to form partnerships. They would be more likely to utilize the method of an unincorporated joint venture if they wished to avoid a permanent legal structure such as a share corporation.

TABLE 2.5   Unincorporated joint venture (consortium)

An unincorporated joint venture is formed by a contract similar to a partnership. The unincorporated joint venture is the most popular of the contractual joint ventures and historically the oldest. Even today, the expression *joint venture* is used when an analysis reveals what is being discussed is the contractual joint venture and not an equity joint venture. Globalization has inverted the choice of investors so that today the equity joint venture is the more dominant form of conducting business in a foreign jurisdiction.

Although the unincorporated joint venture has many characteristics of a partnership, there is one significant difference: The unincorporated joint venture normally is for a specific period of time.

1. Management objectives

Quite specific. The contract has to state for what purpose the consortium has been formed.

2. Management structure

The management structure is created by the parties to the contract. Procedures will be established as to how work is to be executed, bills paid, income distributed. The management structure therefore can be adjusted to the needs of the parties.

3. Due diligence procedures

None is needed.

4. Confidentiality agreement/procedures

None is needed.

5. Accounting complexities

None.

6. Alterations to target company legal structure

None.

7. Company formation

Similar to a partnership.

8. Shareholder approval

Not necessary.

9. Organizational meetings

This would be established in the consortium contract.

10. Investment license

Licensing requirements if they exist would not exempt consortiums. They would be treated as a company with foreign capital.

11. Governmental notices or approvals

They may be required if the consortium will eliminate or substantially curtail competition. Cartels frequently take the form of a contractual agreement.

12. Necessity to obtain licenses and permits

Same as the preceding.

13. Going concern

There is none.

14. Creditor claims/litigation

None.

15. Personnel

They have to be employed.

16. Tax on transaction

No special taxes.

17. Specific tax implications

There are no specific tax implications in the formation process. However, similar to a partnership, the form of an unincorporated joint venture avoids two-tier taxation, as discussed in Chapter Three.

18. Formalities of transaction

As it is formed by contract, the formalities are simple.

19. Necessity to acquire assets

They have to be acquired.

20. Necessity to acquire contracts

Same as the preceding.

21. Necessity to acquire leases

Same as the preceding.

22. Patents, technology licenses, and copyrights

Same as the preceding.

23. Flexibility in payment

Moderate, particularly as some of the parties may contribute equipment or specialized services.

(continued)

TABLE 2.5 *(continued)*

24. Flexibility in financing

Less than that of a partnership since the duration of the consortium is for a limited term.

25. Closing

Similar to that of a partnership, the contract of a consortium is deposited at the commercial conservatory.

26. Summary

The unincorporated joint venture as a method for forming an international joint venture is simple enough; however, its use is limited because the joint venture is habitually formed for a specific purpose for a determined period, such as building a dam or extracting minerals. Not many companies intend to enter into a joint venture for a temporary period. Traditionally, it has been used for the one-time construction of huge industrial complexes where many specialized services are necessary.

TABLE 2.6   Profit-sharing management contract

A management contract is on the legal frontier between traditional joint ventures and contract rights. At times, it has the characteristics of a joint venture; at other times, it has the aspects of typical contracts. The management contract we are analyzing has one entity managing the assets of another entity for a fee, whether fixed or variable, denominated the profit-sharing administration contract.

1. Management objectives

Being a contract, the object is usually quite specific as the motif of the contract is management of a particular asset. There should not be any accommodation necessary to the objectives of management.

2. Management structure

The contract will establish the division of rights and duties between the managers and the owners. It cannot properly be called a management structure.

3. Due diligence procedures

None is needed as the manager assumes no responsibility toward creditors for the underlying asset, for example, a hotel.

4. Confidentiality agreement/procedures

They should not be needed although the manager may wish to keep confidential its manner of doing business on a worldwide basis. This is extremely difficult to control.

5. Accounting complexities

They can be considerable as the manager and the owner must have an agreement as to the accounting procedures that will show accurately the results of the accounting year.

6. Alterations to target company legal structure

None is needed.

7. Company formation

A contract must be drawn.

8. Shareholder approval

The board of directors of the owners of the assets would have to agree to delivering the management of the assets to a third party.

9. Organizational meetings

None is needed.

10. Investment license

The joint venture management contract may require approval by the foreign investment authorities if there are any exchange controls in existence.

11. Governmental notices or approvals

It is unlikely any notices have to be given to entities such as antitrust authorities. However, in theory, even through a profit-sharing administration contract, control of prices could be exercised throughout a particular jurisdiction. If the possibility is realistic, the applicable authorities have to be notified.

12. Necessity to obtain licenses and permits

The presence of foreign capital in the legal form the manager adopts may require a license to manage the asset.

13. Going concern

There is one but this does not affect the managing entity.

14. Creditor claims/litigation

They do not affect the managing entity.

15. Personnel

Any specialized personnel needed are on the staff of the manager.

16. Tax on transaction

None.

17. Specific tax implications
None.

(continued)

TABLE 2.6 *(continued)*

18. Formalities of transaction

None.

19. Necessity to acquire assets

None.

20. Necessity to acquire contracts

None.

21. Necessity to acquire leases

None.

22. Patents, technology licenses, and copyrights

None.

23. Flexibility in payment

Not applicable.

24. Flexibility in financing

Not applicable.

25. Closing

Not applicable.

26. Summary

The management contract is a special niche of joint ventures; or it may be viewed as an iconoclastic branch of contract law. Many hotel chains are managed by nonowners. In this respect, the management contract has an affinity to the franchise contract.

3

THE VARIOUS FORMS
OF THE INTERNATIONAL
JOINT VENTURE SHELTER

PART ONE

3.1 ESSENTIAL JOINT VENTURE CHARACTERISTICS FOR REVIEW BY OWNERS AND MANAGERS

Method is different from form. Our discussion has emphasized this distinction so that the corporate executive will be able to separate out the process of forming a joint venture and realize that a particular method does not necessarily lead to a particular legal form. There is a freedom of choice and it is an important selection. Consequently, different characteristics of a particular legal form must be carefully considered.

Some characteristics favor one joint venture form over another, perhaps ease of transfer of ownership; others may have a serious, negative aspect, such as unlimited liability; others may be completely neutral, or of little outcome, perhaps too much bureaucracy. Most commonly, the various attributes have no inner logic, one to the other.

Tax implications are not logically related to questions of ownership liability. Tax consequences are not dependent on the general internal management structure of a company. Questions of liability are not related to how long the company will endure. Restrictions on the sale of ownership interests bears no relevancy to questions of liability.

Clearly, there are a multitude of topics, questions of concern, that will influence our decision as to what is the most suitable form for any joint venture shelter without any necessary rational relationship between the various items. For owners and managers, the choice of the joint venture shelter involves a weighing of many factors and each individual will have his own private list for those features that have a substantial importance. An understanding of the practical results of a particular legal form is therefore indispensable. Although these effects are legal concerns, they are elementary, easy to communicate, and being "legal" in no way obscures their explanation.

For purposes of international joint ventures, there can be identified thirteen general characteristics that should be taken into consideration when deciding what is the appropriate form to be chosen. The list cannot be exclusive because the facts of each joint venture, the jurisdiction, and the commercial interests of the parties all contribute to influencing what factors have priorities. Still, the list that follows gives some indication of the common characteristics that should be reviewed when choosing the final form of the joint venture and a brief definition or explanation of their relevance in joint ventures. They are the attributes that most entrepreneurs consider when they are involved in the decision-making process.

Their order is empirical, based on what seems to be foremost in the minds of investors, although this sequence is also subject to frequent alteration. Each of the legal forms normally utilized in forming joint ventures is then analyzed in light of the thirteen cardinal properties, for example, "Share Corporation /thirteen characteristics," which is a point-by-point comparison. Our survey first describes the nature of the legal problems in broad terms and then passes to a discussion as to how a particular legal form conditions these legal features.

The order presented is not intended to imply one legal characteristic is more important than another, although the list is in descending order as to what most managers find to be their priorities. This is most evident when considering "termination flexibility," which is at the end of the list. In fact, how interests are terminated is important and complex; yet most managers do not give this topic high priority. No doubt this is due to the emphasis they give to the constructive, creative aspects of forming a joint venture.

For each joint venture, management must decide what elements constitute priority, for example, whether limited liability is more or less important than profit withdrawals.

3.1.1 THIRTEEN ESSENTIAL JOINT VENTURE CHARACTERISTICS

The characteristics of the various legal forms, for example, share corporation or private limited liability company, will affect considerably the day-to-day joint venture operations. The most significant are the following:

1. limited liability (or not) of owner
2. profit withdrawals
3. management structure
4. taxes
5. financial engineering flexibility
6. effect on private agreements of form chosen
7. how ownership interests are represented and transferred
8. restriction on sale of ownership interests
9. formalities of formation and subsequent reporting requirements
10. duration of form
11. familiarity
12. monitoring the investment
13. termination flexibility

A brief description of each characteristic will indicate its significance in international joint ventures.

1. Limited liability (or not) of owner. Not all legal forms confer limited liability to their owners. In a general partnership, all the partners must respond to creditors, financial or others, for debts incurred by the general partnership. A consortium is a contractual joint venture in which one of the participants can bind the consortium and all the other participants. It is thus similar to a general partnership, although a consortium is a temporary, contractual joint venture. It is well known that a share corporation protects the shareholders from claims by creditors. Any legal form is therefore going to determine who has general or limited liability. For any jurisdiction, the particular legal form chosen must address this issue: To what extent are the owners subject, or not, to unlimited liability for the debts of the company?

2. Profit withdrawals. Joint ventures are formed to realize profit as quickly as possible and withdraw it. Consequently, when faced with a solid expectation of profits, many entrepreneurs will assume general liability. Thus, although concerns of general liability rank high in the list of relevant topics for managers, ease of profit withdrawals is of enormous importance.

However, some legal forms permit profits to be received in a more advantageous manner than other forms. At times, profits may be harvested with a different accounting name and different tax consequences. Both these aspects, how profits are received and under what theory, are influenced considerably by the legal form of the joint venture. Naturally, for any joint venture vehicle, we want to know how easily or not profits can be withdrawn, no matter what the guise.

3. Management structure. Profitable ownership is dependent on efficient management. Different legal forms have various manners of authorizing management. There is considerable overlapping among the multiple legal models and management functions can be designed in conformity with the expressed intention of the parties. They are also affected by the laws of the foreign jurisdiction with a great variety of possibilities. Nevertheless, broad valid generalities do exist.

A share corporation is governed by a board of directors with a well-defined hierarchical system of management and responsibility. In a general partnership, unless the articles vary the standard rule, all partners are managers as each can bind the others; there may be an agreement as to who is the general operating manager, but this is an internal agreement made for the convenience of the partners, not the public.

Additionally, in some jurisdictions, there has been in existence for decades a form known as a limited liability company, which has the management structure of a partnership but limited liability for the owners. The management structure usually foreseen in the applicable legislation is a mixture of a share corporate management structure and a general partnership. It is a hybrid that functions very well in small closely held companies. The owners of the private limited liability company are ordinarily the managers. There is a mixture of ownership and management, which at times contrasts and is in conflict with more formalized methods, such as the board of directors and officer arrangement, which distinguishes share corporations.

Each form, as we will see, brings with it a recognized, usual system of management and confers on the joint venture its own management style. This in turn influences greatly the freedom or not of managers. Management structure also affects what controls the absentee owner may exercise in a distant joint venture. Management discipline is substantially dependent on the legal form.

4. Taxes. Many joint ventures involve considerable tax planning because the partners have worldwide activities. In a federal jurisdiction, such as the United States, a U.S. taxpayer, for example, its a corporation formed in one of the states, is subject to taxation on income no matter what the source. Consequently, when a U.S. corporation decides to form, or enter into, a joint venture in a foreign jurisdiction, it must be concerned about the tax consequences in its home jurisdiction.

And, of course, this is true for a number of European jurisdictions as well. It is not possible to make concrete recommendations without being fact-specific. Furthermore, what becomes exceedingly complex is integrating the tax consequences of one jurisdiction with the tax implications in another jurisdiction, for example, the home office of the investor. There is a balance of tax concerns that must be recognized by all partners. However, although we cannot lay down precise tax rules in the abstract, we can indicate the type of questions raised, which bears considerably on the legal form chosen.

Our normal concerns are whether there will be one- or two-tier taxation because of the form chosen. Will profits and losses pass through the legal entity chosen and be reported by the owners directly in their home jurisdiction? Or must first the joint venture pay taxes and then pass on the profits in the form of dividends, these being in turn subject to a withholding tax?

Does the form chosen even admit the concept of dividends? What form is best suited for Investor USA utilizing the tax credits (i.e., the taxes paid) assessed on Italy SA in which Investor USA has an equity interest? Does one form permit retention of earnings whereas another does not? These are fairly common concerns.

A merger may raise accounting questions of valuation of assets (not ordinarily an issue when establishing a subsidiary) that naturally have tax consequences. Another typical question dependent on the laws of the jurisdiction is if the surviving corporation will be permitted to utilize all the losses of the absorbed corporation. Will the combined new assets of the surviving corporation be reevaluated in accordance with the purchase price? What if the price contains a substantial amount for goodwill? To what asset will the value be allocated?

Thus, the legal form adopted ultimately leads to a multitude of tax questions whose responses are considerably affected by the legal form of the joint venture vehicle.

5. Financial engineering facility. The form chosen will ultimately affect access to financing. A private individual, even if permitted to incorporate and do business as "Individual, Inc.," will not have the same flexibility as other traditional forms of company. Few individuals doing business in their individual names float bonds. The prospects look frankly hopeless. But the concern of obtaining financing also goes beyond a simple credit request to a bank. Augments of capital, increasing the stated capital of a company, are more easily achieved through one form than another. Augments of capital are facilitated when a company can retain its earnings, which again is not possible in all legal forms.

A company, in order to secure financing, may be asked to deposit its ownership interests in a credit institution. A company may wish to have recourse to borrowing from its owners. Or a company may wish to declare a stock dividend instead of a cash dividend for tax reasons. The form chosen for the joint venture can facilitate or make difficult such operations. In a private limited liability company, it is not possible to make a stock dividend. There are no shares.

6. Validity of private agreements dependent on form chosen. There are many different types of agreements accompanying a joint venture that find expression in different documents. Agreements contain obligations and, as an illustrative list, we have obligations derived from the following:

- articles of incorporation
- joint venture agreements
- shareholders' agreements
- agreements between members of the board of directors
- contracts affecting the joint venture such as a distribution agreement or technology license
- loan agreement between one partner and the joint venture

The obligations may be affirmative or negative, not to do something. The latter are sometimes described as restrictive covenants. A prohibition of competition; restrictions on transfer of shares; veto rights given to a shareholder; limitations on certain company acts, such as an augment of capital, are typical concerns facilitated in one form, perhaps impeded in another. Such conditions may be contained in the articles of the company, but depending on the restraint desired, it may be necessary to have recourse instead to a private agreement such as the shareholders' agreement.

It would not be sensible to put into the articles of a corporation that its key employees will not compete for X years after terminating employment. This is a typical, simple restrictive covenant often inserted in a private agreement between the key employee and the corporation.

Other rights can be more complex. Rights of representation on the board, rights of first refusal in the sale of an equity interest, rights to participate in an augment of capital, rights to nominate certain key personnel are legitimate ownership and management concerns that must find ease of expression in the form chosen.

Additionally, even if the topics concerned are regulated in agreements, how legally effective are they? Some agreements are easier to enforce than others and this is often dependent on the nature of the legal form of the company. There is a symbiotic relationship among the promise, the document in which the promise is contained, and the form of the joint venture vehicle.

Thus, in a stock corporation, if a shareholder has in his possession his shares, by endorsing them, he can transfer them; he can even write on the back of them: "transferred subject to condition . . ." Anyone receiving these shares is put on notice that there exist conditions affecting these shares and the potential purchaser is obligated to make the necessary inquiries.

But today shares are often not held by their owners. They are traded electronically. The sale and purchase is a bookkeeping entry without a transfer of physical possession. It is not possible to inscribe conditions on the share certificate. Share corporations thus hamper transfer restrictions.

This is to be contrasted with the private limited liability company where in many jurisdictions the ownership interests are not evidenced by share certificates. The equity participation is recorded at the commercial conservatory where the articles of the company are also registered. The public is therefore apprised of any transfer conditions. As a general rule, the more closely held, private, limited liability companies afford a protection to and implementation of partner agreements that do not find the same recognition in a share corporation, not at least to the same degree. We will of course review in more details these concepts as applied to different legal forms.

7. How ownership interests are represented and transferred. When we think of companies, we tend to think of problems of liability, management, or financing. However, some very simple characteristics of a company can bring ease of investment, simple transfer procedures, or a lot of bureaucracy. The vast movement of shares on a national stock exchange is directly a consequence of the mobility of the investment, which in turn is intimately related to the physical representation of the investment, a share. Shares can be bought, sold, and transferred with simplicity, even electronically, with no physical act involved.

In many jurisdictions, such as exist in Western Europe, ownership in various types of companies is not represented by shares, but rather the company is constituted before a notary who records the ownership in the relevant legal folio. This means that an ownership interest in a limited liability company does not have a physical existence such as a share. It is comparable to an interest in a partnership, which is only described in an agreement.

Not having a physical object that represents ownership signifies that the transfer of such an ownership interest cannot be done by endorsement or even signing an agreement. A transfer necessitates the formal act of going before a notary and signing the necessary deed of transfer. Such a formality brings advantages and disadvantages, which we will soon explore beyond the formalities described. Nevertheless, there is clearly less mobility to an investment when transfers can be only consummated by a formal, officially recognized act.

8. Restriction on the sale of ownership interests. The way ownership interests are represented materially affects whether ownership interests can be restricted, partially or wholly, and how. This is one of the characteristics of a particular legal form, which in some joint ventures well may be chosen for that purpose. Many joint ventures are formed with other partners and it is critical to the parties that there be no changes in the ownership structure without the consent of all the other parties. A national manufacturer of glass bottles for wine forming a joint venture with a Canadian manufacturer of decorative crystal may not want the Canadian interest sold without its consent. The legal form chosen can facilitate or impede this objective. One legal form may allow total restrictions and another legal form may only permit partial restrictions. Restrictions on the sale of equity interests require a considerable amount of legal drafting and many economic considerations. The subject of restrictions on equity transfers frequently originates prolonged discussions. Many incipient joint ventures have failed to materialize because the potential partners could not agree on the appropriate clauses concerning restrictions on transfers. In all cases, the legal form of the joint venture establishes limits as to what types of restrictions are possible, permitted in one form, partially allowed in another form.

9. Formalities of formation and subsequent reporting requirements.
Certain legal forms are easier to constitute than others. A share corporation can originate multiple preliminary, preincorporation steps. Some companies due to their legal form can be brought to legal life in the office of counsel; other forms obligate public notices and procedures to be followed before official authorities. There may be multiple documents to be delivered to governmental agencies. Although most entrepreneurs will accept a great deal of bureaucracy in forming a company, the legal annoyances do not necessarily cease on constitution of the company. Changes to articles of incorporation, alteration of ownership interests, and designation of managers may all need to be subject to specific procedures involving "backup" legal documents to substantiate the requested changes. Such steps are a direct result of the legal form chosen.

Closely related to formation requirements are the subsequent reporting duties. Share corporations have to publish annually their financial results. This means every year a fixed expense and an independent review of the financial results are prepared. They are available to the public. The accounts must bear the approval of licensed accountants. The laws of most jurisdictions require the share corporation to have a fiscal council and require independent accountants to oversee and to some degree monitor the actions of the board of directors. This is to be contrasted with private limited liability companies, which in many jurisdictions do not have to file or make available publicly any information about their accounts nor is there requirement for a fiscal council.

10. Duration of form. Oftentimes, a joint venture is formed for a specific term or object in mind. It may be a consortium or it may be a joint research-and-development project. The parties do not want the joint venture to be of unlimited duration. However, in the business community, there is a reluctance to indicate this temporal state in the articles of the company. The laws of most, if not all, jurisdictions require the articles of the company to state its duration. In the average joint venture, the period of time is usually indicated as "indefinite." Even if the participants in the joint venture know that their association is temporary and consequently the articles are able to indicate a specific termination date, the attitude of many business persons is not to state a termination date in the legal documents as this may convey a sense of instability. In view of this public relations dilemma, there are really only two alternatives.

The partners choose a legal structure such as a private limited liability company, knowing the joint venture will only last for some years, but do not declare this in the articles. Or else, there is chosen a legal form, for example, the consortium, which by its nature has a natural termination date on the completion of the construction of the hydroelectric plant. Normally, the duration of a particular form is not a serious element in the choice of a particular joint venture structure. When a consortium is the proper candidate, it invariably will be selected, in spite of its limited duration.

11. Familiarity. There are many different legal forms in many different jurisdictions. They have multiple, subtle differences. Dependent on the home jurisdiction of the foreign investor, a particular legal form may be easily understood, such as the share corporation used in many parts of the commercial world. But a particular legal form may be suggested by the advisors of the foreign jurisdiction whose name or brief description indicates it is different in concept from other familiar legal forms. Whereas legal familiarity does not necessarily convey material information, unfamiliarity may have worse consequences: unperceived problems. Some legal forms are fairly common, others not. It is never wise to choose a legal form without having a simple, articulate explanation of the many features. Frequently, legal forms are chosen because they are recommended. It is helpful for management to prepare an agenda of questions, perhaps prepared by counsel of the foreign investor, as to the general consequences of choosing a particular legal form. This may help management to decide as to the more adequate form for the joint venture vehicle.

On the other hand, managers commonly assume one form of company has the same managerial structure as the form of their own employer because it has a similar name, for example, corporation ("Inc."), private limited liability company ("Ltd."), or partnership. This is not a prudent supposition. There are multiple subtle differences in similar legal forms throughout the diverse jurisdictions of the world. A proper question-and-answer period with local counsel should highlight similarities or differences between apparently similar legal forms in one jurisdiction and another.

All things being equal, familiarity with a particular legal form in another jurisdiction is a sensible consideration; it tends to create a sense of knowledge, it is helpful to have a practical grasp of what will be the results of a particular course of action, but this idea of understanding must be founded on correct information. When there is little doubt as to the similarities between the legal structures of the home jurisdiction and those of the foreign jurisdiction, naturally what is most familiar will prove to be a strong inducement to the foreign investor.

12. Monitoring the investment. Quite frequently, the foreign investor does not assign management to a foreign joint venture. The joint venture is run by the national partner and once a year there is a meeting of the partners. On the other hand, there are times when the foreign partner wishes to be able to fiscalize and supervise closely the activities of the joint venture. Some legal forms facilitate control but not all.

As an example, in many European countries, a private limited liability company has a management structure of one manager who only reports to the partners at the end of the year. Normally, the owners of such small companies are also the managers. An owner-manager does not have the same tendency to conform to reporting requirements as in formal hierarchical structures. This would not suffice normally for a foreign partner who wanted frequent access to managerial events with substantial detail. An owner-manager attitude is often "don't do business with me if you do not trust me." When the purchase of an equity interest means the acquired company is to be integrated into a larger group with a well-defined management organization, attention should be given to this issue prior to completion of the purchase. Postclosing management changes are difficult to enforce.

13. Termination flexibility. There comes a time when the joint venture comes to an end. Any legal form can be dissolved and liquidated. Dependent on the form, this may be a simple procedure or it may be complicated. Furthermore, there are some legal forms that can become, for tax purposes, dormant. It is not necessary to go through dissolution formalities. It is sufficient to file the necessary forms at the tax department and the corporate structure, for all purposes, ceases doing business. This is very cost-effective.

Additionally, there is the problem of one partner wanting the joint venture to terminate and the other does not. How can this impasse be resolved? How does one avoid becoming a captive partner beyond the desired term? This may be possible to avoid in a share corporation but would be more difficult in a private limited liability company. Such a conclusion is derived from the fact that in a share corporation, there cannot be a total restriction on a transfer of shares but absolute restrictions are allowed in a private limited liability company. The ability to exit from a joint venture is an important factor that is directly related to the legal form of the joint venture vehicle.

With this brief description of some of the more important attributes of the various legal forms, and certainly not all of the possible characteristics, the importance each one assumes is clearly dependent on the particulars of any one joint venture. It is now helpful to see the differences, similarities, and to better understand the individuality of the legal forms of some of the more common business structures. This will aid the corporate manager in understanding what legal form is the most appropriate for the joint venture contemplated.

3.1.2 MERGERS

A preliminary observation concerning mergers is appropriate before we begin our investigation. Merger as a method has been outlined previously. One corporation absorbs another. Two corporations transfer all their assets to a newly formed entity, or one already existing, and then the transferors are legally extinguished. If we inquire what is the difference between method and form concerning mergers, the practical response is "none." A merger results in there remaining another entity, which can be a corporation or other business form, that already exists.

Thus, a merger describes what takes place concerning other legal structures and in itself is never a form. A merger can be between two corporations, two limited liability companies, or two partnerships. It is a method that invariably continues with the legal form of the participants. This is not a rigid legal necessity. Two partnerships could merge and adopt a subsequent share corporation form. Or two corporations could dissolve and decide to transfer their assets and liabilities to a new partnership. But this is the exception, the unusual, not the typical merger. It is a rarity in international joint ventures.

Consequently, a merger always describes a method. Of the existing legal forms of the companies involved in the merger, one will remain. From this understanding, we cannot describe the characteristics of the legal form of a merger because they are dependent, not on the merger, but on the form of the companies involved in the merger.

3.1.3 ADVANTAGES AND DISADVANTAGES TO VARIOUS FORMS REGARDING THE THIRTEEN CHARACTERISTICS

Having in mind some of the vital legal characteristics of a particular legal form, our focus will be to summarize the characteristics of the many business forms existing but with emphasis on those features that assume importance for the business community in a joint venture. This cannot be an exhaustive survey because so many jurisdictions have variations on standard business organizations or forms not frequently used. Additionally, there are business forms that have a particular legitimate function, such as a business trust or a "group of affiliated companies," but that have a minor use as a form of creating an international joint venture. These are highly specialized legal forms that the corporate manager is unlikely to encounter when considering a joint venture. Furthermore, there are forms such as the management contract that have many attributes of a joint venture but whose legal aspects are contained within the principles of contract law.

Although not intending to exclude the relevancy of such legal forms and others, our review is with the more widely used legal structures, those that the corporate manager is most likely to utilize when creating a joint venture. There are a few widespread legal forms used in the great majority of joint ventures. Our correlation of characteristics is therefore to the basic legal archetypes on which joint ventures are usually founded. They are the

- share corporation
- limited liability company
- general partnership
- unincorporated joint venture

The profit-sharing management contract is excluded from this discussion, being confined to special industries, such as the hotel trade, and not susceptible to generalized treatment.

PART TWO

3.2 THIRTEEN CHARACTERISTICS OF A SHARE CORPORATION

Most corporate managers when asked what choice of legal form to adopt when entering into a joint venture would probably elect a share corporation without having consciously studied the various attributes of such a legal form. They probably work for share corporations. Many of the characteristics of a share corporation are of common knowledge to corporate executives from personal experience. In spite of there existing myriad, complex corporate law issues with corporations, the simplicity of representing ownership by a share certificate and the owners having no liability beyond their capital contribution have no doubt contributed immensely to the share corporation being a preferred form of doing business. We will understand quickly why the share corporation is so popular for use in joint ventures.

3.2.1 Limited liability

Shareholders in a share corporation are not responsible for debts beyond their subscription obligation. Normally, in corporations quoted on the stock exchange markets, this is not a concern. No one would ask his broker if the shares of General Motors were fully subscribed because a national stock exchange requires compliance with multiple standards. However, when shares are being purchased from family groups, it is important to know that there is in most jurisdictions a liability to creditors by the shareholders up to the amount of their unpaid subscription. To be able to invoke limited liability to a creditor, the shareholder must fully subscribe to the nominal value of the share and pay in the money.

For example, in a Portuguese corporation, on formation of the corporation, a certain percentage of the initial capital must be deposited in a bank but not the rest of the unpaid subscriptions. This is left to the fiscalization of a corporate board, such as the fiscal council or the board of directors. Should the corporation become insolvent, in theory, the creditors could seek the unpaid subscription of any shareholder. But this is a technical aspect seldom causing problems and one that would be discovered with proper due diligence procedures. Beyond the subscription obligation, shareholders do not respond for any of the claims of any creditor.

There is one area that merits the attention of management. The concept of limited liability attendant on the corporate form should not be. The most frequent example of this is when a corporation is thinly capitalized, that is, the stated capital is hopelessly inadequate in face of the purported business. Who would capitalize a company with U.S.$2,000.00 and borrow U.S.$20,000,000 to build an industrial complex, assuming there existed a bank that would enter into such a ludicrous financial program? This is the classic example of the *thinly capitalized* corporation and it symbolizes a frontier.

Dependent on the jurisdiction, the corporate form, when thinly capitalized, may be set aside, *pierced* is the legal expression utilized, and the shareholders personally held responsible for the failure of the bank loan in our extreme example. In such a jurisdiction, shareholders would be personally liable to creditors for the debts of the corporation. The concept of limited liability for share corporations therefore has its reasonable limits.

The rule of piercing thinly capitalized corporations is not universally applied and there are still jurisdictions that follow automatically the limited liability of share corporations if formed in accordance with the local law, whether the capital is a realistic amount. This is particularly true in Europe but much less so in the United States.

Besides insignificant capital contributions, there are similar problems after the formation of the corporation. This occurs when the corporation enters into technical insolvency. This takes place in some jurisdictions when current assets fall below 50 percent of the stated capital, or another statutory measure, and the shareholders are obligated by law to increase the capital, but they do not. In these circumstances, the law may hold the owners responsible for debts if the company continues to trade.

The concept of limited liability confers on the share corporation an attractiveness when forming joint ventures that ranks such characteristic as a prime element for investors. The reasons are easy to understand. The joint venture may involve a capital risk in an unknown jurisdiction with consumer habits not readily understood and there is a fear of possible bankruptcy. An overwhelming majority of joint ventures formed are usually established through a share corporation. Often, purchases made of private limited liability company interests result in later transforming the private limited liability company into a share corporation. But it must always be remembered that the concept of limited liability cannot be abused in practice. There should be a harmony between capital requirements and capitalization.

3.2.2 PROFIT WITHDRAWALS

One of the difficulties with share corporations is that the shareholders normally receive their return on their investment by the time-honored dividend. The term *normally* has been chosen deliberately because it is possible, and oftentimes so planned, that a return on the investment is shifted to another legal category, such as a royalty contract.

As an example, an owner of technology may form a subsidiary with another partner. The partner with the technology makes a substantial capital participation and also licenses the subsidiary. The progress of the joint venture may take some years. The parties agree that the royalty rate to be paid by the subsidiary will be a "healthy" one. This is a way of obtaining a return on capital that is not in the form of a dividend.

Then there is the opposite strategy. The transferor of technology, as a partner, may agree with the other partner that instead of significant dividends, profits will be retained and reinvested so as to promote an expansion of the business. In this case, the technology may be contributed to capital or very low royalty rates are charged as the partners are in agreement as to the future capital expenditures. Dividends are thus not an automatic consequence of a healthy profit-and-loss statement. Choosing the share corporation is no guarantee that there will be dividends, no matter how financially healthy is the company.

A further disadvantage to the share corporation is that to receive dividends, they must first be declared and this requires a voting power. A minority shareholder, unless steps are taken to secure dividend rights, remains subject to the will of the majority. Even when there exists legislation that decrees that the shareholders have a right to dividends, this exigency is easily circumvented by the majority invoking the need for the earnings to be applied to other necessities. Thus, in a share corporation, without special agreements being drafted, the right to dividends can be easily suppressed. Earnings can be used for increased salaries, investment in equipment, augments of capital, expansion into other areas of commerce; there are a number of alternatives to declaring dividends. Fortunately, there exist many legal techniques for bypassing this problem and that fall under the heading of *protection of minority rights*. As a consequence, the real possibility of there being no dividends declared, as a practical matter, can be averted, through proper documentation.

But the theoretical resolution does not always mean it exists as a practical matter. The majority owner may not want to negotiate any special provisions. The minority equity position may be in a substantially large corporation with a diffuse shareholder ownership, and it is not possible to negotiate any special protection. Large market capitalization companies (shares times market price) are therefore not good vehicles for joint ventures. In fact, joint ventures are not often constituted by such corporations. The more sensible route with large market capitalization companies is a merger in which the acquirers cause the target company to disappear and the share structure is completely changed. The formation of a joint venture in which a majority and minority will exist is best confined to the closely held corporation in which there is a reduced number of shareholders. Agreements can be signed between the majority and minority altering the rights of each so as to give more of a voice to the minority owners in the management of the company. In this way, receipt of dividends can be secured.

3.2.3 MANAGEMENT STRUCTURE

One of the substantial virtues of a share corporation is its management structure, which presents similar characteristics in a multiple of jurisdictions, certainly in the common law and civil law countries, such as found in North America, South America, and Europe. This is one of its great advantages as an option for the joint venture form. Managers from different jurisdictions encounter a familiar management hierarchy.

Normally, a share corporation has a board of directors and a fiscal council. This is a fairly common attribute. After that, there are varying differences dependent on the jurisdiction. Sometimes the board of directors are in fact the operating managers; other times, their authority is delegated to a general director, responsible for day-to-day operations; other times, committees are set up to handle specific tasks: administration, finance, production. In some jurisdictions, the workers have a council that must be at least consulted over what the board of directors decides that affects the workers. Although there are many variations, the prime management feature of a share corporation is a chain of command and decisions taken by consensus.

This management structure thus presents a familiar scene to investors from different parts of the world, and the share corporation makes it possible to continue with the same management model even when the partners come from diverse jurisdictions. This familiarity makes it easier for management to transpose its system of administration from one jurisdiction to another and is a strong impetus to choosing the share corporation as the joint venture vehicle.

3.2.4 TAXES

Share corporations present one major difficulty as a legal form for operating a joint venture: two-tier taxation. The corporation receives income and pays a tax on this income. An annual profit is recorded and the board of directors declares a dividend. There is also a tax applied on the dividend. This is what is known as two-tier taxation. The same income, which is generated by the corporate activity, is subject to tax twice. In some jurisdictions, the dividend tax is only applicable above a threshold amount. Alternatively, the taxpayer may receive a credit for dividend taxes against the final income tax.

It is possible to structure joint ventures so that the two-tier taxation is avoided or deferred, for example, if there is a double-tax treaty between the local jurisdiction and the jurisdiction of one or all the partners. Multinationals with commercial operations in various countries can often reduce the two-tier tax effect by creating subsidiaries to be the owner of the shares in the joint venture vehicle and these subsidiaries are established in jurisdictions with whom there are tax treaties.

Furthermore, contingent on the original jurisdiction of the partners, it is possible that the local government will treat the joint venture as a corporation, but the home jurisdiction will permit it to be taxed as a general partnership. In a general partnership, the gains or losses pass through to the partners who then receive either a gain or loss on their tax returns in their home jurisdiction. Consequently, in these situations, there is no two-tier taxation for the shareholder. Besides general partnerships, this passing through of gains or losses is also important even with share corporations because of the concept of consolidated tax returns.

Dependent on the ownership threshold required, some jurisdictions allow ownership of subsidiaries to treat the gains or losses of those subsidiaries on a consolidated tax return, which means gains or losses from all corporate sources are added together to constitute one final gain or loss. In these situations, the investor obtains the best possible treatment: limited liability in the local jurisdiction and tax treatment in the home jurisdiction as if the corporate joint venture were a partnership.

As a general rule, the more modest joint ventures initiated have no recourse to this advantageous situation. The joint venture abroad may be the only foreign commercial operation. Effective tax planning may require extensive legal alterations to existing legal structures of the joint venture vehicle no one wants to modify. It is often the case that the owners are less concerned with the tax aspects, assuming they are standard, and more concerned with the commercial aspects. Frequently, there is no choice. The other partners present the joint venture in a form that will not be altered.

Consequently, the shareholder in a corporation must often accept the fact of dual taxation and weigh this against the benefits of limited liability. Most business people will accept two-tier taxation to obtain the benefits derived from limited liability.

3.2.5 EFFECT ON PRIVATE AGREEMENT OF FORM CHOSEN

One attribute not often considered is the effect the joint venture form has on private agreements executed between the parties. There are many agreements that are executed between shareholders. The most common is a shareholders' agreement, which may regulate a variety of matters between the shareholders, such as dividend rights, voting rights, budget control, nomination of managers, and augments of capital. The list is quite long and such agreements are often essential to the success of the joint venture.

Executing an agreement does not mean the agreement is effective or susceptible of facile implementation. The form of the joint venture vehicle can improve or make difficult the probability of the shareholders' agreement serving well the reason for which it was drawn.

As can be imagined, this practical question has immense consequences for perhaps the joint venture would not have been approved if there was any beforehand knowledge of difficulties with such agreements. In a share corporation, many provisions subject to a private agreement cannot find reflection in the legal constitution of the corporation, which is the articles of incorporation. It is not possible to insert into the articles of incorporation rights between the shareholders as to budget control or capital expenditures. Such is a matter for the internal regulation of the corporation.

This is resolved in some jurisdictions where, besides articles of incorporation, there are by-laws that do regulate the internal operations of corporations and find their place alongside the articles of incorporation as the general rules governing corporate life. However, many jurisdictions do not have by-law provisions; they simply are not utilized or are not recognized by the jurisdiction, and thus the shareholders must fall back on an agreement. As will be demonstrated later in the book, it is vital for a minority shareholder to be able to veto certain acts by the majority, such as on capital expenditure, but this may depend on whether or not the shareholders' agreement has any effective force and passes from the still life of a document into the active voting life of the corporation.

Returning to our initial probe, we find that the efficiency of private agreements in a share corporation is of limited value. The shareholders' agreement is a contract and breach of a contract requires redress in courts, a remedy that may take time and be of little practical value to the litigants if corporate acts sought to be impeded are already consummated. Later, we will see that some of the provisions traditionally inserted in shareholders' agreements should be transferred to the articles of incorporation, such as a requirement on a certain percentage of votes for an augment of capital.

But others cannot be inserted into the articles of incorporation. There are no articles of incorporation that state that the annual budget of the corporation will not exceed X currency. It would be impossible to fiscalize and enforce and yet such an exigency may be of extreme importance to a shareholder. In our discussions concerning shareholders' agreements in Chapter Six, we will indicate what further legal documents can give further support to the rights established between the shareholders. Consequently, insofar as private agreements are concerned, share corporations have substantial limitations and do not offer a guarantee of protection.

3.2.6 RESTRICTION ON SALE OF OWNERSHIP INTERESTS

One of the most common agreements between shareholders is a restriction, partial or total, on the transfer of shares. This may be because one shareholder would not have entered into the joint venture except for the collaboration and capital presence of another shareholder. This presence may be deemed vital for reasons of management, or expertise in a particular industry, or a good public relations image, or an unwillingness to have a joint venture with third parties not chosen by the other shareholders.

However, the effectiveness of such agreements in share corporations is dubious. There are only two ways of restricting the transfer of shares in corporations. Either there is an article to this effect in the articles of incorporation or there is a private agreement among the shareholders. Both meet with moderate success when applied to share corporations.

The basic obstacle in many jurisdictions is that a total restriction on the sale of shares recited in the articles of the company is prohibited. This is because such restrictions would be incompatible with mobility of capital. Some jurisdictions have special laws relating to closely held corporations, often called the *closed corporation,* in which special laws do permit a variation to the general prohibition. But this is not a widely diffused exception in the various jurisdictions throughout Europe. However, what is frequently permitted in all jurisdictions is a partial restriction. The terminology utilized by lawyers is not always constant but the ideas are clear enough.

The shareholder desiring to sell must first offer the shares to other shareholders. This is usually denoted a right of preference conferred on the other shareholders. Or it may be a restriction that on receiving an offer, the possible seller must give other shareholders a right of first refusal. In this case, the thought is being seen in its negative. The right to buy becomes the right to turn down the first offer. These simple examples, and more complex ones discussed in subsequent sections, are only partial restrictions. A sale is possible but only after following certain procedures designed to give the other shareholders a right to purchase the departing shareholder's interests. Thus, even with partial restrictions, there is a substantial amount of legal bureaucracy involved in sale.

Secondly, even with a right of preference or right of first refusal, there is the obstacle of proper enforcement of such a clause. As a practical matter, it is extremely difficult to monitor. It is easy to arrange fictitious prices if one party wishes to exit and has a preference for another entity entering, perhaps a price to be paid outside of the stated transaction. A total restriction is much more effective and there is nothing to fiscalize. It simply cannot be done. The question of preventing a transfer of shares is one of the most common problems presented by joint ventures. Normally, once a joint venture is formed, the original partners do not want to have to accept other, new partners, who, as previously agreed, cannot be part of the joint venture.

As to relying instead on a private shareholders' agreement, whereas total restrictions can be agreed on, the effect is to create contractual rights between the parties. If they are breached, the injured party merely has a right to damages. Even this remedy may be doubtful, for the parties are attempting to by-pass the general prohibition on total restriction by a private agreement. Not every jurisdiction will permit this attempt as it is against public policy.

Of course, there are solutions, but they obligate the choice of other legal forms. Perhaps the parties to a joint venture decide that all other conditions have no importance except nontransferability of the one owner's interest in the joint venture. Then a partnership would be chosen since there can be no transfer of a partnership interest without the consent of the other partners. If such an event takes place, the partnership is dissolved by law. Excluded from this general proposition are special situations of death, assignment for debts, marital agreements, all of which often receive special statutory treatment. However, the general principle is that partnership interests cannot be transferred without the consent of all. No agreement is necessary. Thus, the loss of limited liability is accepted for obtaining nontransferability.

Then there are the intermediate forms, such as a private limited liability company, which often have special, but favorable rules about restrictions of transferability. Many jurisdictions do permit a total restriction on the transfer of interests in a private limited liability company or at least give the company the right to purchase the interest in question. This has the effect of preventing the transfer of the interest to a third party.

In conclusion, when the interests of the parties are critically dependent on share restrictions, the share corporation is not the ideal legal form in the absence of special legislation affecting closely held corporations, which in turn limits the number of shareholders possible.

3.2.7 FINANCIAL ENGINEERING FLEXIBILITY

One of the prime virtues of the share corporation is its pliancy in the face of financial engineering. Augments of capital are easy to understand: more shares are issued and the capital is increased. Loans are easy to arrange. The shares can be deposited for security. It is possible to issue bonds for sale to the public who associate a public raising of funds with corporations. Even with only two shareholders, but a respectable capital, it is possible to make a private, but public placement of bonds, through a credit institution. Both the bank and the public sense a certain comfort in knowing they are dealing with the traditional stock corporation in which ownership is a tangible certificate and security interests can be protected by holding the shares on deposit.

In some jurisdictions in Europe, it is the tradition for banks, instead of loaning money, to take an equity position, provided certain rights are received, such as the right to nominate a member to the board of directors. In a share corporation, this can be achieved by issuing a special class of shares that carries with it the right to nominate a specified number of members of the board of directors. This permits the banks to accompany management on all major decisions.

Profits are distributed as dividends and it is well known that preferred shares can be issued that carry with them the right to an annual dividend. The share corporation lends itself simply to this concept, whereas other legal forms require much more internal drafting or creative structuring. Financial engineering is a prominent feature of share corporations and is often a decisive influence when choosing between various types of possible joint venture forms.

3.2.8 HOW OWNERSHIP IS REPRESENTED AND TRANSFERRED

One of the conveniences of using a share corporation is its ease of representation of ownership. An owner receives shares, a tangible object. A share can be deposited in a bank; it can be endorsed; it can be given as security for a loan. Special rights can be attached to a class of shares and the shares can bear an appropriate indication. Transfer of ownership, the passage of title, can be accomplished by physical delivery of the share. Formalities with transfer of ownership are thus simplified. This concept is well understood.

However, there are multiple legal forms that do not offer this physical evidence of ownership. Partnerships, private limited liability companies, and unincorporated joint ventures all have their ownership interests represented in varying ways: a deed before a notary, contracts drawn between the parties, deposit of documents in an official conservatory. But an owner, to prove ownership, must obtain other evidence of such a fact, such as a certificate from the commercial conservatory attesting as to who are the registered owners. Therefore, owners in these legal forms do not have easy demonstration of their rights of ownership and there are often consider-able formalities involved in the transmission or establishing of other rights concerning such ownership interests. The more bureaucratic the steps in having to prove ownership, the less the business world tends to consider that particular company form.

3.2.9 FORMALITIES OF FORMATION AND SUBSEQUENT REPORTING REQUIREMENTS

Closely related to the question of evidence of ownership are the formali-ties in constituting the legal form chosen. Thus, in a share corporation, the formalities of constitution can be considerable, entailing publications in journals and deposits in a bank to ensure the minimum capitalization re-quired by the law. Additionally, the establishment of a share corporation, dependent on the capital, may involve the intervention of a number of official entities whose function is to ensure that all formalities have been duly completed. This is to ensure that the share corporation does not put into public circulation shares of a fictitious entity. This is to be contrasted with other company forms in which there is little official, fiscal supervision over capital contributions beyond the publication of the articles in a journal and deposit of the articles at the relevant commercial conservatory.

Furthermore, in share corporations, there are the annual reports by the board of directors published in the local journals; the financial accounts are deposited at the commercial conservatory. There is substantial trans-parency. Additionally, it is almost universal that a share corporation will have to have a fiscal council that, jointly with the board of directors, will supervise the financial management of the share corporation. Concluding, the share corporation entails many formalities in its creation and thereaf-ter is subjected to multiple filing obligations and supervision by indepen-dent licensed accountants.

3.2.10 DURATION OF FORM

When the purpose of the joint venture is of an indefinite duration, there are a number of legal forms from which to choose, which certainly in-clude corporations and private limited liability companies. Other legal forms pose special problems due to the personal nature of the joint ven-ture or the possibility of exterior events, such as the death of a partner in a partnership. However, the traditional limited liability companies satisfy quite well the object of duration without termination. Although it is possible to insert in the articles of incorporation that the corporation will terminate on X date, such a provision is highly unusual. When an investor wants a company form with a limited duration, the most probable choice would be the unincorporated joint venture, also known as the consortium.

3.2.11 FAMILIARITY

When doing business in a foreign jurisdiction, there is much to be said for choosing a legal form with which the foreign investor is familiar. This avoids, but only to some degree, making erroneous assumptions based on analogies from prior legal experience. Of course, every jurisdiction has its local variations and there cannot be ever assumed a faithful transplant of the New York law of corporations to the corporate law of Belgium. However, share corporations do present many similarities in the various jurisdictions, enough so that the corporate executive is not at a complete loss as to the nature of the legal form that incorporates the joint venture. Having experience with share corporations in one part of Europe facilitates understanding share corporations in another European jurisdiction. This tends to make the corporate executive more confident in his understanding of the legal form chosen, without avoiding, of course, recourse to counsel on local legal variations.

Additionally, by choosing an unfamiliar legal form, the foreign investor is unable to draw any logical conclusions from the acts involving ownership. How are voting rights exercised? How are managers nominated? What is the legal form of management? Having to constantly seek explanations as to the day-to-day operations of a foreign subsidiary is often a reason for not utilizing any legal form except the well-known share corporation. The lack of experience with a particular form tends to generate a state of insecurity. Other important aspects of a legal form being satisfactory, familiarity with a legal form is a sensible reason for electing it.

3.2.12 MONITORING THE INVESTMENT

Many investments are made by foreign companies that do not place any local personnel on site at the joint venture. Although this may seem surprising to many executives, one simple explanation is that the legal nature of the joint venture permits it to be easily monitored. However, to be readily monitored means having a legal form that lends itself to such vigilance and the share corporation is ideal from this point of view.

Proper accounting books utilizing modern methods of cost accounting, such as the GAAP (general accepted accounting principles); a managerial structure that obligates periodic management reports; a general supervisory management board that bears a duty to all owners; and an independent fiscal council that ensures proper compliance with accounting and tax obligations—form the coat of arms of a share corporation—and are the reasons why share corporations have achieved such prominence in the commercial world. A share corporation forces adherence to a management style of quality and excellence.

3.2.13 TERMINATION FLEXIBILITY

Commercial activity is commenced and one day it ends. The right to establishment is followed by the right of termination. Share corporations present two elements, one of them not duplicated easily in other legal forms and that is of primary importance. In many jurisdictions, it is possible for a share corporation to file a certificate of no longer doing business and the corporate entity goes dormant. It exists, but it does not function. The dormancy produces no tax incidence. The dormant corporation becomes a conservatory ghost, hovering in the records with no activity. For partners who do not want to go through a formal dissolution and liquidation, this is quite convenient.

Although in theory this should be possible with private limited liabilities companies, such company forms often have a general manager who may act for the company. The restrictions on management's powers are less in these company forms and hence the partners may justifiably feel they are running a risk when the company is dormant, but not dissolved. Any unauthorized act of the manager will obligate the company with untold consequences.

The partnership form is also not an attractive company form for ceasing activity but not going through formal dissolution procedures. There is the general liability of each partner for the acts of others, which is ever present. Naturally, partners in another jurisdiction will feel uncomfortable with a possible liability for acts that may be practiced in the future without permission of all the other partners.

For most company forms, dissolution and liquidation are the only means for terminating the joint venture and ending matters properly. These legal procedures are formal, lengthy legal steps involving other parties, liquidators, publications, and eventual deeds of liquidation and distribution of assets, if there are any, to the former partners.

Consequently, the share corporation offers a simple method of cessation of activity and a less costly alternative. The filing of a certificate of

Not Doing Business is an inexpensive alternative to dissolution and liquidation and is often satisfactory as an interim measure.

3.2.14 SUMMARY OF ADVANTAGES AND DISADVANTAGES TO THE SHARE CORPORATION AS A LEGAL FORM

Of the thirteen characteristics we have discussed, the share corporation appears to confer a benefit in eight of the characteristics, which is a healthy majority. Moreover, within the eight are contained important aspects, such as limited liability. We can make a summary as follows:

Advantages

- limited liability
- management structure, a well-structured hierarchy
- financial engineering, permitting issuance of bonds and additional shares
- representation of ownership interests by a physical document
- indefinite duration
- familiarity, understood characteristics in most parts of the world
- monitoring the investment, facilitated by management controls
- termination flexibility, dissolution and liquidation can be avoided

Disadvantages

- profit withdrawal subject to dividends that may not be declared
- two-tier taxation
- moderate efficiency in enforcing private agreements between shareholders; the more shareholders there are, the less probable it is that private agreements will be enforceable
- restriction on sale of ownership interests usually severely curtailed
- formalities of formation and subsequent reporting requirements

The major disadvantage to a share corporation is the possibility of a majority owner withholding dividends to put pressure on a minority owner. This can be circumvented with a shareholders' agreement. Two-tier taxation is a serious disadvantage, but many investors accept it as a price to pay for limited liability and attempt, through tax planning, to mitigate its effects. Therefore, unless the facts of the joint venture do not permit a choice or there are other important concerns, the share corporation offers itself as an ideal form for a joint venture. Similar to the share corporation, but of course with many differences, is the private limited liability company.

PART THREE

3.3 THIRTEEN CHARACTERISTICS OF A PRIVATE LIMITED LIABILITY COMPANY

In many jurisdictions, there exist private limited liability companies that combine some of the aspects of partnerships and share corporations. The private limited liability company is not as universal as the share corporation. It is more a creature of the civil law. In Europe, it is a well-known legal form. It is used also in England and lately has come to be the subject of legislation in various states of the United States.

A private limited liability company is no more private than a small, closely held corporation, one not quoted on an exchange. The word *private* is intended to communicate a restricted number of owners. Such a company is not quoted on any national stock exchange. Besides having a reduced number of partners, the company enjoys the same limited liability of the share corporation. Few partners and limited liability thus converge in a beneficial union.

A brief history of the limited liability company reveals the reason of its characteristics. The source of the private limited liability company had its beginnings in family companies; or in companies with a limited number of partners who knew each other well and in which there was a modest capital structure. They were companies formed by the small merchant who needed limited liability to run commercial risks and did not wish to use the general partnership form. Normally, it might be two or three members of a family or it might be two partners who made a modest investment to see if their commercial ideas would bear fruit. In all cases, management was simple; there was no hierarchical system of administration.

Usually, the articles of the company said the management was to be exercised by *all partners*. The owners participated directly in the day-to-day operations of the company. Management and ownership rights were exercised by the same people; there was no separation of the rights and obligations normally associated with management and ownership.

Consequently, the management structure of a private limited liability company is quite simple, although it is theoretically and technically possible to superimpose the management structure of a share corporation on a private limited liability company. But this would be using a share corporation management style for a legal form that was intended for the opposite, for companies where a certain intimacy is presumed between the partners. Creating a share corporate design for a private limited liability company often meets with resistance from the public officials who supervise and legalize the formation of the company.

As stated, the facts normally associated with a private limited liability company were a restricted number of partners with a simple management structure. The company was intended to be used by a limited number of persons having a solid knowledge of each other. Of course, a lot of this philosophy has disappeared and today private limited liability companies are used by commercial entities that have had no prior experience with each other. The partners of this hybrid share corporation and partnership may be multinationals with activities all over the world.

This transformation has occurred because of the increasing globalization of foreign investment. In those jurisdictions where the private limited liability company was widely used, foreign investors began to utilize this legal form as it was easier to form, easier to capitalize, there was more direct involvement in the management, and the formalities were less. Share corporation formation in many parts of the world has always been a detailed, time-consuming, bureaucratic event. Whereas others saw the private limited liability company as being more suitable for "families," the multinationals reinvented the use of the private limited liability company from a "small-merchant" vehicle to a more simple form for any entity to do business under the protection of limited liability.

Ownership is represented by possessing a *part* of the company; in some countries, it is called a *quota*. This quota has no physical existence, being recorded in an official book much as is a deed of land. Normally, the parties, the future owners, go before a notary, and a deed of constitution of the company is drawn up. Ownership is represented by the names of the owners in the deed and their equity participation. Thereafter the deed of constitution of the company must be registered at the nearest commercial conservatory.

In Europe, the two principal supervisors are the public notary, who forms the company, and the commercial conservator, who registers the articles. Both have to agree to any legal complexities associated with this legal form. Otherwise, there is no formation, or formation that is not registered and therefore incomplete, engendering a terrible legal confusion. A company formed but not registered is like a person without a passport. In Europe, at least, as the official entities still tend to regard private limited liability companies as "family" companies, they are reluctant to mold them along share corporation ideas.

This is of particular relevance because often investors from common law countries tend to want to impose on private limited liability companies as many of the characteristics of share corporations as possible, particularly a management structure along the lines of a board of directors and even the creation of internal regulations, which are the counterpart of by-laws. By-laws are not utilized in most European jurisdictions for any of the company forms. The only source of regulation is the articles of the company. Without by-laws, the normal management controls associated with share corporations are difficult to adapt to private limited liability companies.

Constituting such a company is not as complex as with a share corporation as there are usually less intervening public entities. However, interests cannot be sold or transferred without going to a public official who oversees a deed of transfer. Consequently, in a private limited company, there are usually less formalities on establishment but more on transfer of interests.

Additionally, as the private limited liability company drew its sources from circumstances usually associated with a general partnership—a commercial intimacy between the participants—total restrictions on the transfer of interests are generally permitted if the parties so wish and such restrictions are stated in the articles of formation. Thus, the private limited liability company confers an advantage not associated with share corporations. Ownership interests are captive, if so agreed. Ownership cannot be transferred without permission of the other owners. This is in marked contrast to share corporations in which partial restrictions may be incorporated in the articles of incorporation, such as a right of first refusal, but not a complete prohibition. It is rare to find a jurisdiction that allows a complete restriction on the transfer of shares unless confined to closely held corporations. Thus, the private limited liability company has many features of a general partnership but still has the limited liability aspects of a share corporation, a beneficial union for the foreign investor.

For joint ventures in which the capital structure is of a modest dimension and there are only two or three individual partners or perhaps the partners are medium enterprises, the private limited liability company can be an eminently satisfactory vehicle for a joint venture. And, of course, as already mentioned, a management structure can be designed to accommodate the particular interests of the partners provided there is a compromise on the complexity of the control desired. With this brief description, we can now examine more closely the individual characteristics of the private limited liability company.

3.3.1 Limited liability

Equal to the share corporation, the private limited liability company confers on the owners insulation from creditors. Once a partner contributes
his capital, there is no responsibility for the commercial acts of the
company. In this respect, the share corporation and the private limited
liability company stand on an equal footing.

3.3.2 Profit withdrawals

Akin to a share corporation, profits are distributed by a declaration of
dividends after approval of accounts and the necessary setting aside of
reserves established by the local legislation. However, the comparison to
a share corporation cannot be carried too far. As ownership is not represented by any physical document, there can be no circulation of ownership with anticipated rights of dividends. Moreover, the closer we will
examine dividend rights, the greater will be the chasm between share corporations and private limited liability companies.

Very often, share corporations have different classes of shares whereby
one class has a right to receive dividends, the so-called *preferred shares*. Of
course, it is possible in many jurisdictions to draft articles of association
in a private limited liability company whereby there are created different
classes of quotas that confer special rights to receiving profits. Normally,
however, the granting of a preferred status as to dividends in a share corporation is often accompanied by a restriction or absence of voting rights.
Whether this could be done in a private limited liability company raises
difficult questions of law in various jurisdictions and no valid generalizations are easily formulated.

A further substantial difference between shareholders and quota owners is the exercise of rights in the light of alleged wrongs for failure to
declare dividends. Class actions by shareholders are common enough, an
action where one shareholder, although initiating a lawsuit, purports to do
so on behalf of all other shareholders. One acts for all. In the typical private limited liability company, a party believing itself aggrieved for failure to receive a declaration of dividends would probably have to proceed
in court on a different basis, a more personal one, perhaps a conspiracy by
the other owners to dilute his rights. The enforcement of the rights to profits in this legal form does not have the same strength and insulation from
character assassination as the class action, easily characterized by those
defending the company as a personal aberration of facts by the allegedly

injured partner. Concluding, although the private limited liability company enjoys with the share corporation limited liability for its owners, its corporate aspect cannot be exaggerated.

3.3.3 MANAGEMENT STRUCTURE

The substantial virtues of the management style of the private limited liability company are at once its principal defect: the direct participation by the owners in the management. Normally, the articles of such companies simply state "the management will belong to the owners." This capsule nomination, enshrined in the articles of the company, confers substantial liability on the owner-managers and also makes the company responsible for the acts of any owner-manager, an uncomfortable situation for any minority owner who is also frequently absent.

As to liability, being a manager, and so named in the articles, in many jurisdictions makes the owner-manager responsible, without any negligence being proved, for paying the taxes. This deters absentee foreign investors from wanting to have any managerial responsibilities. Oftentimes, this liability aspect is avoided with recourse to outside managers, employing a person to be the manager of the company. However, anyone with any knowledge of the laws of the local jurisdiction is unlikely to accept such a nomination and instead seek to act as an agent of the legal managers, that is, request a power of attorney from the legal manager(s). This means that acts done by the day-to-day manager are being done in the name of the legal manager who still remains responsible before the authorities for all taxes owed.

On the other hand, with all partners being managers, it is easy to see that the general responsibility of the company is enlarged. Every partner has to be sure that the other partners are acting in accordance with due propriety. Any owner-manager can obligate the company. Furthermore, all partners being managers means that all have access to company funds; every owner can sign in the name of the company; any partner can withdraw or sell assets, acting in the name of the company. The private limited liability company also presents serious obstacles to the efficient management of an international joint venture.

This is because an international joint venture, with its distant ownership, its often majority-minority equity participation, the lack of management involvement by one party, the reliance on delegating management responsibility, the enormous power of authority each partner has, tends to raise problems that can be easily prevented only by agreements on management rights, which conflict with the traditional, direct relationship between ownership and management. The more discussions are held on how to contain management rights and create a more complex management structure, the more the parties tend to be led toward establishing a share corporation.

Of course, it frequently happens that an acquisition is made and the interest purchased represents an interest in a private limited liability company. The parties do not want to change or alter the company structure; perhaps, they want a period of experience with each other. All that can be done is to draft and execute agreements between the partners, what are called *shareholder agreements* when referring to share corporations, and fall back on the contractual responsibilities of all parties for ensuring, as an example, that the company will not exceed X in its annual budget.

In summary, the private limited liability company is quite suitable for more modest joint ventures or as an initial entry in a foreign jurisdiction, but for complex commercial and legal arrangements it is often unsuitable, out of harmony with the jurisdiction of the foreign investor, creating unnecessary friction as the foreign investor is compelled to do business but not as it is done back home.

3.3.4 TAXES

In the jurisdictions where the private limited liability company is recognized, there is also two-tier taxation. The private company earns income subject to tax. Any profits distributed to the partners are also taxed. Dependent on the jurisdiction, the owners may receive a credit for the dividend tax paid when filing individual income tax returns.

However, although the private limited liability company has share corporation characteristics, many jurisdictions of the foreign investor allow this form to be treated as a partnership for income tax purposes. By having the income classified as partnership income, the individual owners of the private limited liability company are able to treat the profits or losses as being directly received on which a tax has been paid with a resulting tax credit in the home jurisdiction.

Even if the home jurisdiction does not permit taxation as a partnership, there is often the possibility of filing a consolidated tax return if the ownership interest of the foreign investor obtains the necessary percentage, for example, fifty percent, and when the income or loss of the subsidiary is then added to other worldwide income.

Thus, the limited liability company actually has an advantage over the share corporation when considering two-tier taxation. The limited liability company in some jurisdictions may be considered a partnership for tax purposes.

3.3.5 EFFECT ON PRIVATE AGREEMENT OF FORM CHOSEN

The enforcement of private agreements between owners in a private limited liability company is simply achieved and confers on this form a substantial benefit when adopted for the international joint venture. As this form permits a total restriction on the transfer of ownership interests and as in this form normally all partners are managers, it is facile for all partners to be prisoners to others only being able to act when there is unanimity. This is a practical observation. The owner-managers can act independently, but then for any one decision taken by a particular owner, the others can undo the same decision. Confusion is only avoided when, as a functional fact, there is substantial agreement among the partners.

Consequently, any private agreement executed between the owners of the company can be enforced easily by inserting in the articles of the company the provisions that "all partners are managers," that all decisions must be by unanimous decision, and that no ownership rights can be transferred to third parties without permission of all the other partners.

The result is that all signatories to the agreement know that any deviations from the agreement will not receive unanimous approval and hence this confers strict adherence to the agreement. Thus, the articles of the company need not reflect many details of the private agreement. We need only to ensure that the voting requirements compel unanimity. We have created a company in which all act together or nothing can be done. There can be no escape from this dilemma as there is no exit for a partner. Each is a hostage to the other.

To the degree that the participants in a joint venture are willing to chip away at this possible complete veto power, the more the private limited liability company will begin to approximate a share corporation, in which management rights are not dependent on unanimous consent by all shareholders. Thus, the articles may provide that a simple majority of votes will prevail except on certain issues, such as augments of capital or mergers. As a legal form for ensuring management is strictly controlled by all partners, the private limited liability company form offers a substantial and effective method, superior to that of a share corporation.

3.3.6 Restriction on sale of ownership interests

In practically all jurisdictions, a total restriction on the sale of shares in a share corporation is not permitted. This is because the theory of the *negotiability* of a share becomes destroyed were this possible. Joint venture participants wanting to ensure there are no unpleasant surprises by having to work with new, different partners should not use the share corporation form if this is the most important consideration. It can be.

For most jurisdictions, a private limited liability company permits restricting completely the freedom associated with ownership. The articles can simply state there can be no transfer of ownership interests "without the consent of all parties." It is simple. It is effective. It is enforceable. As the transfer of ownership can be done only before a notary, he will request a copy of the company document that indicates under what conditions transfers of interests can be made. After the total restrictions are seen, it will be necessary to prove all partners have agreed to the sale.

In share corporations, there are often drafted exceedingly complex articles of incorporation that attempt to restrict partially the transfer of shares by conditioning the sale on "rights of first refusal," "rights of option," "rights of preference," and other provisions, most of doubtful practical application. Such complexities are avoided with the private limited liability company.

3.3.7 Financial engineering flexibility

In some respects, the private limited liability company offers more flexibility than the share corporation regarding capitalization. As an example, some jurisdictions permit capital contributions to be made in intervals, which avoids a formal augment of capital provided this condition is articulated in the company articles. Similar to the share corporation, a minimum amount of capital subscription is obligatory.

However, the financial engineering flexibility of this legal form is practically nil. For financing, there are no shares to deliver to a bank to secure any borrowings. In the absence of holding shares as a security, credit institutions have to rely on guarantees given by the owners. These may be of substantial value if we are dealing with multinationals or others with large resources. Nevertheless, drafting guarantees is not as simple as delivering shares to be held on deposit.

Another possibility is a pledge of the quotas, but in most jurisdictions, this requires a formal deed before a public notary, which adds to the legal bureaucracy.

In lieu of credit, raising further capital by the entry of other partners will require the agreement of the limited circle of partners. Most medium-sized private limited liability companies have articles requiring a unanimous vote for augmenting capital. Even if all the partners agreed, for the company to raise substantial sums means an additional partner but one who would have to have a substantial interest if we are referring to significant amounts. This alters radically the balance of power in the company. Otherwise, many new partners are needed with lesser contributions. Yet it would be absurd to expect one hundred people to arrive at the notarial office to sign the appropriate deed subscribing to the new quotas. The private limited liability company is an antiquated structure if it has to house many occupants.

Issuing public debt instruments is perfectly possible, but then commercial acceptance is probably dubious. Most investors associate private limited liability companies with closed groups in which transparency is not possible and there is less public, official control, tending to equate this, no doubt unjustly, with less financial probity. In any event, since there are always corporate bonds available for purchase, why would an investor select the private limited liability company?

Naturally, if this legal form is to be utilized, and is the only form available when an acquisition is made, partner guarantees are traditional to secure bank financing. This also may be a substantial disadvantage for any partner who is forced to reflect this contingent liability on its consolidated financial statements.

3.3.8 How ownership interests are represented and transferred

Ownership in this legal form has no physical representation other than in a deed, and only by a deed can ownership be transferred. It is similar to an interest in a general partnership. Ownership is contained and expressed in words. It is what lawyers denominate an *intangible* right, one with no seen features; it is not represented in any document you can carry with you, other than a complete set of articles being certified as a true copy of articles filed at some commercial conservatory.

For some international joint venture investors, this is a cumbersome, awkward inconvenience, particularly if the investment is of substantial amounts. Proving to a new member of a board of a company with offices in Chicago ownership in a private limited liability company in Greece will require obtaining an updated version of the articles. There will be written who are the owners. Although not a prime reason for turning down this legal form by any means as a joint venture shelter, the participants in this joint venture form may not understand many of the mechanisms associated with proving and transferring ownership without explanations from their counsel. This often creates a corporate unease with the choice of the joint venture vehicle and frequently, particularly in acquisitions, the private limited liability company is converted into a share corporation.

3.3.9 FORMALITIES OF FORMATION AND SUBSEQUENT REPORTING REQUIREMENTS

In civil law countries (which constitute the vast majority of jurisdictions in the world), the mechanics of constituting a private limited liability company have been alluded to many times. In this legal form, there is a public official, a public notary, forming part of the ministry of justice, who approves the articles as being in accordance with the law, and who attends a signing of the deed, which must bear his signature, and that witnesses the birth of the company. Thereafter, with a certified copy of these articles, given by the notary, the parties bring to the commercial conservator their copy to be deposited and registered, so that all third parties may know of the existence of the company, its owners, and the general contents of the articles. Usually, the first request from a lending institution is for a copy of the company articles from the conservatory.

To transfer ownership, the same procedure is repeated. As there is no physical evidence of ownership, as there is with shares, proof of ownership and its transference can be done only before a notary and compliance requirements at the nearest commercial conservatory. This procedure must take place for any significant act affecting the company.

Although delegation of powers from a manager to an operating officer might not require any formal act before the notary, the company resolution conferring this mandate on a designated person does have to be registered at the commercial conservatory, as otherwise no one would know what was the authority of the chief operating officer. With managers changing for various reasons, this can be an irritating bureaucratic process. Additionally, it impedes the effectiveness of managerial alterations, often a part of modern corporate management. As excellence in management is one of the principal ingredients of a successful joint venture, this excessive officialdom tends to grind down the initiative of the partners and leads to an acceptance of status quo management to avoid constant legal steps.

Until recently, most jurisdictions did not impose any public reporting requirements on private limited liability companies. This was a serious disadvantage to investors who associate capital ventures with public reporting requirements and a solid requirement of transparency in all financial and legal matters. The private limited liability company has traditionally been a closed, secret society with very little accountability to either the tax authorities or other partners. Many jurisdictions now impose moderate reporting requirements in the form of accounts being published and deposited at the commercial conservatory. Nevertheless, such obligations are usually only applicable above a capital amount and may even require a minimum number of partners. To the foreign investor seeking to have multiple legal weapons to compel full and complete disclosure on all financial matters, the private limited liability company is not as beneficial as the share corporation.

3.3.10 DURATION OF FORM

Normally, this form of company is for unlimited duration, similar in concept to the share corporation. It is rare for a private limited liability company to establish an automatic termination date. For investors in international joint ventures who wish a temporary existence, for a specific period, this would not be the chosen form.

3.3.11 FAMILIARITY

Depending on the jurisdiction of the investor, the private limited liability company is as familiar as the share corporation. In Europe, it has well-established roots, a solid judicial experience, and is the subject of much legal scholarship. It is the legal form to which most lawyers and businessmen in Europe are accustomed since it is a form chosen for moderate capital and closed financial transactions. This is probably not the fact in a jurisdiction as the United States, where the private limited liability company is relatively recent. Consequently, if we are dealing with U.S. participants in a European joint venture, there will be a certain unfamiliarity on the part of the U.S. partners. Although this is not an insurmountable obstacle, it is one element that tends to shift the balance of choice toward the share corporation for foreign investors.

3.3.12 MONITORING THE INVESTMENT

Historically, the accounts of the private limited liability company usually have not attained the standard associated with general accepted accounting principles. This has tended to change with the globalization of commerce. Some jurisdictions have enacted more stringent accounting principles to be applied to this form of company. But there still remains a gap, particularly in the requirement of a public auditing group and the publication of accounts.

In many jurisdictions, this form of company does not require a fiscal council and may not even require a publication of accounts. Such a latter requirement is often dependent on the amount of capital. Consequently, for monitoring an investment by documents, such as by financial statements, this legal form leaves much to be desired. Although such requirements can be undertaken by the partners by a private agreement or even by the articles of the company, any default in such obligations leads to a dispute over interpretation of contractual rights and not a failure to comply with the legislation. Financial accountability is one of the important advantages the share corporation has over the private limited liability company.

3.3.13 Termination flexibility

Termination rights in this form are superior to those of a share corporation. Corporations issue either bearer shares or nominative shares. The latter are certificates issued in the name of a person or entity. Bearer shares circulate and it is not possible to know what events affect any one owner of bearer shares. Death, insolvency, a criminal prosecution, the anonymity of the owner, other than as a name on the corporation registry, prevent any detailed knowledge. This lack of personalized knowledge disappears with the private limited liability company.

It is not customary to insert into the articles of a share corporation that the corporation will terminate, that it is be dissolved and liquidated, on the death of a particular shareholder. In a private limited company, there is often used language that achieves this objective. The articles of a private limited liability company can recite that on the death of a particular member, the company has the right to purchase the ownership interest.

Such an option can be extended to other situations such as bankruptcy, attachment of the ownership interest, even action by an owner that will bring the private limited liability company into disrepute. There is great flexibility in such a legal form for conditioning the ownership of an equity interest on a number of external conditions. The private limited liability company is ideal for erecting a virtual firewall preventing the entry of any unsolicited partners, such as the heirs of a former partner.

The personal character of the private limited company permits a dependency on the identity of the partners. If this is an important issue in an international joint venture, in which perhaps the local partner has a very important management function, the existence of the company may be conditioned on such human factors as "continuity of life" of a particular person. In this situation, the private limited liability company is molded to the realities of commercial life. This is to be contrasted with the share corporation, which on springing into life, often veers on a legal course of its own, depersonalized and without roots in the business ambiance into which it was born.

3.3.14 SUMMARY OF ADVANTAGES AND DISADVANTAGES IN THE PRIVATE LIMITED LIABILITY COMPANY AS A LEGAL FORM

By comparing the various advantages and disadvantages of this legal form, the quantity of advantages exceeds by one the disadvantages, but by inspecting closely each of these quantities, the balance really depends on the importance given to the factors in the mind of the investor.

Advantages

- limited liability although participation in management may render this illusory since managers-owners in this legal form may attract personal liability for their acts of negligent administration and tax responsibility
- management structure simple and direct although probably not suited for corporate managers used to hierarchical systems
- two-tier taxation probably can be avoided in the home jurisdiction of partners
- enforcement of private agreements can be highly effective
- total restriction on sale of equity interests is possible
- indefinite duration
- termination facilitated with removal of partners for agreed-on external events such as bankruptcy

Disadvantages

- management in various jurisdictions is exposed to tax liability
- profit distributions are similar to share corporation but more difficult to compel dividend rights
- financial engineering nonexistent
- manifestation of ownership interests is awkward, having to be proved by documents from the relevant commercial conservatory
- formalities of formation similar to share corporations but transfer of ownership interests complicated

- not as well known as the share corporation and the investor is easily induced into an error caused by false legal assumptions
- monitoring is more difficult and not advisable from a long distance

A fair conclusion is probably that the private limited liability company is suitable for modest joint ventures in which a reduced number of participants will take an active role in the management of the company, the equity interests are evenly divided and the obligation to pay taxes is fulfilled. For the medium-sized enterprise with a minimum number of partners and a limited employee staff, the simplicity of the private limited liability company is to be commended.

PART FOUR

3.4 THIRTEEN CHARACTERISTICS OF A GENERAL PARTNERSHIP

The singular advantage of a partnership is its tax treatment and presumed legal intimacy. The latter words no doubt seem strange when applied to trade. Before turning to the tax issues, it is necessary to emphasize this unusual fact of a partnership: When one of the partners withdraws, for example, by demise, the partnership is dissolved by law. In other words, in a partnership, the law assumes the original partners are the essential condition for its existence and no others, or the lack of them, will suffice. Each partner was chosen for his personal identity and no substitutes will be permitted. This does not happen in a share corporation, in which many shareholders are individuals, nor in a private limited liability company, in which ownership interests are often represented by quotas, intangible rights, registered at the commercial conservatory.

Today, this rule of law is easily circumvented by all the surviving partners agreeing to reconstitute the partnership with the remaining partners or admit others. However, one substantial consequence of this personalized aspect of a partnership is that a partner can withdraw at any moment. This is in sharp contrast to the share corporation or private limited liability company in which withdrawal is not possible. A sale can be consummated, but this is not withdrawal.

The other serious result of a partnership is that all partners are liable for the acts of any partner. There is no corporate entity that is responsible. The partnership is the partners. Their personal assets respond to any creditors.

There is no shield of limited liability. There is the reverse. There is unlimited liability.

Nevertheless, it is usually the tax treatment of a partnership that receives the most academic attention. In a partnership, unlike a corporation, there is imposed a tax only once. Whatever profits or losses the partnership has are passed through the collective entity to each partner. This can have important implications.

If there are profits, a tax is paid once by the individual partners and the tax then can be used as a tax credit in another jurisdiction, a credit against taxes due in that jurisdiction. If there are losses, these losses can be used by the partners to offset other income from other commercial operations. With multinationals having sources of income from all over the world, consolidating the total income into one report permits using losses more effectively if such losses can be utilized directly by the taxpayer. Thus, a partnership, unlike a corporation, avoids two-tier taxation.

Unfortunately, the tax advantages may not be enough to outweigh other considerations, particularly the absence of limited liability. Doing business in a foreign jurisdiction and being exposed to unlimited liability are not comforting thoughts. These disadvantages can be mitigated by using corporations as partners, but this can be an unwieldy legal form.

Presently, it is unusual for corporations or other company structures to form partnerships. But there is still a place for establishing partnerships. Even in multijurisdictional operations, a partnership has its relevancy. It is still the preferred method among professionals. Typical examples are the auditing, management consultancy, and law firms that have offices all over the world. Although in some jurisdictions the local firm may have a corporate structure, there is a general partnership agreement to which all individuals or firms worldwide subscribe and by which profits and losses are allocated. The reason is the basic principle: the other partners wish to define very carefully the composition of the partnership. A high degree of professional competence is required and this is still best controlled by a rigid method of selection and prevention of transfer of interests.

3.4.1 LIMITED LIABILITY

The general partnership affords no insulation from liability from creditors. This is one of its substantial disadvantages, and other than for very special reasons, it is difficult to imagine why this legal form would be chosen as the joint venture shelter. This observation is even more ag-gravated when doing business in a less familiar jurisdiction, one where the laws may be totally strange or difficult to understand or there is sig-nificant governmental activity in the management of the joint venture.

In international joint ventures, the general partnership is seldom used as a joint venture shelter, usually confined to an existing situation whereby an acquisition is made of a partnership and then the new partners agree to convert the partnership into another legal form. The prospect of unlimited liability on the part of the foreign investor is a serious deterrent to utiliz-ing this legal form as a joint venture shelter.

3.4.2 PROFIT WITHDRAWALS

Profit withdrawals in a partnership constitute a virtue of this legal form. Both net income and net losses are assigned and allocated directly to all partners in proportion to their partnership interests unless there is any agreement that alters this general rule. Profit withdrawals are usually legally secure since generally all partners partake in the management, all have rights of voting and participate in the decision-making process. As there is not a grave cleavage between management and ownership, the final result is more acceptable, more understood, less contentious.

3.4.3 MANAGEMENT STRUCTURE

The management structure of the general partnership is also simple and direct. All partners are managers. Direct management of course means there is no hierarchical style of management, certainly not in legal theory. A general partnership for purposes of internal administration may create committees equal in function to a board of directors or a fiscal board. But such committees are appointed by the partners and their composition even may rotate frequently. To third parties, the partners are the managers.

Utilizing the partnership legal form obligates the foreign investor to participate directly in the management or assume the risks of general liability for the acts of another partner. Most investors in international joint ventures do not like this combination, unlimited liability for the acts of others.

3.4.4 TAXES

The tax attributes of this legal form are most important and the principal reason usually given for using it. There is no two-tier taxation. All financial results are allocated to the partners in their proportionate equity interests. Such a consequence permits taxpaying entities to use these results in their home jurisdictions. As many joint ventures do not earn income in the initial years, the start-up period, utilizing these losses is of considerable benefit. Losses in the joint venture shelter, the partnership, find their expression in a line-by-line reporting in the accounting records of the partner in his home jurisdiction. This line-by-line accounting of the joint venture shelter, technically known as consolidating income, or the consolidated tax return, is very important to participants in an international joint venture who have worldwide operations.

3.4.5 EFFECT ON PRIVATE AGREEMENT OF FORM CHOSEN

Private agreements between the partners in this legal form are usually not necessary. What would be the agreement that could not find its counterpart in the articles of partnership? As an example, any serious acts affecting the general partnership would unlikely to be realized without the consent of all the partners. Thus, each partner, although in a minority, in fact occupies a powerful position. Imagine a partnership wanting to borrow funds. It is not probable a credit institution will lend funds without all the partners signing.

Even assuming there is a partnership committee, or a managing partner, and even further assuming powers have been delegated to such a group to bind the partnership, the nature of a partnership, the known fact that all partners are personally responsible, will prompt the bank to solicit individual signatures, thus guaranteeing the foreclosure of any questions as to the proper authority of the acting agent.

There is no need for agreements preventing a transfer of equity interests because partnership interests cannot be transferred without the consent of all the partners. Such an event causes an automatic termination of the partnership. This is avoided when new partners are admitted by immediately reconstituting the partnership, but this is what the partners wish.

For a final example, if two or more partners want to have an agreement on how they will vote on any issues, any partner voting agreement would have to rely on the contractual provisions of such an agreement. There would be no way to bind a social organ, such as the board of directors, because there is none. As a private agreement, any disagreement as to its contents is for judicial resolution or arbitration, but between the parties. This contrasts markedly with some jurisdictions in which share corporations are bound by shareholders' agreements deposited at the principal offices of the corporation.

3.4.6 RESTRICTION ON SALE OF OWNERSHIP INTERESTS

As already noted and discussed, the general partnership does not admit the transfer of interests without the consent of all partners. This general rule can be altered by the articles of partnership specifying under what conditions a transfer will not constitute a termination of the partnership, such as death and subsequent inheritance by a family member, or the transfer of an interest to a controlled affiliate. However, the general rule prevails unless altered in the agreement: Any change in the composition of the partnership causes its automatic dissolution. A general partnership would be used only in niche industries in which the predominant desire of the partners is to work with only those people or entities with whom they are familiar. This normally means professional or scientific activities, such as lawyers, accountants, consultants, and researchers.

3.4.7 FINANCIAL ENGINEERING FLEXIBILITY

This legal form has very little flexibility. It requires the consent of all partners to change any capital structure. There are no sophisticated techniques for raising funds publicly. No large sums not within the financial possibilities of the partners are going to be requested because everyone becomes responsible for the debts of the others. Joint liability for the acts of other partners is a consequence of the partnership and thus causes it to be an inflexible financial engineering concept.

3.4.8 HOW OWNERSHIP IS REPRESENTED AND TRANSFERRED

Partnership interests are recorded in a deed and registered at a commercial conservatory. There can be no transfer of interests without altering the original charter of partnership. Consequently, this legal form, although not presenting any unusual formation complexities, is sluggish to adapt to changes. Bureaucracy intervenes. It surely is not the ideal legal form in which exit and entry of partners is going to be a constant feature of the joint venture shelter.

3.4.9 FORMALITIES OF FORMATION AND SUBSEQUENT REPORTING REQUIREMENTS

As already noted, the formalities of formation are not serious. They do not exceed the formalities incurred with other legal forms. Reporting requirements are usually not required by the local jurisdiction. There is seldom any necessity for publishing accounts or reports of management. When the foreign investor wants complete secrecy and to be shielded from public inquiry, the general partnership is a convenient form. When the activity is less commercial and more professional, such as with lawyers or auditors, this may confer a benefit. Nevertheless, this comes with a high price: unlimited liability. For international joint ventures, the general partnership is an infrequent choice.

3.4.10 DURATION OF FORM

A partnership may easily establish an automatic termination date in the articles. However, a foreign investor wanting to have a specific termination event, either a date or an occurrence, such as the completion of a project, would more likely choose a consortium and not a partnership. By its nature, the general partnership is contingent on the composition of its members although in theory it possesses the objective of enduring for an indefinite time. The general partnership is intended to endure for an indefinite period and provisions are made in the articles for this to happen.

Nevertheless, partnerships permit the unilateral withdrawal of a partner and thus what started as a permanent collaboration is suddenly ended. This is a sufficient reason for not choosing the general partnership as a form for the international joint venture. There is a permanent instability that can surface easily when there are any latent conflicts and then the partners face the necessity of reorganizing and distributing the assets. The necessary substratum of permanence needed to engender the commitment to a successful joint venture is absent.

3.4.11 FAMILIARITY

The common features of a general partnership are well understood by most international executives and as a form of doing business would not present any difficulty in comprehension.

3.4.12 MONITORING THE INVESTMENT

Partnerships suffer from the same local customs as private limited liability companies. Being legal forms with a long commercial history, and moreover, often being used by families or restricted numbers of entities, accounting standards can easily reflect the largest common denominator in the local commercial market. This may be of considerable quality. But then it may not. It may even reflect the unspoken intent of the partners not to facilitate matters for the tax authorities. As there are no outside shareholders for whom clarity would be essential, the partnership may be hopelessly inadequate for the international joint venture in which impartial, accurate, transparent financial reporting to third parties is essential. Partnerships tend to be a closed unit and not adaptable to the flexibility required of an international joint venture.

3.4.13 TERMINATION FLEXIBILITY

Termination of this legal form can be simple. In fact, of the legal forms considered, it presents an unusual advantageous feature. In many jurisdictions, a dissatisfied partner can file a notice of withdrawal and the partnership must be dissolved. Contrast this powerful right with shareholders, whose only exit is a sale. In share corporations, to force the corporations into an involuntary dissolution usually requires a substantial majority of the shareholders to so agree. One shareholder, who has a fractional interest, cannot do this alone. In a partnership, one partner can force a premature dissolution. Of course, the partnership can be reconstituted immediately, but at least the dissenting partner has been able to withdraw legally from his participation and be free from future liabilities.

3.4.14 SUMMARY OF ADVANTAGES AND DISADVANTAGES OF GENERAL PARTNERSHIP AS A LEGAL FORM

In a line-by-line count, the partnership legal form has a superior number of advantages. It is the disadvantages, even if reduced in number, that make it an unlikely candidate for the international joint venture.

Advantages

- profit withdrawal rights are easily enforced
- there is no two-tier taxation
- very seldom is there any need for private agreements between partners
- there cannot be any transfer of interests without the consent of all the partners
- formalities of formation are simple enough
- the duration of the partnership can be defined easily
- it is a well-known legal form
- it is easily terminated

Disadvantages

- there is personal unlimited liability
- there is a simple management structure that obligates participation by all members as liability exists for the performance of others. Absentee ownership is dangerous.
- financial engineering is nonexistent
- ownership interests are only confirmed by inspecting commercial records
- it is a legal form difficult to monitor without direct management participation

As a legal form for international joint ventures, the fact of personal unlimited liability and the need for direct management place a severe practical restriction on its use. The most advantageous use of the partnership form is for tax purposes where profit or loss is attributed and passed through directly to the partners. Therefore, the tax reason may be the very reason why such a form is chosen.

PART FIVE

3.5 THIRTEEN CHARACTERISTICS OF AN UNINCORPORATED JOINT VENTURE

The unincorporated joint venture constitutes the principal contractual international joint venture in contrast to the other forms of international joint ventures, the equity forms. It is often referred to as a *joint venture,* leading one to believe that this is the form of an international joint venture in contrast to other international alliances. As demonstrated, the unincorporated joint venture is but one variant, one form of the international joint venture.

Another synonym for the unincorporated joint venture is the *consortium.* We will consequently use the words interchangeably. Consortium and unincorporated joint venture are the same legal creature, the same legal form. An examination of legislation often entitled *unincorporated joint ventures* or *joint ventures* reveals quickly that we are examining the effects of a contract, the responsibilities and liabilities of the various members of the consortium. The unincorporated joint venture is formed by contract, normally a very detailed one, that elaborates what will be the rights and obligations of each of the participants. It is a joint venture based solely on contractual clauses.

The use of the word *unincorporated* reveals its principal characteristic: the absence of a stated capital locked into a legal form, such as the corporation or the private limited liability company. What replaces the typical capital of a share corporation is the consortium fund, contributed by the various members. There is no *capital* as usually associated with other legal forms; rather, funds are made available through contributions by each member of the consortium.

Parties adopt the consortium as a legal form for it is a simple method for temporary alliances, the gathering together for a specific period of various skills to complete a task, to accomplish an objective. Once done, there is no need for continuing the alliance. The unincorporated joint venture thus has a termination date at which the consortium comes to an end.

A uniqueness to the unincorporated joint venture is that the method for forming a consortium is also its form. Other joint ventures have two aspects: how the joint venture will be realized (acquisition or formation of a subsidiary) and then what will be the form of the joint venture shelter, perhaps a general partnership or private limited liability company. A consortium is similar to a merger but with different consequences. In a merger, two or more companies fuse together and then one disappears. In a consortium, two or more companies join together to collaborate by contract and no entity disappears. In fact, one is created. All the participants continue in existence until the consortium is disbanded by the terms of the contract.

A great many international joint ventures are conducted under the form of an unincorporated joint venture. Such a form constitutes a substantial part of international joint venture activity in specialized areas such as construction projects, but as we urged, this form is largely confined to tasks or endeavors that have a relatively short existence and predetermined termination date, projects that involve substantial capital expenditures and a necessity for multiple technical services. It is normally not suited to the average commercial joint venture.

The average consortium does not have the malleability of an equity joint venture. Its reason for being is that the associates envisage from the commencement a specific term for a definite purpose: construction of a highway, a bridge, a tunnel; a research project; a marketing study. The consortium is contract-based. For this reason, it is classified as a contractual joint venture.

Being temporary in nature, the consortium is ideal for parties who do not wish a long-term relationship. Once the job is done, a termination is desired. There is no need to look for investors to buy up any interests. By its terms, the contract comes to its natural end. Naturally, experiences gained by working with other colleagues may eventually lead to a more permanent form of a joint venture.

The principal disadvantage to this method of doing business is exactly its temporary aspect. For those parties who are expecting to engage in a long-term presence in a foreign jurisdiction, a consortium would not be chosen in principle. Furthermore, in a consortium there is no limited liability for partners and, similar to a partnership, one member of the consortium binds all the others. Usually, the terms of the consortium contract will prohibit transfer of interests and thus the parties are bound to their investment with withdrawal not feasible, as it is in a partnership.

3.5.1 LIMITED LIABILITY

This legal form does not confer limited liability; this is obviously one of its major defects. All the participants in a consortium are bound to each other by contract. As the participants form a contractual group that holds itself out to the public as a unified whole, an operating entity, the law obligates each participant to be responsible for the acts of the group, although exercised by one or another of the members of the group.

3.5.2 PROFIT WITHDRAWALS

The concept of profit withdrawals is misplaced in the consortium. There is no company, but only a contractual relationship. Therefore, all income deposited belongs to all members. Of course, the unincorporated joint venture is similar to joint ownership of property. Every owner has an undivided interest and thus owns a part of the whole. Naturally, the consortium contract will allocate income and losses to various members in conformity with a formula, but in theory access to the funds is available to all.

Similar to owning real estate with another person, the consortium fund facilitates the exercise of ownership but makes difficult its withdrawal.

3.5.3 MANAGEMENT STRUCTURE

The consortium will have the management structure the members wish. During the preparation of the contract, management functions will be allocated to the various members, such as purchasing, administration, financing, supervision, and marketing. The management structure of the consortium is thus collegial. One cannot speak of a hierarchical structure. Normally, the members stand on an equal footing although discharging different responsibilities. This of course brings a mixed blessing. The participants are actively involved in the management, but each member is subject to the collective will similar to a partnership.

The absence of a hierarchical form is ideal for a joint venture in which various complementary services are needed for a short duration with each part working independently toward a common goal.

3.5.4 Taxes

This legal form confers the same advantages as a partnership. Profit or loss is passed directly to the members of the consortium.

3.5.5 Effect on private agreement of form chosen

There is no need for any private agreements as the consortium is a compilation of clauses resulting in a detailed, complete contract. Any agreements between a member of the consortium and a third party would be a parallel contract, not obligating the consortium or its members, excluding naturally any contract whose intent is to bind the consortium. Consequently, there are no private agreements in this legal form. Any creditor having a right of action against a member of the consortium could seek to obtain the monies due that particular member. However, this is not a right against the consortium but an attempt to reach funds passing through the consortium.

3.5.6 Restriction on sale of ownership interests

The consortium contract will prevent any assignment of the rights of any member. Allowing the transfer of such rights, denominated an *assignment* in legal terminology, would defeat immediately the object of forming a consortium: the union of the members of a chosen, specialized group who are uniting their efforts. In this respect, the consortium is equal to the partnership.

3.5.7 Financial engineering flexibility

There is no financial flexibility to a consortium because no member can raise funds for the consortium without all other members agreeing.

3.5.8 How ownership is represented and transferred

Being a contractual form of a joint venture, the consortium is dependent on an exhibition of the contract to indicate to third parties the members and their respective rights. There can be no transfer of ownership rights because this requires an assignment. This is only possible if the consortium contract permitted this eventuality, which would be highly unusual. Moreover, creditors of the consortium would have to consent to the assignment, otherwise the transferring party remains still liable to the creditor. In some cases, the attempted assignment is sufficient to make due all credits from a particular creditor as the transfer may be in violation of a credit agreement.

Due to its temporary nature, the consortium does not lend itself easily to a transfer of ownership as most business people would not undertake the extensive due diligence procedures that are needed to ensure the transfer is free from troublesome legal and financial issues.

3.5.9 Formalities of formation and subsequent reporting requirements

The formalities to this form are usually the drafting of a substantially detailed contract, publication of the contract, and its deposit in the appropriate commercial conservatory.

3.5.10 Duration of form

The consortium has the advantage of having a predetermined termination date forming part of its clauses. If there is not a specific date, there may be an external event to which others can refer, such as the completion of a barrage or hydroelectric plant.

3.5.11 Familiarity

The consortium is a well-known legal form with much legislative history and judicial opinion that form a substantial body of law. It thus has a significant body of jurisprudence to which lawyers can refer for advising on any particular issue. Many entrepreneurs think of a joint venture as being typified by the consortium. Contract-based, it presents many similar features in different jurisdictions, which thus confers on it a sense of familiarity and a willingness to use this form.

3.5.12 MONITORING THE INVESTMENT

Being utilized by active participants in a specific task, the consortium grants significant powers of monitoring the investment since the members are present, at least by representation. With the consortium contract allocating management functions and with disperse activities involved, ranging from purchasing to public relations, there is usually created a management committee that keeps all members accurately informed. Furthermore, all members will have access to the financial records, which permits an accurate knowledge of the state of finances of the consortium.

3.5.13 TERMINATION FLEXIBILITY

The consortium presents substantial termination flexibility since the contract, on coming to an end, obligates the disposition of assets according to the percentage interests stipulated, or, in the case of losses, the payment of these amounts. Exiting from a consortium is therefore relatively simple.

3.5.14 SUMMARY OF ADVANTAGES AND DISADVANTAGES IN THE UNINCORPORATED JOINT VENTURE AS A LEGAL FORM

The unincorporated joint venture presents a few advantages that warrant its adoption as a legal form. There is the absence of two-tier taxation, with profit and loss passing directly to the members. The management structure permits active participation. The consortium has a temporary existence, which means there is no unlimited commitment to a long-range project. The public at large does not expect a consortium to have an indefinite existence. It is a method, at times the only means, for pooling considerable technical expertise to accomplish a specific task within an agreed-on schedule. For this reason, its diffuse use is normally associated with large construction contracts or production facilities.

Finally, a consortium is often the only means by which a company can tender a bid. The host country may require the collaboration of a national company concerning the public concourse.

Advantages

- there is direct management participation
- there is no two-tier taxation
- the formalities of formation are simple
- the duration of the consortium is limited in time when this is desired

- it is a familiar form to the investor
- it is easy to monitor the investment
- termination of the consortium is facilitated

Disadvantages

- there is general unlimited liability for each member for the acts of the others
- there can be no profit withdrawals by any partner without the consent of the others
- there is total restriction on the transfer of interests
- there is no financial engineering
- ownership interests are manifested by the contract, which impedes any possible transfer of an interest or an attempt for a member to seek credit unrelated to the consortium

The unincorporated joint venture is a suitable shelter for significant commercial activity in which different skills are needed for a specific task, after which its reason for existing is no longer valid. There is no need for the continuation of the commercial alliance. For temporary difficult construction tasks, it provides many benefits such as direct attribution of income or losses; direct management participation; simple monitoring of the investment; and prevention of other, new members.

However, these benefits are offset by unlimited liability for all members, and thus unless the commercial purpose obligates the choice of a consortium, it is not suitable for the usual commercial activity.

Part Six

3.6 Final practical considerations concerning joint venture formation

Our interest is in the voluntary international joint venture. We are not concerned with a hostile takeover, which is the antithesis of collaboration. Although it is necessary to have some understanding of mergers, the usual international joint venture is not constructed through this legal process. Mergers occurs, particularly in former independent jurisdictions, which have now become part of an incipient, unified economic and legal system such as the European Union. Even in these circumstances, it is often merely a group restructuring: Italy SA and Belgium SA merge to eliminate an unnecessary subsidiary. Mergers are frequent in the same jurisdiction such as the United States or the UK, but again the basic motives and considerations place these acts in another field of study: economy of capital and labor, access to untapped funds, opportunities to manage what has been mismanaged, expansion of corporate activity.

Asset purchases are also not a traditional route to forming a joint venture. In theory, there are various legal routes by which one company could dispose of its assets to another company, and these assets could be used in the formation of a joint venture. However, such a method would be even more rare than a merger. It is the sporadic case that must be isolated and studied for its implications. It is not the usual manner of establishing a joint venture. For the average international joint venture, then, what will be the preferred method and final form?

As to how the parties will enter into a joint venture, whether by acquisition of equity interests or establishment of a new company, some very practical aspects loom significantly. It is helpful to reiterate the usual consequences of the principal methods of acquisition and subsidiary formation before commenting on the preferred final form.

3.6.1 Acquisition or formation of a subsidiary?

The significant virtues of an acquisition lie in the advantage a buyer sees in a going economic concern, with its successful penetration of markets and its physical assets and human resources. Nevertheless, although it appears to be a rapid method to gain an equity position, an acquisition, if it involves any significant investment of capital, is going to require a detailed investigation into the legal and financial conditions of the seller, what is known as due diligence procedures, and as Chapter Seven will make clear, such procedures are time-consuming and costly. No matter what the heart wants to believe, buying, if done properly, involves cautionary steps that must be done by professionals, lawyers and auditors, and this involves considerable expense.

Furthermore, the more complex the economic unit and the more the quantity of the purchase, the more delays will be encountered in the steps toward the closing, the final transfer of title. True, the essential legal aspect of an acquisition is simple, since, for example, in the purchase of shares, title is passed by the physical delivery of certificates. But this is a minor element in the drama, and at times trauma, of a wealth of investigatory steps imposed by proper due diligence procedures, and the ever constant uncertainty that surrounds any dynamic economic unit. The legal simplicity of an acquisition is supported by multiple, complementary legal steps leading into myriad, twisting alleys of investigation that precede the elementary legal act of transfer of title.

The alternative is to establish a new subsidiary in a foreign jurisdiction. Of course, the formalities will be more. There will be local regulations to understand and the necessity of compliance. Management's understanding of the local laws is naturally limited at the beginning. There is not the same sense of familiarity with how things work. There is a greater need for reliance on the local partners.

Doing business in a foreign jurisdiction definitely requires a certain preparation. The formation of a new company requires many formalities. But the opportunity to start from the beginning will confer the most advantages. There is no need for due diligence procedures. There will not be the latent fear of claims or litigation arising subsequently due to a miscomprehension of various acts. Above all, forming a company provides an opportunity for the participants to customize the joint venture vehicle in conformity with the philosophy of the various partners. The purchase of shares or other equity interests often involves amending many of the legal aspects of the existing joint venture vehicle which may not be as easily done as the participants believe. It will certainly involve much discussion and encounter a certain resistance on the part of the remaining owners.

The outstanding merit of the formation of a subsidiary is its custom-made legal suit: it's not secondhand.

Finally, when contrasting an acquisition with a tailor-made subsidiary, there looms the most significant cleavage possible regarding proper distribution of power and the protection of management rights. In a major acquisition, amending articles of the company, seeking particular protection from action by the majority requires a tremendous cooperative spirit by the seller. With competing buyers, such an attitude may not be present. Invariably, major acquisitions obligate the buyer to accept less in terms of a legal structure than is desirable. The lure of profit induces a compliant spirit.

Contrast this with the early stages of discussing the equity distribution that will prevail in a new subsidiary, the necessity for collaboration that will impel the parties toward a central position of compromise. When the parties have sought one another, the enticement of mutual gain generates a willingness to understand, in this case, the comprehension of the rights of others.

One might imagine a more dramatic analogy. An acquisition is similar to being born into a country, with its established rules. Forming a subsidiary is the birth of a new nation, where the citizens agree on the sanctions that will exist. Clearly, often there is no choice. But when management decides first it wants to have a presence in a particular market, instead of an opportunity for a purchase appearing, the natural inclination should not be to find a "good buy" but rather "encounter a good partner."

3.6.2 THE PREFERRED LEGAL FORM OF THE INTERNATIONAL JOINT VENTURE

Suggesting the more practical route to a joint venture, in our case the formation of a subsidiary, is easier to justify than counseling the preferred legal form. Nevertheless, as a suggestion, made with the knowledge that for every participant in a joint venture there will be unique facts justifying another choice, the share corporation initially should be a strong candidate for the joint venture.

In spite of having the inconvenient characteristic of two-tier taxation, the share corporation confers many advantages to the investor, principally limited liability, management control, capital flexibility, enforcement of private agreements, substantial protection of minority rights, ease of transfer of ownership, and, a fact not to be ignored, a legal form with well-known characteristics in multiple jurisdictions throughout the commercial world. Business people feel comfortable with the share corporation. This spirit is beneficial to the success of the joint venture.

PART SEVEN

3.7 SUMMARY OF DISTINGUISHING ASPECTS OF AN INTERNATIONAL JOINT VENTURE

In preceding chapters, we offered a provisional definition of an international joint venture; we listed the characteristics of an international joint venture; we discussed the methods for creating an international joint venture and analyzed the various legal forms. With this preparation, it is now fruitful to summarize the distinguishing aspects of an international joint venture.

Our analysis to date has revealed that the study of joint ventures has two great divisions: the equity joint ventures and the contractual joint ventures. But the overwhelming majority of joint ventures are equity joint ventures. It is the equity joint venture that will command most of our investigative attention. They are normally denominated *capitalized companies*. The parties form a company with a stated capital.

In contrast to the equity joint ventures are the contractual joint ventures, which unfortunately have since their origin been denominated *unincorporated joint ventures*. The contractual joint venture has its legitimate function in specialized joint ventures. It would have been clearer for legal purposes if such joint ventures had been designated *contractual alliances* or *international contractual ventures* to distinguish them from equity joint ventures. Oftentimes, references are made to contractual joint ventures utilizing language more appropriate for equity joint ventures. This is because legal tradition and legislative action have grouped these two distinct forms of joint ventures into one family.

Clearly, a joint venture implies a collaboration between entities. But this is also true of many other forms of doing business. Many companies cooperate through distribution agreements, franchise contracts, agency representations, or supply and purchase contracts. Collaboration is present in all these situations. It is an important feature but not the distinguishing element of an international joint venture. It could not be because collaboration can be sporadic, or temporary, or even without any specific legal form, such as a commission agreement, which may be nonexclusive and terminable at will. If the agent sells the principal's product, he receives a commission. Perhaps nothing ever gets sold. The collaboration is illusory. Although its presence is necessary, common sense dictates that collaboration cannot be the special aspect of an international joint venture. All contracts mean voluntary cooperation.

However, building on the idea of cooperation and collaboration, we have seen that the various methods of forming a joint venture create a stable, formal relationship between parties that takes a definite legal form. It may be a share corporation, a private limited liability company, or any of the legal forms recognized in a particular jurisdiction. This stable, formal relationship normally has an indefinite period. It is in the nature of the various legal forms that it is formed for a limitless period. The parties anticipate a period without end in order to achieve a constant flow of income. There is one substantial exception: those temporary joint ventures for a specific purpose within a determinable time frame typified by the consortium.

Besides the characteristics of stability, an indefinite period, a permanent legal form, the equity joint venture demands a contribution of capital by the parties. Our equity joint venture is thus almost complete. It has recognizable features: participants, legal form, an economic independence, a commercial pursuit, an indefinite time period. Why, then, is this different from any other company? What are the unique features of an international joint venture?

3.7.1 Ownership and investment

All of the characteristics described earlier are true of legal forms in which parties join forces and capital together. The common denominator is the existence of partners. But a share corporation has many participants, multiple, if not fathomless, shareholders, and yet this does not make the typical public share corporation a joint venture. It is probably the antithesis of a joint venture. At most, it is probably a management joint venture with management often in conflict with some of its principals.

Therefore, the plurality of equity owners is not a valid criterion. If we search for a reason for the joint venture, if we return to the origins of the creation of the joint venture, we know it lies in collaboration. But we need an element more than just collaboration. Commercial experience suggests that a key marker for a joint venture is the division of power among the various equity owners. The empirical evidence is that joint ventures are formed between entities with a spirit of collaboration. One party needs the other. The parties cooperate to achieve a commercial purpose. The need for mutual assistance obligates that the rights of ownership and the rights of management are accommodated so that each party senses the responsibility of its rights. Whereas a plurality of owners often is just an investment vehicle, the joint venture is a confederation with each unit having attached to it a constellation of rights and powers. Rights must be allowed to be affirmed and power must be sensibly controlled.

This conclusion is not a mere affirmation. Consider the publicly quoted share corporation. Shares are bought and sold. There are diverse owners. The ownership is a mere legal conclusion. The actuality is that the purchase was an investment. The separation of the ownership from the management and ordinary rights of ownership is so large that the word *ownership* loses its ordinary sense. The ownership of a share is only asserted when a shareholder feels his rights have been abused or curtailed.

Contrast this with the average joint venture formed. The number of parties is limited. A commercial object is envisioned. The parties will collaborate. Given the intimacy of the relationship, the parties are able to discuss problems of ownership and management. Who will manage, when alterations to the company structure will be permitted, how annual budgets will be decided, and the close knowledge of all participants impose on them the recognition of the rights of others. There then begins a phase of negotiation in which each party seeks to achieve his object but is beholden to moderate his normally unfettered pursuit of profit if he wishes to construct a working group. Having sought a collaboration, the parties are thus forced to accept that others have legitimate motives, rights, and functions.

We are thus led to the qualifying criterion of an international joint venture, but one without numerical quantification. There must be reasonable rights of ownership and management reposing with all parties. What is reasonable cannot be mathematically determined. There are various laws that refer to ownership conferring rights of *influence,* although often these laws have an antitrust context. These laws correctly separate the significant distinguishing feature of an influential presence in an international joint venture. Frequently, these laws cite various features that will constitute a presence of influence such as membership on a board of directors or the right to prevent action on a number of issues because of a special veto right.

However, we can skirt the problem of detailing what will be considered influential ownership. Rather, we can state that to the degree the rights of investment become the rights of ownership, the more complete will be the collaboration. In a company that has two partners, one with 60 percent of capital and another with 40 percent of capital, this might be thought of as a joint venture. But if the rule of majority is not altered, if no special rights are granted to the minority 40 percent, what rights does the minority have? How is this any different from an investment of the purchase of a share on a publicly quoted share corporation? The honest answer is none. If it is not different, then stating the two parties have a joint venture is concealing the legal realities.

The more closely an equity interest brings ownership rights and management functions, the more the collaboration approaches the qualitative criteria of an international joint venture. Thus, the field of international joint ventures obligates a study of the sharing of power. It also requires a knowledge of how power can be dispersed sensibly amongst the various owners and what are the legal documents that do this best.

3.7.2 THE SHARING OF POWER

This discussion leads us to a formulation as to the theoretical essence of an international joint venture. It is the sharing of power, power over property rights, power over management functions, exercised within the legal form of a permanent confederation, that is the essential characteristic of a joint venture. Without this aspect, we are dealing with commercial collaborations under various guises or investments. Only when collaboration is combined with ownership rights and management functions in which all parties have a reasonable participation does the international joint venture become a reality. The analogy to a political organization such as a confederation is thus correct.

This affirmation is not imposing on commercial ventures criteria that have been formulated foreign to the experience of the entrepreneurs. An examination of joint ventures, the counseling of joint ventures, the problems the participants bring show an overwhelming concern for compromising the rights of all parties. It is therefore sensible to start from this premise. The manifest intent to collaborate creates the need to share power. When this power is sensibly shared, the joint venture will have the necessary mechanism to develop with the least conflicts possible. It also furnishes a sensible criterion for distinguishing a joint venture from other legal forms of collaboration. The international joint venture is analogous to a civil society. There must be shared rights, shared obligations, sanctions on the majority, and the infrastructure must be created to provide this atmosphere. This infrastructure is documentation.

A study of the joint venture beyond its theoretical foundations is also a study of documentation that has been developed through the years by a specialized corps of corporate financial executives, auditors, and lawyers that lend support to this viewpoint. This documentation seeks the protection of rights and the regulation of management functions and ultimately a division of power. Quite often, the formation of an international joint venture becomes an exercise in reviewing a substantial amount of documents. Unfortunately, the documents tend to overshadow the principal economic objectives and the required division of power.

This causes a loss of perspective that can be regained only by understanding the nature of the documentation, what it is intended to achieve, and the relationship among the various documents. This will avoid being overwhelmed by the amount of legal clauses frequently introduced into the documents in anticipation of problems that have affected or disrupted other joint ventures. Nevertheless, the multitude of these clauses, justifiable due to the accumulated experience of professionals, should never be permitted to detract from the basic, underlying economic objectives being negotiated.

Therefore, prior to initiating a detailed study of the typical documentation associated with a joint venture, the next chapter will be a general review of the economic basis of the international joint venture.

4

CAPITAL STRUCTURE AND NEGOTIATIONS

PART ONE

4.1 INTRODUCTION TO CAPITAL STRUCTURE AND NEGOTIATIONS

Capital structure primarily deals with the amount of capital a company possesses, the percentage of equity interests derived from the capital participation, the relationship of equity to long-term debt, and, of course, any special classes of equity interests represented by, for example, preferred shares.

Concerning acquisitions, negotiations basically seek to establish a purchase price, but normally the capital structure is preserved. With formation of a joint venture, negotiations attempt, among other things, to delineate the various participations of each partner and their mutual rights and obligations. Thus, capital structure and negotiations have a common axis: negotiations invariably include capital structure issues, and agreement on a capital structure is unlikely without negotiations also on a wide range of topics. Our first concern is with capital structure.

If we are purchasing an interest in a joint venture, we are confronted with an existing capital structure whose characteristics are resistant to change. Forming a joint venture permits tailoring the capital structure to the various requirements of each partner. The options between purchasing an interest and establishing a joint venture are not always available. The entrepreneur may have to accept what is offered in order to profit from an existing opportunity. One method may bring advantages over another method.

Thus, in an acquisition, less than 50 percent of the capital may be up for sale. This means for a U.S. investor that consolidation of accounts will not be possible as accounting requirements in the United States for consolidating accounts require more than 50 percent of the capital. Naturally, if the sellers of equity understand this problem, they may be willing to sell an extra percent to permit consolidation. On the other hand, in the formation of a joint venture company, the additional percentage points required to achieve consolidation should not be difficult to secure, particularly if coupled with concessions to the other partners concerning other matters. Thus, the different methods make it easier to achieve one objective over another, in this case consolidation of accounts.

Moreover, capital as the nominal, legal amount of the initial resources of a company is a static concept, but the nature of capital is not fixed, displaying significant variety. Additionally, the consequences of a capital participation are not automatic. Much depends on management's attitude toward various issues.

Thus, the prospective purchaser or founder of a joint venture must bring to the topic of capital structure fundamental policy considerations that will require adaptation to the potential joint venture, whether by acquisition or formation. In the ensuing discussion, the analysis will concentrate on those broad areas affecting capital structure and the more recurring problems investors have to resolve. The general order of discussion will be

- nature of capital contribution
- degree of control to permit specific accounting treatment
- control of capital without a majority interest
- threshold requirements that confer powerful veto rights by law
- profit determination
- alternatives to equity contribution
- raising borrowed capital, that is, long-term debt

4.1.1 CAPITAL STRUCTURE: CASH, ASSETS, AGREED CONTRIBUTIONS, LOANS, AND GUARANTEES

Capital structure is not just with how much equity the company is formed. It also concerns the nature of the contribution, the future needs of the company, the probability of financing, the obligations, if any, of the partners toward financing and the willingness to furnish guarantees. Naturally, the first concern when considering either an acquisition or the formation of a subsidiary is what will be the capital contribution of each of the parties. In an acquisition, there may be simply a cash payment to the seller and the capital structure of the existing company, now the joint venture company, is not affected.

However, when forming a joint venture, the possibilities are substantially more flexible and varied. Capital normally means a cash contribution. But this is not obligatory and very often it is possible to have a substantial equity position, even a majority control, by contributing noncash assets to the joint venture company. As might be suspected, the various laws of the multiple jurisdictions throughout the world display much variation in regulating this topic.

In some countries, there is a limitation on the amount of the noncash distribution. In others, the value of this contribution must be confirmed by professional auditors licensed by the jurisdiction. Some jurisdictions limit what can be a noncash contribution and exclude services, since these is often difficult to tag with a value. When confirmation of a noncash contribution is required, the entity entrusted with this responsibility must justify the evaluation given.

From both accounting and legal aspects, the only condition imposed on what will be capital is that the item have value. There are clearly many differences in the multiple jurisdictions as to what constitutes permitted *value*. In a vast majority of jurisdictions, physical objects such as land, buildings, and equipment, to identify the most common, clearly have value. The use of noncash contributions is usually the subject of legislation, and, consequently, when we refer to *value*, it is legal value and not economic value.

Concerning intangible assets, those that have their existence contained in documents, we can identify the more common as the transfer of technology, patents, or copyrights. We cannot exclude the more tenuous of this category such as trade secrets or know-how. However, we are not discussing the licensing of the joint venture company but the granting to the joint venture company of these intangible rights in the form of capital.

It is natural at first sight that this should appear as a strange concept. How can one give to a company something that is not physically represented? Where is it deposited? However, on closer examination, it will be seen that cash is also an intangible right because originally it symbolized the right of the holder of any note to claim a certain quantity in species, such as gold. We are accustomed to discussing cash as being a tangible right because it has a physical presence and a stamped nominal value. Yet, fundamentally, it is no different from any other intangible right represented by a legal instrument such as a contract for the transfer of technology.

All of these items, both tangible and intangible, represent value, some in physical form such as land, others through the concession of knowledge, such as a patent. The diversity is substantial and as a result the range of what will be a capital contribution permits substantial creative financial engineering by the participants. In all cases, local legislation must be consulted to ensure the noncash contribution satisfies the requirement of the law.

The concept of a noncash contribution to capital has important consequences for the investor in a joint venture. Capital is locked into a legal structure. It cannot be withdrawn without dissolving the company. Dividends can be received, but this is a return on the capital. Capital is permanent. Once contributed, it remains as evidence of the funds with which was launched the joint venture. A capital contribution has few tax consequences. It is practically neutral fiscally. The contributor records the investment on the balance sheet. It cannot be retrieved except by dissolution and liquidation. Dividends are not a return of capital but income earned from the use of assets purchased with the original capital.

A contribution of noncash can have several positive aspects that make it preferential to an investor. The most obvious comes from the contribution not being cash. This means the liquid assets of the investor are not being used. With a noncash contribution, the investor preserves liquid assets for other uses in which intangible goods cannot be used, for example, in making purchases.

It is also a way of disposing of assets an investor has for which there is a limited utility. This does not mean the assets are useless or overvalued. The truth may be just as stated. What has become technologically bypassed in one country may have considerable use in another jurisdiction. The nationals of many countries welcome serviceable technology even if not the most advanced.

There is more flexibility with noncash contributions. Depending on the jurisdiction, they may even include services. Although it is unlikely any sizable contribution could be made with personal services, that is not true of goodwill, which can have substantial value associated with a particular trademark or service mark. One need only think of the soda bottle or fashion industry.

However, goodwill is a highly subjective valuation. Unless there is a purchase of another company, with a price being paid over and above the assets, it is difficult to quantify for accounting purposes. Furthermore, many jurisdictions do not recognize goodwill as a proper item for financial statements, such as amortization of this intangible asset. In such a jurisdiction, the licensor will be restricted to contributing the technology of the product concerned and, with regard to the service mark, execute a license permitting the use of the brand name. It may be even necessary to have recourse to a franchise contract. This way, fees can be used to compensate for licensed good will which local accounting practices may not permit to be recorded as an asset.

Beyond identifying what will be the capital contribution, the parties are well advised to decide the needs of the joint venture company over the proximate years and agree as to any future capital contributions when requested by the board of directors. Thus, a decision as to capital needs is not only a present consideration but a determination as to the future.

Capital contributions therefore raise various questions that are best resolved by the parties identifying what are the needs of the joint venture company; how these objectives can be realized, whether all cash or cash and assets.

4.1.2 CAPITAL STRUCTURE AND CONSOLIDATED ACCOUNTS

The amount of equity ownership in an international joint venture can have important financial and legal repercussions beyond voting strength. The percentage to be acquired therefore must be calculated carefully. For companies with joint ventures in different parts of the world, the accounting concept of a subsidiary becomes important. When a partner owns a certain percent of the voting stock of another company, many jurisdictions permit the financial statements of the partner, frequently called the parent company, and the subsidiary to be consolidated line by line. This is because there is enough equity ownership to be qualified as *control*, a word not as clear as it appears, but for the moment, we will assume it has the common meaning: power to decide without opposition. When this control exists, the investment by one party in another entity is treated as a long-term investment on the asset side of the balance sheet. However, local rules shall determine what is the precise percentage of voting stock needed to permit consolidation.

This means that a net loss in one company, for example, the subsidiary, is offset by a positive net income in the parent. The converse can occur. The subsidiary shows a healthy profit and the parent reports a loss. However, the final results are a "group" reporting into one financial statement. Consolidation can be a strong motive for entering into a joint venture. The group may be willing to suffer losses for a few years in one jurisdiction provided these losses can be used for income reporting purposes in its home jurisdiction.

For publicly quoted companies, this is clearly beneficial as it makes transparent the accounting results of the group. In smaller companies, even for those with only one international joint venture, consolidation of accounts permits more effective tax treatment.

Consolidation of accounts allows immediate benefits instead of dividing company operations into separate accounting parcels spread throughout the world, each with its own results and consequences. In short, consolidation permits financial management and tax strategy.

Since we are dealing with one economic unit, what we might think of as independent legal acts lose all significance. Thus, when consolidation is possible, a parent company cannot loan money to a subsidiary. Although in fact, substantial funds may be sent to an operating subsidiary in another part of the world, with the express provision that they be returned within a specified period, this is not a loan. One does not loan money to oneself. It is a transfer of cash from one department to another since for accounting purposes there is only one company. All legal acts such as leasing, loaning, selling, and borrowing become intercompany events between the parent and the subsidiary.

Nevertheless, the treatment of events as being intercompany is from the viewpoint of the home jurisdiction of the taxpayer. In the jurisdiction where the joint venture is operating, the national tax laws of that jurisdiction may permit intercompany loans to be treated as a loan from a partner to the joint venture. No hard and fast rules can be generalized. Recourse is needed to local tax and legal advisers.

When it is not possible to obtain the percentage required for consolidation, the investor or founder may be able to negotiate an amount that permits the use of the equity method of reporting. This percentage varies from parent company jurisdiction to jurisdiction, but ususally it would be between 20 and 50 percent. This is a large range and some flexibility is possible with the equity method of accounting. However, by definition, we are dealing with a minority owner, which requires some forethought as to dividend policy.

Under this regime, the parent company's investment in the joint venture is treated at cost on the balance sheet of the investor but with one significant alteration. Net income reported by the subsidiary will increase (or decrease if there is a loss) this basis. Dividends received will be treated as income by the parent company and reduce the cost basis of the investment. Under equity reporting, net income of the subsidiary decreases the value of investment or the converse. Dividends reduce equity since cash is returned. The investment rises and falls with book value.

With ownership permitting the equity method of accounting, the investor in a joint venture will ordinarily be inclined to reduce his cost basis as fast as possible since there is no control over the management of a subsidiary, unless special rights have been negotiated by the minority owner. This means less investment in the subsidiary and more emphasis on dividends to pay back the purchase to satisfy shareholders of the parent company. But as the equity interest is a minority ownership, this will require dividend policies to be well regulated, as, for example, in a shareholders' agreement.

Finally, in some jurisdictions, an investment in a joint venture below a certain percentage will be treated on the accounts of the investor at its cost or fair market value and be recorded as one of the assets. Income received as dividends is treated as income from any source.

In summary, under consolidation the investor will receive the maximum accounting benefits from the joint venture investment. Therefore, where there is resistance by the local partner to selling the required percentage or the local partner wishes to limit the equity ownership of a foreign partner in a joint venture to be formed, the benefits of consolidation are absent. If we could give the local partner dividends as if it had majority ownership but in fact it did not, the interests of the foreign partner in wanting majority control for purposes of consolidation and the local partner's demand for more of a return on its investment could be reconciled. This can be done. But the word *control* requires a better understanding. Its significance must be analyzed within a specific context as we will now see. Control can be achieved through share ownership so as to permit consolidation of accounts but the controlling interest will receive less than its proportionate share of dividends.

4.1.3 CAPITAL CONTROL WITHOUT A MAJORITY INTEREST

Many people are willing to give up control of a company if this does not imply relinquishing the right to less dividends. These same investors are willing to dilute the ordinary concept of control by accepting important veto rights on the exercise of their voting rights provided their right to dividends is not impaired. Such a situation of course renders the common meaning of *control* suspect. How does one have control but be unable to exercise the power associated with this word? What does control mean if not the right to receive more profits and make decisions. We will see that control is not a static concept.

In the case of share corporations, it is probably universal that the particular jurisdiction of any joint venture company will permit the issuance of different classes of shares. In addition to common stock, it will be possible to issue preferred shares without the right to vote or nonvoting certificates carrying the right to dividends provided there is net income. We can construct a simple table that shows these results: loss of control by a local investor but the right to receive more of the profit. The foreign investor obtains more than 50 percent of the voting stock, and thus the right to consolidate, but less than 50 percent of the profits. This satisfies the objectives of all the parties:

U.S. Dollars (in thousands)

Capital structure of joint venture company	$1,000.00
Local Partner	
Common stock, voting, 400 at $1,000 each	
Preferred stock, nonvoting, 9%, 150 at $1,000 each	
Foreign Partner	
Common stock, voting, 450 at $1000 each	
Voting Capital	
Total voting common stock	$850.00
Total Capital	
Total subscription	*$1,000.00*

The result is that the foreign partner (our U.S. corporation) has 450/850 (total voting stock), or 52.9 percent of the voting stock, which grants control of the joint venture company, but the controlling interest will not receive more of the profit. It will receive less. Imagine 1,000 (times 1,000) for the distribution:

U.S. Dollars (in thousands)

Local partner, 9% preferred	90.00	(a)
Balance for distribution	910.00	(b)
Local partner, 47% common times 910	427.70	(b × .47)
Foreign partner, 53% common times 910	482.30	(b × .53)
Common stock dividend	910.00	(b)
Preferred dividend	90.00	(a)
Total dividend	*1,000.00*	*(a + b)*

The local partner will receive $517.70 for every $1,000 of available distribution income ($90 preferred and $427.70 common), and the controlling partner will receive only $482.30. The local partner has contributed 55 percent of the capital but has lost control because part of the capital contributed was in the form of preferred nonvoting stock. Of course, contributing capital and not having control are not as grave as it would appear. This situation is particularly ameliorated in small private companies in which shareholder agreements can confer privileges to a group of shares. When companies go public, millions of shares are sold with most of the shareholders not even expecting to appear at any general assembly or have the minimum influence on management. Ownership and management are completely divorced.

Utilizing a simple distribution of common stock and other forms of nonvoting participations such as preferred shares, other partners may be willing to give up control of the voting stock in lieu of more of the profits and of course this may make it possible for the foreign investor to secure the percentage requirement for consolidation. The preceding illustration is not intended to oversimplify the various complex uses of rights attached to different classes of shares. We will return to this concept of rights and shares in Chapter Six when we discuss how we may grant special rights to shareholders so as to protect effectively minority interests.

4.1.4 CAPITAL CONTROL AND THRESHOLD REQUIREMENTS

Beyond accounting issues, there must be considered one of the more important issues of capital structure by the participant in the joint venture, whether it be by purchase or foundation. This topic is the threshold percentage required that permits complete domination of the joint venture company. A key distinction must be understood between having a supermajority ownership, conferring absolute voting power on any topic, and a simple majority, permitting the final decision on ordinary matters. An example of a supermajority issue would be a merger and a simple majority topic would be annual budgets.

Generally, the share corporation has a decided disadvantage in that any percentage above 50 percent, which is a simple majority, will usually confer complete supremacy. This is not true of other legal forms such as the private limited liability company in which a higher percentage of capital, the supermajority, will be needed on a wide range of subject matter such as mergers, dissolution, alteration of articles, augment of capital, to name a few. Each jurisdiction will have its own list. Although these are generalizations, they are valid enough to cause a red alert to the foreign investor and require a more detailed explanation.

By threshold, then, we mean that percentage of vote that is required to implement without voting opposition a decision. For example, in many jurisdictions, if we are dealing with a private limited liability company, the legislation requires as least 75 percent of the votes to approve an augment of capital, merger, dissolution, or the alteration of the articles of the company. This would not be true concerning the share corporation in which 51 percent would grant unfettered decision making on any topic.

In such a jurisdiction, the unknowing investor who purchases or subscribes to a 74 percent interest in a private limited liability company has effectively and substantially diluted his capital subscription because many of the vital decisions cannot be taken without the consent of the minority interest of 26 percent. Of course, from the minority owner viewpoint, 26 percent is the minimum equity stake that should be sought since the same law increases immeasurably the influence of the minority owner. Without his consent, an augment of capital will not be possible.

Thus, if both parties understand the rules, an inarticulated power strategy infiltrates negotiations. The majority investor wants 76 percent of the capital and the minority participant wants 26 percent of the capital so as to block complete voting domination. Or the voting struggle might shift to the form of the joint venture vehicle, one potential partner arguing for a share corporation (where 76 percent of the capital is not necessary), whereas the other insists on a private limited liability company.

The threshold equity we have just discussed relates to special rights or the power to act without consent from the other partners on a variety of special topics already indicated. However, even without this threshold equity amount, a simple majority may be sufficient for another variety of items, such as budgets, hiring policies, marketing decisions, product line determination, research and development, and dividend declaration. Thus, even in those jurisdictions requiring a particular percentage to effect a merger, a 51 percent majority will be sufficient to approve a supply contract. Consequently, we have the concepts of special majority and simple majority thresholds, and they must be related to the economic and legal issues affecting company life.

As a general rule, the legislative majority requirements are what governs if the parties do not otherwise establish different rules. They are the standards that will apply unless others have been created in the articles of the company or by agreement. Thus, the threshold amount can be lowered and when the law might require 75 percent on a particular issue, the owners of the company may be satisfied to be regulated by a 60 percent requirement created by private agreement or in the articles of the company.

The history of each joint venture determines why the parties consent to a lowering of the threshold equity requirements or the acceptance of the percentage as decreed by law. Sometimes, when all parties possess knowledge, it is negotiated. Other times, one party is aware of what the law confers and, if the other parties are not, there is gained an important voting advantage.

The threshold equity needed to confer special rights varies from jurisdiction to jurisdiction and as well as to the specific issue. Regarding the percentage requirement and dependent on the topic, it can be as low as 10 percent and as high as 90 percent. The issues can be as diverse as the right to demand information; copies of resolutions of the board of directors; request a special general assembly; block divestiture of major company assets. A high percentage may bring unpleasant consequences. In some jurisdiction, having a 90 percent equity ownership may obligate the purchase of all other equity interests if such a demand is made.

When we are dealing with a limited number of partners, the achievement of a balanced equity becomes more possible concerning threshold rights. With only two partners, one partner can understand why 80 percent of the capital tends to destroy the idea of a joint venture in which all parties have a healthy share of power and thus there is a willingness to compromise toward distributing more sensibly voting rights. In such a situation, the minority partner must secure an alteration to the normal supermajority and majority rules.

However, the distribution of equity becomes more complex as the number of partners augments. With five or six partners, it is not likely that one partner will have a threshold equity sufficient to implement without effective opposition major corporate changes. By the same token, more partners renders an effective minority interest difficult, for example, when 75 percent is needed to dominate a company.

Five partners each having a 20 percent interest appears reasonable yet any four partners voting together will be able to block any power by the fifth partner. Perhaps this is just where there is an 80 percent agreement on a topic. In the formation stage, if this is not believed to be a fair solution, then recourse must be had to two other legal instruments: (1) the articles of the company and (2) a shareholders' agreement, in which, in both cases, special rights can be articulated and protected so as to require extremely high percentage voting requirements, for example, 85 percent, where five partners each have 20 percent of the capital. As a practical matter, the 85 percent supermajority requirement translates into unanimous approval since no one block of four voters can secure the required threshold percentage.

4.1.5 THRESHOLD REQUIREMENTS AND THE ARTICLES OF THE COMPANY

If ownership of a critical threshold equity is not possible, an attempt should be made to negotiate clauses into the articles of the company that lower the percentage. Such a provision will expressly require unanimous ownership approval for a selected range of topics or a percentage that ensures the minority partner's consent must be obtained. The reasonableness of such a clause will depend on the point of view, whether we are seeking effective majority control or we want to enhance minority right interests.

Unfortunately, not all topics can be the subject of regulation in the articles of the company. It would be highly unusual, most likely not even possible, to insert into the articles of a company that an 80 percent vote is needed for the annual budget. Besides revealing too much about internal operations to the public, it raises issues to creditors and bankers. Is the company operating on a valid budget? Because such a question is frankly unanswerable without an exhaustive investigation, it is probably unenforceable.

On the other hand, having the articles of the company require an 80 percent vote for dissolution is subject to simple confirmation and the articles are the proper place for such a provision. Consequently, dependent on the topic, a decision must be made as to when any variation to the voting requirements normally established by the law will be inserted. As might be expected, the topic is complex and a complete discussion is reserved for Chapter Six.

If recourse cannot be had to the articles of the company, then the parties must consider the possibility of using a shareholders' agreement.

4.1.6 THRESHOLD REQUIREMENTS AND THE SHAREHOLDERS' AGREEMENT

Most topics can be the subject of regulation by the shareholders' agreement. This legal instrument is not as effective as the articles of the company for consecrating shareholder rights. The articles of a company are a matter of public record and, being the constitution of the company, are easily enforced by the courts. A shareholders' agreement is a private contract. Unfortunately, when a party to a shareholders' agreement breaches its clauses, this leaves the other shareholders with only a right of action against the defaulting party. Normally, such a breach does not always invalidate the general assembly of the company or action taken by the board of directors and hence the wrong committed finds its effect. Subsequent court invalidation as a practical matter is frequently too late to rectify the wrong.

However, although a shareholders' agreement is not as invulnerable as the provisions of company articles, it is a powerful, legal instrument whose existence creates a substantial coercive force. Using a shareholders' agreement to regulate a particular topic, we can attempt to synthesize the various possibilities as follows, but then we must indicate the point of view being assumed:

- From the viewpoint of the majority owner: Is there owned the supermajority threshold equity required by law? If yes, the company is dominated and there is absolute control on all issues. There is nothing further to be done by way of documentation. If not, an attempt can be made to lower the supermajority percentage so as to confer complete authority. Normally, this is resisted by the other partners.
- From the viewpoint of the majority owner: Is there a simple majority control? If yes, there must be determined what are the topics that can be decided by this percentage, for example, dividend declarations. This may be satisfactory to the investor. Usually, not all of the objectives of a majority owner can be achieved by a simple majority.
- From the viewpoint of the majority owner: In all cases when there is not the satisfactory percentage requirement, recourse must be had either to the articles of the company, which specifically lower the percentage required on any topic, or a shareholders' agreement to ensure sufficient voting power, either to dominate the company or gain control on a selected range of items ranging from annual budgets to use of the operating profits.
- From the viewpoint of the minority owner: Does the other party have the supermajority or simple majority threshold equity by law? If yes, then an attempt should be made to raise this number so that the minority owner has sufficient voting strength to block decisions on vital issues. If this cannot be done by altering the articles of the company, then the minority owner must attempt by a shareholders' agreement to negotiate the topics one by one, for example, one percentage requirement for a merger, another for capital expenditures.

It thus can be seen that a majority owner will seek to lower threshold voting requirements, whereas a minority owner will seek to raise the threshold voting requirements.

Viewed in the preceding fashion, capital structure is not a simple mathematical division of equity ownership. The division of capital brings with it important voting consequences. The rules of any jurisdiction must be known well to understand the relationship between percentage of equity and what power this confers. Each party will normally strive to either raise the percentage required by law, so as to diminish the power of the majority, or lower the percentage required by law, so as to obtain more control or at least constrain its use on various topics.

A majority of equity may be effectively restrained and curtailed through a requirement in the articles of the company of a supermajority or a share-holders' agreement altering the voting rules and effectively curtailing the mathematical use of voting power. For those seeking total domination, a lowering of the threshold requirements in the by-laws will confer the ab-solute power sought. Thus, one of the first inquiries the investor must make of local counsel is what percentage of capital is required to have the power to effectuate radical changes to the corporate structure. The amount of this percentage becomes an important, at times purposefully unarticulated, concealed issue that needs to be discussed and negotiated. There should never be a subscription to capital in any jurisdiction without knowing this threshold percentage.

4.1.7 CAPITAL CONTROL AND CORPORATE DIVISION OF POWER

The knowledge of how the amount of equity percentage can be determi-nant invariably leads to an even more complex theme: the division of power in any company; the functional gap between management and ownership; the rights of one group in contrast to another. This distribution of obliga-tions, prerogatives, rights, and duties is in part a result of the law and in part a consequence of agreements established between the parties.

As a general rule, the board of directors manage. The owners approve and receive profits. The law confers on management the issues within their competence. The same happens with the general assembly of own-ers. The relevant legislation and jurisprudence establishes to what group falls what responsibilities, what rights, what duties.

A part of this statutory or court-interpreted scheme can be changed by private agreement. In certain jurisdictions, the law will not interfere in the contractual rights the parties create. Other times in other jurisdictions, the law reigns supreme. The law of many jurisdictions obligates the board of directors to consult the general assembly on the issue of augment of capi-tal. An effective minority interest can block any augment. However, in other jurisdictions, the law may leave this decision entirely to the board of directors and thus an effective minority interest is of little value unless the decision-making process in the board of directors is also subject to special rules. When the board of directors has the sole authority to decree an augment of capital, a minority interest can be protected only if it has a legal means of controlling the board of directors to some degree.

Capital structure and capital control can affect substantially the allocation of power within a company whether by determination of the general law or express provisions. In Chapter Eight, we will develop this theme in more detail when considering the interests of minority owners.

4.1.8 CAPITAL STRUCTURE AND ACCOUNTING RULES FOR PROFIT DETERMINATION

The capital structure of a company will affect considerably whether one or more partners receive dividends if there is a majority and minority relationship between various groups, not only because of a vote to declare or not declare dividends. The accounting criterion used will be critical in ascertaining if there is a profit. Such a standard falls within the judgment of the majority partner unless there are agreed-on accounting standards set forth in the joint venture or shareholders' agreement.

There can be no profit if potential operating income is absorbed by exaggerated salaries to executives. Nor is there likely to be profit for distribution if the company is acquiring other companies or making substantial investments in various capital assets. Profit to one partner means dividend distribution, whereas to another partner, it means the company is doing well but the funds should be reinvested in productive assets or augments of capital to provide a more solid equity base.

It is true the laws of many countries require the distribution of a certain percent of profits, for example, 5 percent unless there is an agreement to the contrary. But this is after a decision has been made as to the use of net proceeds. If the board of directors decides to reinvest all profits in research and development, such a business judgment is not going to be easily overturned by an aggrieved minority partner.

From these observations, it can be seen that the destiny to be given to surplus funds in a joint venture should be broadly the subject of an agreement prior to the formation. This cannot be a promise that will affect all income, but naturally it is a general standard, a measure for future action. Reinvestment in equipment, research and development, expansion of markets, additional personnel, and minimum dividends are all proper themes for previous agreement, so that when funds are available, disagreement as to their use is prevented.

Profit is a consequence of the profit-and-loss statement, to be derived from how *expenses* are used as deductions to construct *net operating income* and later in the appropriate financial statement *net income* from which retained earnings may be segregated to leave an amount for distribution to the owners. From the accounting methods used and the theories that surround expenses and retained earnings, several legal concepts can be developed that find practical utility in joint ventures and are subject to regulation partially in the articles of the company and more completely in the shareholders' agreement or joint venture agreement.

Under expenses, we will usually find items such as depreciation, external services, licensing fees, and operating costs associated with research and development. All of these items are usually, in part, not fixed costs but subject to variation. The rate of depreciation used will affect the net operating income considerably. The faster the depreciation, the higher the amount that must be charged initially, at the early stages of the joint venture, which, although not reducing cash flow, does reduce the net income calculation. What items will be capitalized and not charged as current expenses will have the same consequence. Whether debts are treated as short-term or long-term will determine their treatment in the expense line of the profit-and-loss statement.

The problem of dividends actually becomes aggravated when the capital ownership is divided uniformly among various owners. This is because one group or owner cannot impose its will but rather a consensus must be sought. As students of parliamentary democracy know, finding a common alignment of interests with several people is not simple. In the initial stages of drafting the joint venture agreement, basic considerations of an accounting nature must be confronted and discussed in order for the partners to arrive at what they understand by proper accounting treatment. This implies the following:

- Agreement on the accounting methods to be used. This will ensure that the profit-and-loss statement accurately indicates net income.
- Acceptance of the rates of depreciation to be used since this will raise or lower the expenses for the early years of the joint venture.
- Agreement on the accounting treatment to be given to a wide range of topics ranging from capitalization of certain items, the establishment of reserves, the amortization of goodwill or premiums paid over book value for equity interests to the more mundane aspects of depreciation and reserves. These are the items that lower the determination of net income even though there has been a substantial operating profit.

The problem of dividends arises among partners, in part because of differences as to determining proper expenses but also in the definition of the word *profit.* In fact, the profit-and-loss statements of companies generally do not indicate *profit* but *net income.* As a further complement to a satisfactory solution, the partners can agree on both the accounting treatment of various items as well as a definition of how *profit* is determined. This can be made dependent on accounting concepts such as net operating income, net cash flow, working capital requirements, and capital expenditures. Many accounting concepts have a discretionary element involved, and to the extent an agreement among the partners is possible on the precise meaning of these terms, the more reduced will be possible friction and conflict as to the consequences of the financial results.

4.1.9 CAPITAL STRUCTURE AND FINANCING

Closely related to the question of capital contribution is not using equity capital but borrowed capital, or, as it is more commonly called, long-term debt. Many joint ventures are commenced by foreign investors with the minimum capital contribution. The predominant reason for this is not lack of cash, but an unwillingness to invest foreign capital and be confronted with foreign exchange movements that dilute completely the original investment. The capital contribution of U.S. dollars will be converted to the Brazilian real at the time of formation of the company or the purchase of the shares. Thereafter, dividends will be received in Brazilian currency and repatriation of dividends in U.S. dollars requires purchasing them through a local bank.

If the Brazilian currency has devalued substantially, obviously less dollars will be purchased. In countries where there is a small, but steady decline in value of the local currency against major international currencies, dividends, or even royalty income, lose so much in purchasing power that the original investment in *hard currency* is hardly ever recouped. The more the capital requirements are financed by local currency, the less this risk.

With companies having global operations, the currency risk becomes similar to investing in a mutual fund. In effect, transnational commerce results in doing business with a basket of currencies and when one loses in value, another gains, all, of course, with reference to the national currency of the investor, for example, U.S. dollars or Swiss francs.

Examining how long-term debt can be raised, there are four typical ways this can be done, of which the last is the most common:

1. *Instrument financing.* Funds are sought from the general public by issuing bonds with a long-term maturity. This is not a practical alterna-

tive for the average joint venture. Neither the commercial size of the joint venture nor the capital required warrants this choice. It will not be an attractive investment to the general public.

2. *External financing.* Long-term debt may be financed by international banks or governmental financial institutions such as the World Bank. This also is not a viable alternative for most international joint ventures. Unless the client is a major multinational, such banks are not going to reveal much interest in an everyman joint venture in a distant jurisdiction.

3. *Self-financing.* The partners, through the joint venture agreement, can agree to contribute equity according to a schedule. These contributions can be made dependent on the joint venture achieving a target, for example, a certain net operating income. The articles of the company can establish the maximum capital desired with a provision that only a certain percentage will be initially issued. The precise technique will vary from jurisdiction to jurisdiction, but the theory is the same: authorized capital versus issued capital. This will avoid having to convoke general assemblies every time it is desired to augment the capital. Although this method is not legally creating debt, its realization is dependent on results and hence contains the element of uncertainty associated with procuring financing.

4. *Local financing.* This is the most common source of international joint venture funds. However, in many countries, there is either legislation, or administrative control, over what will be the ratio of equity to debt. Emerging economies have discovered that multinationals prefer to finance as much as possible foreign operations with local currency so as to eliminate currency risks. One of the reasons other countries encourage joint ventures is to attract the home capital of the foreign investor. This produces hard-cash capital inflows needed for industrial development. There is thus a conflict between the objectives of the foreign investor and the needs of the local jurisdiction. The former wishes to bring few foreign funds; the latter wants as much as possible. The compromise is a local equity/debt ratio whereby the foreign investor to satisfy the capital needs of the joint venture must contribute a certain percentage. Recourse to local lending up to that threshold amount will not be possible.

Even with local lending possible, the foreign investor must assume that the signature of the joint venture to the loan agreement will not be sufficient. What normally will be required is the additional guarantee of all partners, principally the foreign investor. When the investor is a moderate-sized corporation, the exposure to a foreign loan is not normally a significant deterrent. But if the foreign investor is a closely held family company or a moderately sized corporation, the local bank may require individual signatures. Consequently, local financing often obligates the furnishing of a guarantee and there is no shelter of limited liability. The bank is seeking individual responsibility.

The joint venture agreement therefore must also foresee this possibility; otherwise financing may be impossible to obtain. Many joint venture agreements set forth the terms on which loans will be made to the joint venture vehicle. It is not subject matter to be left to the future and decided as the need arises. When the exigency arises, some of the partners may not be willing to assume any personal risks as lenders.

4.1.10 STRUCTURE AND LONG-TERM DEBT

Determining capital structure invariably leads to the concept of *leverage*. It has relevance in both acquisitions and in forming a joint venture. For acquisitions, it will reveal the possibility of too much reliance on external, nonshareholder funds. Regarding forming a joint venture, it will indicate if there is a strong equity cushion in the event of an economic downturn.

If working capital can be borrowed and if the return on the use of the assets purchased with borrowed funds exceeds considerably the lending cost, it should follow that using someone else's cash will produce more net income. Therefore, leverage is trading on borrowed equity, someone else's money. With a return on assets at 12 percent and bank interest at 7 percent, the target company will net 5 percent provided there are no drastic economic changes on the horizon, since normally many such loans are long-term. The risk to be weighed is whether the margin between the return and the cost incurred by borrowing is significantly large to cover any unanticipated economic downturns or a surge in operating costs.

If the use of leverage were always productive, from the point of financial stability, there would be no need to calculate its preponderance in the capital structure of a company. In other words, if borrowing always meant obtaining more on the assets than you had to pay the lender, capital structures would be held at a minimum. As can be expected, economic miscalculations are frequent. Therefore, it becomes important to at least approximate the risk involved when constructing a capital structure when long-term debt will be a substantial component. Leverage can be measured by different formulas which endeavor to reveal specific relationships.

We want to know how much of the assets are financed by borrowed funds. If a company is capitalized at U.S.$1,500,000 and its assets are the same, the ratio is 1:1 or 100 percent of the assets have been financed by the subscription to capital. Most companies have substantially lower ratios; perhaps only 60 percent of the assets have been financed by the shareholders. This would be true if the company had been capitalized at $900,000 and its assets were $1,500,000 (3/5). In the case of venture promoters, it will be even lower. What is a sensible proper ratio can be aided by looking at the return on assets. This should indicate if the borrowed funds are being used to the benefit of the company. If they are, more can be borrowed, since apparently debt service is not reducing the profit. Leverage can be increased. However, there are other ratios of leverage to consider.

Instead of thinking of leverage for all assets, we may confine the consequences of leverage to fixed assets, those permanent assets without which the company could not even function, such as a plant site, and current assets such as inventory. We might expect funds to be borrowed for working capital needs and have the debt service met with the income produced from the sale of the inventory. However, having high leverage for net fixed assets is putting the heart of the company's assets at risk. Measuring the relationship between shareholders' equity and the value of the net fixed assets will reveal this relationship. The closer equity divided by net fixed assets approaches 1:1, the less there is of leverage and the more secure are the essential assets of the company.

Proceeding with the same line of reasoning, on the balance sheet long-term liabilities are separated from short-term liabilities, those that are needed for current working capital needs. Long-term debt is similar to equity as it is used for major purchases, for example, building a new plant, and therefore it is borrowed equity. The less there is of long-term debt and the more there is of shareholders' equity, the less there is of leverage for presumably fixed assets or assets approaching this category, for example, major equipment. We can, therefore, enhance our understanding of what leverage brings by seeking to determine what percentage of total invested capital is shareholder equity and not long-term debt.

If the total invested capital of a company is U.S.$3,000,000 represented by shareholder equity of U.S.$2,000,000 and complemented by long-term debt (investment capital) of U.S.$1,000,000, then two-thirds of the invested capital is shareholders' equity. The leverage risk is only one-third. Once again, the closer the percentage approaches 1:1, the less use there is of leverage for the fixed assets.

Leverage will be most conspicuously revealed if we see what part share-holders' equity bears to total liabilities. This is because on the balance sheet shareholders' equity is considered a liability. Of the total liabilities, therefore, the larger the shareholders' equity, the less there has been use of leverage. In some jurisdictions, lenders sit on the board of directors and actively participate in the management of the borrower.

In these jurisdictions, the lower the shareholders' capital to total liabili-ties, the less voice in management the shareholders will have. When form-ing a joint venture in such a jurisdiction, it is prudent to have shareholders' equity exceed total liabilities. The exact percentage will be affected by the nature of the company.

These examples of considering the consequences of leverage are not intended to simplify the extraordinarily complex aspect of analyzing a balance sheet when considering an acquisition. Rather, they are intended to raise for discussion the concept of leverage so that the corporate execu-tive will be aware of what further analysis must be done with the aid of corporate financial advisers.

4.1.11 CAPITAL STRUCTURE AND ALL DEBT

Leverage indicates the extent to which the company is using long-term debt to finance its operation. However, when making an acquisition, one of the immediate problems facing the foreign investor will ordinarily be to confront a complex set of financial facts, presented in the form of a profit-and-loss statement as well as a balance sheet. Unlike the establish-ment of a subsidiary, where the financial health of the joint venture is planned from the beginning, the financial statements of the target com-pany in an acquisition do not always reveal patently the true financial situation. Consequently, accountants and corporate financial advisers have devised through the years many approaches to wresting from financial statements facts that convey information.

We will want to know the return on assets. This can be calculated by dividing operating income by assets. This should show if the assets are being productively used. We will want to know the return on common shareholders' equity, which is revealed by dividing net income (not oper-ating income) by the shareholders' equity. We will certainly want to know if management is controlling well its expenses. This can be determined by dividing operating expenses by net sales, which will tell us how expensive it is to achieve such sales.

We will want to know the working capital status of the target company.

Some simple ratios have been created that aid this analysis. Thus, current assets minus current liabilities indicate the working capital available. This can also be expressed as a formula by dividing current assets by current liabilities. The closer the percentage approaches 100, the more liquid is the company. Since current assets may not be as liquid as we would wish, a further refinement of this concept is to determine the short-term liquidity by dividing quick assets (those that can be converted to cash immediately) by current liabilities.

When dealing with manufacturing and retail companies, we will want to know the inventory turnover. This can be determined by dividing the cost of goods sold by the average inventory. The same can be done for the turnover of accounts receivable. We can divide net sales on credit by the average receivables.

All of the above concepts involve many subsidiary questions that must be resolved before the formulas can even be used. How are the liabilities determined? What will be included? How is the average inventory counted? By what method? What accounts receivable are included? They surely cannot all be of the same quality.

The purpose in setting forth such questions, unanswered here, is to emphasize to the corporate executive that a capital structure is not a static concept and, whether making an acquisition or establishing a company, the capital structure involved must undergo a thorough corporate financial analysis. It must never be assumed in an acquisition that the calculations in a profit-and-loss statement or balance sheet are a sufficient revelation. It takes the knowledge, expertise, and collaboration of accountants and corporate financial advisers to analyze such financial statements and draw the correct conclusions.

4.1.12 CAPITAL STRUCTURE AND ALTERNATIVES TO EQUITY CONTRIBUTION

Many of the benefits derived from a joint venture are accessible through technology associated services without requiring a capital contribution to the licensed company. Or at least a very modest one can be made for reasons of quality control or access to accounts as a partner. The technology is not contributed to capital. It is conceded through a licensing agreement.

The licensing of technology is a flourishing industry and offers various simple alternatives to an outright capital participation in a joint venture. There are three general types of technology cooperation: (1) transfer of technology, (2) ongoing technical services, and (3) technical expertise.

The first two assure a flow of income and may be thought of as the counterpart of dividends. Hence, when there is a transfer of technology or ongoing technical services, the need for a capital participation in the licensee is substantially reduced since the fee structure can include a factor of capitalization as if a capital contribution had been made.

With a steady flow of income in the form of royalty payments as an example, the benefit of this cash flow can be discounted to its current worth and thus this present value assumes all the aspects of a capital contribution without any of the risks of participating in the joint venture. This no doubt has accounted for the great popularity of technology licenses: income without capital risk.

Ongoing technical services often form a part of joint ventures in the form of technical assistance contracts. A joint venture involving palm-held computers will surely involve technical assistance when one of the participants is the national seller and the other participant is the manufacturer. In these circumstances, the capital contribution of the provider of technical services, who is also a partner, can be held to its minimum. Royalty income is more certain than dividend income. The fees can be either a percentage of gross sales or a fixed fee. In either case, fees can be structured to provide a return not only on the services performed, but the capital contributed whether or not a dividend is declared.

Ongoing technical services need not be confined to simple repair of electronic or other equipment. They can include training personnel, ensuring quality control, establishing procedures for avoiding technical problems, in short a wide range of technical assistance.

The final category is technical expertise, which is usually furnished once, although its duration may be prolonged. Typical examples are the designing of a plant, the assembly of a functional factory, and the software design of an assembly plant. Such aid approximates consultancy services although it is confined to technology sectors. Not being a continuous service, technology expertise and its remuneration are not as viable an alternative to the capital contribution associated with joint ventures. The flow of income is missing.

4.1.13 CAPITAL STRUCTURE AND COMPETITION LAW: THE PROBLEM OF *CONTROL*

Oftentimes, the inclination to demand a controlling interest must be tempered in view of various antitrust laws existing in many countries. Such laws prohibit concentrations that tend to eliminate competition. Concentrations are not only mergers. They also include acquisitions. What will be considered an invalid concentration is frequently determined by whether one party controls the joint venture. In its simplest expression, control is obviously a majority interest. It also may be other things, such as a right of veto, which renders major decisions dependent on the concurring vote of a particular partner.

Nevertheless, in situations when control may prevent an acquisition or formation of a joint venture, the convenience of a majority position has to be abandoned. Other solutions must be found that can be determined only in light of the actual legislation. The relevancy of this topic to our present discussion should be clear: Capital structure is not just majority and minority interests. It can have serious repercussions in the area of competition law.

Therefore, those joint ventures creating substantial market penetration must be also judged for their antitrust consequences and the concept of control, direct and indirect.

PART TWO

4.2 INTRODUCTION TO NEGOTIATIONS

By negotiations, we mean what information must be gathered concerning the potential joint venture; our conduct and our working attitude toward the future partners prior to the formation of the joint venture; how we will act and represent our principal; a general outline of where we are bound and how to get there. Most of our discussion concerning negotiations has more relevancy to an acquisition rather than the formation of a joint venture. But in both instances, there are general principles that are valid for either method.

When we allude to negotiations, we are not referring primarily to price, which is often assumed to be the paramount feature of negotiations. Price will be determined by a variety of concepts within the province of corporate finance and evaluation of companies. Negotiations and price determination are not the same. We have our idea of price and other important elements, but this will be contained in our presentation.

Negotiations include fact finding, the atmosphere and personal participation surrounding the determination of price and other conditions; our attempt to provide an interactive framework that will lead to a successful conclusion; an eventual agreement that will include price and all the other important conditions concerning the joint venture.

Thus, negotiations is a word that cloaks the manifestation of our commercial personality. Negotiations are often thought of as *price haggling*. This is a limited use of the word. Price is an approximation of value through various techniques and modules. Negotiations are the chambers in which our discussions will take place. *Negotiations* could be replaced by the phrase *fact finding* when only one of the facts to be established will be the price. It is this broad, ample vision of negotiations that is of interest to us.

Particularly when dealing with an acquisition, negotiations often begin prior to a clear idea of the target company; the country in which the joint venture will operate; the basic legal and tax structure of the foreign jurisdiction. With the formation of a joint venture, many of the observations of the art of negotiations are less relevant because the founders of the joint venture normally have a commercial knowledge of each other. However, this is not rigidly so, and in any event, there is still material that can be utilized in both instances.

The haphazard way in which joint ventures evolve does not make it necessarily the better, and a determined effort should be made by the participants not to drift with events as they arise, but rather set about to gather essential facts in a logical fashion. After the appearance on the part of the foreign investor of a serious interest, a natural inquiry is as to the price. But this does not mean price negotiations have to begin against an imperfect knowledge of the parties, jurisdiction, or company involved. The most serious attitude toward a future alliance does not require an immediate agreement on price or capital.

This is one of the functions of the letter of intent: to reveal to the parties the broad outlines of a possible collaboration through the form of a joint venture. The time span between a letter of intent and a final closing will afford multiple opportunities to have discussions as to price as more factors become known. In an ideal commercial and legal setting, interest would be confirmed, an investigation made, and finally negotiations initiated between the parties as to all the conditions, not only price.

Between these two possibilities, hasty encounters plunging the parties toward an agreement on price, and a more reflective attitude permitting knowledge to surface and be understood with thought and implications, lies a business compromise, a willingness to sign a letter of intent, and a delay of the joint venture agreement until more facts are unveiled. Logically, negotiations should follow the gathering of information and not precede it. However, there cannot be an academic insistence on the proper procedure. The reality is often different. What is required, no matter when negotiations are commenced, is an understanding of the necessary factual information to produce fruitful and meaningful negotiations and a few simple guide rules to conduct.

What these facts are will vary from joint venture to joint venture, but some generalizations can be made. Our approach to negotiations will take the following form, a recommended list of broad categories that can be the preliminary outline of material to be gathered. In the nature of commerce, there is never an orderly procession. Events occur that stimulate reactions. The list, whether for an acquisition or the establishment of a joint venture, may be viewed as being a practical guide to be used to confer a general understanding on the nature of the joint venture and the participants. Its timely convocation, whether partially or wholly, will be dependent on the circumstances:

- the cultural and political environment
- general foreign investment considerations
- basic information about target company or partners
- suggestions as to general rules of conduct during negotiations
- determination of the scope of the joint venture
- assets and financing of the joint venture
- legal structure of the joint venture
- operational issues of management and control
- relationship of joint venture company with partners

4.2.1 THE CULTURAL AND POLITICAL ENVIRONMENT

The keystone to a successful joint venture is cultural adaptability, an embracing of the diversity of the human race and the conviction that differences are a celebration, a necessary ingredient to commercial survival, to which the diversity of human knowledge contributes. Many joint ventures take place in jurisdictions well known to the participants. The parties often assume there is a substantial convergence on many cultural aspects, particularly if the language is not an issue, such as a U.S. investment in an English joint venture.

That language assists communication is certain. But no matter what the language, whether understood or not, we have to be clear as to what requires to be transmitted. This does not involve a detailed sociological research study. We will certainly want to have a good grasp of the general political structure. An investment in a country dependent on the decisions of one individual or a selected group subjects the investment to oftentimes arbitrary conditions. The more diffuse and democratic the political structure, the more the joint venture will survive because of its own inherent, sensible economic, unperturbed by external forces.

Beyond the political conditions, we will of course want to understand the general attitude of labor not necessarily reflected in the local laws. This is a cultural fact that is difficult to ascertain, very often merely because of a language factor. There is no joint venture that is going to succeed without a cooperative labor force. At times, the labor laws are not in harmony with current, local political thought, which is hostile to declared official policies and the written laws.

The foreign investor must strive to understand and grasp the prevailing norms. Legislation is often dragged along by social movements and there is a gap between theory and practice to be expected. Forming a joint venture in a social milieu not favorable to foreign investment will not succeed easily. This consequence is probably a corollary of not investing in a joint venture when the political structure is concentrated in an oligarchy. Many multinationals have established joint ventures in such circumstances and to their credit have striven to diffuse many democratic principles into management. Nevertheless for the everyman joint venture, the risk of loss of capital is too great.

It occasionally happens that a joint venture is initiated in a country where the foreign investor is accustomed to more labor discipline and freedom than exists in the local jurisdiction. When the law as written is more favorable to the labor force than desired by the foreign investor, its relevancy cannot be ignored. It constitutes a minimum platform of behavior.

There is an enormous variety of labor laws in the world. For the partners to a joint venture to establish harmonious relations, there must be at least an acceptance of the local labor laws, which does not require a philosophical endorsement. The joint venture to be implemented will be founded on hours of work, days occupied, salaries paid, social benefits required, and at times intervention by employee counsels in the decision-making process.

Although counsel to the joint venture will have the responsibility for detailed responses on the local regulations, a preliminary summary for management as to the broad scope of local labor laws will be extremely useful and indicate many items to be negotiated between the parties, particularly regarding staff requirements and budgets. The right to terminate personnel should always be examined when an acquisition in an existing joint venture is being purchased. It should never be assumed, no matter what the jurisdiction, that employees can be terminated at will without cause.

4.2.2 GENERAL FOREIGN INVESTMENT CONSIDERATIONS

Beyond matters more affecting management, we will need to have an outline understanding of those areas of the law affecting international business, such as

- currency restrictions
- existing foreign investment laws as to foreign capital and any limitations
- approvals needed to form a joint venture
- repatriation guarantees as to earned income and capital invested
- restrictions, if any, on local borrowing
- export controls
- tax incentives as to foreign investment
- relevant tax treaties and the general tax structure
- the nature of the usual forms of commercial companies
- any restrictions on foreign employees or directors

To this daunting list can be added the possibility of antitrust laws being applicable and any legislation affecting specifically the nature of the joint venture. If the recitation of this list appears to be a good inducement to abandon the idea of an international joint venture, just the opposite should be the conclusion. The entrepreneurs that successfully sift through this complex material indeed enjoy and exploit many overseas markets commercially with reliable net income flows and eventual capital gains. But this objective cannot be achieved without the application of knowledge of the locale onto which is grafted a humanistic vision of our commercial globe.

4.2.3 Basic information about target company or partners

Both as to acquisitions and the establishment of a joint venture, the more that can be learned about future partners and the target company, the more realistic will be estimates of the future course of the joint venture and the more effective will be due diligence procedures concerning acquisitions. There will also be brought into relief the existence of any possible problems. No one would consider a long-term emotional alliance without a previous knowledge of the other party and yet all too often companies hasten into a joint venture with most of the knowledge of the other party derived from financial statements. Anyone familiar with financial statements knows that many of the items on the one hand reflect management's optimistic view toward its assets, and on the other hand, a wide discretion as to how to treat various accounting items, whether reported in one year or another. Relevant information would include the following:

- The commercial history of the target company or the future partners. What is its reputation in the local market? Does it have a good public image? Is it associated with any particular family or group, and, if so, what are the implications of this? Does the joint venture company have access to local financing? Are the partners financially strong with interests in other companies? What is the relevance of other companies in which the future partners have interests?

- Much material can be garnered from credit agencies and local banks, often correspondents of international banks. With the formation of a joint venture, this knowledge should be extended to build a comprehensive profile of the future partners. It may appear to oneself that this is building a joint venture on a pessimistic view of future partners. It is best to put aside such considerations and gather as much material as possible, with discretion and in an informal manner.
- The product history of the target company is important so as to confirm commercial experience. This should be complemented by a detailed study of the financial statements. Concerning future partners, insights into their practical experience will make more, or perhaps less, important their observations during negotiations.
- The attitude of the labor force when we are dealing with an acquisition. There is no more inauspicious beginning to a joint venture than a hostile labor force. Some effort should be made to have informal meetings with key personnel so as to obtain a realistic view.
- The attitude of the local government toward foreign investment. If the joint venture will operate in a country with close foreign investment regulation, the legislative pronouncements in the foreign investment laws can be ignored for purposes of understanding the operating climate. No matter that the national parliament declares foreign investment to be welcome. If the functionaries of the ministry of industry have a different view, the joint venture will incur many obstacles. The proper understanding requires visits to the appropriate ministries and talks with the responsible officials. The impressions gathered will probably be accurate and crucial to an appraisal of the joint venture's commercial possibilities, which are particularly dependent on the local jurisdiction.

4.2.4 SUGGESTIONS AS TO GENERAL RULES OF CONDUCT DURING NEGOTIATIONS

Even the most sophisticated entrepreneurs at times forget some of the simple rules that lead to successful They may seem out of place in a technical treatise but they are commercial rules of conduct that are a reality and that can be useful in negotiating a productive joint venture. We may think of them as *commercial manners*, and although their recitation is made with a certain author's hesitancy for fear of being seen as naïve, their usefulness has been proved over time:

- As a corollary to our brief treatment under the cultural environment, no matter how powerful or fund-rich is the purchaser or one of the partners, it should not be reflected in the day-to-day negotiations by any demeanor. If a multinational has been selected in principle as a potential partner, the others know why they made this selection. What is being sought is technical help and capital assistance. The more professional the attitude, with a sincere interest in the opinions of the others, the more welcome will be the foreign investment.
- Reasonableness, even in the face of total aggressive ignorance by others, eventually triumphs, when triumph includes learning it is time to withdraw. We are not referring to capitulating. Showing an understanding sensibility, being willing to listen, and returning to the bargaining table with facts and figures and the right questions will strengthen the position of our purchaser or founder. If, in fact, after a bona fide attempt, the other party cannot understand what the analysis indicates, then the joint venture should be abandoned early. It's a warning sign to be heeded seriously. The reaction should be *exit* and not *win*.
- Always concentrate on policy issues, on sales targets, for example, and not the price of ballpoint pens. A foreign partner is not needed for the nitty-gritty of commercial life. In fact, the local partners are trying to escape from such an environment and looking to the foreign partner for this assistance. A joint venture is not founded on a total dedication to encountering the best local supplier of rubber bands.
- Never squeeze on price for the sake of bringing back the best deal possible to the main office. Even if the local negotiators were, momentarily, beaten into the ground, the next day there will arrive the communication advising all matters are being considered again, or language to that effect. Good negotiations mean a fair deal for all. Once an advantage is gained by one party, the other, when knowing this, will only harbor a permanent grudge or else retreat and wait to gain an equal advantage. Good negotiations are striving for the best for all. This doesn't mean being a fool in a milieu in which success is the prize and not friendship. It is possible to be fair when integrity means adhering to sensible financial and commercial terms.
- Avoid lengthy lists in the budding stage of negotiations. An attitude of listening and being attentive will probably be more productive initially. Begin with calmness.

- From the preceding principle, it is a short step to realizing that it is never wise to make a demand in negotiations that is humiliating or intimidating. Demands, if possible, should be included in a list so that no one request appears threatening. Menacing to break off negotiations if a particular demand is not accepted will probably result in breaking off negotiations. As in all relationships, never rush to a "take it or leave it" alternative. Most people react negatively to such threats even when not in their own interests.
- In the same vein, no demand should be made that would not be accepted if made by the other party. Obviously, any request made by one party is perfectly reasonable if previously made on the same terms by the other party.
- The preceding implicitly is stating that there is no perfect joint venture as to the terms for each party. Compromise is inevitable. For the company that cannot tolerate concessions, the solution is a wholly owned subsidiary.
- Postacquisition problems are inevitable in an acquisition. If substantial management changes are going to be made, they should be discussed early in negotiations so that the harmony created by the negotiators is not destroyed in unanticipated management alterations.
- When it is realized that it is not possible to form a joint venture on a sensible basis, negotiations should be terminated on the best terms possible. The reasons should be explained, not threats made. This may bring the other party to a more moderate stance. When this impasse is reached, a breathing space should be given for all to rethink the joint venture so that the participants realize how genuine the issues are. This means time will pass, which admittedly makes most businessmen nervous. Yet, even if nothing further takes place, a pleasant departure ensures an amiable and, more importantly, a respectful welcome in the future. It is not unusual for negotiations to break off and then be resumed a year later.

4.2.5 DETERMINATION OF THE SCOPE OF THE JOINT VENTURE

Early in negotiations it is helpful to review what will be the scope of the joint venture and in what countries it will function. Normally, the parties are only considering one foreign jurisdiction. But the larger the financial resources of the parties, the more significant their global marketing, the more likely it is that more than one jurisdiction will be involved, particularly if the joint venture will be in an economic union such as the European Union.

We are not discussing the legal object as stated in the articles of the company, but what the partners see as the natural area and course of commercial events. Whether in an acquisition or in the establishment of a company, a concurrence of joint venture objectives, such as the products, the services, the territory of the markets, the necessary contracts from any of the parties, all contribute to a flexible, accommodating atmosphere.

During the negotiations phase, it is opportune for any partner to raise topics such as other complementary enterprises started in the same jurisdiction that may include the present partners. This can become a particularly sensitive issue in the future when very often multinational partners expand into other activities in the territory of the joint venture. An ample but well-defined business plan for a few years should be discussed to see if the partners are in agreement as to the financial objectives of the joint venture. This will contribute immeasurably to a sense of solidarity, which is a positive factor in a joint venture.

At times, part of the objectives of the joint venture will be its function within the group of companies comprised by one of the partners. A U.S. manufacturer of detergents may well have subsidiaries all over the world, but each subsidiary is composed of a local, minority partner. The subsidiary forms part of global activities. Subject to antitrust laws, the headquarters of the group will attempt to coordinate the activities of these local companies so that intersubsidiary competition is kept to a minimum. The extent of this coordination may be severely impeded by antitrust legislation in the various jurisdictions.

Nevertheless, during negotiations, attempts should be made to define clearly the function of the local joint venture. The possible range of activity of any company is substantial and can include manufacture, research and development, marketing, distribution, retail sales, and exporting. With the functions of the joint venture clearly defined during the negotiations stage, the integration of the subsidiary in the group plans will be facilitated. This early knowledge will assist the local partners in wanting to bring matters to a fruitful conclusion. A future is being mapped out that includes the joint venture company.

Even without the existence of a group, the limitation of the functions of the joint venture company may prevent expansionary ideas only held by a few from becoming a source of contention. The early definition of the function of the joint venture company is thus helpful as to imposing sensible limitations on where the joint venture is going in the foreseeable future.

4.2.6 ASSETS AND FINANCING OF THE JOINT VENTURE

Particularly concerning the establishment of a joint venture, the parties will want to quickly formalize what each partner will contribute to the capital of the company to be formed. The more the joint venture company is capitalized, the more significant will become the contribution of each partner. This means a definition of the capital contribution of each party, the identification of assets to be contributed.

Special items such as machinery, equipment, services, and concessions of technology must be reviewed and values given when appropriate. A working method during negotiations is to draw up a list of what the joint venture will require and indicate what partner will contribute to the item in question. We might think of this as a partner's balance sheet whose sum will be the assets of the joint venture. The total contributions must equal the total assets unless leverage or other financing is intended.

Thus, besides assets, the joint venture company will incur liabilities and again negotiations is the time to raise questions such as one partner loaning funds to the joint venture, or at least guaranteeing local loans, or one or more partners assuming liabilities already contracted by refinancing the principal and becoming a lender to the joint venture company. If one of the partners is to loan funds to the joint venture, the basic financial terms should be set forth in the joint venture agreement as an annex or even a simple loan agreement drawn up that will be used as a reference for further elaboration as to the necessary legal clauses. An analysis of how much debt should be raised and financial questions such as use of leverage or recourse to debt equity in the form of long-term loans are more fruitfully discussed prior to the formation of the joint venture company.

Agreed-on augments of capital and their timing would be a sensible topic for discussion. Any criterion for triggering augments of capital should be clearly set forth, such as a certain platform of sales revenue. The more items raised and resolved during negotiations, the less there will be recourse to subsequent conflict.

4.2.7 LEGAL STRUCTURE OF THE JOINT VENTURE

We have discussed in detail the various attributes of the multiple choices of legal forms. As indicated, a number of concerns will influence the final decision, considerations of taxation, accounting, liability to third parties, financial engineering, and simply familiarity with the legal form. This will be further complicated if the joint venture will operate in more than one jurisdiction, which is certainly very probable in countries such as the United States or economic unions such as the European Union. A number of decisions have to be made before the joint venture can be established.

Will the joint venture operate from one jurisdiction or form subsidiaries in other jurisdictions, for example, home office in France but subsidiaries in Italy and Greece? Perhaps a holding company arrangement will be the best, in which the French company is composed of the joint venture partners but the French company owns all of the capital of each of the subsidiaries. The final choice will depend on the technical considerations of taxation and accounting but not entirely. The management philosophy of how these subsidiaries will be controlled will also have a dominant influence. As soon as possible, these typical questions should be raised during negotiations.

Furthermore, we will want to know what are the usual legal forms of doing business in the foreign jurisdiction. This is never a fact to be assumed. In some jurisdictions, share corporations are associated with substantially capitalized companies, require a minimum amount of shareholders, and often have many formalities associated with their formation. Perhaps the share corporation is seen by the merchants of a particular jurisdiction not as a common way of doing business but one used by the global corporations establishing a hegemony. Although such considerations may often have no relevance, they also can be pertinent, affecting existing management relations. Some preliminary inquiries as to local counsel or the future partner will be revealing and useful.

4.2.8 OPERATIONAL ISSUES OF MANAGEMENT AND CONTROL

One of the most important topics to be resolved during negotiations will be the management structure of the joint venture company. Depending on the jurisdiction, a number of alternatives are possible ranging from a board of directors, management committee, to a managing partner. These are not the only possibilities but rather the typical ones.

Substantial attention must be paid to this area for, dependent on the system of management, there will be derived the principles to ensure minority protection and management control. The investor should choose that form of management that will most protect his capital position. If a minority partner, a board of directors offers a satisfactory alternative provided the minority partner has representation on the board and a supermajority of votes is required for a selected number of vital issues. For the majority partner, having management concentrated in one person, such as a managing partner, confers practical dominion over the joint venture company.

When discussing the issues of management, it is also an opportune moment to decide what will be done when the management issues produce conflict or when an impasse arises because of veto rights in one partner. Veto rights create a return to the status quo. Proposed action is prevented. Therefore nothing is done. This is what is meant by an impasse. In the face of such a situation, the partners may decide during negotiations to agree, then, what will be the solution for an impasse, for example, arbitration, buy–sell options, dissolution. These are subjects for discussion in the chapter on conflict resolution, Chapter Nine. However, it is during negotiations that the ultimate solutions will be vented and find their way into the joint venture agreement.

4.2.9 RELATIONSHIP BETWEEN THE JOINT VENTURE COMPANY AND THE PARTNERS

Usually, in a joint venture, the partners are themselves companies with activities in other parts of the world. This raises questions of competition between the joint venture company and the partners. In the EU, such questions have raised difficult issues of competition law. Restricting competition between the joint venture company and its partners is precisely what the EU wishes to avoid. Care must be taken during negotiations not to assume promises that may be invalid. The exact extent of what may be agreed to between the partners in the form of restrictions will require a detailed examination of the local law by local counsel.

Part of the economic view will also be what each partner can do to provide the services the joint venture will need. This can be a supply of materials, cash, personnel training, technical assistance, or marketing expertise. The more the complementary services of each partner are identified, the more the joint venture will approximate its true function of a collaborative effort.

Frequently, one of the partners to the joint venture will be acting in another capacity, such as supplier of goods or technology. It is prudent to identify those contracts that are expected to be celebrated between the joint venture and any of its partners and ensure these contracts are settled as to their terms. It is not a good idea to leave vital contracts to be negotiated after the joint venture agreement has been signed. If there is no agreement on the ancillary contracts, then the success of the joint venture has been put into jeopardy.

On more mundane materials, there may be anticipated intercompany transactions, for example, when one of the partners to the joint venture will also be a supplier. The example can be generalized. When one partner will furnish a service to the joint venture, topics such as pricing and other terms should be discussed prior to the formation of the joint venture.

4.2.10 CONCLUSION

The working agenda of negotiations easily slips into all the details of the joint venture agreement. From the initial stages of negotiations, there will be founded the elements that will become an integral part of the documentation of the joint venture. This is a typical aspect of joint ventures. The frontier between the various phases is not easily defined. However, before proceeding to the general topic of documentation in Chapter Five, it is worth repeating what should be the hallmark of negotiations. The working ambiance of negotiations, the demeanor presented by all the parties, is important. It is the prime moment to display the best of each partner as to technical expertise and vision of the future. From a comfortable, confidence-building atmosphere, the necessary documentation will become a logical extension, in which the language of these documents merely reflects what the parties have verbalized informally.

5

DOCUMENTATION, OWNERSHIP, AND MANAGEMENT

PART ONE

5.1 DOCUMENTATION IN GENERAL

Stepping into the conference room of counsel to a joint venture, the first sight greeting the client is likely to be a plenitude of documents. There are multiple, bound computer printouts with various names and numerous clauses. The participants, sellers and buyers, are invited to review jointly with their counsel the appropriate documents for the joint venture. There then begins the clause-by-clause analysis.

Counsel have a number of legitimate topics and problems to discuss with their clients: budget limitations; executive salaries; allocation of management responsibilities; composition of board of directors; the appropriate forum to hear and determine disputes; what will be the official language of the legal documents; will arbitration be preferred to court procedures; what will be considered force majeure; the effects of nationalization; privatization; who are the designated agents for service of notice; how many authenticated copies will be made of the agreements. Clearly, counsel are responsible professionals who have undertaken to review with a serious purpose the many frequent problems international joint ventures raise.

Nevertheless, for the newcomer, the complex subjects to be resolved

213

can easily make difficult a general, comprehensive viewpoint. The opinions of the clients solicited by their counsel on various practical issues will not find a responsive answer without a broad discernment of the theoretical outline. We want to avoid an apparent meaningless cascading hourglass of topics. There can be little understanding of the formation of an international joint venture without an appreciation of the basic documents needed and their function. In the average situation, the relevant documents are as follows:

- feasibility (or joint study) agreement
- the letter of intent
- formation agreement
- a confidentiality agreement
- a joint venture agreement
- the agreed due diligence procedures
- a shareholders' agreement
- a board of directors' agreement
- a management agreement
- an adherence agreement
- agreed budget and operating plan for a specified period, for example, 3 to 5 years
- confirmation of closing conditions

All of these documents can be combined into one document. Not every one is indispensable. Probably a minimum requirement would be the joint venture agreement. It is not uncommon to encounter a joint venture agreement that encompasses all of the preceding topics. Such a joint venture agreement would naturally be a massive document whose structure and multiple purpose may not be readily apparent.

Current practice is to have separate legal instruments. This permits an isolation of issues without sacrificing unity. Nor are these all the documents. Many more diverse documents can be an integral part of the documentation. There may be ancillary contracts, such as a supply and distribution agreement; there may be loan agreements; there may be agreements for the transfer of technology; there may be consultancy contracts for the tendering of specialized services such as computer installations.

The possible variety is great. Nevertheless, the basic agreements indicated earlier constitute the core of the documentation, and a brief description of their general purpose will materially aid in understanding how an international joint venture is formed and expressed in documentary form. A more detailed topical discussion follows.

5.1.1 THE LETTER OF INTENT

Some introductory words are needed concerning the feasibility agreement and they are more properly made under this section dealing with the letter of intent. A feasibility agreement is normally confined to joint ventures demanding significant capital and involving multiple personnel. There usually exists an uncertainty if a joint venture should be undertaken. The parties want to form a joint venture but the decision is not yet firm. Obviously, the method or final form is not agreed upon.

A contract is drawn, the parties agree, in principle, to form a joint venture and make bona fide efforts toward the creation of a joint venture. As indicated, this document is sometimes denominated a "joint study agreement." Its purpose is to permit more informal market studies to be made as to the viability of a joint venture, permit an atmosphere of discussing how a joint venture could be structured, and simultaneously confine the potential partners to engaging in an exchange of vital, confidential information while not a binding decision. The feasibility joint venture agreement is thus, to a great extent, an elaborate letter of intent, which explains its inclusion in this section.

Being in part a complex letter of intent, the principles of a feasibility joint venture agreement are those described here in Chapter Five relating to documentation. However, there are some differences between these two legal concepts. A letter of intent is always informal, if properly drawn. It is not binding. A feasibility joint venture agreement can contain mechanisms for converting the agreement into a binding contract, such as the serving of notice by one party on another that it is ready to form a joint venture.

If the feasibility joint venture agreement foresees what will be the method of forming a joint venture and the final form of the joint venture vehicles, proposed articles of association may be annexed to the agreement. In this situation, the feasibility joint venture agreement is approximating a formation agreement or the joint venture agreement, both documents considered in subsequent sections. Nevertheless, to truly convey the subtle differences between a letter of intent, a feasibility joint venture agreement, a formation agreement, and a joint venture agreement would require setting forth sample clauses and entering into the area of draftsmanship.

It can be seen that a great deal of variety and possible choices concerning documentation in the field of international joint ventures exist. There are no rigid rules. Adaptability to the facts will enhance commercial success.

Nevertheless, in the great majority of cases, the participants will settle on a letter of intent and then pass to a joint venture agreement. The letter of intent fulfills an eminently practical function and is widely used. There is an exchange of correspondence, or other written communication, including the various electronic forms such as e-mail. Ideas are expressed by one party to another about a possible collaboration. Intentions are expressed, which is the origin of the name of such a document: the letter of intent. It is a written, brief summary of economic aspirations.

The thought of an international joint venture begins to take shape between potential partners. As we shall develop in more detail letter, the letter of intent should be informal and never contain elements to constitute a binding legal document. Its true purpose, its best function, is as an open agenda of the main points on how the parties shall collaborate. Unless drafted by an attorney, it must be unceremonious and be clear as to the lack of any promises: expectations as to commercial opportunities, yes, but not obligations. We shall return to this theme shortly.

5.1.2 FORMATION AGREEMENT

It is possible to bypass the letter of intent and proceed to a more formal document, denominated in joint venture practice as a formation agreement. It is more detailed than a letter of intent and sets forth mechanisms whereby the parties, if they decide to form an international joint venture, can give notice to each other. Its advantage is that it is a document to be drafted by an attorney and will therefore contain all the basic elements that will be incorporated into the joint venture.

Thus, the formation agreement should refer to the proposed capital of the joint venture company, the contribution of each participant and any special rights or privileges to be conceded to one party, the business the joint venture will conduct and under what legal form. The formation agreement also permits an opportunity for parties to conduct market surveys or other joint studies within the framework of a negotiated structure as to the final international joint venture.

Its disadvantage is that being a formal document, it prevents interest from growing gradually. Casual encounters between entrepreneurs at a trade fair may lead to correspondence and eventually expressions of a desire to form a joint venture. This is the usual way business develops and neither side feels pressured into making serious commitments. Consequently, were all letters of intent drafted the way they should be, such a method would be preferable, allowing parties an opportunity to negotiate their way to a joint venture.

For the corporate manager, the decision as to what route to utilize, letter of intent or formation agreement, the alternative chosen will be what is the most adequate response to the circumstances. If the other party shows a high degree of uncertainty over many aspects of a joint venture, it would be more sensible to utilize a nonbinding letter of intent and proceed more slowly. This philosophy is certainly to be preferred when the project entails only a modest capital involvement and there is a need to be circumspect concerning expenses.

On the other hand, joint ventures involving multinationals, with much experience in joint ventures, a large staff of legal and financial support, may well prefer the formation agreement. It reduces quickly the main outlines of the joint venture to a binding document, leaving open the option to proceed or not dependent on the gathering of more facts. Thus, complicated legal questions are resolved early and this leaves the parties free to concentrate their energies on the economic viability of the joint venture project.

However, certainly in the majority of cases, the everyman joint venture project develops slowly in the minds of the participants. There is a preliminary exchange of information, visits to each other's offices, and finally the decision is made to establish a joint venture. There is a limited use of a formation agreement in the everyman joint venture.

5.1.3 THE CONFIDENTIALITY AGREEMENT

When potential collaboration begins to develop, there is naturally a need to obtain information. In an acquisition, the future buyer may need to have more information on the customer base. In the formation of a subsidiary, one partner may wish to know more information about a manufacturing process. Should the acquisition or joint venture never materialize, valuable information will have been given by one party to another. The function of the confidentiality agreement is to prevent this information from being used by the party acquiring its knowledge and impede further disclosure.

The confidentiality agreement may be a separate document or it may be a clause in a letter of intent drafted by counsel. To avoid confusing the informality of the letter of intent with the serious obligations undertaken in a confidentiality agreement, it is preferable that the two documents be kept separate.

The confidentiality agreement is not a mere recitation of "hold in confidence." It should contain procedures on how the information will be obtained and under what conditions, all of which are discussed later in this chapter.

5.1.4 THE JOINT VENTURE AGREEMENT

When sufficient information has been gathered, the parties will decide whether to continue. If the decision is affirmative, one of the basic documents preceding the joint venture must be prepared and executed, that is, the joint venture agreement. The joint venture agreement is the kingpin of international joint venture documentation. Unless substituted by other documents, it is indispensable.

This is a highly technical document. Its purpose is manifold. It states the terms of the joint venture. It contains the promises of one party to another. It indicates what must take place before the acquisition is made or the joint venture company is established.

The joint venture agreement will contain numerous clauses concerning all the conditions that must be fulfilled prior to closing, the warranties and representations of the parties, and the necessary approvals. The joint venture agreement can be seen as a primary source for ownership and managerial rights. It is a fundamental document that defines the conditions on which the joint venture is formed. It is similar to the function of a constitution wherein the parties agree to the social contract that will regulate their behavior.

When dealing with an acquisition, the right to conduct due diligence procedures will be contained in the joint venture agreement.

5.1.5 AGREED DUE DILIGENCE PROCEDURES

No one makes an acquisition without understanding thoroughly the legal and financial aspects of the target company. This requires an investigation and it is a technical process that bears the name of due diligence procedures. Due diligence procedures are intended to permit this investigation. The right to conduct such procedures, the limitations, if any, the object of the due diligence procedures, will all be established in the joint venture agreement. The importance of due diligence procedures warrants a separate chapter in which this process can be analyzed in its various facets, its importance to management can be determined, and the information management should seek can be gathered. Due diligence procedures are a key, critical aspect of forming a joint venture by the method of an acquisition.

5.1.6 THE SHAREHOLDERS' AGREEMENT

The joint venture agreement often contains clauses conferring special rights on one partner. For example, a minority partner may be ensured a certain number of seats on the board of directors. Or there may be provisions that no augments of capital will be possible without the unanimous approval of all partners, regardless of their capital participation. In what document a particular clause should appear is a legal decision and one not entirely free from doubt. This explains why legal documents often appear repetitive or why there are so many.

Concerning rights between shareholders, it is frequent to construct a shareholders' agreement that deals exclusively with these issues. The same topics could be inserted in the joint venture agreement. But there is much to be said for separating the area of shareholders' rights and putting them into a special document. Such a technique permits a more analytic view: What did the shareholders intend to be regulated between them? Instead of searching through a lengthy joint venture agreement, it can be all contained in the shareholders' agreement.

Additionally, as new shareholders become members of the joint venture agreement, their signature may be secured to the new agreement. If amendments are needed, they can be annexed to the shareholders' agreement, facilitating understanding. The shareholders' agreement has a significant role in enhancing and protecting minority interests so as to warrant an individual treatment, found in Chapter Six. It is a declaration of shareholder rights.

5.1.7 THE BOARD OF DIRECTORS' AGREEMENT

An agreement regulating the functioning of the board of directors is not a common document but it is one seriously recommended. Its purpose is to establish how voting will be done on a variety of issues at the board of directors' level. The possibilities are simple majority, supermajority, or a unanimous decision. In both acquisitions and the formation of subsidiaries, this is a highly useful document because by creating a supermajority requirement, for example, 75 percent of the votes on a particular issue, a minority partner only having one-third of the seats on a board can block any affirmative action. Used wisely in conjunction with a shareholders' agreement, the board of directors' agreement permits minority owners to secure an influence they would not ordinarily have.

5.1.8 THE MANAGEMENT AGREEMENT

What the board of directors' agreement does for owners, the management agreement can do regarding specially conceded management rights. The management agreement is a formal document wherein the participants to the joint venture disperse among themselves various management responsibilities.

In those joint ventures in which one partner is to have substantial dominion over a particular department, for example, the financial sector, a management agreement will direct its attention to these issues and the signature of all participants to the joint venture eliminates future interference. Misunderstanding as to what each partner will do in the joint venture is quite common and the management agreement can dilute this potential latent conflict.

5.1.9 The adherence agreement

This is an agreement that is intended to bind new adherents to the joint venture. As new partners enter because of a sale of interests, all prior obligations existing between the founders are assumed by the new partner. This could be done by having all prior agreements signed again. An adherence agreement facilitates the execution of multiple documents.

5.1.10 Agreed budget and operating plan for a specified period, for example, 3 to 5 years

A great deal of time is expended by corporate executives in the preparation of budgets and operating plans for the new joint venture. These are precious working documents that have a legal relevancy. They indicate what the parties planned, the financial limitations of the joint venture, its expansion possibilities, and how money would be spent and on what. Having these documents annexed to the joint venture agreement thus provides an invaluable reference and even a check on the actions of the majority.

5.1.11 Confirmation of events leading to the closing

Before proceeding to an examination of the usual documentation associated with joint ventures in the next sections, it is helpful to have a general understanding of the sequence of events. Multiple and varied documents are associated with joint ventures and it is easy to lose the general pattern and become exceedingly engrossed in individual documents. There is a usual beginning and a natural end. Although the order of occurrences is not invariable, there is a commercial logic to the sequence of events.

- Negotiations begin. Do the parties want a nonbinding working document that indicates the probable outlines of a future collaboration? If yes, proceed to the next step. If not, a detailed joint venture agreement, the working agreement of the parties, must be prepared by counsel.
- Prepare a letter of intent. This can be informal or formal, dependent on the availability of time. Its most appropriate use is as an agenda. Whatever the contents, it should be emphasized by appropriate language that the letter of intent is a provisional articulation of ideas. Are the parties concerned about issues of confidentiality or exchange of trade information? If yes, a confidentiality agreement must be drawn and executed. A letter of intent with no clauses concerning confidentiality is not a confidentiality agreement. Although the clauses can be obligatory, and thus avoid the informal, nonbinding aspect of a letter of intent, it is best to have a separate binding agreement on the obligation of confidence.
- Does the buyer first want more information about the target company before proceeding further? If yes, an agreement must be drawn up, an amendment to the letter of intent or a separate agreement, providing for due diligence procedures. Such procedures grant to the buyer the right to investigate the legal and financial aspects of the target company. It is the radioscopy the medical profession uses to determine the state of health of the object. This is a highly technical document that must be drafted by counsel in accordance with the commercial objectives of the client.
- It is too soon for further investigation but the parties are satisfied to enter into a binding agreement leading to a joint venture. Whether an acquisition or the formation of a company, a detailed joint venture agreement will be drawn and executed. Concerning an acquisition, if due diligence procedures have not been conducted previously, they will take place once the joint venture agreement is signed. The formation of a joint venture company does not necessitate due diligence procedures.
- During the term of the joint venture agreement, various objectives must be achieved. These are naturally dependent on the facts of the joint venture and who the parties are. But essentially there will be a need for consensus on capital participation of the parties, articles of the company, any special rights to be granted to any group of owners and division of management functions, obtainment of any necessary approvals, and, of course, notices may be necessary to governmental authorities ranging from central bank exchange controls to antitrust notices.

The joint venture agreement is a lengthy recitation of various clauses, some of which are relevant to management and others of a strictly legal nature. Are any special rights to be granted to any participant in the joint venture? If not, there is no need for an additional agreement known as a shareholders' agreement. If yes, proceed to the shareholders' agreement.

- The shareholders' agreement will provide for division of powers between the various blocks of owners; management rights and who will have jurisdiction over what department are typical considerations. These considerations raise other problems of a legal nature discussed in subsequent chapters. However, if the parties to the joint venture have negotiated any special rights in relationship to one another, the shareholders' agreement assumes a primordial importance.

- Have all the approvals for the purchase or the formation of the joint venture company been obtained? If not, the joint venture agreement should determine whether there are any extensions of time involved or the agreement is terminated. If yes, there must then be executed any contracts that form part of the joint venture agreement, for example, distribution contracts, supply contracts, transfers of technology. All ancillary contracts are signed; we are now ready to proceed to closing.

- Closing procedures follow a typical design. The parties notify each other they are ready to proceed. If we are dealing with an acquisition, the seller must furnish the buyer with various documents, the most important being a disclosure letter and often a letter from counsel for the seller assuring the buyer that all is in order to proceed.

The disclosure letter is a statement by the seller that in relation to each and every warranty and representation in the joint venture agreement, there has or has not been a change of circumstances. For example, perhaps a major asset was sold. The disclosure letter would state that in relationship to title to major assets there has been a change and set forth what it is.

The legal opinion of counsel to the seller is to confirm there are no legal impediments to the transaction, such as lack of corporate approvals or shareholders' consent. If the disclosure letter and the legal opinion are satisfactory, then proceed to closing. If we are forming a joint venture subsidiary, there will be no need for a disclosure letter as there is nothing to disclose.

— Closing procedures will vary depending on whether there is an acquisition or the formation of a new company, but the outlines are generally:

— delivery of title of equity ownership

— constitution of the company

— payment to seller or deposit of capital

 — publication of articles
 — registration of company at commercial conservatory
- Simultaneously, or immediately subsequent to delivery of title documents or constitution of company, various management acts must take place, namely:
 — destitution of prior management
 — appointment of new members to the board of directors and key personnel

The preceding flow of events can be seen as:

- negotiations
- agreement on multiple conditions
- due diligence procedures
- obtainment of necessary approvals
- assurances that there have been no major economic changes to the target company
- formation of the company or purchase of shares
- compliance with local legal requirements such as publication of company articles
- appointment of new managers

This is a very broad description. The details of the documentation are substantial; it is important to keep in mind that all documentation, no matter how extensive, normally contributes to the same purpose: fulfillment of promises and transparency.

PART TWO

5.2 HOW DOCUMENTS CONTRIBUTE TOWARD EFFECTIVE OWNERSHIP AND MANAGEMENT

The objective of any international joint venture is to exercise ownership rights and implement management decisions. One naturally thinks of management functions as being a result of ownership, the mathematical consequences of the powers conferred by proprietary interests. Under this view, one can be a majority or minority owner or there can be a deadlock (50%/50%). This usual mathematical view is not correct.

There exist many legal techniques for granting more rights than would be expected from the quantity of equity participation. It is perfectly lawful to have a corporation issue shares conferring on the owners, no matter how minimal their ownership interests, the right to elect a specified number of directors to the board of directors. In theory, a person with a 10 percent equity participation could be granted the right to elect one-third of the members of the board of directors. This may not be common but it is legally possible.

Naturally, in public corporations, this technique is not very common. With a very large shareholder base distributed among millions of owners, special rights could not be implemented as it would negate against the negotiability of the shares, raising fears of undue influence by one group of shareholders. Furthermore, it would destroy the isolation from shareholders that management usually enjoys.

However, in small privately held corporations, the so-called closely held corporations, it is to be expected that the participants in a joint venture will expect certain rights over and above those resulting from their equity participation. Even with a division of ownership in 50–50 (50%–50%), it would be sensible to define what partner will have jurisdiction over what area. If management frontiers and prerogatives are not clearly defined, the potential conflict surfaces more quickly. Management is decision making. Strategy and corporate objectives are highly subjective opinions that can cause disagreement between the various partners.

The only way to chart a sensible ownership and management course is through the proper use of documents. There is no need for legal instruments to be a wasteland of semantic incoherence, a lawyer's undecipherable lexicon. But even granted the need for some legal terminology, the basic purpose of the various documents should be clearly understood by management.

This chapter, difficult in that it reviews the various appropriate documents that are normally drafted by attorneys, will explain what is required and why. The drafting, the actual clauses, and the logical sequence of the clauses are exclusively the province of lawyers. But not their purpose. Documents are an indispensable aid in the distribution of ownership power and management functions.

It is natural to think of legal agreements as being a self-contained unit, with no need to search outside the document for further clarification, as in a lease, a deed, a mortgage, or a bond. The entirety of legal rights and obligations is usually believed to be contained within the physical confines of a instrument. This is only a partial vision.

Legal rights are not as compartmentalized as we would wish. We can see this easily in the case of an owner of realty who obtains a loan to construct a residence. Normally, ownership of land and buildings carries with it a rather extensive list of rights, conferred by the deed. However, these rights can be diluted easily by clauses from other sources. The bank may restrict structural alterations to the house in its mortgage clauses; the fire insurance policy may prohibit the presence of certain products on the property. The local municipality may restrict the use of the premises through zoning laws, obligating it to be solely used for residential purposes. Legal documents are thus affected by other acts entered into, either by the parties or as a consequence of the legal community to which they belong.

Relational effects increase with the presence of multiple documents. An examination of legal relations involving several instruments will reveal that normally four events are taking place simultaneously:

1. rights are being created
2. rights are being modified
3. power is distributed
4. power is weakened or augmented

Reverting to the residence owner, the right of ownership is created with a purchase; then modified by the granting of a mortgage; the power of use normally associated with ownership is distributed between the owner and the authorities of the municipality through the effect of zoning laws. The power of the owner is weakened.

When confronting international joint ventures involving companies, which is the great majority of cases, there is a further consideration. Besides the applicable legal documents, the laws of the external legal jurisdiction in question, the relevant judicial decisions, there must be carefully studied the internal legal constitution, which is, of course, the corporate articles of incorporation and by-laws, or their equivalent.

All of these spheres of legal activity—documents, legislative and judicial acts, and the company charter—create an interlocking system of rights and obligations. In any legal relationship, there is a flux of legal rights, a circulation of power and its consequences.

These multiple aspects of documents can be agglomerated of course under the expression *the rights* of the various parties. But such an expression is not elucidative. For analytical purposes, it is helpful to bear in mind the objectives of any document or part of them; separate them out; verify to what extent they have been modified; confirm the extent of power being conferred and to search for any restrictions on these powers that may be contained in other sources, such as the relevant legal jurisdiction or the corporate charter.

Thus, understanding the multiple aspects of legal relationships, that is, the creation of rights and their modification, the distribution of power derived from rights, and the alteration of the normal exercise of any power will aid in the construction and understanding of complex legal arrangements. It focuses attention on the practical aspects of any legal act.

Rights of ownership may not be as complete as imagined. This in turn requires the power of another party to act to be curtailed. This legal tetrad (group of four) of any document ensures that the rights established in one clause, or agreement, will not be dissipated inadvertently by another clause or agreement and obligates the participants to confirm the consequences of their legal acts due to being inserted in a particular legal environment, whether legislative, judicial, or corporate.

Although all this may appear obvious, the formation of international joint ventures at times obscures this process due to the substantial documentation that has become a commonplace feature of international alliances. The common occurrence of transnational mergers and international acquisitions has generated enormous quantities of legal documents. Each joint venture brings its own characteristic set of documents. Yet, beneath the landslide of paper are the realities of power. In this chapter, when referring to the various relevant legal documents, we will frequently call attention to the part they play in our legal tetrad.

However, the building of a house necessitates at least an agreed sequence of documents, starting with the floor plan. The international joint venture also requires a minimum of documents. There are no rules or regulations that decree what these documents will be. Rather, the traditional documents utilized have been a result of industry practice, what other parties expect. From this viewpoint, relevant documents can be classified as being preliminary, such as the letter of intent, or essential, such as the joint venture agreement; there are many optional documents that can accompany the formation of a joint venture.

We have indicated the usual basic documents and given a brief description. We will now study these more common documents from their functional aspect. How does the document in question assist in achieving the objectives of the parties?

5.2.1 PRELIMINARY DOCUMENTS: THE NEGOTIATIONS PHASE

Our first concern is the preliminary documents. Preliminary in the international joint venture context means in the negotiations stage, a period that is prior to the signing of contracts. The typical preliminary documents most utilized are (1) the letter of intent and (2) the confidentiality agreement; they should complement one another. They do not have to be executed simultaneously. Most likely, they would not. They are documents utilized during the bargaining phase.

Another document belonging to the negotiations stage and used at times is a feasibility, also known as a joint study, agreement. This latter documents is intended to determine if there is a sensible basis for proceeding toward a joint venture. In this respect, it serves the same function as a formation agreement in which it is foreseen the parties will have an interval to decide whether to proceed. There is probably no limit to the variety of documents preceding a formal declaration of intent. The most common still remains the letter of intent.

5.2.2 THE LETTER OF INTENT

Due to the nature of business, the first document to appear is normally a letter of intent. Nomenclature is very variable in international joint venture formation. The letter of intent has many names. It may be called "memorandum," "precontract," "agreement on principles," "letter of commitment," "heads of agreement" and even the French expression *"aide-mémoire."*

If carefully prepared, the letter of intent is a nonbinding document, a statement of purpose, a declaration as to what the parties will eventually do. It is frequently thought of as a legal document. But it is not. Its purpose and legal effect must be clearly understood; it is not a contract; its function is limited; it can serve a useful purpose.

The origin of the letter of intent is the natural desire of entrepreneurs to outline what they understand are the general points of common understanding. The difficulty is there are so many aspects to an acquisition or forming a company that most letters of intent either concentrate on the more vital issues or on points on which there is agreement; the letter of intent is incomplete in many respects. This causes no obstacle provided the letter of intent has not become a contract or, more gravely, an incomplete contract.

On the other hand, if a letter of intent is prepared in detail it begins to become, if it does not become, a contract, creating obligations from which the parties cannot retreat. This is not a good idea as often initial commercial decisions need to be revised. Letters of intent should be kept broad and be written in generalities. The objective should be to studiously avoid any contractual responsibility.

The objectives of the letter of intent should be as a working schedule for the parties. It is certainly helpful to provisionally list in the letter of intent what are the basic elements of the joint venture. An indication of the identity of the participating companies, the object of the joint venture, the proposed capital, the capital contribution of each participant, even any special rights one of the members of the joint venture knows it will require, such as a specified number of members on the board of directors, all this enumeration will be positive steps toward the formation of the joint venture.

5.2.3 Declaration of informality

As soon as possible, somewhere in the communication from one entrepreneur to another should be a statement that the communication in question is a mere expression of an interest. This should be buttressed by statements in the appropriate place that the author of the letter does not have any formal authority to bind any party, reminding the recipient that all authority for establishing a joint venture depends on the final terms, which must be approved by the proper corporate authorities. It would not be an exaggeration to close the letter reminding the recipient that what has been stated are mere ideas, an exchange of information, a possible basis for a collaboration that necessitates much more investigation, or thought. Of course, all of this can be contained within expressions of genuine interest in a collaboration and the necessity for further information.

5.2.4 Points of no return

A fact stated in a letter of intent cannot be renegotiated. It almost always causes an irritation in the other party and creates a climate of no confidence that spills over into other areas and only undoes the steps toward a dynamic collaboration. Rather than state facts, it is more prudent and helpful to refer to issues. Questions of parties, capital contributions, amount of equity participation, and the nature of the company to be formed can all be framed in the generality and made subject to further meetings or the furnishing of more information.

5.2.5 Form of the letter of intent and its function

The preceding considerations naturally raise the question if the letter of intent must comply with any specific legal formalities. Since it is not a legal document, it is clear no particular form is required. However, it certainly is good business practice to pass to writing the contents of the letter of intent for its prime purpose is to indicate the desire to collaborate and the points to be negotiated.

The function of the letter of intent should be to indicate the agenda the parties intend to follow toward the formation of a joint venture. Of course, the more legal-like the letter of intent seems, the more it may be construed to be a contract or an offer to contract that can be accepted by the other party. Consequently, the more formal the letter of intent becomes, the more it is imperative the same letter contain disclaimers that it is not an offer to contract.

The letter of intent is thus one document, the only one, of all the documentation accompanying a joint venture, that should be purposely informal, not bear the hallmark of being written by a lawyer, with constant reminders that the points being raised are for discussion. All final decisions rest with the respective boards of directors.

5.2.6 ADVANTAGES AND DISADVANTAGES OF THE LETTER OF INTENT

The lack of contractual obligations is the great virtue of the letter of intent. It permits parties to exchange views without fear that what is being written will constitute a firm promise, enforceable in court. However, its great virtue is also its significant defect because very often, in commercial enthusiasm, statements are made in the letter of intent that do constitute promises, which may entail responsibility for the author, and yet the ideas expressed were only partial thoughts, without reference to other issues.

Were all corporate letter writers wise users of the word, the letter of intent would provide significant benefits, a casual, nonthreatening approach to the building of a joint venture. This balancing of advantages and disadvantages in the letter of intent is even more difficult when many joint ventures are comprised of parties from different legal systems, particularly the common law and civil law jurisdictions, and issues of good faith arise.

5.2.7 THE LETTER OF INTENT IS NOT A CONTRACT

There is a significant theoretical cleavage between common law countries, such as the United States and England, and the civil law countries, many of whom are member states of the European Union, such as Germany and France, regarding the implied terms of a contract. In common law countries, a document to be a contract must fulfill many requisites. If these are missing, the parties are free to pursue other commercial interests. There is no obligation to strive to form a contract. Until a contract is formed, each party may desist.

Within limits, civil law countries imply a term of good faith into all legal relationships, even those that are clearly not yet within the bounds of a contract. The parties are under an obligation to negotiate in good faith, not to shrug their shoulders and discontinue contact merely because the documents, in this case, letters, have not attained the status of a contract. This is particularly so when one party has relied on the contents of a letter of intent and suffered a prejudice because of this reliance. Once again, the only way to surpass the possible assumption of any contractual liability is to make it clear, repeatedly, that all exchanges of ideas are exploratory and subject to final review by the ultimate corporate authority.

PART THREE

5.3 THE CONFIDENTIALITY AGREEMENT

The confidentiality agreement appears when the parties, even operating with the clear understanding that they are in an exploratory phase, are asked to exchange or give access to information of a confidential nature, trade secrets that should not be known by competitors. It would not be unusual for a confidentiality agreement to be executed after considerable negotiations between the parties and it is an agreement naturally prepared by legal counsel.

The confidentiality agreement has become an important complement particularly in industries or services where the secret of the business is not in patented rights or technology licenses but in trade secrets, commercial practices that cannot receive formal, written protection, such as a copyright, but that nevertheless are crucial to the success of the enterprise. A typical example is a specialized mailing list built up through the years and that is productive for mail-marketing purposes.

No information should be disclosed without a proper agreement defining the responsibility of all parties. It is not that the law requires a written agreement. A verbal agreement may be perfectly enforceable. However, if the information is of serious commercial value, the vagueness and ambiguities that characterize verbal agreements are sufficient for choosing a formal agreement instead. The agreement should be reduced to writing and the solemnity of its terms emphasized. This will contribute to its being voluntarily implemented.

Breach of a confidentiality agreement subjects the defaulting party to a claim for damages. However, this right is more theoretical than practical. When large corporations are involved, the agreement surely has an important moral force. Nevertheless, plaintiffs seeking damages for breach of the confidentiality agreement have a difficult burden of demonstrating what are the damages incurred and, if the information is disclosed to unauthorized third parties, its circulation in the commercial world cannot be prevented easily.

Inserting a statement as to the agreed-on damages for default in the confidentiality agreement may not be a valid clause, a question for local counsel, but in any event, unless the amount is very high, out of proportion to the value of the secret, it is an invitation to disclosure if the information gained is worth more than the penalty to pay.

There is a serious dilemma in confidential transactions for the seller. For the buyer to request to have access to the records and information of the seller is a normal solicitation. It may not even be possible to seriously consider a joint venture without having more information. There thus arises a conflict: If information is not revealed, there can be no further progress; if information is revealed but negotiations fail, valuable information has been given away. How can this be resolved? Two suggestions are a clear delineation as to what is the confidential information and then its managed disclosure according to some simple rules. The possibility of damages should be considered as a last resort.

5.3.1 DEFINING THE SUBJECT MATTER OF CONFIDENTIAL INFORMATION

The most important subject matter is what it is that is being considered confidential. Merely stating that all information given is confidential does not contribute to clarity; nor stating that all information of a commercial nature constitutes a trade secret; nor claiming all confidential information belongs to the seller. A serious effort must be made to define as well as possible what is meant by confidential information; such a description then can be followed by general clauses of confidentiality. The more detailed the description, the more important will seem the material sought to be protected.

5.3.2 THE MANAGEMENT OF CONFIDENTIAL INFORMATION

Negotiations begin. An interest is confirmed. Further information is requested. Even with an agreement, there is no need to rush to deliver all confidential information available. Certain guidelines can be established subsequent to the signing of the confidentiality agreement:

- Management should separate vital knowledge from information that is a natural activity in most companies. How to make a product is very different from where you purchase the materials. The latter is also important but not critical. Insider information then should be divulged in harmony with the advance of negotiations. As negotiations become more close to a contract, the quality of the knowledge being given can also increase, become more unique in its application.
- Information should be given only after a certain level of agreement is reached on major issues. One does not reveal confidential information merely because another party may have interest. The level of interest is difficult to determine but there surely should be agreement on price and the equity contribution of each party.
- The information can be given initially in written summaries. This establishes a reference for what areas are considered confidential and the buyer is put on notice.
- Representative information can be given. It is not necessary to furnish a copy of an entire client list broken down by city and products. Sample information can be given.
- The buyer or potential partner should have to channel his requests in a formal procedure, and if possible to the same party. This tends to make personal the assumption of the confidentiality obligation and also establishes a simpler method of proof should the condition be broken.
- For the same reason, releasing the information should be done in the same room and in a formal manner. This emphasizes the seriousness of the information being given. A rapport may develop between the participants, which contributes to honoring the promises of confidentiality given.
- A point often overlooked is a failure to place a limitation on the copies of information made and in general controlling the copy process. The more there are formalities, the more serious the information received will be considered. It would be perfectly advisable to record how many copies have been made of any item, to whom given, and when.
- The entities entitled to receive the information should be defined as narrowly as possible, for example, auditors, financial officers, attorneys, and specified categories of key personnel.
- A decision has to be made as to the consequences of a misuse of the information received. Two options are to make all parties responsible

who misuse the information and the other is to have one primary party responsible, the buyer who must take the necessary precautions with third parties, such as employees. It is simpler to place the responsibility on the inquiring buyer as this is likely to be a corporation and be able to respond in damages.

Part Four

5.4 The joint venture agreement

The joint venture agreement and the shareholders' agreement are the two fundamental documents in the formation of an international joint venture. They can be combined into one document. However, as will be developed, this is not the most efficient use of the legal concepts contained in these documents. Nomenclature concerning the joint venture agreement is not as variable as that of the letter of intent. At times, it is referred to as a *preincorporation* agreement or *joint venture formation* agreement, which accurately describes its place in the negotiation process: The parties have agreed and reduce to writing their agreement with only the formation of the joint venture to be done. The *joint venture formation* terminology should not be confused with the *formation agreement* terminology. Unfortunately, there is a duplication of words. The use of *joint venture agreement* appears clear and unambiguous; it is the term we will use.

The joint venture agreement is the floor plan of the joint venture. It details all the interior structure of the corporate house to be constructed as we will see when we discuss some of the elements. The shareholders' agreement is an agreement between the members of the house, legal neighbors if you will, and it purports to regulate various aspects of this relationship. Stone walls make good neighbors, and the more the rights of the shareholders are regulated amongst themselves, the more successful, or at least free from conflict, the international joint venture will be. Although the two documents may contain repetitions of the same ideas, their separation is useful as it segregates the different objectives of each document. This will become more clear in the discussion of the shareholders' agreement. For the moment, it is convenient to emphasize some essential aspects of the joint venture agreement before a more profound description:

- It is the constitution of the rights of the participants. By its terms, it must not disappear with the closing.
- It defines the beginning of the joint venture but it should also provide for withdrawal.
- It will be composed of clauses affecting rights of ownership and rights of management.
- It will be a blueprint of each and every essential condition on which the joint venture is founded.

It can be seen now why the kingpin in documentation is the joint venture agreement. It is truly the document for all questions concerning the formation of the international joint venture. It is a document that will continue during the life of the joint venture and it may even be amended from time to time to reflect changing economic necessities. But the joint venture agreement is more than stating how parties will begin to collaborate.

5.4.1 WITHDRAWAL FROM THE JOINT VENTURE

On the one hand, the joint venture agreement defines the conditions under which the parties have agreed to cooperate. Wisely drafted, it will also provide a mechanism for the withdrawal of any party. We will certainly develop this topic in more detail in its appropriate place. However, there is no point in pegging partners down irrevocably because those who wish to leave the joint venture will procure reasons, motives that no lawyer could have foreseen, even seeking a solution in litigation. Commercial necessity surpasses legal creativity. Consequently, entrance and exit demand a dignified articulation in the joint venture agreement.

5.4.2 INTERPRETATION SOURCE FOR OWNERSHIP RIGHTS AND MANAGEMENT FUNCTIONS

With the passage of time, the original reasons for the joint venture tend to become blurred if for no other fact than personnel change. A well-drafted joint venture agreement should be able to serve as a master source document of interpretation in the case of litigation. The joint venture agreement therefore looms as a primary document whose importance will be reaffirmed various times during the life of the joint venture. It is a highly technical work of legal draftsmanship but buried within the clauses are important ownership and managerial concepts.

The joint venture agreement contains numerous clauses with an enormous amount of supplementary material annexed. The overwhelming majority of clauses are of an exclusively legal nature in that they address problems that experience has taught lawyers often recur and merit special attention so as to protect their client. Typical clauses falling within this category are those that concern outstanding capital stock, definitions, title to assets, list of encumbrances, consents and approvals, compliance with laws, preservation of business records, absence of material changes, various representations and warranties, force majeure, applicable laws of the contract, expenses and costs, notices and authorizations for signatures.

These are fairly typical legal clauses that counsel prepares and is unlikely to consult his client, the manager, over their contents, unless negotiations begin to focus on a particular legal problem. They are clauses that are far removed from the immediate, practical, commercial issues in the mind of the corporate manager. Concerning such clauses, the businessman will only want to have a reasonable appreciation of their function.

Parallel reasoning cannot be applied to those clauses that affect matters of substantial interest to managers, the denominated management clauses. They still have to be drafted by counsel. But in this case, their reason for being included in the joint venture agreement should be of paramount concern to managers, who need to know why they are present and what problems they are addressing. We will review the most important of these clauses.

5.4.3 Survival of the Joint Venture Agreement

The temporal validity of the joint venture agreement must be considered. Is it a document that is only transitory, leading the parties to the final closing after which its existence comes to an end, or should it have a presence during the life of the joint venture, thus also taking on the characteristics of an *operating agreement?*

Here legal concepts begin to lose their frontiers and a certain confusion may arise for often the shareholders' agreement is also referred to as an *operating agreement* as the principal role of such an agreement is to regulate the actions of the participants during the life of the joint venture. With such substantial variety of documents possible with a joint venture, it is to be expected that the precise meaning attributed to any document must be sought in the specific collaboration. To avoid confusion, we will continue to only use the expressions *joint venture agreement* and *shareholders' agreement.*

The joint venture agreement should expressly contain provisions that ensure its survival after the formation of the joint venture. Naturally, what has been accomplished cannot survive. The clause stipulating the price becomes a promise of the past after payment. It is a principle of law that promises are merged into the final legal act. A promissory contract for the purchase of land has its clauses merged into the final deed. It is the deed as registered that determines the rights of the owner before third parties.

Many corporate executives assume once the joint venture is formed, the promises therein contained no longer have validity. This is not an obligatory legal conclusion. By its terms and drafting language, the joint venture agreement can be made to be a valid reference document for the term of the joint venture. Some promises will be naturally self-fulfilling and hence extinguished.

Contribution to capital, execution of a loan agreement, transfer of a technology license, conveyance of equipment, all these are typical acts that, once promised, are realized by completion and the promise vanishes.

But many others can survive. This is of supreme importance. The problems to be addressed by a survival clause are also issues of a philosophical nature. Stated differently, among the multiple technical legal clauses in a joint venture agreement are important commercial, even ethical, questions that continue long after the joint venture is formed:

- Purpose, broad or limited? Why did the parties form a joint venture? Was it for a very specific purpose, for example, operating a chemical plant, or was it of a broad, general nature, for example, to import an electronic product in a local market? This dichotomy becomes important because often the parties, after several years of collaboration, while maintaining the joint venture, branch off into other activities and attempt to bypass the joint venture company.
- Managerial functions, divided or accumulated? The growing tendency is for the legal documents to be more and more technical and lengthy, and there is a rift developing between the philosophy of the joint venture and its implementation. The participation of minority interests in management becomes negligible. Management should strive to ensure that the joint venture agreement reflects management philosophy as initially negotiated and that this philosophy is articulated.
- Profit or growth? A common cause of discord between partners will be the application of net operating income. Dividends or reinvestment? The joint venture agreement should address this topic. A detailed joint venture agreement can serve as a guideline for future financial decisions.
- Compromise or conflict? What constitutes a solid basis for a continuing collaboration where conflict is minimized? A statement in the joint venture agreement as to the duty of the various partners to cooperate and

strive for compromises is a healthful, effective statement of principle that the founding partners and their successors can utilize in their search for solutions to the periodic conflicts joint ventures seem to generate. This problem also can be facilitated with a proper clause of mediation in the joint venture agreement. The two together create a strong moral duty on the part of the upper echelons of the corporate partners to bypass local conflict and seek a compromise.

• Good faith or partner beware? The joint venture is initiated in a spirit of collaboration. The joint venture agreement should impose on all partners the duty to act in good faith toward the joint venture company and the other partners. This is not chivalry but common commercial sense and such a clause will be useful for unanticipated situations.

In conclusion, a well-thought out joint venture agreement will have its survival expressly declared as to those clauses whose purpose and function are a continuing activity. This ensures that long after the original parties, or at least their representatives, have left, the vision of the joint venture as foreseen by these executives will have its purpose consecrated and be a guide to interpretation should conflict emerge.

5.4.4 THE BASIC CLAUSES OF A JOINT VENTURE AGREEMENT: PURPOSE AND DRAFTING

Under present-day joint venture practice, the main document, the joint venture agreement, is always reduced to writing. We will not discuss if a joint venture agreement can be implied or constructed from partial exchanges of correspondence between company executives. Our objective is to indicate the most preferable and most effective way of establishing a joint venture. Of course, it should be an entire document, containing all that is necessary, with carefully drafted clauses, and bearing the signatures of all the parties.

There are two aspects to the reading of a legal document. One perspective is the purpose of a clause. This is not necessarily a simple task. Some legal clauses are worded in such a manner that even lawyers would have trouble understanding them. Part of this has to do with the history of words; much antiquated language is still current in legal documents. Other times, the clauses have as a reference legal concepts that require a solid formation. There is naturally a tendency by the corporate businessman to skim much material in a joint venture agreement. After all, counsel has the final responsibility for ensuring material topics are present.

Then there is the drafting viewpoint: How will we put into words knowing what the agreed purpose of the clause is? This is clearly the sole function of an attorney. However, although the drafting language used may employ archaic language or a highly specialized vocabulary, an understanding of the purpose aspect should not be abdicated by corporate executives. If the purpose of a clause is not understood, than it cannot receive the approval of the client. There is no clause whose purpose is so complicated that it cannot be explained simply. If it cannot be stated clearly, why is it in the agreement?

The approval of basic legal documents by management must entail a certain responsibility by the businessman jointly with counsel. This duty will assure management that various key clauses, whose purpose is crucial to the success of the joint venture, are properly in place. The effective drafting of a joint venture agreement thus becomes a sensible division between counsel and management. There must be a dialogue as to relevant material, a communication of the commercial and managerial importance of various topics.

Consequently, our subsequent analysis is of those essential clauses that should be present in the joint venture agreement, some that traditionally fall within the province of counsel but others that affect considerably the exercise of ownership and management functions. We are not concerned with their legal wording, or drafting, but their function; what they are and why they are needed. Counsel will draft, but the corporate executive will identify those clauses that the particular joint venture renders essential.

Our first five topics: (1) identification of the parties, (2) territory and objectives of the joint venture, (3) price/capital, (4) loan contributions, and (5) joint venture form, are routine items, but still important, whose consequences for management must be appreciated. However, beginning with *share structure,* in what follows, we will enter a domain which most managers shy away from or at least feel it is a lawyer's province.

Within this technical province there is a drama to be discussed, whose crucial consequences cannot be ignored by management. They affect directly ownership rights and management responsibilities and afford all interested corporate executives with an opportunity to participate in creating a tailored joint venture. As technical as these concepts may appear because of their presentation in legal documents, these ideas are the thoughts of legislators and judges who have striven to ensure that all owners will have their rights protected. They often encompass libertarian ideas whose legal authors have given them a special expression. They are concepts often utilized by a minority to secure substantial influence. Our efforts will be to show how these concepts can be utilized by management and to explain them in accessible language. Our presentation, it is hoped, will be readable and comprehensible.

Finally, in a separate section, we will refer to the investigatory steps known as *due diligence procedures.* These are procedures that accompany any major acquisition. It is a topic adjacent to the formation of international joint ventures that has assumed such critical importance that it is often studied as separate material. We will review its importance although reserving a detailed survey for Chapter Seven.

Presently, it is first necessary to have a general view of the necessary clauses affecting ownership rights and management functions to a joint venture agreement.

5.4.4.1 Identification of the Parties: caution is needed

The very first issue to be decided when confronted with a joint venture agreement is the decision as to who will sign the agreement. Obviously, we can expect the future partners to be signatories. But there is also the joint venture company, if we are considering an acquisition, and a future company, one not formed, if we are contemplating the formation of a subsidiary.

The joint venture company will be a signatory to the joint venture agreement insofar as there are obligations imposed on the company, as distinct from the partners. The variety of topics is substantial. Thus obligations concerning dividends, location of board meetings, capital expenditures, sale of corporate assets, and augments of capital all involve actions to be taken by the joint venture company, and its signature to the joint venture agreement is important if the latter contains obligations assumed between the partners regarding these topics.

If we are dealing with a company yet to be constituted, the joint venture agreement can be made conditioned on the company signing the agreement as soon as the company is formed. If it fails to execute the joint venture agreement, the joint venture agreement may be considered terminated as this same agreement will provide the mechanisms for dissolving and liquidating the joint venture company. Such a situation is extremely rare.

After resolving the issue of the joint venture company signing or not signing the joint venture agreement, the first natural concern will be the parties to the joint venture. Initially, it might seem a useless exercise in analysis, indicating who will be the parties to the proposed joint venture. Clearly, everyone knows who the parties are. They are those that signed the joint venture agreement.

In fact, this is an initial question that can assume a substantial importance. This has to do with the concept of contractual assignments, meaning that the contract, in this case, the joint venture agreement, can be transferred to a third party. In some jurisdictions, an assignment can be made without seeking the permission of the other party if the joint venture agreement is silent on this issue.

In other jurisdictions, assignments cannot take place without the consent of the other party even though the joint venture agreement is silent on this point. The problem is further exacerbated by the fact that normally common law countries permit assignments, unless the contract states to the contrary, and in civil law jurisdictions, the opposite rule prevails: Assignments are not permitted unless expressly conceded in the agreement. With so many international joint ventures taking place between common law countries and civil law jurisdictions, each party is operating under a different legal reference.

Why is this important? What are the relevant managerial concepts implied by this simple clause? It is failure of control over the final result that interests us: one entity signs on as a joint venture partner and another entity takes its place on the formation of the joint venture. As an example of just one reason, joint ventures are often negotiated by executives from a well-known corporation, but the board of directors may decide that it would be preferable to have a subsidiary or even a company formed for purposes of being a partner in the joint venture. This is a simple method of containing financial exposure.

Capital is injected into the newly formed subsidiary and this represents the total commitment of the parent company. The joint venture must be autosufficient. It may be that a U.S. company wishes to set up a joint venture with a Belgian corporation, but by a subsidiary *controlled* by it. We can indicate this as a three-step process:

1. Corp. US forms a wholly owned subsidiary > Corp. US1.
2. Corp. US assigns the joint venture agreement to Corp. US1.
3. Corp. US1 becomes a partner in > International Joint Venture Company.

In many cases, this is not what the other partner wanted. The inducement to the joint venture was to have an active collaboration with a well-known U.S. multinational. The creation even of a wholly owned subsidiary of the U.S. multinational to be a partner was not the result of an agreement.

We can vary slightly the preceding sequence:

1. Corp. US forms a subsidiary > Corp. US1.
2. Corp. US owns only 51 percent of Corp. US1.
3. Corp. US assigns the joint venture agreement to US1.
4. Corp. US1 becomes a partner in > International Joint Venture Company

Of course, Corp. US controls US1 even though it is not a wholly owned subsidiary. However, simply by adjusting the ownership of Corp. US1, Corp. US may pass from having control to being a minority owner in the group. This will exacerbate the possible negative reaction of the other partner.

From the point of view of the multinational, it is a perfectly sensible financial decision to separate a subsidiary since there is a close identity of resources and knowledge between the subsidiary and the parent company. This may be perfectly correct and the other potential partners may have no objection to an assignment of the contract under certain conditions. These conditions are that the subsidiary be controlled by the parent, preventing the multinational from taking a minority position.

This can be achieved by stipulating in the joint venture agreement that assignment to a subsidiary is permitted provided the parent company owns a specified portion of the capital. There is no magical number, but it should be high, between 80 to 100 percent and with voting rights corresponding to that percentage. Otherwise, the other party, with the joint venture agreement in hand, can sell off its rights for a good price to a third party. This is surely not what the parties intended.

Obviously, the joint venture agreement also can provide that no assignments are possible without the consent of all partners. This eliminates having to draft and consider all the possibilities under which an assignment is possible. With closely held joint ventures, this is a viable alternative. Regarding a joint venture including a multinational, it is unlikely that an outright prohibition will be accepted, which then means a *control* clause is essential.

5.4.4.2 Territory and objectives of the joint venture: management's view to the future

Inseparable from the commercial activity of the joint venture company will be where the joint venture activity is to take place. Legal terminology designates this with the technical name of *territory*. This has important implications particularly if one or more of the parties has a company in neighboring jurisdictions or perhaps a well-developed distribution system.

Although in such jurisdictions as the EU, sales cannot be prohibited from crossing national borders, the active solicitation of sales outside of a jurisdiction may be restrained by agreement. Furthermore, noncompetition agreements between the partners in the event of one withdrawing from the joint venture will be directly dependent on its efficacy for the definition of the territory as stipulated in the joint venture agreement. Thus, the formation of a joint venture obligates a definition of its geographical frontiers.

Once there is defined where the joint venture company will be operating, the parties must equally decide what they are going to do. It might be thought just stating "all commercial activity" would resolve having to make any immediate decisions. Unfortunately, many jurisdictions, particularly when foreign capital is involved, do not permit such a broad, unlimited range of activity. The foreign investor must state with more precision what will be the activity of the joint venture company. The wording of the *object clause,* as it is designated, can thus present a grammatical difficulty but one that must be resolved.

When the local jurisdiction permits the parties to define the object clause in accordance with their intentions and not conditioned by foreign investment laws, there are some benefits to be derived from attention to this topic as the object clause will fulfill two useful functions:

1. A very common cause of disagreement between joint venture partners is, after a while, one of the partners begins another business in the same jurisdiction with profitable results. The experience learned in one product line, with a knowledge of the market, is applied to another commercial item. It is not only the multinational partners who launch diverse activities in a foreign land. It may be the local partner who, having learned substantially its lessons from its multinational partner, decides to branch out.

   The issue of expansion must be considered by all the parties. It can be raised after the details of the joint venture have been settled. It becomes the general philosophy of the collaboration. How extensive will our collaboration be? Is the joint venture only for a limited purpose or are the parties foreseeing a broad cooperation in the local jurisdiction? Whatever the answer, it should be set forth in the joint venture agreement so as to avoid future misunderstanding or to enforce what are seen as original negotiating promises. Such clauses are difficult to implement but their moral effect is considerable and businessmen usually comply with such obligations.

2. In many jurisdictions, the formation of the joint venture may raise questions of antitrust law. If any of the partners have activities in geo-

graphical areas forming part of a larger economic zone, such as the EU, permission to form the joint venture may be conditioned on containing the joint venture's activities through a narrow object clause.

These two examples are contradictory. One advocates the benefits from generalities: The partners are prevented from entering other markets in the same area of the joint venture company. The other suggests specificity, so as to avoid infringement on competition law principles. These are the realities of the international joint venture. The dilemma, if it does exist, obligates an exchange of ideas with local advisers. The preference usually should be for a general statement of collaboration as that will prove the most beneficial to the joint venture within the limits conditioned by the local antitrust laws. An object clause stretched to the limits of the local competition laws will create a cohesive joint venture company.

5.4.4.3 PRICE AND CAPITAL: MANAGEMENT'S FLEXIBILITY

The joint venture agreement will recite what are the capital contributions of the various parties when dealing with the formation of a company. Price will be what is tendered in an acquisition. The capital contributions to the formation of the joint venture company must be obligatory and define with precision the percentage interests the capital contribution represents. In some joint venture agreements, there are *capital contribution* notes or documents signed that indicate the total capital, the contribution of each party, and when the payment is to be made. The formalities surrounding the capital contribution obligation will depend to a great extent on the magnitude of the joint venture, the prior experience of the parties with each other, and, of course, the formalities, or lack of them, attendant on the corporate culture of any of the participants.

The concept of capital presents the most flexibility and possesses more variation in international joint ventures than does price. In both cases, price and capital contributions do not have to be given all at once. They may be tendered in a schedule. Price can be tendered partially and subsequently out of earned income. In other words, the seller may accept the concept that part of the sales price is dependent on the future performance of the joint venture company. Similarly, capital contributions according to a schedule may be conditioned on a platform being reached, for example, annual gross sales.

The notion of price is normally more static. Price is the giving of something for purchasing a capital investment in the joint venture company; in its most narrow meaning, it is merely cash. An immediate distinction in commercial practice takes place between national and international joint ventures.

In joint ventures and mergers in the same jurisdiction, it is common for the purchaser of an equity interest to give part of the price in cash and another part of the price in something that also, it is hoped, has value, such as shares of stock in the purchaser's company. Quite frequently, there may be no cash tendered in a merger with one group of shareholders receiving only the shares of the acquiring company.

This is not the usual situation with international joint ventures, which, besides formation of a joint venture, include acquisitions of shares and mergers. It would be highly unusual for a foreign entity to sell its equity position for shares in the purchaser's company. Price in international joint ventures is invariably cash.

The fact that price is usually cash does not mean its amount is unalterable. Besides being paid according to a schedule, or partially out of earned income, it also may be reduced if the assumed net income projections of the seller should prove too optimistic. If the price can be reduced, then the possibility of putting part of it in escrow must be considered. An escrow arrangement may be necessary, not only because of anticipated income performances, but to ensure that promises made by the seller are fulfilled.

These promises have the technical name of *warranties* and not all warranties can be completed prior to closing. Perhaps the verification of the veracity of such warranties may be dependent on a more thorough examination of the accounts of the target company subsequent to the closing. The escrow deposit is a financial method of enforcing warranties given by the seller. An acquisition therefore permits more flexibility in when payments will be forthcoming and less in the form of the value given, which is invariably cash. Some of the important conditions to be considered are as follows:

- payment schedule: when and how much on each date; nor does it have to be equal amounts
- payment out of earnings: some of the price can be paid out of future earnings, a condition possibly acceptable to a seller of a company in distress; it is an inducement to the buyer to take on the risk and salvage the economic unit and its employees
- payment adjustments: as the investigation of the target company continues, due diligence procedures may indicate adjustments to the price, either increased or decreased

- escrow accounts: it is advisable to have the payments deposited in a financial institution in an escrow account pending the final closing
- retention of last payment: in the purchase of an exceedingly complex economic unit with perhaps multiple affiliates, it would be proper to hold back the last payment pending postclosing verification as to the state of the company bought and the warranties given in the joint venture agreement. Perhaps the amount of the accounts receivables was overestimated

5.4.4.4 LOAN CONTRIBUTIONS FROM PARTNERS: THE RIGHT DOCUMENT

The subject of loans raises a question of considerable importance for a fledging joint venture. To what extent are the founding partners willing to ensure its survival and for what period of time? All companies, being formed for the first time, go through a transitional period of trial and error. It is often a wise decision for the original partners to agree to restrict access to local loans, which may require too much debt service, and agree to make company loans, from the parent company to the joint venture company, at low interest rates. If there is a considerable currency risk, this can be circumvented by the parent company guaranteeing a local bank that is willing to make a loan on favorable terms. There are, of course, multiple variations on this financial topic.

However, our immediate concern is slightly different. Where should such a commitment be put? In what legal document? Some attorneys would advise in the shareholders' agreement since the promise to make company loans is a personal issue negotiated between the original shareholders and that is one of the functions of a shareholders' agreement.

In Chapter Six, we consider in depth the topic of the shareholders' agreement. For the moment, we can confirm there is nothing objectionable to this preference except it is partially incomplete. Although the breach of the shareholder agreement gives a right of one shareholder to sue another, what about the joint venture company? It is the latter that is the intended recipient of the loan and it, too, should have a right to enforce the commitment to make a loan. Consequently, the most secure ground is not only to include the obligation in the shareholders' agreement, but also in the joint venture agreement.

5.4.4.5 THE JOINT VENTURE FORM IN ACQUISITIONS: CHANGE IS PERMITTED

The choice of the form of the joint venture operating company was considered extensively in Chapter Three. The possible alternatives are considerable and each joint venture is fact-specific. When forming a joint venture, naturally, the potential partners will consider the various characteristics of different legal forms and make the appropriate decision.

Faced with an acquisition, it is convenient to emphasize to owners and managers that all usually can be changed. Private limited liability companies can be converted into share corporations. The general partnership can become the private limited liability company. One company with one legal form can be merged into another, with a different legal form. The joint venture legal form should never be what it is because it is there. Not, in any event, if there is a choice. It is during the negotiations stage that the most flexibility exists and this opportunity must be seized.

5.4.4.6 SHARE STRUCTURE: MANAGEMENT'S BEST OPPORTUNITY TO SECURE INFLUENCE

When we begin to examine the theory of share structure of a corporation, or how, in general, ownership is represented in any company form such as a partnership or private limited liability company, we enter into the creative aspect of organizing a joint venture and we must begin to understand how various legal rules can play a primordial part in protecting ownership interests and management rights no matter what the amount of equity interest. Generally, three basic considerations should be in the minds of the founding partners of a joint venture:

- what powers will be reserved to the owners, for example, the shareholders
- what type of management structure the joint venture will have
- what will be the powers of management

On the last issue, if nothing is stated in the articles of incorporation, or other company charter, the law will make the division. This may or may not be suitable. Ordinarily, in a share corporation, the board of directors have extensive, wide powers. In nonpublic, small companies, it is a healthy precaution to specify what are the powers distributed between the governing board and the owners. All that is required is to create various classes of shares with different rights. This is a certain way of protecting minority rights and also preventing abuse of management by a board of directors.

The formation of a joint venture should never be undertaken without examining what will be the consequences of the proposed ownership structure. Many times founding partners agree that the capital will be proportioned 51/49 (in order to avoid deadlocks) and with nothing further legally established, the company is formed. All discussions between the original partners as to division of functions, and what will be a modus operandi, disappear into the atmosphere as executives leave and new ones arrive. In the end, what rules is the reason of the majority, and with 49 percent, even if you have contributed millions, your voting objectives can be suppressed.

Creating classes of shares requires that the articles of incorporation provide for their existence and what rights they will have. Thus, whereas the wording of the article may require a certain legal expertise, its general outline is quite straightforward. Corporation X will have so many classes of shares with an enumeration of their rights.

A list of what can be achieved through this technique is very informative:

- Representation on the board of directors can be assured by attributing to the various classes (class A shares, class B shares, etc.) the right to elect so many members to the board of directors. This ensures a voice in management. This method can be combined with another technique to ensure proper expression of minority interests. If the articles of incorporation require a specified percentage of votes on the board of directors for a particular topic, for example, merger or augment of capital, a minority partner can calculate easily what amount of shares is needed to block decisions on important, major company issues. In Chapter Eight, we will discuss and develop this idea further.
- Being a special right attributed to a class of shares, its exercise is not dependent on contractual promises, for example, a shareholders' agreement whereby the shareholders agree that so many members will be elected by what shareholder. What if one shareholder refuses to fulfill his promise and alleges a good reason? A contractual right, which if broken, does not vitiate the general vote in a general assembly. However, a right attached to a class of shares is an inherent right attached to a share and cannot be bypassed. Broken promises in a shareholders' agreement only have redress in a court of law but the voting consequences may have been already implemented by the joint venture company.
- Various rights incident to ownership, such as the right to receive dividends, associated with preferred shares, which are a special class of shares, or rights on dissolution as to certain assets, can be associated with classes of shares.
- The articles of incorporation can provide that a specified class of shares will not be able to represent more than 50 percent of the board of directors. Sometimes in negotiations, stating you should not have *abso-*

lute power is accepted more readily than requesting *the right* to elect a specified number of members of the board of directors.

We have been discussing share corporations. The same concept can be applied to other legal forms. It is a question of legal drafting. From jurisdiction to jurisdiction, there are many variations to traditional legal company forms and the rules are not always consistent. Implementation of the preceding ideas to any particular legal form requires a solid formation in law. But the route to management security is clear: a judicious use of different classes of shares, or its equivalent, dependent on the legal form chosen.

5.4.4.7 SPECIAL VOTING RIGHTS: MANAGEMENT'S FURTHER WEAPON FOR PROTECTING RIGHTS

Legal concepts often overlap. The compartments are not as clearly separated as we would wish. Creating classes of shares clearly confers special voting rights to the owners of these shares. It is one way of ensuring representation on the board of directors. However, there exist other techniques that are very useful to management in its quest for securing rights negotiated prior to the formation of the joint venture. This is by establishing rules in the articles of incorporation as to how votes will be counted. It need not be a mere mathematical summary related exclusively to voting power derived from the nominal value of the equity interest. There are four traditional methods, although one, the last, is really a prohibition.

Voting in a block

The articles of the company may provide that owners representing less than X percent of capital (and here it is necessary to specify a percentage) may join their votes together so as to vote as a unit. This could be done by the owners conferring a power of attorney on one of the shareholders who then votes in the name of his principals. In some countries, this percentage requirement is established by law. It forms part of the company code in that jurisdiction. If the limit of percentage established is 5 percent, then owners who can aggregate this amount of capital participation or less can have all their votes added and cast as a block on any single issue. This is normally sufficient to ensure representation on the board of directors, although it is not a guarantee.

Cumulative voting

This is a method that can be permitted by the articles of the company or may be established in the local law. In the case of corporations, cumulative voting can be defined as allowing a shareholder to multiply the votes represented by his shares by the number of members to be elected to the board of directors. In a closely held corporation, this is sufficient to ensure a minority owner a right of representation on the board of directors. The precise number of shares needed to give effect to cumulative voting can be known beforehand by the following formula, assuming all shares have the same nominal value:

$$\frac{\text{(total number of shares outstanding)} \times \text{(number of directors desired)} + 1}{\text{total number of directors} + 1}$$

This is the formula the parties can utilize when it is agreed cumulative voting will be applicable for election of members of the board of directors in the joint venture agreement. Imagine a five-member board of directors. If cumulative voting is applicable, for the minority interest to nominate two members, and the total amount of issued shares is 2,000 units, then the minority owner will need to own the following percentage of capital:

$$\frac{2,000 \times 5 + 1}{5 + 1} = 1,666.83 \text{ votes}$$

With this result, a minority owner would have to have at least a 42 percent interest to control the nomination of two directors:

$$0.42 \times 2000 = 840$$
$$840 \times 2 = 1,680 \text{ votes}$$

The preceding formula assumes no special rights are attached to any class of shares, for the same result could be obtained by stating in the articles of incorporation that, for example, class A of shares will have the right to designate two members of the board of directors composed of five members.

Plural votes

Not all jurisdictions permit this system, which states that for any share or unit, votes may be multiplied by a predetermined number. This has to be done without identifying a particular shareholder, for example, applicable to a particular class of shares. Many jurisdictions do not permit this system and so it is a legal area that always has to be investigated.

Limitation on votes

Some jurisdictions permit that the articles of the company may prohibit the counting of votes above a certain number. If the capital structure of the company is of 3,000 units, the articles may prohibit counting votes above 1,500 units. This is clearly to prevent a majority from suppressing any minority representation. In those jurisdictions that do permit this method, it cannot be used to discriminate against any particular shareholder or owner. It must be a rule applicable to all owners of shares.

5.4.4.8 QUALIFIED MAJORITY PROVISIONS: AN INDISPENSABLE TOOL FOR MANAGEMENT

Up to now, we have concerned ourselves with some aspects of shares and how votes may be counted. Subjacent to all of this is a question that perhaps has already occurred to the reader. Who votes on what? What is the division of power between the board of directors and the owners?

At one extreme, often exemplified by the public corporations, the management of the company is entrusted to a board of directors; the owners, arriving at an annual general assembly, hear the report of the board of directors and can either approve or disapprove it. The other extreme is within the closely held corporation in which the board of directors during its annual report makes recommendations to the owners, the general assembly, and these options are voted on. All of this can be summarized by the use of the words *reservation of powers* or *delegation of powers* or *grant and reservation of powers.*

The company is seen as a civil society. Its citizens, in this case, the owners, grant to management various rights. They may be substantial. The owners may withhold some rights. If nothing is said, the applicable company law in the jurisdiction makes this grant and reservation for the owners, much as in a country where the constitution decides what rights have been granted to the executive and what withheld.

The affect of the local laws of course will have to be consulted prior to a final agreement. But regardless of the amount of equity participation, it is wise for all parties to establish what issues are so important as to require a specified number of votes and then agree that on this topic, and others, the general assembly, and not the board of directors, must obtain a majority of votes, attaining at least, for example, 80 percent. This would mean that if the capital of a company were divided 60 percent to 40 percent, no one owner could muster sufficient votes by himself to vote in the proposal, for example, an augment of capital.

This is known as the concept of *qualified majority* or *supermajority* voting as it requires more than a simple majority. There is no magic number that can be recommended. It is a method that clearly is a power play. When introduced, it enhances the power of one group over another. It also reduces the power of one group over another.

In the example given, an augment of capital would only be possible with the approval of all owners. Although not common, as it appears unreasonable, it is legally possible to establish as a qualified majority a unanimous vote of all shareholders.

Even without an agreement among the partners by way of a requirement in the articles of incorporation, there are many jurisdictions on which a qualified majority vote is required for certain topics and how much is the majority required. Normally, these are minimum requirements. If an augment of capital can be voted only by a 75 percent vote of the shareholders, this does not prevent them from changing the rule. The articles of the company may establish that 76 percent is required, where it is known that the capital will be divided 75 percent to 25 percent.

Note that this qualified majority rule is also withdrawing the power to make the decision of an augment of capital alone from the board of directors. The particular law in question is stating that on this topic, the board of directors must submit to the general assembly the issue of an augment of capital and have it approved. Our quest for efficient management control, therefore, can be made even more secure and not left to legislative chance by stipulating in the joint venture agreement what are the subjects that should be approved by the owners and not the board, and what percentage of votes is required.

It is a clear affirmation of the special rights of owners that cannot be circumvented as it will be part of the articles of the company and the first topic to be subject to the qualified majority rule is precisely the articles of the company. They can be changed only with the votes of X percent and provided the majority owner has one vote less than the X percent, the minority owner is fully protected.

We will consider in more detail in Chapter Eight exactly what are the topics that should be subject to general assembly approval and even be joined with a further requirement as to a qualified or supermajority vote.

Some particular items now merit mention for their importance and also as illustrations of the principle under consideration:

Amendments to the articles of the company and joint venture agreement

Clearly, a qualified majority vote should be required on changing the articles; otherwise, everything that had been negotiated and inserted in the articles could be eliminated by one swooping amendment by the other party and render many of the clauses in the joint venture agreement superseded.

Although the joint venture company is not always a party to the joint venture agreement, in those cases when it is, where, for example, the joint venture company obligates itself to alter its articles so as to comply with a clause in the joint venture agreement, any proposed course of action affecting that obligation should require a high percentage of approval by the general assembly for the same reasons indicated in the preceding paragraph.

Augments of capital

Augments of capital can be used to force a party into an even more minority position. If the majority owner of 51 percent of the capital can by simple majority augment the capital, then if he has more financial resources, he can augment the capital, forcing the other party to either "come along" or see his minority position worsened.

Imagine an initial capital of 1,000 units. The capital is divided 510/490 units (51 percent/49 percent). The majority partner calls for an augment to 1,500 units and the minority partner has not the financial resources available to purchase his pro-rata share. The majority owner subscribes entirely to the 500-unit increase. The minority partner now has only a 32.66 percent equity interest:

$$\frac{490 \text{ units}}{1,500 \text{ units}} = 32.66\%$$

The minority owner now has even less of an equity percentage. Thus augments of capital, similar to amendments to the articles of a company, can destroy qualified majority provisions on other topics by increasing the voting power of a party. The effect will be to eliminate the qualified majority previously existing.

If in our example, a 52 percent vote is necessary to alter agreed-on budget limitations, by augmenting the capital, the 51 percent interest, which could not alter the budget, passes to 67.44 percent, which is more than sufficient to dictate all aspects of the annual corporate budget.

Mergers, legal alliances, dissolutions, and other transformations

For similar reasons, but others also, the joint venture company as a complete legal unit should not undergo any change without an extremely high concurrence of votes, if not unanimous. Otherwise, the joint venture may become an entirely different legal vehicle, in which the rights of the parties are substantially altered.

The most drastic would be the joint venture company being merged into another in which the parties receive equity interests that confer significantly less management possibilities. Any permanent legal alliance can affect the rights of the partners as represented in the original joint venture. Purchases by the joint venture company of equity interests in other companies may substantially alter management responsibilities. The setting up of a subsidiary may be contrary to the interests of one of the partners. Then, there is dissolution, which is the extinction of the company. So drastic are these possibilities and so contrary to the joint venture spirit that it is usual to have all parties unanimously agree before they can be implemented, or at least have the matter decided by a high qualified majority of the possible votes in a general assembly.

5.4.4.9 TRANSFER OF SHARES: GENERAL CONSIDERATIONS

Practically every joint venture agreement contains provisions concerning the transfer of shares, or other equity interests; practically all company articles deal with the same topic. It surely will be no surprise to learn that the shareholders' agreement also can deal extensively with the same topic. The possible restrictions range from a total prohibition on sale; to a restriction for a set term, such as 5 years; to a partial restriction whereby the shares can be sold but they must first be offered to either the company or the other shareholders.

What alternative will be chosen is not entirely a free selection. The local law may prohibit a total restriction, or only allow a total restriction if used in a specific company form. Restrictions are normally allowed, but their precise nature is very much a reflection of the local legal system. Considering that enormous amounts of time are usually spend in negotiating a joint venture, why do the parties devote such extraordinary drafting ability to determining how they will depart? Were the same sequence of events to precede a civil marriage, it would probably never take place.

The answer, of course, calls for various responses, but surely we can agree that when a joint venture is not working, there may be still something to sell. Or it may be the joint venture is successful but one of the partners has sold its interest elsewhere in the same industry to another entity. It is this entity that is the proposed transferee. Sometimes partners enter joint ventures for a short term. They do not want their capital invested on a long-term basis. This would be particularly true in joint ventures formed to test new products or services. Should the product be successful, one partner may wish to obtain his capital gains and move on to another investment. Again, one of the partners may feel another, third partner is needed for a variety of reasons, ranging from capital needs to access to new markets, and is willing to sell a part of his equity interest.

Most parties to a joint venture agree that there should not be a total restriction on the sale of an equity interest. In some jurisdictions, a total restriction on the sale of a share in a corporation, as distinct from other companies, is not even possible, not even if all the shareholders agree. It is prohibited by the legislature as being contrary to the freedom of capital movement characteristic of share corporations and consequently an invalid clause that cannot be enforced. Rather the controversy, or choice, seems to be: What restrictions will be possible or are desirable? But even before considering this, we may inquire what the managerial reason is for wanting to restrict or not restrict the transfer of an equity interest.

Reasons why management may prefer substantial restrictions

The most valid reason for wanting restrictions in closely held corporations, and in closely held joint ventures, is that the rapport established that has led to the joint venture, the tailored joint venture agreement, and the agreement on division of management responsibilities is the sine qua non of the successful operation of the joint venture. The distinguishing feature of a joint venture is that it is not an investment, a purchase of shares on an exchange. It is a personal involvement and commitment by the original partners that may have its roots in long-term commercial relationships on a less formal basis, such as an agency or distribution contract.

The average joint venture is a collaboration of different skills and a commercial harmony. The introduction of another party may disrupt this feeling of confidence. End consumers may appear as statistics on market survey reports, but the corporate executives who decide to reach these end consumers are usually people with substantial experience and who are reluctant to entrust any responsibility to others not based on a supposition of competence. This is not a conviction created one day to the next.

The multiple visits from one head office to another; the exchange of ideas, confidences, trade secrets; and the revelation of future plans eventually converge toward the spirit of mutual trust, or at least the absence of suspicion, and thus the joint venture slowly begins to take form. The introduction of a new entity is akin to the appointment of a new executive president. There is suddenly necessary a new alignment of economics and politics and a period of adjustment is necessary. The power structure feels threatened. A restriction on the transfer of shares hedges this insecurity.

Reasons why management may not prefer restrictions

Entrepreneurs generally agree that all entities should have a certain amount of commercial liberty. Even with the most auspicious beginnings, the founding partners of a joint venture, if asked, would agree that the future is always uncertain; management must be flexible and adaptable; no one partner can be a prisoner to an equity investment. It is not in the interests of the shareholders or the ultimate owners. Capital is movement. It doesn't have to be flight; but then it cannot be tethered.

From this medley of reasons and often conflicting reactions, there have emerged several techniques for permitting restrictions on the transfer of equity interests but within a framework of commercial reasonableness. There are various modes of restriction but a general introduction will be beneficial.

5.4.4.10 TRANSFER OF SHARES OR OTHER EQUITY INTERESTS: VARIOUS ALTERNATIVES

Joint venture agreements often provide that restrictions on transfers will not apply if the transferee is an affiliate. This makes good commercial sense since at the time of negotiating the joint venture agreement, the final corporate entity, which will be one of the founding partners, may not yet be chosen. However, the word *affiliate* is vague, not by itself having any precise meaning. Consequently, if the parties are agreed that, in spite of transfer restrictions, the equity interests can be transferred to affiliates, this should be carefully defined, for example, the degree of control. A reasonable rule of thumb is at least 51 percent since by this criterion, the transferor cannot claim it has no administrative control over the acts of its subsidiaries.

Additionally, there should be a provision that on the transferor ceasing to be an affiliate, the equity interest must be transferred back to the original party. Finally, affiliate or not, the transferee must agree to be bound by the terms of the joint venture agreement and the shareholders' agreement. We can now consider the various types of restrictions in more detail.

Total restriction

As a general rule, a total restriction on the transfer of shares is invalid. There are jurisdictions where this prohibition may be allowed, but this would have to be confirmed by local counsel in the jurisdiction where the joint venture will have its principal offices. If the parties decide that a total restriction is indispensable to the proper functioning of the joint venture, then a joint venture legal form must be chosen that permits this provision.

There are good reasons why share corporations cannot have total restrictions on transfers in their articles of incorporation. Total restrictions are totally incompatible with share corporations quoted on public exchanges. It would be impossible to effectively fiscalize such restrictions, and in any event, they would only contribute to destroying the mobility of the capital markets. In multiple jurisdictions, this sensible legislative policy for public corporations is also applied, wisely or not, to private corporations, that is, those whose capital is not open to the public.

On the other hand, many jurisdictions permit total restrictions in the case of closely held corporations or private limited liability companies. Private corporations are not synonymous with closely held corporations. Each jurisdiction will have its definition of what constitutes a closely held corporation in terms of permitted number of shareholders and legal capital. As reviewed in Chapter Three, this advantage has to be seen in the total light of the other characteristics of the joint venture legal form. Once it has been concluded that a total restriction is possible for a particular legal form, the natural inquiry is how this restriction is formalized so as to be effective.

Restrictive provisions can appear in a variety of places. The most secure are the articles of the company, in which their publication is a notice to all parties and the public and no one can claim ignorance of such restrictions. Beyond the articles of the company, the same provisions may appear in the joint venture agreement and the shareholders' agreement.

These restrictions appear in the joint venture agreement because the partners are agreeing that the applicable articles of the company will contain such a restriction. This is quite common. The legal articles of the company, prior to its formation, are settled. The restrictions also appear in the shareholders' agreement because it is intended to regulate the relationship of the owners. Of course, having a restriction on transfer appear in two documents is repetitious, but it causes no harm and serves to emphasize its importance.

Block sale requirement

This is a clause that, when a transfer of equity interests is permitted, the seller must dispose of his entire interest. It cannot be fragmented. The reason for this is eminently practical. A good manager can lead a multitude of people, but a plethora of managers cannot run an organization. A three-partner joint venture may be functional, but as the number of partners increases, the extent of rapport decreases. It makes perfectly good sense for a clause to appear in the proper legal document obligating the partnership interests to be sold only in a block.

Right of first refusal or right of preference

This is one of the most common restrictions found in joint venture agreements and also in the articles of the company, whatever its form. It states that if one partner receives an offer to sell and is willing to sell, the shares or equity interests in question must be first offered to the other owners, pro rata. The other owners have the right to refuse to purchase or a right of preference in the sale. It is the same concept although with different words. This idea can be *rolled over.* If one owner with a right of refusal waives the exercise, it passes in totality to the others. If owner A has an 18 percent interest to sell and there are three other owners, the right of first refusal is first 6 percent for each, then 9 percent for two, and finally 18 percent for the last remaining but purchasing owner.

Although the idea behind this concept is simple enough, its application can cause complex problems. What if the offer to purchase is cash and something else, for example, a share in another company? If you use this same example, does this mean the other three may have to own the share in common? How will something other than cash be valued?

What about the equity interest being sold? What method of valuation will be used: market value, book value, capitalization of earnings at a determined rate, nominal value, outside appraisal? In a closely held company, the value of the equity interest may be difficult to determine. Some jurisdictions do not permit goodwill as a balance sheet entry. This may be contrary to the realities of the investment. It is notorious that the most difficult aspect of a joint venture is in the start-up. Even if this effort finds no balance sheet item, shouldn't a successful survival have worth?

The difficulties with the application of the right of first refusal have not diminished its popularity, but the questions already raised, and others, must find resolutions with the aid of the corporate financial officers of the partners.

Modified right of first refusal

In the typical right of first refusal, the initiative comes from a buyer. An offer arrives; if an owner is interested, the others have the right to first say "yes." In the modified right of first refusal, the initiative comes from the seller.

The seller decides he wishes to transfer his equity interests and a price is established. The equity interest is offered first to the other owners. On a lack of interest from the other owners, the intending seller has a stated period of time in which to offer his equity interest to other third parties. To this modified freedom, there may be attached a further condition. If the seller receives an offer, he must go back again to the other owners. Only on a final rejection would the seller be free to go forward. Of course, the same problems of unraveling the value of the offer as discussed in the right of first refusal also apply here.

5.4.4.11 TRIGGERING EVENTS AND BUY–SELL MECHANISMS: MANAGEMENT'S EXIT

Transfer restrictions are the introduction of obstacles to the free transferability of equity interests. Each party will have its own philosophy. However, what if during the term of the venture, which usually is for an unlimited term, one party fails to live up to its contractual commitments? These could be varied: a failure to make a promised capital contribution or a loan; one party goes insolvent; there is a breach of a complementary contract, such as a supply contract by one party to the joint venture. The most common events are situations of deadlock, in which the parties cannot seem to agree on the major issues, and due to clauses in the joint venture agreement or the shareholders' agreement, there is no possibility of breaking the deadlock. The majority may find itself manacled by the minority.

If the parties have this foresight when they negotiate the joint venture agreement, they may agree on what are called *triggering events* followed by *buy–sell mechanisms*. A triggering event is the existence of a fact that gives one or all parties the right to exit from the joint venture under various alternatives. What constitutes a triggering event is the definition given to it by the parties to the joint venture. It could be deadlock on a sensitive issue such as a capital augment for a specified period; it could even be the passage of time.

Equally subject to definition in the joint venture agreement are the possible buy–sell mechanisms. Their objectives are the same: to allow the parties to exit from the joint venture that has become a troublesome collaboration. These mechanisms are therefore an important tool for management. Typical buy–sell mechanisms are set forth in what follows.

Joint venture roulette

In this rather menacing-sounding technique, once a triggering event has occurred, any party may advise the other party it will buy at a stipulated price. This is called "roulette" because the receiving party can buy out the seller on the same terms! This method is only valid if the other party is limited to only one of two choices: sell at the quoted price or buy at the first party's stipulated price.

Modified roulette mechanism

This technique is not so drastic. When the other party receives the offer, it can introduce a third element: make a counteroffer that the first party can accept or offer to buy at the price indicated. The process stops only when an offer to sell is accepted or a purchase made. This does not appear a practical clause although it is used in international joint venture documents.

Auction procedure

An auction is no more than the parties using their freedom of contract. No matter what the joint venture agreement states, all the parties can agree to amend it and if one wants to sell and the others agree, the joint venture agreement is simply modified. An auction then can be held in which the other partners bid for the offered equity interest. Few benefits are derived to the joint venture company from this technique. It pits the remaining partners against one another.

The popularity of the right of first refusal is no doubt due to its suave procedures. When confronted with a valid offer from a third party, the other shareholders can decide whether to preserve the original nucleus of the joint venture.

5.4.4.12 TAG-ALONG RIGHTS

A combination of clauses on restrictions and triggering events can create a certain degree of apprehensiveness as to who will be the new partners; questions such as "Do I want to be in the joint venture with different partners?" or, perhaps, "Shouldn't I be able to also exit from this collaboration if others are leaving?" are seen as legitimate.

In other words, the initial spirit of the partners who form the joint venture may be "we are all in this together or not at all." Should this be the prevailing philosophical tone, then there must be inserted a clause in the joint venture agreement whereby if for whatever reason one party has the right to sell to a third party, then all can sell to the same party. It is not necessary to go around and ask each partner. Once permission is given to one partner to sell to a specified potential buyer, then all the others also have this right, should this be the wishes of the buyer.

5.4.4.13 DRAG-ALONG OBLIGATIONS

This clause can be draconian. Its effect is if one party sells to a third party, then all others must sell. This would most likely find its place in a joint venture in which one partner has a very high degree of equity percentage and does not want its commercial value diluted by a small minority that may be reluctant to sell. The only reason for accepting such a "drag along with me" obligation is that the conditions under which the seller is permitted to make a transfer obligatory by other partners are extremely advantageous to the drag-along partners. A substantial capital gain is foreseen for all. Even so, it is not a clause to be undertaken lightly.

PART FIVE

5.5 REPRESENTATIONS AND WARRANTIES: WARRANTIES ASSIGN RISK

Representations and warranties weave through the fabric of international alliances and at times it is difficult to perceive their function. Warranties assign responsibility to a party who makes assertions, what we call *prom-*

ises, and, concerning international joint ventures, they are principally made by a seller. However, some also will be made by the buyer. A typical warranty of a seller is that the seller owns the equity interest being sold not subject to any claims by other, third parties. A buyer warrants that it has full corporate authority to make the purchase. Our principal concern is with the warranties of sellers. Warranties given by buyers seldom present legal problems.

Furthermore, we are basically interested in warranties affecting ownership rights and management functions. A joint venture agreement contains myriad warranties, many of which are addressed to specialized legal problems that, although of substantial importance, will not affect seriously the negotiations of sellers and buyers. Such a typical warranty is that the articles of incorporation reflect all amendments to date. Of course, this is important and counsel will undertake the necessary review to ensure the warranty is correct at the time of closing. But our preoccupation in this book is a concern with the practical warranties that will affect directly the activities of owners and managers. The warranties concerning technical legal issues will be drafted by counsel.

In a partial acquisition, every joint venture agreement will contain a clause entitled "representations and warranties." No major acquisition can be undertaken without representations and warranties in the joint venture agreement. A unit in a going economic concern is being sold and the buyer will have many questions concerning the target company. Additionally in the everyman joint venture with its reduced number of partners, the sale of a partial acquisition usually will take place only with the approval of the other partners and the status quo of the target company as a continuous enterprise is the basis for the partial acquisition of equity. Warranties thus ensure continuity in various aspects.

Although a joint venture agreement in the formation of a joint venture company might contain some representations and warranties by the signatories, for example, the necessary knowledge to manufacture a specific pharmaceutical product, the scope of such representations and warranties would be restricted, never as wide-ranging or extensive as in an acquisition. The formation of a company does not require any substantial representations or warranties. Many conditions will be dictated, such as capital contributions, loan provisions, desired clauses in the articles of the projected joint venture company, and contracts to be executed between a partner and the future joint venture company.

But representations and warranties as an inducement to another party to form a joint venture company play a restricted role. A company is being formed without any economic history. The scope of any warranties leading to the formation of a company will be minor compared to those present in an acquisition.

Warranties are the vertebrae of the partial acquisition structure. Lawyers draft the language of representations and warranties, and their object is to ensure that what the parties believe they are buying is as represented. As we will see shortly, the material covered by representations and warranties is varied. The kernel of the material will be a blueprint of the economic, financial, and legal aspect of the seller as well as a comprehensive list of items of major concern to the management of the buyer, for example, employee information, trading practices, and accounting procedures.

When considering an acquisition, the buyer should not neglect to inform counsel what additional information needs to be backed up by representations and warranties for every business has its specific characteristics. Although counsel who specialize in this material have developed clauses that have substantial application for a great variety of joint ventures, every commercial enterprise is fact-specific and requires tailored representations and warranties.

What are these representations and warranties, words that in international joint ventures have assumed such a predominant place and importance? Representations, warranties, covenants, promises, and affirmations are almost synonyms for the same thought: a statement of fact. However, almost does not mean equal. Sometimes a person makes a statement of fact and sincerely believes it to be true. We call this a *representation.* Other times, a person makes a statement of fact and warrants it is true, meaning that even if he is acting on the best information available, should the statement not be true, then there has been a breach of contract. This is a *warranty.* A layman might call this a *guarantee,* but legally a guarantee is liability for someone else's promise.

Covenants used to be promises under seal in the ancient English common law. Nowadays contracts with or without seals have little significance except for perhaps consular or official documents. Promises are statements that form part of a contract and affirmations are just words in common use to describe behavior approximating a contractual relationship or to convince a person to enter into a contract. They are verbal marketing. Normally affirmations are not enforceable.

When properly used, all these words convey a wide variety of information. Warranties have a more serious meaning as liability is imposed whether or not they were made in good faith. A representation if made in good faith may not create a liability. In deference to the uncertainty the law often engenders, lawyers use a shotgun approach and join the two words as if they were brothers instead of cousins.

Representations and warranties speak twice and often more. At the time of the signing of the acquisition contract, those representations and warranties made are speaking of the present. But they also look to the future. They are intended to be valid also at the closing date. In the midst of the interval between the date of the joint venture agreement and the closing time, there will be conducted the due diligence procedures to ensure there have been no changes. Moreover, some representations and warranties speak even farther into the future, assuring the buyer that certain events as promised will take place, for example, a cash flow or gross income that has been projected for an accounting year subsequent to the closing.

Furthermore, when properly used, warranties go further than just reassuring the buyer as to the state of affairs. Such warranties are ongoing declarations as they confirm a continuing state of facts. Since we are dealing with a going economic concern, we want to ensure the viability of the investment will not be impaired by any conduct not consistent with prudent standards of business conduct. Between the date of contract and the final closing, the buyer wishes to ensure that there will be no major purchases of additional assets, or the sale of same, or a sudden increase in salaries to key personnel, nor the undertaking of significant contractual obligations not part of the ordinary course of events.

The final test of representations and warranties occurs at the closing. There is a crescendo of activity spearheaded by the representations and warranties with due diligence procedures as the whiplash that is finalized in one of the last documents to be issued at the time of the closing. Prior to the transfer of title and final payment, the seller will deliver to the buyer what is called a *disclosure statement*. This document is intended to confirm either that no changes are necessary to the warranties given or that some exceptions must be made.

Perhaps a major lawsuit has begun, and in the promissory contract, the seller warranted that there was in course no litigation nor was any anticipated. At the time of closing, the seller will deliver a disclosure statement that will relate the litigation in course and that has arisen since the date of the purchase contract. This is denoted as an *exception* to the representations and warranties.

The origin of the terminology is clear. The warranty continues correct *except* for the statements that ensue. Dependent on the purchase contract and its definition of what is a material fact, one that is of extreme importance to the purchaser, the buyer may have the option of not proceeding further, or reducing the sale price, or requesting a reserve to be established to satisfy any possible judgment.

Every acquisition has its particular representations and warranties. What will arrest the attention of the participants is what management decides are the vital economic aspects of the sale. Attorneys naturally have multiple clauses suitable for most joint ventures. For a joint venture agreement to be customized, owners and management must be prepared to discuss with counsel the commercial objectives and their rationale. There is a practical reason for this dialogue.

The representations and warranties are multiple clauses that cover all the vital legal and economic facts of the selling unit and our affirmations by the seller concerning these issues: We have title to the assets; we have the necessary approvals; we will conduct the business during the investigation stage in accordance with sound business practices; we will make no disposal of major assets; all assets and liabilities are correctly stated on the balance sheet; there are no undisclosed serious contingent liabilities; there are no secret contracts with key employees; our accounting practices follow international standards; we have good internal controls; we have not engaged any brokers; no commissions are due anyone.

Many are the clauses and diverse are the topics. There will be topics that might be loosely called *strictly legal* such as a reference that any construction is in good and usable condition or that the seller is duly incorporated under the laws of the local jurisdiction. All clauses are intended to protect the purchaser, but there also will be clauses that might be called *managerial* or *operational*. Such clauses are within the everyday experience of the average entrepreneur and are founded less on legal compliance and more on business practices. Thus, dialogue between client and counsel will make more useful the cleavage between technical, general legal warranties and customized warranties directed toward the economics of the joint venture.

It is useful to review in detail some of the more common economic warranties for they will highlight important day-to-day commercial events that ensure a fruitful acquisition. Although there are many, the concepts are relatively straightforward. It is also a practical agenda for the corporate executive when reviewing the broad aspects of a proposed acquisition. An overall view can be summarized as follows:

1. Statements are made, which are called warranties and representations.

2. An investigation is made to see if they are true. These are due diligence procedures.

3. The seller must disclose at the time of closing if there have been any alterations to the warranties and representations. This is a disclosure statement. This might cause an adjustment to the price or even the right not to proceed to the purchase.

4. At the time of closing, the attorneys and auditors for the buyer will advise their client that there have been found no exceptions of a material nature from the representations and warranties. Seller's counsel also will be asked to confirm that there are no material divergences from the representations and warranties.

5. Dependent on the complexity of the acquisition, there may be a waiting period, with funds in escrow, to see if the warranties and representations continue to be valid, for example, a period of 6 months to see if any claims are made.

6. Representations and warranties must therefore survive the purchase. This is accomplished by having the joint venture agreement expressly provide for such survival.

7. Due diligence procedures may be conducted postclosing dependent on what has been represented as being true, for example, various accounts receivable being paid within a specified period of time.

8. Should there be a breach of any of the representations or warranties, then the party in default will be liable to the other party. This is denominated a *right of indemnities,* which the injured party has against the defaulting party, and is discussed in more detail in section 5.5.11. Indemnities include the right to claim a loss for damages. But the phrase is also intended to cover liabilities incurred, such as taxes, or costs, even the imposition of an environmental fine or the necessary alterations to the installations demanded by the authorities. Indemnities in legal documents will be defined to include losses, damages, deficiencies, and liabilities. Indemnities are more ample than *damages.* Having to pay a tax fine is not necessarily damages. But tax fines are reimbursable as indemnities.

In conclusion, warranties and representations and due diligence procedures complement one another. What is warranted and represented must be eventually subject to confirmation. Any divergences from the facts warranted and represented must be noted as an exception on the disclosure statement handed to the purchaser in time for review shortly before the closing.

5.5.1 GENERAL WARRANTIES OF PARTICULAR INTEREST TO MANAGEMENT

These warranties, and all others that follow in the subsequent sections, normally have a special wording, technical phrases used and resulting from judicial interpretation of disputes through the centuries. In our discussion, no attempt is made to indicate the legal drafting. Rather, the examples given are intended only to foster understanding of what is the purpose of the warranty rather than dwell on drafting language. We shall concentrate on specific warranties:

- As a general rule, the seller must warrant that all information given prior to and during negotiations, leading to and including the contract terms, either by the seller or its representatives, is correct. Everything the seller knows has been disclosed. The information given is certain, not misleading, and complete.
- As a corollary, the seller confirms that all the information given is material to the buyer. This prevents, when an asserted fact proves to be incorrect, the seller claiming that the fact was immaterial whereas the buyer argues it was extremely material.
- It would be appropriate for the buyer to make the same warranties.

5.5.2 WARRANTIES CONCERNING TRADING TERMS

The buyer wants to have all assurances that "business will be conducted as usual."

- It is vital there be no interruption of business. Consequently, warranties are given that the important customers or suppliers will not stop trading with the seller, nor will there be made any significant changes to the existing terms. This, of course, is intended to ensure that no unpleasant commercial surprises are being concealed or occur shortly before the closing.
- The seller's usual terms and conditions of sale will not be altered for any material contract. This prevents unfavorable contracts being signed prior to the closing or at least on terms the buyer was not anticipating.
- If the seller's business is not dependent on any one customer, then it would be appropriate to include a clause that no entity has contracted to purchase X percent of its goods or services for a particular period from and to the closing date. This prevents the buyer acquiring an interest in a joint venture company that suddenly becomes dependent on one customer.

5.5.3 WARRANTIES CONCERNING PRECLOSING BUSINESS PRACTICES

Between the signature of the acquisition contract and a final closing, a great deal of business may transpire. The buyer will want to ensure there is compliance with various standards.

- Above all, and as a fundamental principle, business will be carried on in the usual way so as to keep the business going according to acceptable standards for the industry in question and transfer the business to the buyer in the best condition possible. In other words, until the closing, the highest standards of management will be imposed.
- This means that the policies of the seller prior to the acquisition contract will continue uninterrupted unless there have been any clauses concerning this area in the joint venture agreement.
- As a necessary complement to the preceding, the seller will cooperate with the buyer so that there is a smooth transition from one managerial style to another. This includes preparation that the buyer deems necessary and that will not disturb or otherwise prejudice the present management of the seller. Naturally, there are gray areas where common sense must prevail.
- There will be no sale of, or acquisition of, any major assets except in the usual course of business.
- The same must be stated regarding capital expenditures.
- Other than foreseen in obligations already undertaken, there will not be assumed any significant additional borrowings or other forms of debt, nor amendments to those already assumed. Naturally, this extends to the giving of guarantees, which is a potential debt.
- The same must be stated regarding long-term contracts or any serious obligation not part of the everyday affairs of the seller.
- No significant litigation will be undertaken.
- No action will be taken to affect the capital structure.
- No dividends will be declared that are normally due. The declaration of any dividends should be foreseen in the joint venture agreement.
- No important resolutions of the owners or shareholders of the seller should be passed that represent a deviation from prior practices. Any resolutions prior to closing should have been anticipated in the joint venture agreement.

The objective of the preceding warranties is to preserve the overall ownership and management structure of the target company.

5.5.4 WARRANTIES CONCERNING ASSETS

As the acquisition concerns an existing enterprise, its operational aspects must be assured.

- The company must have all the assets it needs for the conduct of the business and pursuance of its economic objectives. If it doesn't, then there must be made any relevant exceptions in the joint venture agreement.
- Thus, the seller must have all the equipment it needs and inventory. The inventory has to be of good, salable, merchantable quality. If we are dealing with a distress sale, this must be highlighted in the joint venture agreement.

5.5.5 WARRANTIES CONCERNING THE ACCOUNTS

These warranties are designed to force disclosure of any irregularities in the accounting system.

- Foremost, the seller must warrant that the accounts have been prepared and audited in accordance with generally acceptable accounting principles. If the buyer wishes to make a reference to the standards of his home jurisdiction, this is a prudent criterion and will eliminate any erroneous assumptions being made by the buyer. The joint venture agreement will require the interim audit that has been made to be updated at the time of closing. At times, there has been no serious audit when the contract was signed. In these circumstances, it is normal to require a full audit prior to the closing.
- Besides being prepared in accordance with certain standards, the accounts must show an accurate view of the assets and liabilities of the seller. In other words, from worksheets to final compilation, there must be a steady flow of correct and complete information. The accounts will have a date that must be made current at the time of closing.
- The accounts must also be in conformity with the laws of the locale of the seller.
- Normally, accounts receivable have a standard payment schedule. It may be that no account receivable is due for 90 days from the date of invoice. Whatever are the typical schedules in the particular jurisdiction, the seller should state what they are and warrant that there are no overdue accounts receivable for more than X period. This is important

as concerns the cash flow of the seller and on which the buyer may be relying.

- All necessary reserves and provisions for potential liabilities have been made. This is protection for the buyer should litigation no one expected suddenly appear.
- Often, the parties base their purchase price on the results of the profit-and-loss statements for prior periods, perhaps as much as five years. It is necessary that the seller warrant that the profit-and-loss statements used as a reference have not been affected by any unusual circumstances, or items that do not occur often. The practical use of prior profit-and-loss statements has to do with the reliability of seeing trends. This requires the absence of unusual circumstances in any accounting year.
- Besides having a purchase price related to the profit-and-loss statements, it is natural that the net worth of the company and the value of the net tangible assets have also been taken into consideration. The seller must warrant there will be no changes in these figures at the time of closing. This does not prevent substituting one asset for another. Rather, it is only intended to ensure there is not a total change in valuations.

5.5.6 WARRANTIES CONCERNING EMPLOYEES

When the acquisition involves a considerable number of employees, the warranties have to be very complete in order to justify due diligence procedures in depth. Furthermore, multiple employees naturally contribute to a significant part of the fixed liabilities, which affect the net worth of the seller. Typical clauses are as follows:

- There are no amounts owing to employees, directors, or officers of any significance.
- There are no material amounts owed to any governmental agencies connected with employees, such as social security. Very often, employers are behind in their payments to social security and the exposure is significant.
- There have not been signed any contracts altering the basis of remuneration to the preceding groups in the foreseeable future. When collective contracts may obligate periodic increases, such a warranty forces the seller to disclose what they are.
- The company has adequate records to support the preceding statements.
- Dependent on the details the buyer wants, the warranty can obligate that the records include at least certain details and they should be listed in

conformity with the buyer's needs, for example, name, age, starting date, classification, and accrued benefits.

- There are no special contracts with any director, officer, or key employee. This warranty seeks to force disclosure of contracts favoring a family group.
- There is the necessity for any employee's union representative or similar entity to concur with actions taken by the board of directors or to be informed as to major business decisions.

5.5.7 WARRANTIES CONCERNING INSURANCE

The subject as to when a sale or transfer passes title to goods is one of those topics that has little drama associated with it until the goods are destroyed. Who has the risk is who has title. To avoid an often difficult legal question, which can involve astronomical sums of money, it is essential there be warranties as to the existence of insurance, the extent of its coverage, and the beneficiary. Whatever has been negotiated should find appropriate reflection in the warranties. Indicated in what follows are some typical arrangements:

- All material assets are insured to their full replacement value.
- All risks have been covered for the particular industry in question.
- The policies are all current. There are no premiums in default.
- There are no claims outstanding under any of the policies.
- The seller has not engaged or committed any act which would render any of the policies voidable or void.

5.5.8 WARRANTIES CONCERNING THE ENVIRONMENT

With mounting public concern over the effect of industry on the environment, it is now standard to include warranties, when applicable, that are designed to prevent environmental problems being passed to the buyer. Although the nature of the warranties varies with the industry, typical concerns are as follows:

- The seller is not engaged in a hazardous business or the products will not be considered same.
- The premises of the seller are not storing any hazardous material.
- If any waste or hazardous material is being produced, it is being treated in accordance with the law.

- The seller is in compliance with all zoning laws and any special laws affecting the industry.
- No notices of zoning or industry violations have been received by the seller nor are any anticipated.

5.5.9 WARRANTIES OF A LEGAL NATURE

Reference has already been made to there existing multiple warranties that are of a legal nature. By this is meant that legal training is needed to know what are the warranties that should be made. Setting forth a list would confer a moderate benefit. They are warranties that are of a general application. They appear as clauses in contracts for probably the majority of joint ventures. They do not need a particular joint venture to make sense.

Typical legal warranties as to easements, rights of way, peaceful possession, full corporate authority, no deviation from corporate object, possession of operating licenses, good and marketable title to the shares, free and clear from all liens, are fair examples and that businessmen invariably dismiss as the concerns of lawyers.

Such warranties have their essential function and without them, a joint venture agreement would be incomplete. The choice must be left in the competent hands of counsel. We have already discussed warranties of immediate concern to owners and managers. There are many others we will consider under due diligence procedures for the warranties only make sense when we understand what we are seeking to uncover during the investigatory phase.

The purpose of due diligence procedures is, in part, to ensure the warranties are correct. The other part is to understand better the economic, financial, and legal situation of the target company. The subject material between the two is thus similar. Due diligence procedures can be justified only by the quest to determine if the representations and warranties as given are free from error. An artificial division has been made into two separate chapters to facilitate comprehension. Much of the material discussed in Chapter Seven under due diligence procedures will be the object of a warranty clause.

5.5.10 WARRANTIES OF A FINANCIAL NATURE

It might not appear to be so, but legal defects or infirmities are quicker to detect in a going concern than financial irregularities. A review of the records at the local land office will determine easily if title to the buildings are in fact held by the seller. To determine if the mortgage payments are being made to the bank requires only a simple letter.

Incomplete accounting records when there is an avalanche of records requires complex methods of detection developed by auditors. Financial information concealed is hard to detect because the people who want to conceal it have normally substantial experience in their field. It would be unthinkable in a major acquisition to proceed without financial due diligence procedures; these are reviewed in Chapter Seven with an emphasis on the viewpoint of the corporate manager.

5.5.11 INDEMNITIES AND DAMAGES

The purpose of having an extensive, complete joint venture agreement is to lay the foundation for one party to have a right to indemnities or damages from another party. The words *indemnities* and *damages* are not always used with clarity. If one party breaches an agreement, the injured party has a right to damages. The amount of damages may not be easily ascertainable. A default occurs and the party claiming damages will quantify what is believed to be just compensation. But there is often a subjective element also involved, such as vilification of a name or reputation. Thus, damages have no definitive mathematical context. It is ascertained by a judge or jury.

On the other hand, imagine one party relies on the warranty of another that no taxes are due and payable by the joint venture company in which an interest is being purchased. They are in fact due and levied after the acquisition. The defaulting party, besides having to respond in damages for an inaccurate statement, will have to indemnify the party who pays the taxes to the extent of the amount levied. In our example, this will be the joint venture company.

An indemnity thus replaces a loss sustained because of a contractual responsibility not assumed voluntarily. Damages will be awarded for general misconduct. Indemnities replace a specific loss. Indemnities and damages raise two fundamental issues: What causes the right to indemnities and damages and what will be the extent of the claims permitted?

The foundation for having a right to indemnities or damages will be derived from general contract principles and the stipulations of the parties. The clauses in the joint venture agreement thus assume primordial importance. For this reason, the agreement must be complete and cover the contingencies and conditions foreseen by the parties and their counsel. As a general rule, any breach of a warranty will give rise to either an action for damages or a claim for indemnities. For our purposes of analysis, it is not necessary to describe how it is determined whether a claim for damages or indemnities or both should be determined. This is the task of counsel and draftsmanship. The more detailed the list of expressed representations, warranties, and statement of facts, the easier it will be to claim compensation when there is a breach.

However, having a right to assert a loss does not tell us what will be the ambit of the loss. Will it be a direct, measurable loss confined to the present? Or will we be able to look to the future and claim the consequences of a breach? Perhaps a representation as to an important client contract was made and the contract was terminated, with good cause, a month after the acquisition but with reference to facts prior to the purchase.

Here we will have difficulty in ascertaining future, potential loss because we do not know easily what profit a contractual relationship brings over a period of time. The parties must therefore consider such topics as loss of commercial opportunities, possible profits, and goodwill as potential items for inclusion in damages or not. The well-drafted joint venture agreement will resolve these vague areas where much can be claimed. But these familiar items of loss are not the only ones permitted by the law.

The ground of indemnities and damages is without horizon. From unarticulated but accrued labor claims to pollution issues, human nature fails in its obligations. Although certain topics can be selected and described in the joint venture agreement, it will be necessary to fall back on broad descriptive language in order to include events that can be foreseen in their generality. What can be detailed and anticipated should be. The balance of ideas must fall back on generalities. The pronouncement of what should be done is simple enough but the language task is formidable.

It is also important that there be a clear vision of who has the right to claim indemnities. There are two classes. The joint venture company and the partners form two classes that will have the right to assert a claim for indemnities. A failure by one partner to honor his promise with the joint venture company, for example, refusing to grant a loan promised in the joint venture agreement, will give the joint venture company a right to claim damages.

However, indirectly, a partner is also injured as to the extent of his equity interest. It is not a prudent course of action to allow any claim for indemnities in a joint venture agreement, or other legal document, to be confined to the joint venture company. A partner indirectly injured may not be able to muster the votes necessary to have the joint venture company take any action. With a right of action residing in the joint venture company and all partners, this potential impediment is effectively bypassed.

Thus, even when we are clear that the joint venture company is the direct beneficiary of an obligation, having the partners also execute the relevant document will make enforcement of the joint venture company right attainable.

5.5.12 DUE DILIGENCE PROCEDURES: THE DISCOVERY OF RISK

In the formation of a joint venture company through a partial acquisition, it is incumbent on the buyer to investigate all facets of the target company. With substantial monies involved in an acquisition of a partial equity interest, due diligence procedures may precede the execution of a joint venture agreement. However, in the everyman international joint venture, often this is not the case and there is instead an informal exchange of information prior to the drafting of the joint venture agreement. As there is anticipated a continuing collaboration, the due diligence procedures prior to any agreement are to clear up any major doubts. Once the joint venture agreement has been signed, due diligence procedures must be commenced in depth and detail if we are dealing with a substantial investment. The search is for revelation of risk.

The prolonged investigation of the target company, or due diligence procedures, has thus become a standard facet of acquisitions leading to a joint venture. The joint venture agreement will contain a clause defining the terms and conditions of these procedures and when they will take place. The object is to ascertain exactly what are the financial and legal facts concerning the seller. With a complex, product-varied seller as the target, this can be a daunting process and requires a significant amount of skilled human resources to work as a team. The practice of due diligence procedures is itself a specialty and we will study all the ramifications of these procedures in Chapter Seven.

5.5.13 TERMINATION OF THE JOINT VENTURE AND DISPUTE RESOLUTION

There is rescission of the joint venture agreement; there is termination of the joint venture agreement; and there is termination of the joint venture. They are all different concepts, often intermixed. Rescission means that an agreement, in this case, the joint venture agreement, will be rendered void. There may be many reasons for this, including the most obvious, that the joint venture is no longer possible, for example, a license for import of foreign capital is not obtained. Instead of a license from the foreign investment authorities, there may be necessary a zoning alteration. The parties are aware of the possibility of failure and have already agreed that without such licenses, or any condition the parties stipulate, the joint venture cannot go forward. The realization of the joint venture will not take place for it is legally impossible. All of these contingencies are expressed in the joint venture agreement.

Termination of an agreement occurs when an event gives one party a right to consider the agreement is no longer being performed by the other party and thus the first signatory to the agreement terminates it, usually with a right of action for damages against the offending party. The seller makes a warranty that is not fulfilled, such as to the existence of certain assets. Prior to closing, the whereabouts of the assets are not confirmed. A party has agreed to make a specific contribution and on the appointed day for payment, it is not consummated. Such serious defaults give the other party the right to terminate the agreement as having been breached, which naturally occurs prior to the formation of the joint venture company.

In all of the preceding situations, the joint venture company is never formed. One cannot establish a company in a foreign jurisdiction without securing the necessary legal approvals and a company needs a legal capital. A foreign investor is not going to make an acquisition if the warranted assets are not discovered. The proposed joint venture never materializes. These situations, and many others, relate to problems prior to the formation of the joint venture company. The possible reasons for failure of completion are of course limitless. They may be expressed in the joint venture agreement or they may result from the law.

Finally, the joint venture agreement may provide for mechanisms that all parties agree should lead to a cessation of the joint venture. Termination of the joint venture means that the common enterprise between the original founders is finished whether by one of the partners selling his equity interest or the joint venture company is dissolved and liquidated. A typical clause in a joint venture agreement of this nature would be an agreement by the parties that if the management of the company becomes deadlocked on various issues, this will trigger certain acts, one possibility being a buyout of another party's interest, or even a dissolution of the joint venture company. These alternatives must find expression in the joint venture agreement or else they have to be negotiated between the parties after the problem arises.

Rescission, breach leading to termination, and termination are also allied to questions of dispute resolution and all of these topics will be treated separately in Chapter Nine. How these problems are resolved finds its articulation in the joint venture agreement.

5.5.14 Closing conditions

The joint venture agreement will define the conditions that are a prerequisite to the closing. The expression *closing* has several meanings, ranging from the acts leading up to the solemn legal event of formation of a company before a notary or similar official, to indicating the legal events taking place before the notary, to meaning the entire process until all the terms of the joint venture agreement are completed. Although a closing is often understood in the commercial world as being the formalities of an acquisition or formation, with exchange of documents and payments, in reality, a closing is a series of episodes that is continuous and is often not concluded until after the company is formed if postdiligence procedures are foreseen. The usual sequence of events is described in Chapter Ten.

5.5.15 Miscellaneous clauses: assignment, expenses, notices, and brokers

There are many stipulations that form part of the joint venture agreement that are restrictive. Some are very technical, such as the breach of one clause not invalidating the entire agreement. But there are others whose indication will be useful to the entrepreneur.

The importance of the survival of the joint venture agreement has already been mentioned. There are naturally expenses in connection with an acquisition or the formation of a company and these must be allocated between the parties. Where notices should be sent should be indicated so as to avoid irritating episodes such as where to send a necessary registered letter. Finally, the eternal thorny issue of intermediaries and brokers must be clarified to verify if there are any possible claims for fees or commissions.

Part Six

5.6 Recommended, optional documentation

The earlier suggested clauses are not a complete recitation of the standard paragraphs in a joint venture agreement. They are a selected group of topics that are of particular interest to management. There are many more issues dealt with in the joint venture agreement that counsel will insert as intending to foresee typical recurrent problems. The professional joint venture agreement and its clauses are a net sweeping out intending to catch and collect all possible problems. Management also has to focus on the basic elements that are the foundation of any business: the annual budget, the capital expenditures, and the business plan.

Since they are standard management tools, it is natural that these documents are discussed early between the partners. That such documents will be the subject of lively debate is a frequent occurrence. Many joint ventures are formed with these documents reviewed, exchanged, often the agenda of many meetings, and eventually filed away. Nevertheless, it is a good idea to take a more formal attitude and annex at least four documents to the joint venture agreement. They serve as an excellent reference for the general philosophy of the joint venture and are discussed in what follows. In all cases, these are optional documents although highly recommended as to their inclusion as part of the joint venture documentation.

Budget

The importance of the annual budget is of course well known to entrepreneurs and managers. It defines the priorities of the company, indicating what money will be spent on what activities. It is a sweeping financial blueprint of how to construct the financial and operational goals of the joint venture. It is an essential set of working papers.

It would be unthinkable for any company to initiate its activities without such a written plan as to the future. This can range from expansionary purposes, such as advertising, to research projects. But the budget also has an important, although indirect, legal consequence. It conditions what will happen to income during the year, and, obviously, the more income that is spent, the less there is for distribution of dividends.

The availability of dividends is often a contentious item. One partner wants to maximize profits for distribution; another wants to reinvest income into the research and development of new products. Time spent prior to the launching of a joint venture on an agreed budget for a period of years, perhaps 3 to 5 years, is beneficial and serves to reduce conflict. During the preparation of a budget, it will become apparent what is expected to happen with available income, and differences, if there are any, are much better thrashed out prior to the formation of the joint venture.

The budget confers a well-defined managerial perspective; it indicates what problems there may be and therefore they can be anticipated. It is an invaluable management tool that has its complementary legal side.

Capital expenditures

The preparation of the budget will reveal quickly if any partner is contemplating reinvesting income into assets. The purchase or expansion of company assets normally requires an asset to be depreciated and therefore disposable income is going to be reduced in the annual profit-and-loss statement. Once again, this lessens income available for dividends. Similar to the budget, the capital expenditure plan reveals the commercial objectives of the partners, and its review, prior to the formation of the joint venture, affords multiple opportunities as to the appropriate dividend policy, and shows what will be the priorities of the joint venture.

Working capital requirements

The excess of current assets over current liabilities is denominated *working capital*. It represents the amount of liquid assets available to service debt and is thus a standard indicator of debt-paying ability. Clearly, maintaining a solid working capital is vital to the success of the joint venture and it is an item on which the partners should agree as soon as possible. This will avoid conflicts during the operational phase of the joint venture as to what is a proper, healthy working capital.

Business plan

The negotiation phase of the joint venture is the proper time for the parties to discuss their future plans as to what the joint venture will do; and what will be its short-term objectives as well as long-term plans. This is the best moment for the partners to verbalize if they have other plans for the same market and what they will be. In this way, there will be no surprises nor disappointments.

Such a business plan need not be a formal document. A recitation in the joint venture agreement or even a clause in the joint venture agreement will be sufficient. What is important is that the facts of the future of the joint venture and its partners be open for discussion and transparent. This contributes substantially toward a harmonious collaboration.

5.6.1 BOARD OF DIRECTORS' AGREEMENT

It is usual and certainly good practice for the joint venture agreement to indicate any particular agreements that have been reached on the composition of the board of directors; how it will function; if any special majorities are needed. It is also recommended that such agreements, rather than being buried in the already complex joint venture agreement, be removed to a separate document where their importance will be more readily seen and even can be used to secure the signature of incoming new partners.

In an acquisition, if the articles of the joint venture company do not have any special treatment of this problem, the board of directors' agreement assumes particular importance if the incoming partner can obtain the consent of the other partners. The more effective method is to have any provisions concerning voting set forth in the articles of the company.

Regarding the formation of a joint venture, the joint venture agreement, or a separate board of directors' agreement, can provide that the provisions of the agreement will be transposed to the articles of the joint venture company when established. This is the more secure route. However, at times, counsel are satisfied to leave the board of directors' agreement as the sole authority without any reference to this topic in the articles of the joint venture company. This is not the best procedure for as a private agreement its breach may not offer a satisfactory remedy.

The board of directors' agreement will be an agreement amongst the partners, not the members of the board, as to what topics will require what majority of votes. An agreement between the members of the board of directors is possible only as to how the voting will take place. Members of the board, having the duty to supervise and administer the company, cannot compromise themselves in advance on whether they will vote favorably or not on a particular problem. Normally, the joint venture agreement or shareholders' agreement will specify how many members of the board of directors will be elected by what group of partners. These may also be special rights attaching to a particular class of shares.

Nevertheless, the right to nominate has no bearing on how many votes will be needed on the board of directors for a particular topic. On all issues, it may be a simple majority; or it may be necessary a supermajority on certain matters; or it can even be a unanimous requirement on very important items such as dissolution, merger, augment of capital, and purchase of equity interests in other companies. This certainly will be true in the closely held international joint venture company.

5.6.2 MANAGEMENT AGREEMENT

The same reasoning applies to the reasonableness of having a management agreement. Although the joint venture agreement may indicate what partner will be in charge of what department, securing management rights will be more solid with the execution of a separate agreement, either between the joint venture company and the partner who will perform certain services.

The partners to the joint venture agreement can also execute a separate management agreement, clearly defining the jurisdictional competency of each partner and over what department it will have fairly exclusive jurisdiction. In this way, the division of power becomes more than just a separation of rights; it becomes a contractual right of one partner that can be enforced. Matters relating to this theme must be the subject of a private agreement. It is not usual to incorporate into the articles of the joint venture company reference to one class of shares or one partner having jurisdiction over a particular department.

5.6.3 ADHERENCE AGREEMENT

Of all the many rights that will be created, in whatever document, there is the inevitable limitation of all contracts: they are effective as they were between the original parties. But what can be done toward new, incoming parties. How will they be bound? If a new partner enters into a joint venture, what can the other partners do about ensuring their rights on various topics, such as the right to make certain key personnel appointments?

To solve this problem, there has been developed what is denominated as an *adherence agreement*. When executed, the signatory obligates himself to all of the existing agreements as if he were one of the original parties. However, how to secure the signature to an adherence agreement raises certain problems. Normally, the problem would arise when there is a sale of an interest. On this event, if other partners have a right of preference or right of first refusal, and do not wish to utilize such a right, then the sensible procedure is to advise the selling partner and the potential buyer that there are no objections, provided an adherence agreement is executed.

Most transferees, that is, potential buyers, when so advised will execute the agreement. It is not usual to enter into a joint venture with a climate of hostility. However, in many instances, joint venture legal forms are utilized that permit total restriction. In such cases, securing an adherence agreement becomes the condition on which consent will be given.

However, there will be instances where there are no restrictions or where they are not possible and a transfer is made without there being signed an adherence agreement. Unless the buyer has knowledge of the prior agreements, or should have known of them, it is not likely he will be bound by them. Such situations are rare and not the usual set of circumstances.

5.6.4 JOINT VENTURE AGREEMENT: CONCLUSIONS

The joint venture agreement is a critical document in the formation of a joint venture. It affords various opportunities for owners and management to have consecrated special rights for owners and management and be able to enforce them. Oftentimes, there is no other major document beyond the joint venture agreement.

For many professionals, the joint venture agreement is seen as a basic document, one that defines the important features of the joint venture and ensures, in the case of acquisitions, that the warranties and representations made are validated by the thorough due diligence procedures that will be conducted. From this perspective, the joint venture agreement is on the one hand a document similar to a constitution defining under what conditions the participants will cooperate and on the other hand an agenda setting forth multiple financial and legal conditions that must prove to be true.

But, of course, in a joint venture, there are matters that are of particular concern to the owners and yet they speak of details, matters that are more an operational manual as to multiple aspects of the joint venture vehicle. We are referring to agreed budgets, expenditures, salaries, and job functions as typical items. The joint venture agreement can be all these things, the specific and the general, and often is. However, many professionals prefer to see various details affecting the shareholders relegated to a separate document: the shareholders' agreement.

The shareholders' agreement creates and protects specific ownership and managerial rights in detail. It usually addresses these issues in a specific fashion. It is not a published document. It is a private agreement that operates between shareholders or between shareholders and the company. It can be as detailed as indicating ceilings on salaries, what amounts will be annually spent on fixed assets. Yet it can also be as general as setting forth how votes will be counted on the board of directors.

Although all of these data can be included in a joint venture agreement, this naturally tends to increase the complexity of the joint venture agreement. Furthermore, separating out and placing into a separate document matters regulating issues between shareholders and between shareholders and the joint venture vehicle permit a legal and visual separation from other clauses in the joint venture agreement.

This facilitates analysis, discussion, and subsequent amendments in a direct, simple form. Current professional practice is to have a separate agreement, and in our detailed discussion to come in the next chapter, we will discuss the multiple aspects of this important tool for owners and managers, sufficiently effective that minority interests can easily obtain a significant participation in the major decisions of the joint venture company.

6

THE SHAREHOLDERS' AGREEMENT

PART ONE

6.1 THE SHAREHOLDERS' AGREEMENT: A PRIMARY TOOL FOR MANAGEMENT

In international joint ventures, the shareholders' agreement has become the legal tool to regulate rights between the shareholders of a company. It is a legal instrument that is no longer confined to stock corporations. Even if it were, it would still figure as an important document in international joint ventures as the share corporation is a prevalent, common legal form adopted for this objective. However, with careful drafting, it can be utilized in most legal forms of companies, certainly the more common. It is widely used in the private limited liability company and the closely held corporation.

The shareholders' agreement is employed more frequently in the formation of an international joint venture, but it surely has its place in a partial acquisition. When acquiring an equity interest in a private closely held corporation, the other partners may want to establish certain rights and obligations vis-à-vis the new partner. Nevertheless, the shareholders' agreement has a primary role in the formation of a joint venture as it permits customizing the various rights among all the founding members.

Properly used, the shareholders' agreement is the bill of rights of the owners of equity, no matter what the legal form. It is a private agreement and in many jurisdictions not deposited or recorded anywhere. In other jurisdictions, such as Brazil, to be effective against third parties, including the corporation, it has to be deposited at the home office. However, deposit requirements are intended to determine the effect of the shareholders' agreement regarding only third parties. As between the shareholders, or other forms of equity ownership, the agreement is effective as any contract, deposited or not.

The shareholders' agreement attempts to establish rules that are more proper for a partnership than a share corporation. It seeks to modify general principles of law and regulate in details various matters of interest to the signatories. It permits owners of a company to vary considerably the natural consequences of the share corporation, or other, form of the joint venture vehicle chosen. It allows minority owners to prevent abusive action by the majority. It fosters a fair distribution of power, whether through ownership or management, by requiring the majority to seek the consent of the minority on a variety of topics.

The shareholders' agreement has little utility in an international joint venture involving share companies quoted on national share exchanges. With a share base of thousands, there have to be rules that nourish market flexibility and transparency. There must be legal guidelines that stimulate reliance on public information, such as the articles of incorporation. A shareholders' agreement not of public knowledge contradicts this philosophy. Private agreements cannot affect the rights of dispersed shareholders who have no knowledge of such agreements nor are there any references in the articles of the company to this legal instrument.

However, the adequacy of the shareholders' agreement for the everyman joint venture is undisputed. Much of the practice orientating small and medium companies forming international joint ventures is dealing with circumstances totally different from the large, capitalized public companies. The average joint venture vehicle may be a share corporation, but with the minimum amount of shareholders that can vary from jurisdiction to jurisdiction. Five is a fair average. Other times, the preferred joint venture vehicle may be the private limited liability company, which can have as little as two equity owners. The existence of the shareholders agreement will be known to all the owners. The owners, unlike in a public corporation, will probably have an active participation in the management. If all do not partake, they nevertheless want to keep a vigilance, to have the right to know what is happening, without a lot of cumbersome obstacles being erected.

Consequently, a substantial part of the ensuing analysis is intended for application to medium capital joint ventures, what would be generally classified in the United States as a closely held corporation. Naturally, with fifty separate jurisdictions and a federal system of law, there are count-less variations to the general principles. In Europe, the special concepts affecting closely held corporations in the United States do not find their counterparts. They are not needed as there exist throughout these jurisdic-tions private limited liability companies that have the limited liability of a share corporation but function as a general partnership. Therefore, there is no conflict in treating a limited liability company as a partnership for that is what the legislators intended.

For a long time, the shareholders' agreement met forceful opposition from European jurists on a number of grounds; when legislation was passed in various sovereign governments, it was of a general nature, without much detail, but authorizing in principle the validity of such agreements. Con-sequently, on the one hand, we have a rich background of U.S. legal his-tory to help formulate helpful suggestions for a shareholders' agreement, and on the other hand, there are no hindrances to transporting many of the U.S. legal ideas to Europe.

Besides problems of a theoretical nature concerning the validity of a shareholders' agreement, the existence of such a legal instrument can col-lide with traditional views of how management is divided in a typical corporation between the shareholders and the board of directors. This com-plex area of the law can be summarized as follows:

- Local legislation will define what is the distribution of management power between the board of directors and the shareholders. Generally, the shareholders elect the board of directors or remove a director for cause. Under this principle, the shareholders have few powers.
- In such jurisdictions, minor alterations to this scheme are permitted if all the owners agree on a particular item, that is, there is a shareholders' agreement on the issue.
- Other jurisdictions obligate the board of directors to seek approval from the owners on major issues such as a merger or augment of capital.
- Many jurisdictions do permit substantial alteration of the traditional powers of a board of directors if we are dealing with a closely held corporation. The usual international joint venture will fall within this category.
- Regardless of the dimension of the corporation, many jurisdictions per-mit alterations of the distribution of management power if contained in the articles of the company.
- In all cases, if all partners have some representation on the board of directors, private agreements executed by the principals of the directors strongly tend to be honored.

- This outcome can be secured by establishing what percentage of votes is needed for a particular topic through the company articles. Here drafting creativity is needed, but most of the details established in the shareholders' agreement thus can be implemented.
- An alternative to a provision concerning supermajority votes in the articles of the company is an agreement, or clause in the shareholders' agreement, on votes needed for validating a decision at the board of directors' level.
- No agreement is valid that compromises the votes of the nominees on the board of directors ahead of time.
- There is no perfect agreement or solution to every problem. In the overwhelming majority of cases, businessmen honor voluntarily the agreements they sign.

Against this background, our study of shareholders' agreements will be instructive and beneficial. Before examining in detail the practical aspects of a shareholders' agreement, it is helpful to indicate what it is not.

6.1.1 POOLING AGREEMENTS

A pooling agreement is a contract whereby shareholders, or partners in another legal form, agree to vote as a block for certain directors or they will vote on any issue contained in the contract as a unit and it is hoped that the contract provides the necessary instructions. The shareholders' agreement for use in international joint ventures is of more broad utility. For our purposes, we consider the pooling agreement too narrow in scope to be used in the average joint venture.

In Europe, such an arrangement might be classified as a *defense syndicate,* meaning that various shareholders band together to defend a particular point of view. Such an application is of limited use in a joint venture and would be better served by being a clause in the joint venture agreement conferring special voting rights to a class of owners or establishing a qualified majority voting requirement on a specific issue.

6.1.2 VOTING TRUST

It is possible to convey title to shares, or other equity interests, to a trustee who, vested with the title, votes the shares according to predefined instructions. The advantage of a voting trust over a pooling agreement is that there cannot be dissent as there could be between the members of the pooling agreement prior to the vote. Once title passes, the trustee has the power to vote. Naturally, one has to be concerned that the trustee will vote as instructed. Patently, a voting trust is substantially different from a shareholders' agreement. It would not be practical to create a voting trust with broad powers to endure for many years because it would not be possible to devise preordained instructions for the varying circumstances that arise during the life of a company. Conceding powers to a trustee to vote on all issues in his best judgment is a severe, drastic step and not normally associated with the average international joint venture.

6.1.3 IRREVOCABLE POWER OF ATTORNEY

Frequently, a shareholder cannot attend a general assembly meeting. He passes a proxy to another shareholder. A proxy is a power of attorney whereby one shareholder gives another the authority to speak in his name. The concept can be enlarged to include an irrevocable power of attorney in which one shareholder grants a power of attorney to another and this power cannot be revoked. Such a legal concept could be utilized by a group of shareholders who grant an irrevocable power of attorney to a third to vote all shares in question in a certain fashion. The irrevocable power of attorney is normally for short duration, the next general assembly. Contrary to its name, such powers of attorney in fact are not irrevocable, although an action in damages may lie for its cancellation. The irrevocable power of attorney is similar to a pooling agreement and a voting trust but far more temporal. Of course, it cannot have the diversity of use as a shareholders' agreement and is not a legal instrument particularly associated with international joint ventures.

6.1.4 THE TRADITIONAL PRIVATE USE OF THE SHAREHOLDERS' AGREEMENT

As our understanding becomes more complete, we will see that the shareholders' agreement has a primordial position in all operational aspects of the international joint venture. It is the equivalent of by-laws in corporation law, but it is more than just a set of rules on what authorizations are needed for a particular item and how the authorization will be obtained.

It can, and should, purport to regulate on a multitude of subjects that cannot be conveniently put into the articles of incorporation. Company articles speak in generalities and not in particulars, such as the annual budget, what are the capital expenditure limitations, ceilings on salaries, and what is the business plan for the next 5 years. These are not matters for the general public, not for revelation to competitors. Company articles are filed and available to third parties and the internal economic aspects are not to be divulged.

Beyond the operational aspects of a shareholders' agreement, there are various topics that are traditionally treated in this document. Typical examples are preestablished augments of capital; creation of any special reserves; division of profits not dependent on equity ownership; accounting policies; remuneration of directors; election and reelection of managers of the company; agreements by one partner to loan money to the joint venture; and obligation of a partner-licensor to continue furnishing technology to the joint venture company in the event the owner-licensor sells his interest to another party.

However, the ease with which these matters can be drafted into a shareholders' agreement should not obscure the fact that in many cases their recitation only in the shareholders' agreement may not prove sufficient. When there are clauses in a shareholders' agreement that may later prove to be uncomfortable for one of the partners, there will certainly be attempts to diminish or reduce legally the effect of such clauses.

To a great extent, therefore, the proper structuring of a joint venture involves complementary clauses in other documents, specifically, the articles of the company and the joint venture agreement, so that the shareholders' agreement is impregnable and effective, a powerful tool in the hands of management. All of these techniques will be covered in detail in this chapter and Chapter Eight.

Additionally, at the end of this chapter, we will list again the topics to be inserted in the shareholders' agreement and explain summarily why such items are not suitable for recitation in other legal documents, or, if so, it is the rare exception. For the moment, we must shift our attention initially to the general aspects of a shareholders' agreement and then the detailed contents in order to better understand their relevancy.

Previously, it has been stated that all the contents or a partial list of a shareholders' agreement can be a clause(s) in the joint venture agreement. Many joint ventures are formed with the joint venture agreement as the only ancillary document and the clauses that would normally be in the shareholders' agreement are scattered throughout the joint venture agreement. Nevertheless, there is a strong tendency to have the same clauses inserted in a separate document, the shareholders' agreement, to facilitate ease of analysis and to permit other new partners to adhere to the document. Furthermore, in those jurisdictions where the shareholders' agreement may be deposited, it would be awkward and too commercially revealing to deposit an entire joint venture agreement.

In addition to the joint venture agreement as an alternative to the shareholders' agreement, it is to natural think of inserting the items to be regulated by the shareholders' agreement in the articles of incorporation. Some can, but not all. General restrictions on the transfer of shares can be put in the articles of incorporation. But if two shareholders wish to have an agreement relating to them and no other shareholders, it would not be legally possible to insert any applicable restriction into the articles of incorporation.

Unless we are dealing with classes of shares, clauses affecting restrictions could never speak in particulars, that is, restrictions affecting shareholders X and Y. Once shareholders X and Y transferred their interests, the clause would not have any effect. An amendment would have to be effectuated to the articles of incorporation. Clauses in the articles of incorporation always speak in generalities so as to be able to apply them without any doubt.

Furthermore, there are many clauses that speak in particulars that could not be inserted in the articles of incorporation for there would be no way for third parties to monitor them. Clauses concerning debt limitations, annual budgets, limitations on capital expenditures, assignment of key personnel, salaries to be paid, internal control procedures, methods of taking inventory, refer to details that the general public cannot confirm and that would further turn the articles of incorporation into a manager's manual. It would be tantamount to indicating in a shareholders' report what shirts and ties the board members usually wear!

For example, a bank when asked to make a loan would have to call for a complete investigation of the company's activities to determine if the loan requested was within the debt limitations stipulated. It would have to inquire if the company was appraising its inventory as mandated. It is far easier and more effective to have the partners in a company agree as to these particulars and thus the managerial conduct of the participants is regulated in accordance with a particular philosophy.

Likewise, we may legitimately inquire why not just make a general reference to the shareholders' agreement in the articles of the company or, if we are dealing with a share corporation, simply endorse on the certificate a reference to the existing agreement. In this way, the public and purchasers are put on notice and they can request a copy of the agreement to study it.

This is possible, if impractical, in a closely held corporation but not in other legal forms of companies in which no shares are issued. The most common form of a closely held corporation in Europe is the private limited liability company, which does not issue share certificates. There would have to be a reference in the articles of incorporation as to the existence of a shareholders' agreement, which would render the conduct of business too cumbersome. Anyone dealing with the private limited liability company would need a certified copy of the articles of association, updated, which means daily trips to the commercial conservatory.

Many U.S. jurisdictions, by case law or legislative act, have expressly permitted the endorsement or notification on the certificate of a shareholders' agreement provided the company in question fulfills the requirements of a close corporation. The definition of a close corporation varies from state to state and there is needed strict compliance with the law. However, as already noted, a domestic joint venture in the U.S. between closely held corporations presents different problems and issues from the international joint venture. Thus, although the viability of the stamping on the share certificates of a closely held U.S. state corporation "subject to shareholders' agreement dated . . ." is useful, the same technique is not easily available for international joint ventures.

In Europe, it is rare to find legislation concerning close corporations. There is legislation affecting private limited liability companies, which approximate very closely the U.S. closely held corporation, and there is the general corporation law. In many jurisdictions, if there is legislation permitting shareholders' agreements, it is general and perhaps regulates in detail only a specific requirement, such as requiring the shareholders' agreement to be deposited with the joint venture corporation or indicating the subject matter proper for a shareholders' agreement.

Consequently, with such a varied approach to the material, the frequent practice in international joint ventures is not to make references to the shareholders' agreement in the articles, for this would only provoke third parties to make inquiries. If there are no deposit requirements, the existence of the agreement is unknown. Regarding endorsements on shares, this appears to meet with reluctance by most owners of small closely held corporations regarding international joint ventures. The shareholders' agreement is understood to be a private matter.

For all these reasons, the shareholders' agreement continues to have widespread use as a private document. It can be substantially beneficial to a proper functioning of the joint venture, but it continues to be treated as a confidential matter between the owners. Transparency to third parties is not usually associated with the shareholders' agreement. It remains a highly important, private document, functioning as a bill of rights between owners of equity.

Before turning to the matters that are appropriately regulated in a share-holders' agreement and the use owners and management can make of this all-important document, it is useful to review some of the basic aspects of the shareholders' agreement.

6.1.5 THE CHARACTERISTICS OF THE SHAREHOLDERS' AGREEMENT

Many techniques have developed through the years for minority share-holders to protect themselves against the voting strength of the majority. This is usually done by a group of shareholders uniting under various legal forms to form a voting block. A study of shareholders' agreements also can be a study of the multiple legal devices developed in the United States and Europe, such as voting trusts, voting syndicates, or pooling agreements in which the declared purpose is to forge a united voting block by a group of shareholders. For our objectives, this is too limited a perspective without any significant utility.

Regarding international joint ventures, we are concerned with a broad agreement, multifunctional, one that will encompass many rights, voting rights, but also additional themes. The shareholders' agreement used in such joint ventures is not only a legal agreement whereby a minority share-holder can be granted special rights. This also could be done by creating a special class of shares or having the articles of incorporation require a supermajority for quorum purposes in the general assembly. The share-holders' agreement as used in international joint ventures can be drafted to regulate not only voting rights, but also myriad ownership and manage-rial functions. This has not been the function of the voting trusts or voting syndicates. Consequently, we will look for certain characteristics that will identify the standard shareholders' agreement forming part of many inter-national joint ventures. Although we refer to shareholders, we always mean equity owners. The description is not intended to be only confined to a share corporation. The characteristics of this comprehensive document are as follows:

- Obviously, the agreement concerns shareholders and their relation-ship within a particular company. An agreement between a share-holder and a creditor is not a shareholders' agreement. It is a loan agreement with security. This requirement for shareholders has impor-tance when we realize certain jurisdictions obligate a shareholders' agree-ment to be deposited with the corporation to be effective. If an agreement between a shareholder and a creditor were considered a shareholders' agreement, it would have to be deposited with the corporation to be valid.

- The agreement should not only relate to restrictions on transfer of shares or how voting will take place. Legal literature is abundant with devices such as voting syndicates that permit a union of shareholders to form a voting block, and often in treatises concerning shareholders' agreements, these legal arrangements are included as a form of a shareholders' agreement. Frequently, such a clause restricting transfer of shares appears in a joint venture agreement and it is referred to as a shareholders' agreement. For our objectives, this is too confining and limiting in function.

- When implementing an international joint venture, we will want an agreement that will permeate both the ownership and managerial aspects of the joint venture vehicle. The shareholders' agreement therefore will be multipurpose. It will go beyond mere voting rights. It will address ownership issues and managerial rights. It should be a complex document rich in creating and detailing multiple aspects of the internal life of the joint venture vehicle and not just transfer restrictions. Although we will not deny the status of a shareholders' agreement to documents which regulate a few or even one issue, such as a transfer restriction, our focus is on a broad, utilitarian document that will be a positive aid to management on diverse operational matters.

- The shareholders' agreement must relate to functional matters affecting the corporation. This is a practical requirement. We are not interested in regulating the rights of shareholders on issues of representation at a general assembly or even a requirement of the rotation of the chairman of the board of directors. The shareholders' agreement as an integral part of the international joint venture must address ownership and operational issues. Otherwise, agreements with very limited subjects can find their expression in clauses in the joint venture agreement.

- Unfortunately, it cannot be expected of a shareholders' agreement that it will be unlimited in duration or in the material sought to be regulated. These latter two topics have never been satisfactorily resolved by legal theory and some knowledge of the legal history of shareholders' agreement is necessary to understand the reasons. Very generally, many European jurisdictions showed an initial hostility to shareholders' agreements and their present recognition in the law has been secured by the persuasive power of many eminent jurists and legal theorists writing in this area of the law and advocating valid reasons for their recognition. U.S. and English jurisprudence recognized earlier the validity of a shareholders' agreement but agreements of an unlimited duration have always troubled jurists from English common law and continental civil law countries. It is prudent to limit the time duration and material encompassed with its provisions.

- For the same reasons, the shareholders' agreement should never contain any clauses that might be construed as requiring action against the interests of the company or as attempting to obligate a management organ, such as the board of directors, to vote in a particular fashion on an issue. They surely would be declared invalid and might result in the entire agreement being declared defective and unenforceable. The object of the shareholders' agreement is to protect various rights of the diverse shareholders, not manacle the board of directors.

These preliminary words of caution should not be construed as being an indication we are dealing with a marginal document, one whose use is suspect and looked on with judicial disfavor. This is certainly not true in common law jurisdictions, such as the United States and England, where their varied and flexible use has been put to imaginative application by lawyers without many problems. Presently in Europe, many jurisdictions have legislation regulating the shareholders' agreement and it is possible to affirm that its employment will also find a welcome reception there. This is to be expected as so many international joint ventures are formed between companies of common-law and civil-law origin. The shareholders' agreement is a good example of the globalization of commercial law.

6.1.6 FORMALITIES: THE PARTIES

Normally, the shareholders' agreement is a written document. Of course, it could be pieced together from correspondence among the parties. However, in some jurisdictions, a shareholders' agreement to have any effect concerning the corporation must be deposited with the company. Consequently, it is customary and advisable that the shareholders' agreement be a complete, coherent legal document prepared by counsel.

Under ordinary circumstances, all shareholders will execute it. Whether or not the corporation should also sign the shareholders' agreement is not a pacific question. Some legal writers see no need for this as the agreement intends to regulate only the conduct of the shareholders. This may be true in legal theory, but it is an eminently practical idea because at least the corporation has notice of the contents. This becomes important in those jurisdictions where there are no mandatory deposit requirements concerning the shareholders' agreement and there are multiple jurisdictions who are silent on the issue.

As an illustration, imagine that shareholder A has agreed with shareholder B that the latter may nominate two members to the board of directors. During the general assembly for the election of the board of directors, shareholder A, in violation of his agreement, and with sufficient voting power, elects the entire board of directors! If the corporation is not a party to the agreement, shareholder B is forced to go to a court of law to enforce his rights; this is a difficult remedy since shareholder A may allege, honestly or not, that shareholder B violated the agreement and it is no longer in effect. The court naturally has a dilemma that requires proof. Nor does shareholder B have an immediate practical solution. Most likely, the corporation will operate pending litigation with the board of directors elected by shareholder A.

If the corporation is a party to the agreement, shareholder B has a simpler solution since as a shareholder, he can allege, and correctly so, that the corporation cannot accept a board of directors in violation of an agreement to which it is a party. The corporation has agreed that shareholder B will elect two members to its board and this cannot be affected by disputes between shareholders A and B. Although this may appear technical, it should be evident that when possible, having the corporation sign the shareholders' agreement can and will bring added efficiency to the implementation of the shareholders' agreement. Securing the adherence of the corporation to the shareholders' agreement can lend only more support to the provisions it contains.

The same reasoning can be applied to a number of other topics. If an annual budget is agreed to, the corporation, not just the individual shareholder, is responsible for its breach. The same applies to internal controls, accounting procedures, salaries, and personnel assignments; the more the corporation is obligated with the shareholders, the more the agreement tends to become invulnerable. This is a powerful deterrent to a shareholder breaching the shareholders' agreement and hoping that while litigation is pending, the wrong is being implemented, for example, the capital expenditures are exceeding the limits agreed to.

6.1.7 FORMALITIES: DEPOSIT REQUIREMENTS

Although it cannot be ruled out, it would be rare for a jurisdiction to require a joint venture agreement to be recorded or deposited in an official conservatory. Some jurisdictions require the shareholders' agreement to be deposited at the home office of the company, thus ensuring the company will know if there is compliance with any agreed voting arrangements. Deposit requirements also make it possible to confirm the validity of representation at a general assembly. If deposit requirements are not fulfilled, the representatives of the corporation, in the event of any dispute, may have to take a position, as a judge would. This is a moot issue with many legal writers and some have suggested the shareholders will have to go to court to resolve their differing interpretations. A corporation is not a court of law. Obviously, compliance with deposit rules, if they exist, is far simpler.

6.1.8 FORMALITIES: DURATION

The shareholders' agreement displays a wide diversity as to its duration when drafted by counsel. Most jurisdictions are silent on the length of term a shareholders' agreement may have and most practitioners do not fix any term to the shareholders' agreement. We are thus faced with the most distressing of all legal situations: an agreement that is indefinite and in theory to last forever. Is this possible?

Without entering into a legal analysis of various theories, which will be inconclusive in any event, it is wise to put a term into the agreement, even if distant. An indication of a period of time is better than none. Some U.S. jurisdictions indicate a period of 5 or 10 years. Most European jurisdictions do not indicate any term. Some legal writers find it horrific that one generation of shareholders could bind their grandchildren and suggest that by law, the shareholders' agreement is terminated on the death of the last original shareholder. Wisely or not, there is much opposition in legal literature to long terms and it is prudent to adopt a middle ground: choosing a term neither too short nor indefinite.

6.1.9 PROHIBITED ASPECTS OF THE SHAREHOLDERS' AGREEMENT

A shareholders' agreement cannot either have as its object an illicit purpose or invade the competency of the management boards of the company, for example, the board of directors or a fiscal board. As to an illegal purpose, this is not a very serious issue that will deter us. We have indicated early in this book that our concern was not with how to form cartels or monopolize markets nor to suggest indirect ways to control the management of other companies.

Nor, of course, can we sanction a shareholders' agreement whose principal function is to group together shareholders to systematically offer a contentious attitude toward management when there is no good cause. Obviously, the use of shareholders' agreements toward these ends is irrelevant for our studies. Rather our interest lies with the establishment and implementation of the ordinary international joint venture, not its self-destruction. Consequently, our focus is on the legitimate use of the shareholders' agreement as a document to settle many operational aspects of the joint venture.

Concerning the shareholders' agreement encroaching on the powers of management, this is substantially dependent on how the powers of the board of directors and general assembly are divided and the flexibility of this division being recognized by the operating company's laws. Some jurisdictions are rigid as to what will be the division of powers between the board of directors and the shareholders. The shareholders' agreement must operate within this framework and will seek to influence, but not obligate, management through a disperse presence of shareholders on the management board. In this view, the shareholders elect the board of directors and the board is the supreme power, managing and hiring the officers of the corporation.

In other jurisdictions, the board can act independently, except on certain matters such as mergers, dissolutions, augments of capital, but the law permits more flexibility in the distribution of powers between the two groups. In these circumstances, the general assembly must be heard and the shareholders' agreement will affect more topics.

No matter what the jurisdiction, powers granted by legislation or the articles of the company to the board of directors cannot be curtailed or vitiated.

6.1.10 The theory of the self-enforcing, no-exit legal circuit

Agreements whose enforcement is dubious create a perilous state. People think they have rights and on their breach discover how ineffective are the remedies. The shareholders' agreement can fall easily into this category. Many rights may be regulated in the agreement but their breach may be compensated only long after the event and the damages awarded may be only an illusory victory.

If the shareholders' agreement prohibits an expenditure for fixed assets above a certain limit, and the ceiling is exceeded, and the corporation becomes insolvent, of what value is an action for damages against the defaulting majority partner who is the other signatory to the agreement? It will probably be a noncollectible judgment.

Thus, one of the fundamental functions of documentation in joint ventures is to establish what are the operating guidelines, which is what the shareholders' agreement does, and then attempt successfully to ensure they are implemented, not in contradiction or contrary to the powers of the board of directors, but rather by finding support in other clauses in the articles of the company when possible. It is the situation of more is better, referring to legal instruments.

The shareholders' agreement must be surrounded by safeguards that will ensure its effective implementation. It is possible to construct the joint venture vehicle so that there is a self-enforcing, no-exit legal circuit to compel compliance. This requires a careful construction and integration of the joint venture agreement, the shareholders' agreement, and the articles of incorporation. A sensible conception of a joint venture vehicle will include a close symbiotic relationship between the various clauses and articles composing these basic elements of a joint venture. Properly integrated, the effectiveness of the shareholders' agreement is considerably augmented.

In Chapter Eight, we will study and explore this topic in more detail and make specific suggestions. Furthermore, at the end of this chapter, there is a summary as to the preferred documentary source(s) for any particular item in the shareholders' agreement.

6.1.11 THE OWNERSHIP AND MANAGERIAL EFFECTIVENESS OF A SHAREHOLDERS' AGREEMENT

Many special rights to be conceded to owners can be inserted in the articles of incorporation. Quorum requirements, supermajority provisions for votes on issues on specific topics such as augments of capital or mergers, general assembly notices that give a true opportunity for other shareholders to attend, all can be regulated easily by the articles of incorporation. However, the range of possible topics for the articles of incorporation is limited. Other legal instruments need to be used.

U.S. corporations use by-laws, a document that regulates all the minute details of the internal bureaucracy. Numerous jurisdictions in the commercial world do not have provisions for by-laws. To some extent, a shareholders' agreement is a substitute for by-laws, setting forth many aspects of the internal governance of the company. It is only to some extent, as by-laws are normally concerned with corporate bureaucracy. The shareholders' agreement refers to a wide range of topics of substantial importance that would never be part of the by-laws.

A better appreciation of this view can be obtained by actually examining typical items inserted into the shareholders' agreement. They are a mixture of various ownership issues and managerial aspects that should form part of a shareholders' agreement. The subjects selected are those that most affect ownership and management issues. Naturally, there will be many other clauses of a strictly legal nature which will be included in the shareholders' agreement. Our sole concerns are those most directly dealing with ownership and operational issues. Some of them can be inserted in the articles of incorporation. Duplication in such a case is merely emphasis. All of them could be included in the joint venture agreement.

PART TWO

6.2 PROTECTION AGAINST UNFAIR TACTICS AND PUSH-OUT ATTEMPTS:
A GENERAL VIEW

As suggested in the Introduction, the practice of international joint ventures is the art of power. Many of the items indicated as being appropriate for a shareholders' agreement are defenses in anticipation of foul play by another partner. A partner cannot withhold dividends in an attempt to squeeze out a minority partner if the company is obligated to declare dividends with a specified cash surplus. Cash flow cannot be diminished by exorbitant salaries if this is prohibited by the shareholders' agreement. Operating profit will not disappear because the board of directors executes a contract with a member of someone's family on lucrative terms to the family (to be divided, naturally) but prejudicial to the company if insider contracts are prohibited.

In short, the construction of a list of preferred topics for a shareholders' agreement takes into account possible nasty methods used by a majority owner. This is one of the outstanding features of the shareholders' agreement as a stand-alone document. It is a neat, tidy document that can serve as a ready reference for owners basically concerned with the protection of ownership and managerial rights. Thus, the discussion developed in what follows is a mixed agenda; some items are indispensable to a well-run joint venture and others are designed to prevent abuses by one partner against another.

It is relevant to repeat a theme already reviewed. In all cases, it must be borne in mind that in any jurisdiction, the law may prescribe limits to the powers subtracted from the board of directors. Thus, the use of the shareholders' agreement is not completely subject to the will of the parties in every jurisdiction. Nevertheless, as a general rule, there is a great deal of flexibility permitted.

The ensuing discussion reviews the typical problems joint ventures create.

6.2.1 AMENDMENTS TO THE COMPANY ARTICLES

The very first precaution to be taken is to establish a high supermajority for the amendment to any articles of the joint venture company. If this step is not taken, then whatever rights are established in the company articles or affect the company by virtue of its being a signatory to the shareholders' agreement can be destroyed, of course, by simply amending them. Scheming shareholders have no limits. If the shareholders' agreement stipulates shareholder B will have the right to 2 members on the board of directors (not expressed, note, in a percentage), a simple amendment of the articles raising from 4 to 6 the number of directors destroys the deadlock power of shareholder B.

When the company articles have been the careful result of negotiations between the parties, particularly in the formation of a joint venture company, the entire benefits of these negotiations can be swept aside if one owner, through voting power, can alter the articles. The higher the threshold voting requirements, the more secure will be the rights of the other partners.

6.2.2 NAME OF THE JOINT VENTURE COMPANY

A great deal of goodwill is rightly associated with the service or trademark of a company. The name of the joint venture company may bear, in part or entirely, the name of one of the partners, for example, US Petroleum and Gas Corp., S.A., a French subsidiary of a U.S. company (US Petroleum and Gas Corp.). Should the U.S. partner at some future date withdraw from the joint venture, the U.S. partner may not want the French company to continue to use its name. The reason is clear. Not being a partner, the U.S. company has no control over what commercial events may occur in the French subsidiary and possible consequences to its name.

On the other hand, even if a partner prior to the sale, the U.S. company may not be able to muster the necessary votes to change the name of the subsidiary as this act requires a change to the company articles. Thus, as often happens in the law, a seemingly simple task—a change of name—requires a legal act, in this case, a general assembly meeting, or its substitute, to achieve a change of name.

The average joint venture does not endure indefinitely. There is frequently an exit and entrance of new partners. Many potential sellers, when faced with the prospect of not being able to withdraw the use of their name from a joint venture, will not sell. The possible consequences are too substantial, a potential liability for the acts of others through the inducement generated by third parties believing they are dealing with an authorized agent, in our example, a subsidiary of US Petroleum and Gas Corp.

The shareholders' agreement can cover this contingency easily and provide for the change of name of the joint venture company should the partner who lent his name withdraw from the corporate joint venture. The joint venture company will naturally be a party to this agreement as it concerns a company asset: its name.

6.2.3 RIGHT TO INFORMATION

Most commercial codes and the laws affecting companies provide for shareholders or other forms of equity ownership to have access to and to be able to demand information relevant to the company in which they have an ownership interest. Oftentimes, there is a minimum interest, a threshold amount, beyond which this right then can be exercised. The statutory *right to information* is often curt, brief, and may only refer to being able to see the resolution book of the board of directors and certain financial information. Frequently, this statutory right is repeated in the articles of incorporation so that all owners are aware of its existence. This does not amplify its scope.

The right to information that is contemplated for insertion in the shareholders' agreement is more diverse, more demanding, more factual, and would not be normally inserted in the company articles. The partners should have the right to monthly financial statements sent to the home office in the language of the partner. The minutes of all meetings of the board of directors should be subject to the same requirement. However, besides financial information, it should be clearly agreed that any partner may request any information it wants, without restrictions as to capital participation, as long as it is held in confidence. This is another reason why the company should be a party to the agreement. By being a party, the obligation is enforceable against the joint venture and the delivery of the information is assured.

6.2.4 DISTRIBUTION OF DIVIDENDS

Most jurisdictions state that the shareholders "have a right to receive the profits." Nevertheless, these are accounting concepts and oftentimes there is not agreement among the various partners as to how to define profits nor what will be done with the profits. Application of funds is often an ardent discussion. Not uncommonly, this matter is regulated by the shareholders' agreement.

Prior to the formation of the joint venture vehicle, the parties agree what will be done with profit over the next few years or even as a permanent philosophy. Will there be consistent and continual reinvestment? Will this only happen after each partner receives an agreed rate of return on its capital contribution? These and other related accounting issues are both ownership issues and management decisions easily regulated by the shareholders' agreement and further developed in Chapter Eight.

6.2.5 NOMINATION TO BOARD OF DIRECTORS

If there is a special class of shares, it is a simple matter for each class to have the right to nominate a specified number of directors to the board. This would be stated in the articles of incorporation. However, particularly in an acquisition, this provision may not exist for different classes of shares and there may be strong resistance on the part of remaining partners to alter the corporate statutes. This means then that the only recourse for a minority buyer to have any special nomination rights concerning seats on the board of directors is through the shareholders' agreement with the signature of the other partners. Without the willingness of the other partners to execute a shareholders' agreement, the prospective purchaser should desist.

When we are dealing with the formation of a joint venture, great care must be exercised in drafting and ensuring that minority interests will have a representation on the supreme management organ of the joint venture company. The shareholders' agreement must clearly condition the formation of the joint venture by calling for the company, as soon as it comes into existence, to become a party to the agreement.

6.2.6 VOTING ON THE BOARD OF DIRECTORS

Although it has been urged as a separate document, it is not yet frequent for joint ventures to have a complementary contract that regulates voting on the board of directors. This is normally handled by a clause in the shareholders' agreement. The matters to be considered will be what topics can be passed by a simple majority, what are those that require a supermajority, and what are the items that must have unanimous consent.

Such voting provisions are best remitted to the articles of incorporation where they constitute a binding obligation on the conduct of the board of directors; such a clause is more and more common in the formation of an international joint venture. As stated before, in an acquisition, there may not be such a clause in the articles of the company and the other partners do not want to make any changes. The only alternative is the shareholders' agreement.

However, an agreement between partners as to how members on the board will vote is not an agreement between the members. There is a substantial difference. It is true that as a practical matter, the nominees of partners consult their principals on important issues. But this is not a legal obligation, and once a vote is properly taken on the board of directors, it is valid even if it violates the terms of the shareholders' agreement.

The parties may agree that on routine matters, a simple majority is sufficient. On the other hand, disbursements above an agreed ceiling might require two-thirds of the votes and augments of capital might easily necessitate unanimous approval. It can be seen that dependent on the nominations each partner can make and the total number of board members, a minority partner can have an influence disproportionate to his equity participation.

The same reasoning can apply to any issue that in the jurisdiction will be within the province of the board of directors. This will include many operational items. Annual budgets, capital expenditures, asset disposals, expansion plans, and approval of salaries are normally within the competency of the board of directors. Management, whether majority or minority, must review the various matters that will fall within the province of the board of directors and strive to achieve those voting requirements that will render majority tyranny on major issues impossible, for example, a unanimous voting requirement or a supermajority in which the vote of the minority partner then becomes indispensable.

As to how to further buttress these provisions in a shareholders' agreement, a solution will be found in the division of powers between the board of directors, or other management structure, and the general assembly. Such matters will be considered again in Chapter Eight.

6.2.7 LOCATION OF BOARD MEETINGS, NONVOTING OBSERVERS, AND TECHNICAL COMMITTEES

It is a sensible provision to require board meetings to take place on a periodic basis at the various home sites of the partners. This affords each party to become acquainted with the culture of the other partner and hopefully bridge any difficulties caused by language. Also, contact with the other party's installations and personnel creates a personal bond that helps overcome communication obstacles due to language and perhaps different business methods.

Additionally, if one of the partners does not intend to be present at many board meetings, a clause should be contained in the shareholders' agreement whereby the absent nominee of the partner can send a nonvoting observer to the board meeting. This make it possible for the absentee partner to be better informed, particularly if the nonvoting observer speaks the language of all the partners.

Additionally, beyond the formalities of the board of directors lie many areas of the company necessitating exchange of information between all partners, areas where perhaps each partner has a specific expertise to contribute. In these situations, the creation of informal nonstructured committees of personnel from the partners will assist in forging a solid, helpful working ambiance.

Of course, the corporate articles will provide for meetings on a regular basis and even state they may be held out of the jurisdiction; but the alternate method, the presence of an informal nonvoting observer, the setting up of technical committees, is more gracefully accomplished through the privacy of a shareholders' agreement. Furthermore, these provisions, if they are put into the corporate articles, apply to all owners, present and future. It may be easily the case that the concept of alternate site meetings is only a temporary measure, one conceded by the other partner as a measure designed to facilitate a more congenial working environment that will be eventually abandoned in favor of having the meetings always at the home office. It is far easier to delete such a requirement from the shareholders' agreement than to alter the company articles, at times a tedious, bureaucratic formality.

6.2.8 SECRET PURCHASE OF MAJORITY SHARES

When there are no rights of preference established by any of the documents creating the joint venture, each partner is free to market and sell his equity interests. It may happen that in a clear majority/minority cleavage, for example, 81/19 percent division, a buyer might approach the majority owner, pay a substantial premium, and then later offer to buy the minority shares at a reduced price, coupling this with implied threats of a management that is not very concerned about the rights of the minority.

This would most likely happen in a company with few partners, where one of the original partners is deceased, and the heirs do not feel the same business loyalty to the minority partner. Does the majority owner have a duty to inform the minority partner of the offer? If not, what can be done? These questions will find varying responses dependent on the jurisdiction.

A practical solution is to circumvent potential litigation and to avoid the problem entirely. This can be done in the shareholders' agreement by inserting a requirement that, even without restrictive transfer clauses, the partners have a duty to inform each other of possible offers. This takes out the element of surprise, makes it possible for a minority partner to consider his alternatives, to understand the terms of the sale without relying on the version proffered by the purchaser, and perhaps even to make a better offer of purchase to the selling interest.

6.2.9 ONE PARTNER BUYS EQUITY INTERESTS AND DOES NOT INFORM THE OTHER PARTNERS

Closely related to the buy-out-the-majority and intimidate-the-minority strategy is the situation in which in a joint venture with a reasonable number of partners, perhaps 6 or 7, one partner begins to purchase the interests of others, and if there are no restriction transfers, what might have been a fair distribution of power becomes a majority/minority relationship. The consequences of a majority/minority relationship, which was not the original design of the joint venture, can be avoided by a clause in the shareholders' agreement compelling either predisclosure of the intent or what would be better, compelling the possible seller to prorate his sale among the remaining owners, or even conduct an auction procedure within the company. Of course, this amounts to a transfer restriction.

6.2.10 ANNUAL BUDGET, CAPITAL EXPENDITURES, EXPANSION PLANS, AND DISPOSAL OF ASSETS

Much information relating to the financial operations cannot be inserted into the articles of the company. Financial details are not for public record. Agreements between partners as to how much they will spend will only find their recitation in the shareholders' agreement. The annual budget is a typical example.

During negotiations, the partners may have had budget projects for a number of years, anywhere from 3 to 5, and this is a beneficial obligation that should be inserted in the shareholders' agreement, and, if possible, the company should be a party. The most frequent managerial conflicts that arise are precisely with how much money is being spent.

The same is true of capital expenditures, expansion plans, and disposal of assets. Everything that has been said of the annual budget applies with equal logic to all these categories. The more the financial management of the joint venture is subject to specific guidelines, the less likely conflict will arise. This is because a consensus prior to the formation of the joint venture has been reached.

6.2.11 LOAN PROVISIONS, GUARANTEES, AND ENCUMBRANCES

The obtaining of loans by the joint venture company encumbers the assets of the company and of course reduces the net worth of each partner in the joint venture vehicle. There is nothing more distressing to an absentee owner than to receive financial documents indicating the existence of new loans agreed to by management. It is prudent and beneficial for the partners to have an agreement as to the limits of loan liability the managers of the joint venture vehicle can contract. In legal forms other than share corporations, for example, private limited liability companies, there may be one manager, one person who is administering the company, and his powers are substantial. This authority must be curbed.

What is applicable to loans is of course applicable to guarantees assumed by the company. A guarantee becomes a loan when the guarantor is called on to make good the default. There are many ways to create debt and the shareholders' agreement will contain broad enough language to encompass the typical forms of debt creation. In the initial phase of a joint venture, working capital needs may be insufficient and there is a strong temptation to resort to debt financing. Reasonable limits on the assumption of debt established by the shareholders' agreement will ensure that there is a convergence of opinion among the owners.

6.2.12 PURCHASE OR DISPOSAL OF EQUITY INTERESTS

The same prudence concerning the creation of debt must be exercised by the management of the joint venture company concerning the acquisition or disposal of interests in other companies. Such assets are normally significant. The board of directors of the closely held company should have preestablished guidelines and, when possible, subject to the confirmation of the general assembly. This is particularly important in the everyman international joint venture that is not intended to be a holding company.

6.2.13 DISPUTE RESOLUTION

Normally, the articles of incorporation of the joint venture will recite that any dispute or litigation between the members will be subject to the law of the forum (the host country) or arbitration. Practically all jurisdictions have their own arbitration procedures and there are many international arbitration groups, such as the International Chamber of Commerce at Paris, the London Court of International Arbitration, the American Arbitration Association in New York. In Chapter Nine, we will review the various alternatives as to how partners to a joint venture may resolve their differences and what are the advantages and disadvantages of each method.

For the moment, it is convenient to call attention to one informal mechanism that could not be recited in the articles of a company. This is what is denominated an *internal dispute clause*. Its function is to defuse conflict at the operating company level and have the matters referred to a superior hierarchical level where if the conflict is a clash of personalities, at least this element is removed. Often what is seen as a crucial issue at stake at the board of directors' level is viewed as a mere ripple to be overcome as quickly as possible without causing any disruption to the joint venture.

A typical approach is to require the representatives of the partners in the host country to submit their grievances to the managing directors at the home office of each partner but that the joint venture continue to operate. At the higher managerial level, the relevant boards may call in outside experts or attempt to resolve the matter between themselves within a specified period of time, for example, anywhere from 45 to 90 days. This road to removing local conflict to a distant shore is very beneficial, usually productive, resulting in a solution.

As an informal, unstructured process, its most adequate expression will be in the shareholders' agreement.

6.2.14 LITIGATION AUTHORIZED BY THE BOARD OF DIRECTORS

The commencement of major litigation should always require a supermajority of votes by the partners. Defending a lawsuit is almost involuntary, but initiating a lawsuit is costly and a step only to be taken when there is a high consensus of opinion amongst the partners. Although the decision may be taken by the board of directors, the shareholders' agreement can provide that such a step requires a specified majority of votes by the partners. Alternatively, the matter can be covered by a provision in the articles of the company as already indicated for other topics.

6.2.15 NEW LABOR POLICIES

The introduction of new labor policies, such as profit sharing, reduction of hours, layoffs, reorganization of the personnel scheme, and bonuses, may not have the intended results, and a disturbed labor force means an unprofitable joint venture. Without intending to limit the examples, any major labor policy before being introduced should require the unanimous consent of all partners with substantial equity interests.

6.2.16 PROVIDING ADDITIONAL CAPITAL

Not infrequently, a joint venture company is initially undercapitalized. The partners want to start slowly, to see if their market predictions are correct. In countries where foreign investment is regulated, there may be a minimum capital requirement or the financial projections for a certain initial period may be subject to review. The working capital requirements of the joint venture company may augment substantially in the early years. Rather than having to debate at a critical stage what further contributions of capital should be made and how the money may be raised, it is circumspect to have the shareholders' agreement stipulate that when certain conditions are fulfilled, for example, a market share platform, then the partners will make additional contributions to capital in a defined quantity. Such a clause finds its ideal expression in the shareholders' agreement.

6.2.17 AUGMENTS OF CAPITAL, ISSUANCE OF AUTHORIZED SHARES, AND STOCK DIVIDENDS

The caution needed concerning augments of capital has been discussed already. Although appearing to benefit the company, by increasing its stated capital, an argument of capital can be used to put pressure on a minority owner to sell his share. This is because in order to accomplish an augment of capital, either the company is going to use accumulated reserves or it will call for further subscriptions to the capital. Either case can create a problem for a particular owner.

Utilizing reserves means there will be less funds available for dividend distribution. Frequently, corporations are formed with a permitted capital, but there is a first issue. Should there be a second issue and a shareholder cannot afford to make the purchase, the shares not bought can be purchased by the other shareholders. This very quickly disrupts any planned balance of power in the original equity arrangement.

Undesirable results also can be achieved with stock dividends. In order to achieve this accounting operation, it will be necessary to transfer, from surplus, funds into the capital account. Once again, there may not be a declaration of dividends or, if made, a very modest amount. This can cause concern to a minority shareholder dependent on dividends for needed income. Augments of capital, issue of further shares and stock dividends, should require approval by the general assembly and a high percentage of votes, enough to protect the minority interest. If this is solely a function of the board of directors, recourse will be had to the technique of a board of directors' agreement.

6.2.18 ACCOUNTING POLICIES

When entities such as U.S. companies go abroad, they quickly discover the enormous variety of accounting methods and many of them do not adhere to GAAP, general accepted accounting principles. Improper accounting procedures, those that do not conform to acceptable international standards, those that deviate substantially from GAAP, are a source of strife and distrust after a very brief interval in any international joint venture. It is obligatory for the parties to agree in the shareholders' agreement as to the accounting policies to be adopted because this is always a sensitive issue in international joint ventures.

6.2.19 EXORBITANT SALARIES: CONTRACTS

One way of receiving dividends if you are a majority partner is to become a managing partner and pay yourself well for this difficult task. Or, as a majority partner controlling the board of directors, the appointment of officers, and key employees, there is always the alternative of employing the whole family. Such situations can be avoided by the proper language in a shareholders' agreement.

In order for the minority being protected from having income siphoned off by a majority partner through the board of directors having a contract executed with a third party in which a majority partner has an undisclosed interest, there should be a clause in the shareholders' agreement stipulating that such contracts are void and cannot be executed. It prevents an abuse of power and confidence. Worded generally, it applies to all partners, both the majority and the minority. What has been said for the company and partners applies with equal force and reasoning to contracts with directors.

6.2.20 APPROPRIATION OF CORPORATE ASSETS

Closely allied to the problem of unfair contracts is preventing one partner with management functions from utilizing company funds for general expenses, which can include unnecessary expense accounts, uncontrolled use of credit cards, and certainly undeserved holidays. This problem is another view of the right to have information. It would not be conducive to a partnership spirit to insist for detailed limits on various items in the shareholders' agreement. What might be established in the smaller joint venture company with a reduced number of partners is a general amount, an estimation of what will be entertainment expenses, traveling expenses, all of this included in the agreed annual budget so as not to create an atmosphere of distrust.

6.2.21 SALE OF CORPORATE ASSETS OR CONTRACTS WITH THIRD PARTIES

With a scheming partner in a management position, it may happen that this partner forms a company he controls, although his ownership is concealed, and then assets or products are sold at very favorable prices permitting a lucrative resale or contracts are executed calling for the furnishing of services highly favoring the third party company. While concealment is just that, a prohibition on this conduct eliminates the argument of proving unfairness in the dealings, a probable requirement needed to set aside the transaction. The shareholders' agreement should provide for any such dealings to be obligatorily divulged prior to execution of any contract.

6.2.22 PROFITING FROM INSIDER INFORMATION OR OTHER OPPORTUNITIES

It is inevitable that directors and managers in a position of authority will learn of other opportunities that, instead of being offered to the company, are directly, but mostly indirectly, appropriated for personal use. Instead of having to litigate whether there is a duty to disclose, it is far simpler for the shareholders' agreement to provide that such behavior is prohibited.

6.2.23 MATERIAL CONTRACTS ABOVE A CERTAIN AMOUNT

When the joint venture has substantial commercial operations, a sagacious precaution is to require all major contracts above a certain amount to require a high percentage of votes on the board of directors, sufficient so that the consent of the minority partner is required to achieve the platform. This prevents *insider trading,* in which the local partner favors a particular supplier without getting competitive bids and instead receives a *kickback.*

6.2.24 PLACEMENT OF KEY PERSONNEL

The proper administration of the joint venture is significantly dependent on the assignment of key personnel to sensitive management areas. If one or more of the partners intend to make certain appointments, or to have this right, this should be expressly stated in the shareholders' agreement and the company should be a party. This ensures that this all-important right will not be overridden by the board of directors or simply breached by one of the partners, particularly if the latter has a majority vote. Selection of personnel, and other matters affecting personnel now to be discussed, are best treated in the shareholders' agreement.

6.2.25 LANGUAGE ABILITY OF PERSONNEL

Although not often considered, as it does not occur to the negotiators, having key personnel speak the language of the partners fosters a harmonious collaboration. Perhaps it is not always possible, especially in countries where the local language is totally strange to the foreign partner. When this is not the case, expectations of key executives who can speak various languages are realistic and should be an obligation, unless recruitment proves impossible.

6.2.26 TERMINATION OF EMPLOYEES

All partners with any material interest in the joint venture company should have the power to discharge any employee for cause that is not arbitrary (purely personal) or discriminatory (racial or religious). Inserting a requirement that the termination must be for *reasonable cause* or *just cause* is tantamount to rendering termination impossible.

Reasonable and just cause refer to standards amounting to grave conduct, which is rarely the case. If termination is possible, and not all jurisdictions allow termination of employees, a partner not wanting an employee is a better partner when he can exercise this judgment. It prevents staffing the company with employees for reasons other than competency. It is rare for such a provision to be applicable other than to key personnel, but of course the clause should be worded in very general terms so as to be applicable with great flexibility.

6.2.27 PROHIBITION ON DISMISSED EMPLOYEES WORKING FOR ONE OF THE PARTNERS

Very often a foreign company will form an international joint venture with a local entity that may have several other companies and the joint venture constitutes an opportunity to enter into a new field. The local partner may second an employee from one of his other companies to hold a key position in the joint venture. This is common and ordinarily presents no problems.

Using a trusted employee may confer on the local partner a belief and trust in the competency of the management of the joint venture. However, it may happen that sometimes the transferred employee is not entirely impartial, or his position is used to gather information for use by the other companies belonging to his employer. There may be other abuses.

Discipline, or fear of it, is not possible if the employee knows that on his termination he can return to his former employment. A clause in the shareholders' agreement prohibiting a dismissed employee from again working for his former employer is a strong stimulus to perform his functions in conformity with standards of excellence.

6.2.28 CHANGE OF CONTROL, DECEASE OF A PARTNER, OR PROLONGED ILLNESS

If companies are partners, there is usually little concern as to personal circumstances of one of the partners affecting the validity of the joint venture. But this is not always true. When corporations are partners, there can be a change of ownership in the corporation-owner that results in a different management style or different objectives, and the other partners believe the joint venture will no longer succeed or its future is seriously compromised. With individuals as partners, there are different concerns, such as death, having to deal with heirs, prolonged illness, or bankruptcy of a partner. A shareholders' agreement can deal with these by simply listing the relevant conditions that are of concern to everyone and then introducing compulsory buy–sell provisions.

6.2.29 TERMINATION OF THE JOINT VENTURE

Under this heading, we are not only referring to situations of bankruptcy of one partner, or an attachment of a partner's assets, which may include the interest in the joint venture, or even conduct by one partner that brings into disrepute the joint venture. Many joint venture agreements provide that such events are cause for automatic buyout provisions of the offending partner. Nor are we referring only to dissolution or agreements to sell off the assets of the joint venture and put an end to its activities, what might be called a *voluntary termination* of the joint venture.

We are also referring to *deadlocks,* one of the more troublesome areas of joint ventures. This is when the partners cannot seem to agree and a general malaise becomes prevalent. A stupor and lethargy assume control; the maneuvers begin to either force one partner out or reduce losses and sell out as quickly as possible. A properly structured joint venture should reduce substantially this possibility and this can be done by requiring specific majority votes on a wide range of issues and other protective mechanisms we will discuss. However, there always exists the probability that if there is no legal deadlock, then there is a moral deadlock." "We don't agree with these expenditures, but we cannot claim they are in violation of any agreement we made." Managerial philosophies change. What was agreed to a decade ago may seem completely inappropriate at the moment.

The solution is to identify what will constitute deadlock and what will be the consequences. The entire subject area is technically treated in the shareholders' agreement. It is necessary to compile a list, albeit probably general, of what will be clear signs of a deadlock. Typical indications of a deadlock are as follows:

- The board members are continually, evenly split on major policy issues and neither side can muster the needed majority.
- The same happens at the general assembly of the shareholders or owners.
- Important contracts to which one of the partners is a party are legally terminated, or not renewed, which places the success of the joint venture in jeopardy. The owners cannot agree on a substitution.
- The management of one of the partners changes because of change of control at the partner level and there is a clear clash of management philosophies. There are no violations of any agreements, but there is complete disharmony between the managers of the partners.
- The joint venture needs capital, but the partners cannot agree on how to capitalize it further nor can further financing be arranged because of the lack of harmony between the partners.
- The joint venture return on capital is far below expectations.

Each joint venture will have its own deadlock signals that will be incorporated into the shareholders' agreement. The solution to such a situation should be anticipated prior to the execution of the shareholders'

agreement. This is, of course, the ideal strategy, the proper planning before the event happens. Often, this does not occur and the parties limp
through the problem, eventually coming to a solution. When there is a
thought-out policy, the partners, and here each will have his own perspective,
should anticipate whether they would wish to remain in the joint venture or
sell out. We considered what this implies earlier in Chapter Five.

6.2.30 CONTINUATION OF BUSINESS AFTER THE JOINT VENTURE HAS BEEN TERMINATED

When the joint venture is terminated, the partners agreeing that it has
served its purpose or that collaboration has become impossible, what is
the permitted future course of action? Can one of the partners start up the
business again, in its own name? This will naturally depend on the economic strength of each partner. Generally, it is the local partner who wishes
to continue, having learned the business. One solution is to have the shareholders' agreement prevent either partner from inaugurating the business,
for a reasonable time, and let the negotiation process work out a
solution. The qualification of a reasonable time is a requirement of antitrust legislation, when existing, that does not favor absolute prohibitions
on economic activity.

Another solution is for one party to know beforehand what it wants,
and perhaps if we are dealing with a multinational it will agree the local
partner can commence again with a license fee for a reasonable period. The
philosophy here is that the student, having learned, on graduation should
pay his enrollment fees. These solutions, and others that management and
counsel will suggest for any particular joint venture, find appropriate regulation in the shareholders' agreement.

6.2.31 DISPOSAL OF ASSETS AFTER THE JOINT VENTURE HAS BEEN TERMINATED

The thoughts expressed about a future course of action in the event of a
termination must implicate the disposal of assets, if there are any. This
would naturally occur when we are dealing with an industrial complex. If
the export market dries up, it may be natural that the parties will want to
agreeably terminate the joint venture. What will happen to the multimillion-
dollar industrial complex sitting in the free trade area?

Under the rules of dissolution and liquidation, either the assets are sold
and the cash distributed or there is an agreement between the partners as

to who will receive specified assets. In moderate capital or service joint ventures, the disposal of assets is unlikely to become a serious issue. With large-scale projects, the partners should decide, before they proceed, what will happen to the complex should the joint venture terminate. The solution negotiated will be reflected naturally in an appropriate clause in the shareholders' agreement.

6.2.32 POST-TERMINATION OBLIGATIONS

Although the joint venture may be terminated, there will be various promises assumed prior to its formation that will continue to have their effect after the legal collaboration has ended and their importance must not be underestimated. Typical concerns are as follows:

- *Confidential information.* During the joint venture, much information of a confidential nature will be obtained as to the business and commerce of each participant. Access to highly important commercial secrets is inevitable. Visits to each other's home offices, attendance at joint meetings of the respective board of directors, reviews of intercompany memoranda will enhance significantly the commercial knowledge each partner will have of the other. The shareholders' agreement must sanctify this knowledge and prevent its use by others. As it is likely due diligence procedures will require the execution of an agreement concerning confidential agreement, the latter should not be confused with posttermination requirements.
- *Continuation of contractual relationships.* Partners in a joint venture company may quite frequently have independent commercial relationships not related to the joint venture. Participants in a joint venture involving the operation of a megashopping center can quite easily be suppliers to each other of goods in their separate capacities. Although termination of a joint venture should not ordinarily affect other, independent contractual relationships, the logic of litigation can be crafty and wily. It is comforting if the shareholders' agreement makes it clear that whatever reasons surge for the dismemberment of the joint venture, other separate contractual relationships are not affected.
- *Noncompetition.* We have referred to this topic before. It is an area of the law in which perceptions of justice are often in conflict. Many jurisdictions do not sanction restrictions on the commercial or professional activities of parties, as they restrict competition, for bargaining strength is often not equal amongst contracting parties, and there is a strong social

policy in support of individual freedom. On the other hand, parties who train others and contribute to substantial formation in the hopes of a continuing collaboration, beyond a disappointment, do not relish seeing their efforts fail and be resurrected in the form of a competitor. Between these two currents of thought lies a possible compromise in which the restrictions on the time and geographical area will be of moderate duration and territory.

• Within the fear of training a competitor is the realistic vision that a former partner may begin to solicit employees of his former partner to assist him in mounting a possible competitive enterprise. Here, legal concerns shift from a restriction on competition to unfair business practices. We thus can expect clauses prohibiting the solicitation of employees of a former partner as having moral support and legal approval.

PART THREE

6.3 TEN PRACTICAL CONSIDERATIONS

Without question, a shareholders' agreement will have a substantial influence in the life of the joint venture. Besides all the operational aspects that have been indicated earlier, there will be various legal clauses inserted. Nevertheless, what we want finally is an agreement that is effective, practical, comprehensible, and produces the desired results. Some general observations as a reference during negotiations may be helpful:

• Explain in the preamble of the document why a shareholders' agreement has been executed. This is useful when there is a dispute or litigation.
• Distinguish very carefully between obligations affecting the owners and their nominees, the directors. The independence of directors cannot be compromised prior to their election. As a practical matter, nominees do follow the advice of their principals, but this should not be a contractual obligation. A semblance of independence must be maintained; otherwise the shareholders' agreement will be considered an invasion of the legal responsibilities of the directors or other form of management utilized.
• If there seems any doubt as to a possible derogation of the powers of the directors, a good fallback position is to have the shareholders' agreement recite that whatever amendments are necessary to the company

articles to implement the provisions of the shareholders' agreement will be made.

- Another alternative is to have the shareholders' agreement recite in a separate clause that the articles of the company will be prepared in harmony with the agreement. This is of course only possible when the parties are forming a company for the first time.
- Ensure that there is no conflict between the shareholders' agreement and the company articles. If there is, very likely the company articles will prevail.
- To the extent possible, the language should be direct, simple, accessible. Oftentimes people who are not lawyers are called on to interpret a clause.
- The shareholders' agreement should recite that the invalidity of one clause will not affect the general validity of the agreement. The house should not be demolished because there is a leak in the roof. This requires an attentive examination as many joint ventures involve multiple documents.
- Avoid an indefinite term. Once an agreement is reached on a reasonable term, then there can be added a renewal clause whereby the parties agree to renew on the same terms and conditions unless there has been a radical modification of the conditions that led to the formation of the joint venture. This is not as illusory as it would appear. Many jurisdictions impose a good faith requirement in dealing, and if we are structuring a joint venture involving responsible companies or parties, the obligation to renew is normally honored, or it starts a new negotiation process.
- All shareholders or owners should sign and there should be a clause requiring the company to sign when formed, or if it is already formed. The more signatories, the less likely there will be exceptions or deviations to the agreement.
- There must be a requirement that any transferee of any equity interest will sign the shareholders' agreement or a separate document known as an adherence agreement.

The preceding list of items recommended to be put into a shareholders' agreement can be amplified, or reduced, in conformity with the particular international joint venture. The previous examination has been to underscore the relevancy of the item for managerial purposes. In preparation for a study in Chapter Eight as to what further steps can be taken to ensure the proper implementation of the clauses that will be of aid to management, it is convenient to emphasize once again that the mere recital of an agreed obligation or special right conceded in the shareholders' agreement is no assurance that it will be automatically enforceable. The knowledge that the clause negotiated will be applied can receive further help: other clauses in other documents, principally the articles of the company, that provide support to, and prevent breach of, the clause in question.

Prior to initiating our detailed list it is appropriate to again confirm that any item that should be in a shareholders' agreement of course can be inserted into a joint venture agreement. Where the text indicates that the shareholders' agreement is the proper or only document that can be used, the words *joint venture agreement* can be substituted. Although these documents serve basically different purposes, many practitioners, for reasons perhaps of expediency, do not draft a separate shareholders' agreement.

This is unfortunate because when two possible sources exist for protecting rights, one may prove more effective than another for reasons we cannot anticipate at the time of creating the joint venture. The following schedule is based on the more important topics that arise in international joint ventures and why one documentary source is better than another, if such a choice exists. The discussion is a review of material just considered but in more summary form and with less explanation as to its relevance.

Our objective is to underscore when a clause in the shareholders' agreement also can find support in another company document. Oftentimes it cannot.

Part Four

6.4 Amendments to the Company Articles

The company articles must provide that they can be altered only on a supermajority vote of an acceptable percentage to the partners present at the general assembly or other organ where voting takes place by the owners. The reason for this is clear. Requiring a high voting quorum (this is the technical phrase to describe an obligatory presence) eliminates the diluting of any rights receiving special protection in the company articles or for that matter in the shareholders' agreement.

If there is a clear conflict between any provision in the shareholders' agreement and the company articles, the latter will prevail being a more solemn act. Particularly in Europe, the company articles are seen as a social pact, an agreement between equity owners, and contract principles will apply. If two contracts conflict, the one with the more solemn formalities will prevail, that is, the company articles.

The entire shareholders' agreement must be protected from adulteration by the articles of the joint venture company requiring:

- a high qualified majority vote on major issues
- alteration of the shareholders' agreement
- presence of a specified percentage of owners at the general assembly

6.4.1 NAME OF THE JOINT VENTURE COMPANY

Although the shareholders' agreement can easily regulate this aspect of one partner lending its brand name in some form to the joint venture company, fortunately, this can also find simple, statutory support in the articles of the company. It is only necessary to declare that the name of the company will be what it is while a certain partner owns part of the equity. On any transfer of this equity interest, the name will have to be changed.

6.4.2 RIGHT TO INFORMATION

As previously stated, most jurisdictions confer on shareholders the right to demand access to various items of information, holding the same in confidence, but often there is a minimum equity interest imposed. Such rights are general and limited to the most basic financial information. Assuming the articles of the company could lower the percentage threshold, there still remains the scope of the information subject to request.

In legal theory, it is permissible to insert a detailed list of what any owner could request from management in the company articles. Although possible, it would surely convey the image of partners who had little confidence in their managers, or else, overzealous owners anxious to monitor all aspects of the administration.

Either alternative indicates that it is best to save the minutiae for the shareholders' agreement, but it would be also beneficial to repeat the general right to information in the company articles, perhaps even amplifying the vagueness of the material that could be requested and lowering the percentage requirements or not imposing any. A broad sweeping charter provision confers substantial protection to all partners.

6.4.3 DISTRIBUTION OF DIVIDENDS

Similar to the right to information, most jurisdictions state that the owners have a right to *profit*. The word *dividends* may not be used in the applicable legislation. Moreover, it is traditional when drafting company articles to insert a clause that after reserve requirements, the owners will participate in the profits. The problem is how will profits be determined? What will be done with the surplus, if there is one? Reinvestment? Research and development? Are these decisions to be conditioned only when a certain level of dividend distribution is possible? Such questions could not be remitted to the articles of incorporation. The shareholders' agreement is the only place where all the various criteria can be set forth.

6.4.4 NOMINATION TO THE BOARD OF DIRECTORS

The right to nominate a specified number of members to the board of directors is an item that can and should find double support: once in the shareholders' agreement and once in the articles of incorporation. This is one of the few items that can find expression with ease in the company articles and it is in accordance with traditional professional practice. Various alternatives exist, such as a special class of shares or, if we are not dealing with a share corporation, simply conferring on one or more partners the right to nominate a specified amount of the administration. All of this can be stipulated in the articles of the company. Thus, company articles and the shareholders' agreement complement one another. The signature of the joint venture company when formed to the shareholders' agreement will ensure successful implementation of this right.

6.4.5 VOTING ON THE BOARD OF DIRECTORS

Indicating how votes will be counted on what items can be, and often is, a subject for the shareholders' agreement. However, it must be remembered that the board of directors, or other management entity, has a duty to the owners to discharge its functions with good judgment and exercising an independent will. Consequently, having the shareholders' agreement, to which only the shareholders and perhaps the corporation will be signatories, cannot and will not be binding on the directors as to how they will vote, only how their votes will be counted.

Whatever the signatories agree to is not going to bind the directors. That the directors are nominated does not alter their independent status. Judges, when elected, are not beholden to the political party that nominated them, nor does anyone expect they will be. In fact, the proper place to establish voting procedures, what majority is needed on what issue, is the articles of incorporation. Unfortunately, the articles cannot become a laundry list of all possible voting issues. It is preferable practice to only indicate in the articles of the company the more important, vital issues, such as augments of capital, mergers, and dissolutions, but preserve for the shareholders' agreement the more operational issues.

A further support document could be the board of directors' agreement that will not dictate how to vote but how many votes are needed on a particular issue. For this important topic, an excess of documents may irritate the clients but eventually prove providential.

6.4.6 LOCATION OF BOARD MEETINGS, NONVOTING OBSERVERS, AND TECHNICAL COMMITTEES

It is necessary to have language in the articles of the company as to meetings, when they will be held, language as to whether meetings may be held out of the jurisdiction, and even how the presence of directors will be determined. Nonetheless, when much detail is needed, such as nonvoting observers, alternating meetings, and setting up technical committees, then this material must find its expression in the shareholders' agreement.

The articles of a company are not for discretionary material, since they offer no definite guidance and one cannot know if they are being satisfied or not. However, the shareholders' agreement can be less dogmatic, more suggestive, without infringing the certainty the law requires. If the shareholders' agreement says, "when possible . . . ," this is inserting an element of goodwill and good faith into the conduct of the owners. There is a criterion in the law for determining this state, although it is certainly difficult to have rigorous standards predefined. Thus, the company articles and shareholders' agreement must complement one another.

6.4.7 SECRET PURCHASE OF MAJORITY SHARES

When there are restrictive transfer provisions in the articles of the company, the danger of a majority bloc sale to an unfriendly third party will be considerably reduced if not nonexistent. In the absence of such a clause, the efficacy of restrictions in the shareholders' agreement is moot. With no deposit requirements applicable, the purchaser may be a purchaser in good faith, which in the law has a special meaning. He will not be affected by private agreements of which he has no knowledge. Thus, the elaborate drafting inserted into the shareholders' agreement will be rendered useless without being transposed to the articles of the company. Of course, breach of a contract, in this case, the shareholders' agreement, permits recovery of damages, and in many cases, a collectible judgment is obtained. The shareholders' agreement is a powerful deterrent to its repudiation.

6.4.8 ONE PARTY BUYS EQUITY INTERESTS AND DOES NOT INFORM THE OTHER PARTNERS

Everything that has been said for a purchase of a majority share applies equally to this problem. The only distinction will be that the wording of the shareholders' agreement will be different regarding this issue.

6.4.9 ANNUAL BUDGET, CAPITAL EXPENDITURES, EXPANSION PLANS, AND DISPOSAL OF ASSETS

None of these items could appear anywhere except in the shareholders' agreement. It would not be feasible to convoke frequent general assemblies to consider such operational issues even admitting this division of management was permitted by the local jurisdiction.

6.4.10 LOAN PROVISIONS, GUARANTEES, AND ENCUMBRANCES

None of these items could appear anywhere except in the shareholders' agreement for the reasons cited before.

6.4.11 PURCHASE OR DISPOSAL OF EQUITY INTERESTS

In the closely held corporation, it is conceivable that there should be put into the articles of the company a general prohibition against the purchase and sale of equity interests without the permission of the general assembly. It is an important company step and, not being the business of the joint venture company, to seek confirmation with the general assembly seems correct.

Additionally, the shareholders' agreement will regulate the matter.

6.4.12 DISPUTE RESOLUTION

The articles of a company often recite that differences, litigation, or interpretation of the law will be subject to the law of the country in a court of law or whether there will be recourse to arbitration. The shareholders' agreement may be a faithful repetition of these ideas, also.

For pacific solutions, mechanisms established on an informal basis, with first recourse to the internal hierarchy of each partner and then possibly mediation or even conciliation, could only be expressed in the shareholders' agreement. The articles of the company cannot set forth the details of internal dispute resolution, it being not strictly legally enforceable but rather resting on morality for its support.

6.4.13 LITIGATION AUTHORIZED BY THE BOARD OF DIRECTORS

Any restrictions concerning when litigation can be initiated must be expressed in the shareholders' agreement. It is not convenient to attempt to grant any power to the general assembly on this issue as it needs quantification, which, in company articles, will appear awkward, as if the company were anticipating litigation. When possible, a board of directors' agreement on the percentage of votes needed for authorizing litigation above a certain amount will be ideal.

6.4.14 NEW LABOR POLICIES

This all-important topic only can find proper expression and direction in the shareholders' agreement.

6.4.15 PROVIDING ADDITIONAL CAPITAL

When dealing with further contributions of capital to be made, it is possible to have a provision in the articles of the company to the extent that there is an authorized capital and an issued capital. Frequently, the articles of a company provide for an authorized capital, but the full capital contributions are realized in steps. For example, a joint venture company can initiate its existence with capital issued for U.S.$2,000,000 but have an authorized capital of U.S.$12,000,000. This will eliminate the necessity of seeking permission from the general assembly for a further call for capital.

The articles could stipulate further advances are required when the net worth of the company at the end of the fiscal year falls below a certain percentage as indicated by the published balance sheet. In fact, many jurisdictions require this as a matter of law.

If more subjective criteria are to be utilized, such as accounting ratios, then these standards could not be indicated in the articles. As has been stated various times, the articles of a company must be susceptible of application with the least doubts possible. Additionally, indicating to the general public what are the accounting ratios a company uses is too revelatory and mandates that such conditions be a confidential matter finding expression only in the shareholders' agreement.

6.4.16 AUGMENTS OF CAPITAL, ISSUANCE OF AUTHORIZED SHARES, AND STOCK DIVIDENDS

Rules concerning when these corporate acts are authorized can be satisfactorily regulated by the articles of the company if by authorization we are referring to the necessity for the general assembly of the shareholders to approve such steps. Further protection can be achieved by requiring a specified supermajority of votes. Thus, in this case, we have two possible alternatives: the company articles and a shareholders' agreement. If there is a choice, the company articles are the preferred source as this constitutes public notice and hence will bind any future buyers of any sold equity interest.

6.4.17 ACCOUNTING POLICIES

The standards of accounting in many countries are of excellent quality. Many of the prestigious U.S. and English firms have partnerships with local accountants in diverse jurisdictions throughout the world. Naturally, they have brought with them their knowledge and their professional requirements. But not all joint ventures involve multinationals.

Small enterprising companies do go abroad in search of partners and the latter may very likely not use one of the international accounting firms. However, it is natural that a small firm from a country such as the United States or England will already have general acceptable accounting procedures whereas their local counterpart may not. This is because the official accounting requirements throughout the commercial world vary considerably. Until the advent of international accounting firms, it was not chauvinism to claim that the average U.S. or English accounting standards were a model of excellence. The gap is closing but it still exists.

When an acquisition is being made, a clause in the shareholders' agreement requiring general acceptable accounting procedures in conformity with international standards, or even a reference to the home jurisdiction of the foreign partner, will ensure that the necessary rectifications will be made. The problem is less serious when a new company is being formed because if one of the partners has a satisfactory technical accounting system, the other partner has little cause to refuse to adopt it.

Inserting accounting requirements into the company articles will not be workable. The most that could be expected is that the company articles require an accounting system in conformity with the law. But then, this is obligatory without being stated. If the official accounting system is satisfactory, then there is no need for concern. But when this is not so, having the company articles provide for an accounting system in accordance with international accounting standards is not a feasible reference. Although not vague to the experienced, it is devoid of content to novitiates. The matter is more satisfactorily treated in the shareholders' agreement in which the standard required can be detailed with multiple examples and references.

6.4.18 EXORBITANT SALARIES: CONTRACTS

One of the typical patterns for pushing out a minority owner is to have the majority partners pay themselves exorbitant salaries. Then, there is no need for dividends and the minority partner receives no return at all on his investment. One might think this situation could be rectified in court, but, in fact, what is a just salary is subject to so many variables that courts invariably hesitate to intervene.

Putting a clause in the company articles prohibiting directors from being paid is self-defeating. Many, if not most, directors are competent, serious, hard-working, and fair executives. Their services are needed and they should be paid. What has to be regulated is the amount. Two solutions are possible. The company articles can permit such contracts but require the general assembly to approve same unanimously and the same provision can be put into the shareholders' agreement. The latter is the usual alternative.

What has been said about controlling the quantities directors pay themselves, either through salaries or contracts, should not be subject to avoidance by having family members or friends on the payroll. This is a delicate matter that cannot be articulated in the company articles. Such a control has to be remitted to the shareholders' agreement. However, if the company articles will require unanimous approval of directors' salaries and contracts, then it is a simple matter to insert the phrase *directly or indirectly* when referring to the prohibitive acts and this should be more than sufficient.

6.4.19 APPROPRIATION OF CORPORATE ASSETS

To control expense accounts, misuse of company assets, using the company car to frequently travel to a faraway weekend home, exaggerated entertainment bills, and assets purchased but used at home all can be controlled easily by a detailed annual budget that is established and approved by the partners. This topic can be satisfactorily regulated only by a shareholders' agreement as the detail required exceeds what is usual for company articles nor is the subject matter for public exposure.

6.4.20 SALE OF CORPORATE ASSETS OR CONTRACTS WITH THIRD PARTIES

More insidious is creating dummy companies to siphon off money from the joint venture company to one controlled, apparently or not, by one of the joint venture partners. Again, it might seem that the courts would condemn such an act easily, but again the standard as to whether the contract in question is fair and just is ripe with variables and one cannot count on the court's concurring judgment that a fraud has been perpetuated.

However, unlike a company article prohibiting the payment of salaries to directors or officers who are partners, the company articles can state that any partner will not be a partner, directly or indirectly, in any company having business with the joint venture vehicle. This sets a high standard of ethics perfectly acceptable. Obviously, the same provision should appear in the shareholders' agreement.

6.4.21 PROFITING FROM INSIDER INFORMATION AND OTHER OPPORTUNITIES

Profiting from insider information does not only refer to dealing in the company stock when confidential information has been obtained. It also can mean, in our context of learning of collateral information, information brought to the attention of a director-partner because of his privileged position.

In general, there should be a general obligation on any partner that any company commercial information obtained or any other commercial opportunities presented to the company during the tenure of the director must first be offered to the company. Company articles are not the proper place for such a general interdiction.

6.4.22 MATERIAL CONTRACTS ABOVE A CERTAIN AMOUNT

It is not feasible to control all aspects of company life. A commercial organization means delegation of responsibilities. In all joint venture companies, the temptations for a partner-director or partner-officer to require a supplier of goods to set aside a private commission certainly exist. Nevertheless, it is difficult to isolate such acts, which are easily submerged in a quantity of accounting information.

Therefore, what can be controlled are only the limits of authority delegated by the board or retained by the board. In large organizations, the limits have to be higher; otherwise the board of directors will be intervening in all operational aspects. What is a sensible platform is dependent therefore on the facts of the particular joint venture. Nevertheless, limits should be established whether powers are delegated or not and above these limits the approval of the board of directors must be necessary. There can be two standards. Above one limit, the board's approval is required by a simple majority, and above another limit, a supermajority is required. These provisions are exclusively for the shareholders' agreement.

6.4.23 PLACEMENT OF KEY PERSONNEL

A frequent clause appearing in shareholders' agreements is the right conferred on one partner to indicate personnel for a particular department of the joint venture company. This is a critical, valuable right. If the joint venture is in good part founded on one partner's aptness, naturally, the right to administer this expertise must be preserved. It may be supervision of the accounting department; it may be in the production facilities, or quality control. Whatever it is, management's right to ensure its implementation must find adequate expression.

This can be done effectively only through the shareholders' agreement. Indirectly, it is a result of choosing one or more members of the board of directors. Therefore, if a board of directors' agreement is utilized, this can be one of the clauses that requires a supermajority: so many votes for nomination of the head of the accounting department. Unfortunately, requiring such a supermajority may result easily in a deadlock. The shareholders' agreement avoids a deadlock since it does not refer to votes but confers a right. The company articles cannot be used for this issue.

6.4.24 LANGUAGE ABILITY OF KEY PERSONNEL

Perhaps this seems odd. The joint venture is operating in France and the shareholders' agreement requires the managing director to speak French and English. Why isn't French sufficient? It is if all the partners speak French fluently; otherwise, what will happen is only the local partner who speaks French will be able to make rapid, day-to-day decisions based on the information provided by the managing directors. Immediate reaction to a problem hardly can be dependent on receiving a translation of the facts.

If such were the case, in effect the non-French speaking partners have turned over the management of the joint venture to the French partner. Such a consequence can be avoided without harming national pride by having the shareholders' agreement provide that key personnel will comply with various requisites and amongst many will be the language requirements. The shareholders' agreement is the only place for this provision.

6.4.25 TERMINATION OF EMPLOYEES

Many a joint venture has foundered on one employee souring relations between the partners. The most common reason is the belief of one partner that a particular employee is incompetent and not suited for the job. This judgment may appear reasonable to the complaining partner but not to the other partner. The latter hired the employee and, due to cultural identity with the employee, many see qualities not easily transparent. And so it goes on.

There is a complaint by one partner and appeal to reason by another, and friction slowly builds. Far better for partners with a reasonable participation of capital to be able to exercise their judgment, erroneously or not. With such a provision in the shareholders' agreement, and that is the proper place for this right, each partner feels his judgment can have practical consequences.

6.4.26 PROHIBITION ON DISMISSED EMPLOYEES WORKING FOR ONE OF
THE PARTNERS

Often enough, the local partner has many activities in the jurisdiction and the joint venture is a new commercial experience. One or more key personnel may be transferred from one of the local partner's other companies. In principle, this may confer substantial benefits. The competence of the employee is known; there is a feeling of trust.

When, however, there has not been a lot of commercial experience in common between the partners, there is the danger that the employee's loyalty will be first to his former employer. This is natural. Abuses are possible, the most notable being that a failing joint venture will precipitate the former employee into acts benefiting his former employer.

To some degree, this can be prevented by having a clause in the shareholders' agreement wherein a terminated employee cannot be reemployed by his former employer, directly or indirectly. Due to antitrust provisions, which dislike restrictions on the freedom to work, such a clause in the shareholders' agreement would have to be of short duration.

6.4.27 CHANGE OF CONTROL, DECEASE OF A PARTNER, OR PROLONGED ILLNESS

When companies are partners, the original negotiating partners frequently are assigned to other functions and they may never have contact again. Those who were responsible for the establishment of the joint venture are not present to act as spokesmen with their respective boards. The boards may change. There may be even a change of control in the company-partner. An entirely different management philosophy takes charge and the joint venture may assume less importance.

With similar consequences is the death of a partner or his prolonged illness. It all amounts to the same practical consequence: The same parties are no longer doing business with each other. It doesn't matter that the company-partner hasn't legally changed. Its management has and the joint venture may receive scant attention.

The once dynamic partner is gone and in his place are complacent disinterested heirs. Illness sows its seeds and the inability to work is the undesired flower. The solution for these varied problems is both in the company articles and the shareholders' agreement.

For the company articles, provisions can be established that will result in compulsory retirement of the equity share or a buyout prerogative on the part of the other owners. This would be applicable only to individual owners because one reason could be the *demise* of the partners. Clearly, this is not possible with a company, since, in theory, it endures indefinitely. Thus demise is not possible with a company.

Concerning change of control and *illness* or *inability to work* for an individual partner, the proper governing document would have to be the shareholders' agreement in which these concepts could receive more elaborate treatment. They then could be subject to the same redemption rights or buyout provisions as established in the articles of the company.

6.4.28 TERMINATION OF THE JOINT VENTURE

The parties can agree to a multiplicity of reasons that cause the joint venture to come to an end. There are the voluntary reasons, the expressed desire of the parties to end the joint venture through dissolution and liquidation of the assets. Such a provision would appear in the articles of the company.

Another termination may occur de facto, that is, for all practical purposes, the joint venture ends because one partner is legally forced to sell out his interest or his equity is redeemed for an amount fixed in a formula. Common causes, when attributable to a partner, are bankruptcy, attachment, even nationalization of the equity interest of a particular partner. Such provisions would appear in the company articles.

The more difficult criteria are those that lead to a deadlock. These situations have been mentioned before. The commercially sound agreement will identify those situations in which the parties cannot achieve anything or move the joint venture forward. Due to the distribution of voting power, there are never mustered enough votes to take any action. The company clearly needs further injections of capital, but the minority votes are sufficient to block any affirmative action.

In order to avoid these situations, the only solution is to have the shareholders' agreement provide, and this is the only document in which such a clause could appear, what will happen. One partner will sell or one partner will buy. Before this clause can be written, the parties have to know what position they will occupy or wish to occupy. This then becomes a negotiating point.

6.4.29 CONTINUATION OF BUSINESS AFTER THE JOINT VENTURE HAS BEEN TERMINATED

Once the joint venture has come to an end, it is not unusual that one partner may want to continue with the business in a different company. Putting aside what will be the attitude of the other partners, the only document by which this can be regulated is the shareholders' agreement. Having the company articles treat this problem is not advisable since by law the company articles cease to exist when the joint venture is dissolved.

6.4.30 DISPOSAL OF ASSETS AFTER THE JOINT VENTURE HAS BEEN TERMINATED

By law, on a dissolution of a joint venture company, and assuming there are no creditors, the assets of the company would be distributed to the partners in proportion to their equity interests. But how do you divide a building? As you usually cannot, the result is the building is sold and the cash is divided.

If such a solution appears satisfactory to the partners at the time of the joint venture, there is no need to have any document refer to the issue at all. Yet, this is rarely the case. If we are dealing with an industrial complex, it may well be one partner wants to retain the complex as a unit and wish to pay the other partner his equity interest in the asset.

By now, it should be clear that the formation of a joint venture requires thoughtful consideration as to what will take place when there is a termination of the joint venture. Although this is not the usual approach, it is still a preferred course of action. If such a point of view is possible, then the shareholders' agreement is the relevant document to settle the disposal of the assets. The material is usually too complex for company articles.

6.4.31 THE SHAREHOLDERS' AGREEMENT: THE KINGPIN OF CONFLICT RESOLUTION

Given that so many important issues can be satisfactorily resolved only through the use of the shareholders' agreement, its documentary presence is obligatory in any major joint venture. The traditional use of the joint venture agreement as the operating agreement and reliance on the company articles will provide limited flexibility when confronting the variable problems joint ventures raise. Once the joint venture is formed, the partners often relegate the joint venture agreement to the offices of counsel.

Even if the agreement provides that various clauses will survive the formation of the joint venture company, the partners tend to dismiss this as a legal technicality. This results in the hindsight of counsel being dismissed as a professional exaggeration. The company articles can offer important but modest help for they are often too generalized and too vague to solve the majority of partner conflicts. This leaves the shareholders' agreement as the kingpin of conflict resolution.

7

DUE DILIGENCE PROCEDURES: COMMERCIAL, LEGAL, AND FINANCIAL

PART ONE

7.1 A DEFINITION

When dealing with significant investments, there should be no purchase of an interest in a company without due diligence procedures. Due diligence procedures are intended to reveal the most possible about the target company, the company in which an equity interest is up for sale. A necessity for such procedures arises when a joint venture is to be formed through the method of a partial acquisition.

Since the seller cannot speak for the remaining partners, their consent and cooperation in the due diligence procedures are usually indispensable. As the articles of companies normally contain restrictions on the sale of an equity interest, any permission given for the sale will mean that the remaining partners are keen on having a new partner and welcome the injection of new capital, ideas, methods, and opportunities.

Due diligence procedures have minimum relevance in the establishment of a joint venture company, in which all parties subscribe for the first time to the initial capital. Although the future partners forming a union for the first time will naturally want to know a great deal about each other, such information is assembled through prior knowledge, data gathered through meetings, the natural exchange of facts furnished during conferences, or recourse to available public information.

One does not solicit the interest of a third party in forming a joint venture company and simultaneously request the same entity to submit to a rigorous internal investigation. It would be the unusual set of circumstances. Who would propose .to a loved one and, in the same tremulous voice, request a curriculum vitae, even a brief one? Discretion will consummate the commercial conquest.

In a joint venture by acquisition, the terms of sale will be contained in the joint venture agreement. Before making a purchase, the buyer will want numerous assurances on a wide range of topics affecting the target company. These are the representations and warranties discussed in Chapter Five. Such statements, however, if left unchallenged, would merely be the hopeful, but, it is hoped, honest conviction of the seller. One additional step is necessary. One of the clauses of the joint venture agreement will permit the buyer to thoroughly analyze the target company as to its economic, financial, and legal aspects prior to the closing. This permission and the resulting investigation have the official designation of due diligence procedures. We can think of this as a total, factual revelation of the target company.

The objectives of such procedures are to confirm the seller's presentation of the target company, assure ourselves all is well, and discover the virtues and the weaknesses of our purchase prior to the closing. In a joint venture, due diligence procedures protect and predict. They are an indispensable aid to the investor for an intelligent appraisal of the projected investment.

Although a standard of investigative conduct, the precise meaning of a due diligence procedure will depend on the circumstances. But we know it means a sincere bona fide attempt to uncover all relevant information. It is a preventive legal step completely analogous to the practice of preventive medicine. In both cases, the cost of a cure exceeds the expenditure of judicious prevention.

Due diligence procedures are intended to reveal to the incoming partner as much as possible about the joint venture company for the benefit of all. The grand symphony of representations and warranties distributed throughout the joint venture agreement without such procedures might easily terminate in an awkward silence, a lawyer's gasp when confronted with the subsequent realities of the target company, and a buyer's rage at the variances of the facts with the affirmations in the contract of sale.

What value have warranties when the purchase price has been passed but the inventory is worthless due to its obsolescence, stock the seller thought truly still had sales potential? What remedy is there when a major client contract is canceled after the closing and such a fact could have been predicted with a preclosing telephone call? Clearly, then, when acquiring an interest in a company, warranties by a seller without a careful investigation of the financial and legal status of the target company would be fruitless. Warranties and due diligence procedures are inseparable.

Although with a different spirit, due diligence procedures are also a commercial inquisition. In a partial acquisition leading to a joint venture, due diligence procedures are also concerned with discovering any omission of facts. But if a joint venture is intended, it is unlikely these facts have been deliberately concealed. It is of course possible, but highly improbable. More likely, the seller was also unaware of the uncovered defects or deleterious facts. If this is true, due diligence procedures provide a further, constructive mission concerning the joint venture avoiding postclosing, embarrassing situations and certainly potential litigation.

Thus, besides seeking to confirm the facts of the heterogeneous legal structure embodied in the word *company* and the complexity of information contained in the financial statements, the procedures are intended to uncover problems that may not even be known to the seller. It is the small shopkeeper counting his inventory now transformed into a complex corporation. But the object remains the same. What do I have in my shop? Do my records accurately reflect what transpired during the year?

Accordingly, due diligence procedures are a broad, wandering quest for information that may not appear at first sight, whether through ignorance, negligence, or perhaps even because the information was not easily available to the seeker, being buried in records rarely consulted. From the buyer's viewpoint, the purpose of due diligence procedures in an international joint venture can be succinctly summarized: to ensure that the representations of fact made by the seller that have led the buyer to make an acquisition are true. From the honest seller's viewpoint, they are procedures designed to confirm what he reasonably believes to be correct.

But in order to know the genuine economic and legal picture, many aspects must be reviewed. Of course, the extent of due diligence procedures is commensurate with the amount of the investment and the complexity of the joint venture. Due diligence procedures are time-consuming and very costly. Ordinarily, one is not going to spend more on due diligence procedures than on the amount of capital invested. On the other hand, due diligence procedures often highlight the difference between investing and gambling. The proper balance is the moderation that usually guides ordinary human conduct.

As previously explained, the formation of a joint venture by an acquisition will be by a partial acquirement, the purchase of less than the entire capital of the target company. There must be equity interests remaining in the possession of others. This is the definition of an acquisition that leads to a joint venture: collaboration with another entity.

Because we are dealing with a joint venture, the spirit of conducting due diligence procedures is both less aggressive and less stressful than in a total acquisition, in which the selling party will no longer be available for consultation; or in an unsolicited takeover, in which the buyer proceeds in an atmosphere of hostility and even purposefully created obstacles.

Due diligence procedures in a joint venture therefore may be defined as methods intended to obtain an assessment of an economic unit and to ensure that the facts match the warranties. However, contained within the words *methods* and *assessment* resides much of the complexity associated with this process. Moreover, due diligence procedures have multiple applications and it is necessary to distinguish those due diligence procedures associated with joint ventures from the ones that have other objectives. A brief survey aids in obtaining a broad perspective.

7.1.1 APPLICATIONS OF DUE DILIGENCE PROCEDURES OTHER THAN IN JOINT VENTURES

Our interests are in those due diligence procedures that will form part of the steps leading to a joint venture. Nonetheless, due diligence procedures have an important function in other significant legal events. In spite of sharing a common name, due diligence procedures fulfill various functions to achieve different objectives dependent on the transaction. As with other phrases used to describe legal procedures, the same phrase does not necessarily mean the same procedures or objectives. The use of due diligence procedures in a joint venture is different from the same verbal concept applied to other situations. Due diligence procedures have their relevancy in various broad categories, not all related to international joint ventures. They are used to

- assist in capital financing, whether through equity subscriptions or debt, such as the sale of shares or bonds to the public; representations must be made in the prospectus, and the investment bankers want assurances from their counselors that the representations are correct.
- avoid liability imposed by various laws for failure to use a reasonable and prudent standard of investigation when confirming facts to the public

- provide a solid basis of information about the target company in a total acquisition or merger
- ensure compliance with any representations and warranties in a contract of sale of a partial acquisition
- indicate present troublesome areas and assist in analyzing solutions when material omissions have been discovered in a target company, usually leading to an adjustment of the sales price
- constitute a legal basis for terminating a contract of purchase and sale concerning a joint venture

Of all the possible uses, it is in the last three categories where due diligence procedures are realized under the most favorable and least adversarial conditions. Within the setting of a collaborative atmosphere, the seller will make it possible for the buyer to consummate a total understanding of the target company, its legal and financial history, its merits, and even its defects. In the absence of such cooperation, serious reservations about the future success of the joint venture are clearly pertinent. A partial acquisition implies a voluntary cooperation by the seller with the assistance and consent of the other partners. Otherwise, there is no purpose in forming the joint venture. It should be abandoned.

7.1.2 THE PROPER PLACE AND TIME IN WHICH TO CONDUCT DUE DILIGENCE PROCEDURES

A better understanding of due diligence procedures can be gained by asking two questions:

1. How do we go about conducting due diligence procedures?
2. When are they conducted?

They cannot be conducted from the confines of an office. The only way to conduct due diligence procedures is to go to the premises of the seller and physically inspect the site, examine the books, speak with key personnel, review all relevant legal and financial documents, which allows conclusions to be reached about a variety of matters ranging from title to assets to proper, or not, accounting methods.

Material gathered can be collated and studied within the sanctity of an office. But first and foremost, due diligence procedures require a physical dislocation and familiarity with the premises of the seller, its personnel, the location of its records, and informed opinions as related by employees.

All of these steps will be initiated by the advisers sending a letter to the target company outlining what information they will be seeking, broken down into categories and with sufficient detail to leave no room for doubt as to what is wanted and needed. However, the letter is not a substitute for personal involvement by the advisors. With the information obtained, a number of purposes can be achieved:

- In the contractual phase, a potential buyer can determine if he wishes to continue with negotiations.
- Once a contract has been signed, we can verify the truthfulness of the multiple warranties made.
- Thereafter, complete legal and financial analyses of the target company are achieved.
- Risk to the buyer may be discovered and quantified.
- Adjustments may have to be made to the sales price.
- The advisers are in a position to issue their professional opinion confirming matters are in order, or not, to proceed to a closing.

Oftentimes, these procedures are referred to as an *audit* of the seller. This is not technically correct, because an audit is a verification by a team of accountants that the accounts of the seller are being accurately represented, that the company method for gathering information is in accordance with acceptable standards and is being factually reported in the accounts.

Audits are a recurring annual event for companies, whether there is a joint venture and are usually restricted to the state of the accounts, the identification of any fiscal problems, and any special requests of a consulting nature requested by management. Due diligence procedures do contain many of the steps of an audit. Auditors form part of the team conducting due diligence procedures. However, due diligence procedures are not an audit. They just utilize a similar methodology.

In contrast to a hostile takeover or a total acquisition, in a joint venture, the natural and probably most beneficial moment to begin due diligence procedures is after the contract has been signed when the parties can foresee a lengthy association. With a set of representations and warranties in hand, it is natural that the potential partners will seek to unravel matters that need further clarification.

7.1.3 Classification of due diligence procedures

Due diligence procedures are normally divided into legal and financial categories and the work is divided between the auditors and the attorneys. These procedures follow a well-defined pattern intended to ferret out the truth. Financial and legal due diligence procedures are indispensable to a successful closing and there is no substitute for their thoroughness. Although this is the traditional division, there is, however, abundant information useful to management buried within the records of the target company and that should be developed in accordance with the interests of the purchaser's corporate executives. This we denominate *commercial due diligence procedures* and they are the ones we will review first. Our final classification of due diligence procedures in order of presentation is, therefore,

- commercial
- financial
- legal

Matters of interest to management could be divided easily into issues affecting the governance of the joint venture and those affecting human resources. Commercial due diligence procedures are not usually denominated as such but included in the information collated by the professional advisers. Commercial due diligence information, no matter by whom gathered, will make a critical and vital contribution to the success of the joint venture. It will reveal those aspects that most concern the managers: the issues of governance, marketing, distribution, production, research and development, human resources, and, finally, new corporate horizons to be explored.

Our first focus will be on those commercial due diligence procedures management should either undertake or request to be undertaken, with an explanation as to their importance. It is hoped that this will contribute toward constructing a methodology for commercial due diligence procedures.

At the end of the discussion on commercial due diligence procedures is a brief résumé of the due diligence procedures auditors and lawyers conduct to afford a more complete understanding of the entire process. The shortness of such a survey should not be taken to convey a sense of simplicity of these areas. On the contrary, they constitute some of the most complex questions surrounding international joint ventures and their responsibility falls to the financial and legal advisers.

Before turning to an examination of the multiple areas that are properly a concern of commercial due diligences, it is helpful to understand what risks, if any, exist for buyer and seller in these procedures. Although they are not substantial, they are present and their consequences should be understood by the participants. The risks derive from warranties made.

7.1.4 SELLER: WARRANTIES THAT SHOULD NOT HAVE BEEN MADE

A promissory contract is executed and the seller is convinced his warranties are based on accurate facts. In fact, they may not be and the due diligence procedures reveal a breach of one or more warranties. This results in liability to the seller, in one form or another, damages, reduction of the sales price, or cancellation of the promissory contract. Many a successful business is more the result of a dynamic management team and less that of an accurate accounting system.

Sellers must have a factual understanding of their warranties. They are more than promises intended to be kept. They must be fulfilled. It is not an issue of good faith. Warranties should not be declared without a firm conviction in their accuracy. In other words, warranty clauses should not be assumed in a sales contract because they have been presented in the legal form of a contract. Economic realities lie behind these declarations.

7.1.5 SELLER: BUSINESS IS NOT AS GOOD AS REPRESENTED

The natural enthusiasm of the seller as to attractiveness of the equity interest being sold may not withstand thorough due diligence procedures. The buyer discovers various problems, and dependent on what stage of the procedures the parties are, the sales price will have to be revised.

Serious participants to a joint venture should restrain making quantified assertions and rather rest on general assertions of optimism and confidence, but not sales projections and cash flow. Marketing pronouncements are not a prudent accompaniment to a joint venture agreement. Once transposed to a promissory contract, they create potential obligations of a pecuniary nature.

7.1.6 SELLER AND BUYER: REVELATION OF POTENTIAL SALE

The buyer runs the danger that once it is known that a particular equity interest is for sale, and there is as yet no contract in existence, other buyers can appear and of course start competitive bidding. Although this is possible, in most incipient joint ventures through partial acquisitions, the parties do manage to maintain a low profile; this risk should not be exaggerated.

Furthermore, with medium and small companies, the attractiveness to a joint venture is usually not in an inactive asset base, for example, prime realty that can be developed or excess cash lying fallow in bank accounts.

The average joint venture is predicated on a complement of skills and joint efforts. Thus, the possible disclosure to the public of an equity interest in a closely held corporation is minimal.

Part Two

7.2 Commercial due diligence procedures: general objectives

Before reviewing some selected areas of commercial due diligence procedures, it is convenient to summarize what are the general objectives. We seek information for a purpose. We are striving for comprehensive discernment of all aspects of the joint venture company, not a collection of isolated facts. All the data gathered should contribute to useful knowledge revealing a meaningful pattern.

Company profile

Because the parties to a potential joint venture know one another from prior commercial dealings, it is natural that negotiations will provoke an exchange of much information to be followed by due diligence procedures once the contract is signed.

The degree of familiarity of the future partners may vary considerably from joint venture to joint venture. In some cases, it will be hazy and vague so as to justify completing due diligence procedures prior to the signing of a contract. However, even in these circumstances, the initial due diligence procedures will probably be low-profile, a shying away from any overt action that could be misconstrued.

There is a third middle ground, one that might be more accommodating when some knowledge is formed of the other partner, but more is desired of a general nature without implying the proposed partnership is founded on distrust. Good sources of additional material are stockholder reports, business periodicals, financial newspapers, credit agency ratings, opinion of local banks, suppliers, customers, and reports on file at any public bureau.

Negotiations between the parties usually involve visitation to one another's offices and such moments can be further exploited by exploratory conversations with senior management and production chiefs. Normally, such visits include a senior financial officer of the foreign investor and a joint review of financial material is natural to occur. During these interviews, much additional material is obtained and this may engender further questions and a request for more clarifications. All such information received complements commercial due diligence procedures but does not replace them.

Group structure

Ordinarily, the everyman joint venture will not be part of a worldwide corporate organization. On the other hand, nothing can be taken for granted. We therefore must understand all the major commercial relations, economic and legal, that the joint venture company has with other enterprises. This requires an inquiry into the interrelationships between the joint venture company and others. This inquiry will afford a comprehensive understanding of the dynamics of the joint venture company.

Management structure

When entering into a joint venture by acquisition, it is wise to look at the target company management in all its aspects. Is it satisfactory? What is wrong with it? What are the lines of authority? Does it make sense? Is it a system compatible with the acquirer's style? The elements of sound management and its existence in the joint venture company will have an enormous influence on the success or failure of the collaboration. As soon as possible, information concerning the hierarchy, the methods of payment, the scope of the retirement plans, and the offering of bonuses should be collated and studied.

Goods and services

What has the joint venture been doing in the past and what is it doing now? Although current commercial relationships will divulge the present easily, the past has some utility. The incoming partner perhaps is thinking of further product lines that did not have any success. Current products under license have critical importance that must be known immediately. The existence of such licenses would be revealed by legal due diligence procedures, but the importance of these products is above all a commercial determination.

The same reasoning applies to services in which technology and consultancy mix. At times, the consultancy services cannot be separated from the accompanying technology, such as human resources assistance, and the needed software may be under license.

Economic and geographical environment

The joint venture company is not operating in a cloistered boardroom but is an active participant in the macroeconomic realities within a specific geographical area. There are other companies. There are trade organizations. There is a general labor attitude toward employers in general and perhaps different for foreign employers. The search for a solid, working knowledge of the locale of the joint venture requires an effort to understand the culture and its political economy.

7.2.1 COMMERCIAL DUE DILIGENCE: COMMON PROBLEMS

We are ready to begin to examine those areas that are the natural terrain of the corporate executive. A joint venture is fact-specific and what will have a particular interest to managers for any given joint venture is very variable. Nevertheless, the broad purposes of commercial due diligence procedures should be always kept in the forefront. The investigator is seeking to appraise the business of another entity and to assess the efficiency of its management. With these general commercial objectives in mind, we can begin to isolate the various subjects.

The areas indicated in the ensuing discussion are those that seem to have the most broad application. However, beyond a mere listing of those areas of general interest to managers, further information is needed:

- an explanation of its relevance
- what latent risks does the information convey
- suggestions as to containment of the risk

These questions can be given the shorthand description of relevance, risk, and resolution.

Accordingly, the material we are suggesting for commercial due diligence procedures will follow this sequence. Under the topical description, we will list some typical information that should be solicited without attempting to be exhaustive. This part of the due diligence procedures is more concerned with managerial issues.

Our review will not only describe the information sought but suggest remedies. Of course, not all risks have legal or management solutions, but the focus on potential discordant material prior to a closing will lessen its abrasive effects on the joint venture once the purchase is consummated. The element of surprise is replaced with the determination to seek a solution.

7.2.2 OTHER JOINT VENTURES: RELEVANCE

Our own joint venture will naturally occupy our complete attention. However, it must not be forgotten that the joint venture company may itself be a party to another joint venture agreement or other form of alliance. Although such knowledge ordinarily should be communicated to the negotiating parties early, the size of our joint venture company and its hierarchical arrangement may mean the local negotiators do not have any specific knowledge.

Multinationals do not necessarily inform their local subsidiaries or other joint venture companies with alacrity. Clearly, other joint ventures involve considerable management attention and an incoming partner will certainly want to be apprised of this fact early, if possible before the signing of any joint venture agreement. Essential information includes

- copies of all other joint venture agreements and similar arrangements
- letter from counsel to the joint venture company that all such contracts are in vigor and there are no defaults

7.2.3 OTHER JOINT VENTURES: RISK

Other joint ventures may have provisions similar to share preference rights among shareholders. It will be recalled that these obligate a selling shareholder to first offer his equity interest to the other shareholders. We may face the same legal situation if the target company is a shareholder in another joint venture vehicle. A change of ownership in the target company may trigger rights to buy out the target company's interest in the other joint venture. There may be antitrust considerations as there is being constructed a chain of interests between various companies. This may suggest to authorities an attempt to influence prices through management control. What started out as a straightforward partial acquisition becomes an involvement with national antitrust agencies.

Additionally, the target company being a partner in another joint venture may have multiple financial obligations. Guarantees given by the target company and liability for further capital contributions are simple examples. Whatever the consequences, the ramifications of the target company's participation in another joint venture have to be known prior to any closing concerning the target company.

7.2.4 OTHER JOINT VENTURES: RESOLUTION

The existence of other joint ventures involving the target company would be covered normally by representations and warranties and the details set forth in a disclosure letter. The partaking of the target company in another joint venture would be a material fact required to be divulged by the target company prior to closing and the resolution of any risks will range from renegotiating of the terms of the joint venture to desisting.

7.2.5 ORGANIZATION CHART: RELEVANCE

Of great concern to managers assigned to a joint venture will be the hierarchy of the joint venture. Questions such as: "What powers of management will the local joint venture have?" "How autonomous will local management be?" "Where will final decisions be made?" "Is there any recourse from acts of the local management to the main office?" "Will any partner have more or less exclusive jurisdiction over a particular department?" and many others can be determined only when the managerial structure of the joint venture is revealed in detail.

Particularly in joint ventures by acquisition, the incoming partner finds itself with a preexisting management structure that can be adapted only with great difficulty to the home office structure. The managerial style of the new partner may be sufficiently different from the existing joint venture organization so as to impede communication and implementation between the partners and between the purchasing partner and the personnel it assigns to the joint venture.

The organization of the joint venture must be thoroughly studied, understood, and facts solicited that reveal its structure in detail. The way a joint venture is managed leads either to its success or failure. Illustrative of information that should be solicited are

- organizational diagram
- flow chart of authority
- mechanisms of recourse from one level of management to another
- detailed nomenclature for all recognized positions and their corresponding identification, such as code number or database reference, whatever system the company uses

- list of employees occupying what are understood as key positions, those to which the foreign partner might either be assigning personnel and over which authority will be exercised
- identification of those positions to be fulfilled solely with personnel supplied by one of the partners

7.2.6 ORGANIZATION CHART: RISK

Two recurring troublesome areas in joint ventures are the degree of autonomy the local managers have over different departments and recourse from decisions made by supervisory local management contrary to this local autonomy. These are dilemmas that frequently occur and they may give rise to conflict between the foreign investor and the local partner; or a clash of managers representing the various partners; or, even worse, decisions taken that do not meet the approval of one partner, thus causing a deterioration of relationships.

Joint ventures generally are a happy combination of different management skills, perhaps one partner contributing his financial knowledge and another his production skills. This results in a natural tendency for one partner to assume more authority in the accounting department and the other in the production facilities.

Nevertheless, these are often de facto arrangements and it is common to see personnel in authority crossing departmental lines. The risk here is of unnecessary interference, challenges to authority, leading to counter orders from a general manager, and operational differences break out into open conflict. A proper understanding of the organizational structure should indicate where problems are likely to arise.

7.2.7 ORGANIZATION CHART: RESOLUTION

Once the organization structure of the joint venture is mastered, the resolution is at hand. The first decision is if the foreign partner will have any jurisdiction over any particular department and to what extent this authority will not be subject to supervision except at the partner level. Thereafter, the partners will have to decide whether any foreign personnel will be assigned as employees or as consultants.

If the latter, they are then similar to independent contractors and not subject to the same internal management controls. Many multinationals assign one of their key employees to the foreign joint venture in which the executive holds a dual position. He is at once an employee of the foreign partner and also a consultant of the local joint venture, which pays another part of his salary. The solution to be adopted will depend to a great extent on the local laws.

The resolution to avoiding conflict at the organizational level is for the partners to come to a consensus at the contract stage; the solutions decided are inserted in the joint venture agreement and the shareholders' agreement. This will substantially compel adherence to the management philosophy as negotiated at the beginning. It will make clear what the partners expect of management; what are the powers of management; what they can or cannot do; whether their decisions at a local level are final; if not, what are the procedures.

The more detailed the responses, the more harmonious will be the joint venture. Local conflicts can be dissipated in the appeal process. Often, management at the home office encounters a sensible compromise to the distant squabbles that became more serious arguments. When management style disparity exists, it is helpful for the partners to create a project team composed of key employees from all partners to meet frequently and discuss ways of conciliating the different managerial philosophies.

A good commercial due diligence procedure will uncover the different styles of administration and a proper agenda will therefore elaborate the multiple points of difference. Rather then allowing different camps of management to crystallize, it is more productive to lead everyone toward a common goal and style. The presence or lack of such unison can be determined by direct questions to the managers of key departments to verify

- how departmental decisions are reached and implemented
- what decisions require further approval and from whom
- if there is any necessity for a formal request to the ultimate management authority
- whether one department has more authority than another
- if the chain of management is horizontal, emanating from one superior board, or if it is strictly vertical
- specific features of the management structure
- the articulated role of managers vis-à-vis employees as implicit in board of directors' directives or pronouncements

As for the articles of the joint venture company, they may contain the skeleton of management, that is, what boards will govern the company; what powers the board will have vis-à-vis the owners, or general assembly. But the day-to-day details of management cannot find satisfactory expression in the articles of the company.

Nor would it be feasible to insert the company procedures for management appeal in the articles. They require too much detail. These are private matters confined within the company structure. Thus, an itemized chart of corporate organization revealed by due diligence procedures should be complemented with a consensus among the partners as to management responsibility and attitude. That is one of the purposes of the due diligence procedures: to bring into relief any possible problems.

7.2.8 LABOR FORCE: RELEVANCE

Whether created through a partial acquisition or formation, a joint venture will need a labor force, but of course there is a vital difference in the two methods. By acquisition, there is received a structured labor nucleus that is a part of every department. So pervasive is labor that it would be unthinkable to proceed to an acquisition without having obtained the basic facts.

Management will want to know whether there are any glaring weaknesses in the labor force that will be the support for the entire economic unit being partially acquired. Were we dealing with the formation of a subsidiary, the labor force could be customized to the perceived needs of the joint venture. However, in an acquisition, the margin for customization is significantly reduced in most jurisdictions. In those countries with strong social policies concerning employment, there is none. Consequently, there is a minimum amount of data that must be solicited:

- We will want to know the answer to the simplest of all questions: How often are personnel paid? In some jurisdictions, it is weekly; in others, it is monthly. This fact will influence our calculations on cash flow.
- We will want to know the standard work week and hours per day, compulsory paid holidays, authorized leaves, and obligatory benefits, for example, maternity payments. This basic information is often thought to be fairly standard throughout the industrial world or easily altered. This is not true.
- The number of employees and a breakdown by category, department, function, age: all the human resource elements should, in a partial acquisition, already be compiled in a database or other form and the results analyzed. Conclusions derived, whether the joint venture vehicle is strong in some labor skills, but weak in others, will be useful in proposing, if possible, alterations to the other partner.
- We will want to know existing human resource training. Beyond dismissal, which is normally not possible in most jurisdictions, the intro-

duction of any modifications to the existing organization of the labor force will depend to a great extent on voluntary formation by the labor force.

7.2.9 Labor force: risk

Collating basic information about the nature of the joint venture human resources is in part an organizational necessity, tools that management needs to fulfill its functions. However, the knowledge gathered is also needed to ensure a smooth transition to the new composition of the joint venture. The risks a new partner faces result, in part, from an attempt sometimes made to impose different standards on the labor pool but also at times a failure by the new partner to recognize the cultural differences present in people associated with a joint venture.

The dilemma might be called *new partner integration* and it is a reality of joint ventures. Economic units such as companies are also minute clusters of culture and belief. The knowledge of these divergences in economic philosophy or style of management between a new partner and the present labor force should be used to achieve suitable compromises to avoid conflicts. In fact, the more these differences are known prior to the entry of the new partner, the more time the latter will have to make the necessary adjustments to its own philosophy. In those jurisdictions where the labor force has strong social and legislative protection, it is invariably the new partner that has to cede before any labor conflicts with management.

7.2.10 Labor force: resolution

Possessed with sufficient data, the potential new partner may make it a condition of the joint venture agreement that certain changes have to be made prior to the finalization of the sale. Assuming an extreme case, in which the incoming partner wants a substantial reduction in the labor force, it can be made a requirement in the joint venture agreement that the joint venture company will request from the applicable authorities permission for collective dismissals or reorganization of the company.

Whatever changes the potential purchaser believes are necessary that will affect labor must be negotiated and included as a condition in the joint venture agreement. After the closing, the new partner is a captive partner, subject to the laws of the local jurisdiction as are the nationals. The only escape from the confines of the local laws will be either a sale of the newly purchased equity interest or the termination of the joint venture.

7.2.11 EMPLOYEE BENEFITS: RELEVANCE

The human resources aspect of any economic unit is a fundamental factor in its success. A significant part of the cash flow of a company is devoted to various benefits accruing to the employees beyond salary requirements. In our search for relevant information, we will want to know the details of all employee benefits. These must naturally include the rights of employees to purchase equity interests in the target company.

Additionally, the local jurisdiction will have a wide range of social legislation that may be as variable as there being no right to dismissal of employees without just cause to conceding extended maternity leaves of absence with full pay. The material to be reviewed is considerable and is a partial part of the legal due diligences but also in part commercial due diligences. Managers occupy a substantial part of their time with employee relationships. Furthermore, an early appreciation of the social legislation may be a deterrent to the plans the potential partner has concerning the target company.

A partial illustrative list will include the following:

- Beyond plans existing by virtue of the target company employee policies, there must be understood the general requirements of the local jurisdiction concerning the rights of employees, such as mandatory retirement, health facilities, sick leave, and permitted maternity absences. General characteristics of existing employee benefit plans include details of group health, accident, and life insurance.
- Any share purchase plans
- Any profit-sharing plans
- Details of any deferred compensation plans
- Rights to retirement that can be anticipated earlier than provided by law
- Confirmation of all necessary reserves and funding required to support these broad categories of benefits

7.2.12 EMPLOYEE BENEFITS: RISK

All employee benefit plans have to be maintained. They are essential to the proper functioning of the target company. Beyond the financial implications, when these plans exist, considerable time will be expended by management in their proper administration. These plans and employee rights also constitute a social philosophy that is not expected to be contested in the local jurisdiction.

If one of the partners is from a liberal employee market, meaning employees are hired and dismissed at will, but the local jurisdiction is zealous in its concession to and protection of employee social benefits, there is usually no margin of compromise possible. Consequently, the sooner these facts are determined, the more thoughtful will be the response of the investor toward its intended acquisition.

7.2.13 EMPLOYEE BENEFITS: RESOLUTION

Employee legislation and private plans installed by a company are not likely to be altered in any degree whatsoever. If by resolution is meant amending substantially their impact, then there is no resolution. With an investment in a joint venture with a social philosophy considerably different from that of the foreign partner, efforts should be made to understand the reasons and rationale of the local culture and sufficient adaptation displayed so as not to cause the joint venture to founder. This will surely happen if generalized conflict becomes present.

7.2.14 SUBSIDIARIES: RELEVANCE

Part of the organization analysis must determine whether the joint venture company is part of a corporate group. An adequate understanding of all intercompany relationships is necessary. This particularly will have importance to a minority interest partner. He will want to know to what degree the target company can pursue its own business policies and to what extent it is seen by others as a captive client, a prisoner to the interests of the group as a whole.

In joint ventures that may indirectly involve a substantial amount of companies, it is common to have created *management boards* or *advisory councils* whose sole function is to coordinate the various activities of the multiple subsidiaries. All of this will determine to what extent the management of the joint venture is an independent unit or forms part of a larger, integrated group. Partners will surely want to know the degree of permitted action their joint venture vehicle will enjoy. Illustrative information required includes the following:

• Sufficient details to be able to understand the chain of share ownership. When one of the partners to a joint venture is a share corporation, it is not apparent where the ultimate authority and ownership lies. This must be uncovered, and at times, the route is long and contains surprises.

- Responses to questions that will evidence if we are dealing with unstructured management boards with no official statutory recognition yet that act as a cerebral guide for the entire group. A bona fide investor does not unwittingly step into an informal cartel.
- A list of the business activities of those companies comprising the group. This will testify as to whether the joint venture company is going to be able to pursue an independent economic course.
- Information as to any informal management councils existing that are supposed to make suggestions as to the activities of the group as a whole and the objectives it will pursue.

7.2.15 SUBSIDIARIES: RISK

When purchasing an interest in an existing company, and especially when dealing with a subsidiary of a company with global activities, there is a substantial risk that the policies of the local joint venture will be a reflection of larger macroeconomic events and less those of the jurisdiction in which the joint venture is operating.

It happens frequently enough that a multinational majority partner in a modest foreign joint venture pays little attention to its investment and is guided by considerations originating from a board of directors of whom the minority partner has absolutely no knowledge. Such information should have been obtained prior to the signing of the joint venture agreement, but it surely must be uncovered prior to any closing.

A further risk resulting from integration in a larger unit is the imposition of unfavorable contracts on the joint venture company when the other contracting party is another subsidiary controlled by a member of the group. This is just a subterfuge for withdrawing income from the joint venture company without denominating it *dividends*.

7.2.16 SUBSIDIARIES: RESOLUTION

The issue of concealment of true ownership is a good example of how simple clauses that appear to be unnecessary prove to be immensely fruitful. The joint venture agreement should contain language that identifies the seller and also includes as seller any company controlled by or controlling the seller. This is a standard phrase inserted by counsel that besides being repetitive seems at first blush to be musical jargon.

But it ensures that the representations and warranties given by the party with whom the buyer is dealing are also applicable to those other parties not named, the companies that, having a majority interest, may dominate the joint venture partner indirectly.

Imagine company A owns the majority interest in company B, a partner in the joint venture Company C. But company A is controlled by company D and the latter is controlled by another company. The chain of control may stretch a considerable distance. The value of the warranties and efficacy of the due diligence procedures are dependent on dialogue with the ultimate responsible corporate entity.

The solution to knowing ultimate ownership of a company in which a minority interest is being purchased requires a well-drawn joint venture agreement complemented by thorough due diligence procedures. The resolution to a global mentality being applied mechanically to a local company is to have a shareholders' agreement that will affirm the independence of the local joint venture company and its pursuit of commercial interests in light of the local jurisdiction.

7.2.17 HARMONIZATION OF DEPARTMENTS THROUGH KNOWLEDGE MANAGEMENT: RELEVANCE

Companies are divided into administrative units. There are the manufacturing and production department, the sales organization, the marketing section, distribution centers, computer sector, both hardware and software, human resource offices, advertising department, and communications division.

Proper commercial due diligence procedures will compile the details of all these areas, and of course others of interest to a particular joint venture, and then proceed to harmonize the prevailing methods being used by each department so as to ensure there is a common foundation of knowledge management.

Such an integration effort will be productive toward a successful acquisition. Quite frequently, the differing states of knowledge of the various departments are considerable and unnecessarily friction is created when no concentrated attempt is made to ensure a common core of knowledge and experience is accessible to all.

Departments operating with less knowledge than other departments invariably result in an out-of-step joint venture. Productive commercial due diligence procedures will seek out these differences and take steps toward creating a general integration project for the joint venture. A sample questionnaire would seek answers to the following:

- the way information is recorded in every department and if it is inserted in databases
- determining what access each department has to the others' databases
- verification if the information from all departments is collated on any schedule and if conclusions are extrapolated from same
- the frequency of interdepartmental meetings
- the existence of departmental recommendations that refer to knowledge within the province of another department
- the percentage of personnel employed in knowledge management
- the degree of authority of knowledge management personnel
- the frequency with which recommendations from knowledge management is implemented
- a sampling from personnel in all departments as to their perception of the degree of effectiveness of their department in relationship to other departments

7.2.18 HARMONIZATION OF DEPARTMENTS THROUGH KNOWLEDGE MANAGEMENT: RISK

Without knowledge from any department available to others, there cannot be safely assumed that the ultimate repository of management, the board of directors or its equivalent, possesses the necessary knowledge to conciliate the interests of all partners. An effective and successful joint venture requires all partners to be able to make decisions drawn from an accurate base of facts.

If the accounting department is using sophisticated models of financial projections whereas the production department is relying on published official statistics, it is unlikely that they will reach the same conclusion as to the growth of the joint venture company. The larger and more complex the joint venture company, the more critical becomes knowledge management.

7.2.19 HARMONIZATION OF DEPARTMENTS THROUGH KNOWLEDGE MANAGEMENT: RESOLUTION

Installing a proper system of knowledge management is only possible through directives from the board of directors. Such an attitude can be stimulated only by commitments in the shareholders' agreement as to what the partners see as being necessary to ensure a viable joint venture. Unfortunately, often the vision for these corrective measures comes after the acquisition when experience is gained.

As a practical matter, implementing computer programs to ensure simultaneous access to all departments and a daily updating of available information are not going to be the subject of any legal provision in a joint venture document. The risk can be resolved only with a wise selection of management personnel.

7.2.20 WORKER ORGANIZATIONS WITH MANAGEMENT FUNCTIONS OR POWERS: RELEVANCE

There is a great variety among the various jurisdictions as to the extent of powers the employees have concerning management decisions. In some countries, decisions made by the board of directors affecting critical areas such as termination of employees, restructuring of the company, pension policies, indemnities, and reclassification of jobs require the approval of a committee composed of workers' representatives, or at least that the committee be heard.

The degree of collaboration between management and the labor force will be variable, obviously reflecting the prevalent social philosophy of the particular country. Normally, these facts would be uncovered by due diligence procedures conducted by counsel. Such differences may become evident when, as an example, a partner from a free, liberal, no protection to the employee market purchases an interest in a company in a country highly sensitive to the social aspects of employment and extremely protective of these rights.

Between these two extremes are many variables and it is surely one of the vital aspects of commercial due diligence to uncover the specific role of employees in the management of the joint venture. To this end, there will need to be obtained material revealing a number of facts:

- the existence and nature of employee organizations
- whether employee organizations are dependent on company policy or legislative mandate
- the percentage of employees adhering
- the extent of powers of the organizations concerned with management functions
- on what issues, if any, management must advise any employee organization
- the freedom of management to disregard action proposed by management
- a determination if employee organizations are seen as being powerful interlocutors or cosmetic legislation

7.2.21 Worker Organizations with Management Functions or Powers: Risk

The dependency of management on the concurrence of any employee organization can be seen as positive or negative only within the traditions of the local jurisdiction. This of necessity requires that the members of the joint venture have more than a cursory acquaintance with the customs of the country.

An effort has to be made to acquire meaningful insights. Imposing a free market philosophy on a work force used to substantial collaboration with management will result only in disaffected, not dissatisfied, employees. The risk of the existence of strong employee groups exists only if the philosophy of any partner is in disharmony with the prevailing practices.

7.2.22 Worker Organizations with Management Functions or Powers: Resolution

There is no resolution. Whether by company policy or statutory mandate, it will not be possible to make any substantial changes in practice and policy to date. The real solution is for the potential partner to be aware of employee practices and to make a decision prior to any contractual commitments as to whether such a joint venture is viable under these circumstances. Unfortunately, many entrepreneurs underestimate their own level of tolerance.

A possible compromise if the facts are learned late is to grant substantial autonomy to the local joint venture combined with other provisions, such as establishing a high dividend requirement or otherwise obtaining profits by grants of intellectual property rights. This makes possible a return on the investment without a participation in the management.

But insofar as management is concerned, the less the home office has legally to do with the local management the more the various organs of the subsidiary will feel responsible for the well being of their company.

7.2.23 Expatriate Laws: Relevance

An expatriate is a person working in a foreign land. Another word often found in the relevant law is *nonnational*, meaning someone who is not a citizen of the country where the joint venture is operating. Normally, such laws permit that only a fixed percentage of the employees can be nonnationals. Or nonnationals can be employed only in a job for which a national cannot be found.

When the requirement involves a fair amount of subjective opinion, the bureaucracy can wreck the incipient joint venture. No government official is going to admit that there cannot be found a national for a particular job. The most sensible solution is for the acquisition to be conditioned on obtaining the necessary approvals, at least in provisional form.

Under these circumstances, the philosophy becomes different. The foreign investment will not be made unless a certain amount of places are reserved for expatriates. The same government official is not going to deny employment to various nationals by refusing to grant the necessary approval. With this reversal of strategy, some success is usually obtained.

As will be readily understood, what is required is a clause in the purchase agreement conditioning the realization of the sale on the necessary preliminary approvals. What is sought is not the consent of the seller or other partner, but the concurrence of the official entity. The information to be obtained is relatively simple:

- a summary of the law on employment of foreigners
- a determination if there exist restrictions on employing foreigners
- the exceptions permitted
- verification of the approvals needed to employ foreigners
- the entities involved in issuing approvals

7.2.24 EXPATRIATE LAWS: RISK

Without competent key personnel, there will not be an effective joint venture. Freedom to hire therefore must be secured. If this is not going to be possible, the joint venture is probably condemned to the status of providing work to local employees with precarious economic benefits to the partners.

7.2.25 EXPATRIATE LAWS: RESOLUTION

There are resolutions. The shareholders' agreement should define what percentage of the joint venture company may employ foreigners and for what functions. The joint venture agreement will condition the acquisition on obtaining the necessary approvals. If the licenses in question are required to be renewed, the application to the authorities must foresee this contingency and attempt to secure permission for all renewals in advance. Normally, the relevant ministry at least can issue a comfort letter.

7.2.26 COMPENSATION OF DIRECTORS, OFFICERS, AND SHAREHOLDERS: RELEVANCE

Commercial due diligence must uncover, if any exist, multiple facts about the relationship of the members of the board of directors, senior executives, and shareholders with the target company. We are seeking to uncover any contracts that will constitute an onerous obligation to the target company.

We want to know if there are any forms of compensation other than annual fees. When there is a change of control in the target company, which would be the case if the potential purchaser will have a majority equity position, key executives may have the right to golden parachute payments. This is a compensation given to designated personnel that is triggered by the change of ownership control. The information to be compiled is diverse. If the number of personnel is extensive, the information can be provided in a schedule. Sample data for all categories are as follows:

- in addition to employment contracts, all forms of payment including bonuses, stock options, deferred compensation, gross-up payments, severance penalties, and golden parachute arrangements
- employee plans that must be maintained after termination of services, such as retirement and medical benefit plans, all forms of insurance coverage, such as group life, accident, or disability
- the terms of any loans made and whether forgiveness of debt is contemplated
- the terms of any contracts such as consultancy or service agreements

7.2.27 COMPENSATION OF DIRECTORS, OFFICERS, AND SHAREHOLDERS: RISK

The purpose of compiling the information of course is to determine the complete extent of the target company's financial exposure, not only at the moment of the joint venture agreement, or even at closing, but as a continuous obligation. Future payments to be made will affect anticipated cash flow. Furthermore, having fixed monthly payments for former directors or officers is an indirect method of obtaining a higher sales price. It's just being amortized.

7.2.28 COMPENSATION OF DIRECTORS, OFFICERS, AND SHAREHOLDERS: RESOLUTION

As we are dealing with obligations already created, the only possible compromise is if the incoming partner believes them to be onerous, there must be an agreement that above a threshold amount, a monetary platform agreed to between the parties, the sales price will be reduced.

The possibility of this occurring should be ideally determined before the signing of the joint venture agreement. This really is concerned with a determination of the proper sales price. In this case, due diligence procedures would have been better prior to the execution of any agreement. With smaller, low-staff joint venture companies, such information is usually divulged early with exchanges of information. The larger the target company, the more likely this information becomes less visible. However, prior to any agreement being signed, preliminary financial information will be requested and the financial advisers will usually note or request the appropriate data.

7.2.29 RESIGNATIONS AND APPOINTMENTS TO THE BOARD: RELEVANCE

Ordinarily, an incoming partner expects to have some managerial influence. This is one of the significant differences between an investment and a joint venture. Although a new partner does not have to make personnel appointments to see its policies implemented, this would be substantially less true concerning the board of directors. Even with an absentee owner, it is normal for the new partner to have representation on the board and attend the scheduled meetings.

Presence will distinguish collaboration that merely expects an anticipated rate of return on the amount of equity held. But even this symbolic appearance may not be sufficient to instill the sense of a team that is important for the usual joint venture. Particularly with international joint ventures, shared experiences are effective in uniting around a common goal and overcoming cultural differences. Whatever the attitude of the participants, the required information will be a complement to the data assorted under the compensation heading. We need merely to identify the directors and officers to be replaced. We want to know

- the names of directors and officers that will be substituted
- the normal expiration term of their office

7.2.30 RESIGNATIONS AND APPOINTMENTS TO THE BOARD: RISK

The possible prejudices associated with this heading are not being able to make designated appointments that will naturally reduce the managerial influence the new partner expected to have. Fortunately, when an incoming partner does expect to participate in the operational aspect of the joint venture company, this is invariably part of the negotiating agenda.

Even when the potential purchaser does not intend to collaborate in any managerial aspect, it is prudent to secure the right but not necessarily exercise it during any one term. In other words, the exercise of power that management confers may be suspended for a period of time but should not be contractually abandoned.

7.2.31 RESIGNATIONS AND APPOINTMENTS TO THE BOARD: RESOLUTION

When one partner is leaving and a new one enters, the latter will surely have some managers he wishes to appoint, either to the board or to key positions. This is a two-step process. First, the joint venture agreement will contain various representations of fact as to the managerial structure of the joint venture company. There will be discussion between the partners as to the amount of directors each group will be able to appoint. The joint venture agreement will recite any agree- on alterations to the articles of the company detailing the management structure. The shareholders' agreement will further detail the apportionment of director nominations among the partners.

The second step occurs prior to the closing (the purchase) or simultaneously with it. Resignations are handed in. Contracts are voluntarily terminated by the employee or executives in question. Resignations should be obtained prior to the final payment involved in the acquisition.

Employees are notorious in discovering why their former employers have not honored their obligations, and if the resignations are not secured at the appropriate time, they are unlikely to be obtained without further payments or a protracted lawsuit. In simple language, the slate, if it is to be partially wiped clean, must be done so prior to the final legal acts of the acquisition.

Shortly after the acquisition or the establishment of the joint venture, there should be an organizational meeting. The partners elect members to the board of directors, nominate officers, adopt any special by-laws agreed on. The precise contents of these meetings vary from one jurisdiction to another.

From the managerial point of view, it is imperative that the first organizational meeting take place as early as possible subsequent to the formation of the joint venture. As soon as possible, all new members of the board should be operational and key employees appointed. The optimism of the new enterprise makes all this possible in a cooperative ambiance.

The resignation of one group of key employees is followed by the appointment of new executives, which may in turn require the signing of special contracts. These appointments may be the result of nominations by the board of directors or they may require the execution of contracts with the individual employees.

Bonuses, stock-option plans, premiums for performance, all such privileges require the consent of the employer, the joint venture, and this in turn necessitates the approval of the majority of the partners. Such contracts should be executed prior to or simultaneously with the closing.

When the acquisition takes place, or when the joint venture is formed, these contracts should be all signed with no further formalities. Reference to these contracts will appear in the joint venture agreement. But their validity is independent of the joint venture agreement and such contracts have their own rights and obligations.

Waiting to execute such agreements after the formation of the joint venture is not as free from strife, even in the beginning, as one would wish. Often, there seem to arise objections over the person chosen. Perhaps one of the partners had a different employee profile in mind. Securing the execution of the employment contract prior to the acquisition avoids such a problem.

7.2.32 ENVIRONMENTAL ISSUES: RELEVANCE

Green laws intended to protect the environment have proliferated throughout the world as healthfully as the wild underbrush threatened. For the overwhelming majority of jurisdictions in which joint ventures will be formed, there will be multiple legislation affecting the use of property, the manner of production, the disposal of any waste, zoning regulations, and numerous permits to be obtained and renewed.

There is an ambiguous line of compliance that has its natural determination in the investigatory powers of the local and national governments. Strict adherence to all applicable ordinances is the only sensible response. The field is vast and very often special consultants are retained to ensure that due diligence procedures do not overlook any area.

It would serve no purpose to develop a comprehensive list of items for this would be substantially conditioned on the jurisdiction and industry. A proper schedule of information must be left to the incoming partner or consultants familiar with the industry. What will be more useful in our context is to call attention to some aspects that are common whenever there are environmental concerns:

- verification that there exist reserves on the balance sheet for potential environmental liabilities
- there should be reflected in the annual budgets estimates for equipment and maintenance that may need to be replaced
- the existence of insurance policies with adequate coverage for environmental law violation should be confirmed
- confirmation that all environmental permits or licenses are in vigor and that the acquisition will not have any effect on their validity
- a request for any notices of any environmental violations
- interviews with neighbors and local authorities are often revelatory and highly recommended

7.2.33 ENVIRONMENTAL ISSUES: RISK

The associated risks with environmental violations are well known. They are substantial.

7.2.34 ENVIRONMENTAL ISSUES: RESOLUTION

Similar to accrued employee benefits, there is not any resolution to environmental issues other than taking into account their existence, the implications these have for the parties, assurances of there being financial reserves adequate for continuous compliance, and verification of no existing defaults. As to legal obligations, the joint venture agreement will contain the necessary representations and warranties. Regarding adequate reserves and potential litigation, the warranty clauses can be extended to include all of these contingencies.

PART THREE

7.3 FINANCIAL DUE DILIGENCE PROCEDURES: GENERAL OBJECTIVES

The commercial due diligence procedures suggested concern areas of natural and initial interest in matters directly related to corporate governance. They were presented first as the material gathered that will assist management in obtaining early a comprehensive view of possible problems. Yet much more data are necessary.

It is of general knowledge that acquisitions necessitate knowing a substantial amount of information of a financial nature concerning the target company. What is now needed will be the due diligences procedures to ensure the accounting data are in strict conformity with the financial records, which are usually annexed as exhibits to the joint venture agreement, or referred to with sufficient precision by the agreement.

Financial due diligences in this context are therefore basically a review of internal accounting procedures so as to lead to a hopefully well-founded conclusion: The financial records correctly reflect the state of affairs of the target company. If not, there is a breach of the joint venture agreement.

Whatever has been the basis for our price calculations, the economic records of the target company will once again undergo scrutiny in financial due diligences. But there will be an important difference between what was our objective prior to the joint venture agreement and procedures subsequent to its signing.

Provided the warranties have covered the essential material, all that financial due diligence procedures can achieve after the signing of the joint venture agreement is to confirm the veracity of what has been said. We are not going to renegotiate our price unless the joint venture agreement allows this. In the average international joint venture, this is not usual.

Of course, the joint venture agreement will recite that the seller warrants that the financial statements are correct in all material aspects. And this is what we will require from our due diligence procedures: verification of this affirmation. The emphasis is on the word *material* since the more one probes, the more likely some differences will surface. However, the difference between inventory listed at 1,000 and inventory correctly valued at 999.5 is not likely to cause either managerial or legal concern.

Our objective is to uncover material, relevant, substantial deviations from the financial records that, in the opinion of reasonable businessmen, would affect entrepreneurial judgment had such information been correctly recorded. Financial due diligences are thus a search.

This is not a simple task. The examination must be meaningful. To be consequential, there must be understood the reason for the data collected. Moreover, we are confronted with financial statements utilizing accounting concepts and the task is thus even more complicated. We need to know if the concepts used in the financial statements make sense. Net income in one jurisdiction will have different components than in another jurisdiction. The accounting systems differ materially. Yet both jurisdictions have the same objective: an honest determination of what in that jurisdiction is considered net income.

Consequently, financial due diligence procedures tend to become an examination of the way information is collected, how it is reported, and the use, correctly or not, of accounting concepts but from the point of view of the buyer. How else will the buyer know if the warranties are correct? If these possible differences are not raised during negotiations, the warranties will make reference to generally accepted accounting principles. This can be amplified by reference to internationally accepted accounting principles. It can be narrowed even to accounting principles in conformity with the standards used by the buyer or a professional group such as the U.S. Financial Accounting Standards Board (FASB). The precise criteria will depend on the choice made by the buyer in consultation with counsel.

Experience has demonstrated what are those areas most likely to induce error in the managers entrusted with bringing the joint venture to a completion. Such executives will usually be accompanied by technical personnel from the potential buyers who are substantially competent in corporate finance and who will undertake the comparison of the financial data given as correct with the underlying records. However, it is useful for management to have a comprehensive overview of what is intended and a broad idea of areas that often raise problems. In résumé, it is helpful to know what the buyer's auditors are seeking and for what purpose.

7.3.1 ACCOUNTING PROCEDURES

The financial records that have formed the basis of negotiations will be absolutely useless if they are founded on erroneous information or on procedures that are not in accord with those of the buyer. This is not to make a value judgment that the accounting procedures of one jurisdiction are superior to those of another country. Perhaps they are. But the purpose of due diligence procedures is not to discover these differences that, once uncovered, confirm the preference of one methodology over another.

A further requirement is necessary, a standard against which accounting procedures may be compared. Buyers, when making price calculations and risk estimates, make them on financial records in accordance with their own systems. As indicated before, normally, the joint venture agreement will warrant that the financial statements are in accordance with general accepted international accounting principles or other standards. However, the more narrow and detailed the reference, the more the other party will want to know what are the recommendations of this professional group. There is thus initiated an endless discussion.

A compromise has to be sought between a reliable general paradigm and the desire to indicate a satisfactory source of detailed rules. The use of the phrase *internationally accepted accounting principles* usually satisfies the negotiating parties, and, in fact, such a standard is reasonable, valid, and will serve satisfactorily should divergences appear between the accounting procedures of buyer and seller.

If the sellers of the target company have reason to suspect their accounting methods are not consistent with good reporting practice, any doubts should be raised during the negotiation stage and prior to the signing of the joint venture agreement. Consequently, the first items for consideration will be the following:

- examination of how management reports accounting information
- verification of accounting policies and whether they are in compliance with general accepted accounting principles
- confirmation as to whether the accounting system accurately reports the state of the company's accounts
- determination if the target company has created reliable internal controls
- reporting requirements from one department to another
- operational controls
- transparency of financial statements
- approximation of financial statements to accounting records
- review of the target company's computerized accounting system and a determination if it is reliable

What we are seeking to discover is if revenue is being accurately recognized and if the cost attributable to the revenue is being fairly allocated. Financial ratios such as how much net revenue assets will generate are useless if not based on the proper determination of the revenue and the underlying cost.

Fundamental to the recording of proper financial information are the controls the seller utilizes to ensure revenues and cost are supported by the necessary documentation. Our financial due diligence procedures will include a statistical sampling to confirm that the seller's management has controls over purchases, records that correctly report inventory, that there are barriers against fraud, that the information is current, in general, a system that leads to the dependability of the accounting information presented.

Dependent on the size of the target company, the investigation can be considerable. The departments to be examined will include cost and general accounting. Each of these departments will have relied on ledgers and records. Some of these documents will be examined to see if the information therein contained is finding its way either into the general computing system or being transmitted to the next administrative hierarchy. Experience has shown that the more dispersed and specialized are the functions of the personnel of the target company, the more likely the information is being correctly recorded.

Conversely, in those joint ventures that have a reduced number of employees, those that perhaps have had a family in control for many generations, responsibility over the accounts tends to be concentrated in a few hands and the reliability of the information has to be scrutinized carefully. Contrary to first impressions, the smaller the target company in terms of owners and managers, the more there is risk that less than satisfactory standards of accounting are being utilized.

7.3.2 DISCRETIONARY ITEMS THAT AFFECT JOINT VENTURE RESULTS

Many accounting concepts involve an element of discretion. What decision is taken will have its immediate reflection in the financial statements. This can be seen from the examination of the most notorious.

Depreciation schedules

Machinery and equipment are bought. Since they have to be replaced, accounting systems all over the world permit an amount to be deducted from gross income to be set aside for replacement. The official rate of depreciation varies from country to country. However, more importantly, within the same jurisdiction, there will exist alternative methods of depreciation. One will be a uniform percentage rate of cost permitted for a specified number of years. Another method will permit a larger depreciation rate at the initial phase and the rate will decrease with the passage of time.

The rate of depreciation affects the net income reported. Aside from choosing the method most appropriate to the equipment, a discretionary act, there is another element of choice to be considered. Is the official rate even realistic? The more advanced the technology used, the more likely it will be affected by improvements. Therefore, the net income figure reported can contain serious errors of judgment and yet the warranty states the net income is as reflected on the financial statement. Has there been a breach of the warranty? This will depend on the degree of divergence between the rate used and the standards used internationally.

Sales returns

The profit-and-loss statement indicates goods sold resulting in gross income. What is the percentage of goods sold being returned? This will obviously affect materially the gross income. There is an element here of substantial discretion dependent on the product being sold. With a high volume of sales, we will expect a larger rate of return. The accuracy of the profit-and-loss financial statement is directly related to the dependability of the estimated returns. One cannot say the warranty is breached if there is an honest and reasonable disagreement over the rate chosen. Yet, the buyer may honestly believe the gross income figure is overstated and not in conformity with commercial expectations.

Treatment of expenses as a capital expenditure

In accounting theory, money spent in one year that produces benefits in subsequent years cannot be treated as an expense, thus reducing the income for that year, but rather as a capital expenditure to be amortized over a period of time. This has the result of reporting more income annually, or at least in the first year. What will be allowed to be treated as a capital expenditure depends on the reasonableness of the anticipated future benefit. This can produce a lively discussion and obviously involves a substantial amount of discretion.

Reported net income

One would think the most sacred number in the profit-and-loss statement—net income—would be rigidly defined. In fact, many factors can affect its veracity. The method used to calculate inventory, not just the question of undervaluing or overvaluing, which is treated subsequently, but the system used will have incalculable consequences. With inventory moving in and being sold off, what is the cost of the inventory sold? Is it the oldest inventory being sold, with a lower cost, or is it the more recent inventory, with the current costs? If the older, more net income will be reported, yet the replacement value becomes higher.

The company in which an equity interest is being acquired may have recently changed its accounting system, which will of course affect a variety of calculations. A simple change from a cash basis to an accrual basis will have significant repercussions in the reported net income for the first year of changeover.

These two simple examples are an alert as to the flexibility of many accounting concepts, which means financial statements cannot be taken as static, impregnable statistics, but rather a line-by-line analysis is required coupled with a knowledge of the accounting history of the joint venture company. This difficult task will be completed by the auditors, but the corporate manager must guide the inquiry toward those accounting items that have influenced considerably the decision to enter into the joint venture.

7.3.3 COST OF GOODS SOLD

The profit-and-loss statement, which is frequently circulated among the negotiators at the conference table, indicates "Sales" against which there must be deducted "Cost of Goods Sold" to eventually arrive at "Gross Profit." From there, we will descend to net revenue which is clearly dependent on accurate cost reporting. We will want to know how the target company is calculating its cost of goods; otherwise, the profit-and-loss statement being discussed is a useless fantasy of someone's idea of profits.

Are they doing it by calculating the total cost for each unit, known technically as the job order cost system, or are they doing it by the process cost system, whereby as the product, or service, moves through each department, an added value takes place, with a resulting departmental cost?

A job order cost system will require more details; a process cost system will divulge an average cost. Both these systems require detailed accounting records to substantiate their conclusion. It is these records the auditors will want to see to determine if the cost accounting system accurately records direct, indirect, and overhead costs. Cost accounting is a specialized area and subject to various theoretical considerations. It can never be assumed that the line "Cost of Goods Sold" on the profit-and-loss income statement is a rigid conclusion merely necessitating mathematical confirmation. It involves theory and accurate cost reporting, both requiring considerable experience in the field of cost accounting.

Since many financial ratios are dependent on this key number and since the whole profit-and-loss statement will be influenced by its accuracy or lack of it, the cost accounting records merit considerable confirmation, an area carefully reviewed by the buyer's technical staff. Improper cost accounting will affect substantially the net revenue calculation and may give rise to substantial differences between the financial statements used between the parties and the realities. Cost accounting seeks to determine the production cost to put the product into its final salable stage.

7.3.4 Inventory

Cost of production affects the profit-and-loss statement. An accurate accounting of inventory is required to have an accurate balance sheet that is used to determine the net worth of the seller. There is no more important item on the balance sheet or profit-and-loss statement than the use and determination of this inventory value. Correct inventory reporting is fundamental in verifying the reliability of a company's financial statements.

Its representation on the balance sheet must be verified by due diligence procedures for it is a key element in the valuation process and has surely been considered by the buyer.

However, besides affecting the value of the balance sheet, it is also a critical factor in the profit-and-loss statement and its valuation is at times deliberately erroneous for tax purposes and for enhancing the acquisition value of the company.

From gross profit or sales, we have to deduct the cost of the goods sold, which, in addition to the production or manufacturing costs, includes purchases made during the year to generate these revenues. Inventories are assets used in the revenue-producing process. Not reporting the inventory correctly will permeate the entire profit-and-loss statement and lead to false conclusions.

The most common stratagem is to either overstate or understate the inventory. This is because during the year our accounts reflect the beginning inventory to which are added purchases of inventory made during the same accounting period. Cost of goods for a tax year will be the sum of beginning inventory plus inventory purchased.

Understating the final inventory count means more has been purchased to make the sales in question. If we understate the inventory, our unit cost rises. If we overstate the final inventory, our cost of goods drops, since less expenditures were needed to generate the same sales income.

Further complications arise from an incorrect statement of inventory. Errors committed in one year are obviously carried over into the other year with different results. If the final inventory is undervalued in year 1, then in year 2, the cost of goods will be understated by the same amount of error since less purchases were needed to produce the sales for year 2. There will be an increase in net income by the amount of the error.

This is because the amount of sales has been generated with apparently less inventory than was needed, which raises the profit margin and, all things being equal, ultimately net income. It will be observed that the error in year 1, understating the net income, was corrected by overstating the net income in year 2. This canceling effect is not innocuous. It may reflect incorrect patterns. In our example, it would mean revenues from year 1 to year 2 showed a trend of rising net income, exactly what a seller would wish to demonstrate.

Although it may seem contradictory, in fact, the following rules can be enunciated:

1. Understating final inventory understates net income. The reason is that the understatement in inventory results in overstating purchases.
2. The reverse is true. Overstating final inventory overstates net income. The reason is that the overstatement in inventory understates purchases during the tax year.

These errors prolong themselves into the subsequent tax year.

3. With the beginning inventory understated, the net income for the subsequent year will be overstated. More sales revenue has been generated with presumably (but false) less goods.
4. With the beginning inventory overstated, the net income will be understated for sales revenue will be attributed (but erroneously) to more purchases.

Subjacent to this analysis is a question we have not yet addressed. How will the inventory be valued? We can understand readily enough the importance of the year-end inventory valuation. But when we speak of understating or overstating, what are the criteria being used?

Unfortunately, there is not one method that is satisfactory for all situations and there is considerable disagreement among professional accountants as to which is the best method for valuation purposes for any one company. Besides being dependent on the economic unit in question, the applicable macroeconomics is a contributing factor, that is, whether prices are rising and there is inflation or deflation.

A review of inventory pricing is a subject for the principles of accounting. However, the corporate manager must be aware that accurate inventory counting does not ensure realistic inventory accounting and this can be determined only by the audit team.

In addition to the problems of determining inventory and its value are other more general related problems.

Dependent on the target company, management should take steps to ensure the inventory included is the inventory of the target company, not inventory held on consignment, or other legal situations in which title to the merchandise does not pass to the target company. This aspect of goods and title will be reviewed by the attorneys but it must be accompanied by management's investigation into operational aspects.

Additionally, no one better than the incoming management will know whether the goods on hand are obsolete or inventory that can be sold readily. If we are dealing with a target company in the electronics industry, technological changes are occurring so rapidly that short time periods often render inventory, if not obsolete, at least difficult to sell.

The proper evaluation of inventory and its accurate status affect both the balance sheet on the assets side and the profit-and-loss statement as an entry within the cost of goods. With such pervasive influence, in-depth due diligence procedures are warranted under the direction of an auditor or professional equivalent.

7.3.5 Cash or its equivalent

One would think a simple entry on the asset side of *cash* would not raise any questions. Either the target company has the cash, or else there is terribly inaccurate reporting. Depending on the degree of transparency, the truth of the amount of cash may not be evident. This may be caused by what is known as *compensating balances*. As part of a loan agreement, a bank may require the borrower, in our case, the target company, to maintain a specified amount of cash at the bank as a permanent balance.

This is a cushion to the bank. It is hoped that the bank will have recourse to that amount in the event of a default by the target company borrower. These compensating balances reduce to a degree, dependent on the balance, expenditures of the target company for the year. They function similar to overdrafts in which the accepting bank establishes a line of credit that must be reduced before further overdrafts will be granted.

Financial due diligence procedures will seek to discover these compensating balances by making the necessary inquiries at the lending banks. Although the requirement of compensating balances does not reduce the cash asset on the balance sheet, it does reduce cash available in practice and should be taken into account. This restriction of a compensating balance is quite common in medium and small capitalized companies.

Some balance sheets will include *marketable securities* or expressions of a similar nature. In the average joint venture, which is a one-product-line company with modest personnel size, assets readily convertible to cash are not likely to be a prominent item. Naturally, as the size of the target company increases, and the amount of its revenues rises, there is a possibility surplus cash will be diverted to income-producing, short-term investments other than in bank accounts. Care has to be taken to ensure any near-cash items listed are also not being held on deposit as collateral by a lender or subject to other restrictions that would prevent their conversion at will. Normally, on audited accounts, these restrictions should show up. However, there may not be audited accounts.

7.3.6 ACCOUNTS RECEIVABLE

In addition to the current assets of cash and inventory, which will be used to generate cash flow, there are the accounts receivable. On the balance sheet of the target company, there will be indicated an amount for accounts receivable that may constitute a considerable asset in terms of the total valuation of the target company. To what extent are these accounts actually collectible? Just listing them as being due and owing does not mean they will be paid. In fact, sometimes the seller's best opportunity of having them paid is by the sale of the equity interest that will be based on the asset value of the target company. In other words, the risk of collection is being passed to the new partner, the potential buyer.

Particularly in smaller companies, these risks can be substantial. Of the total amount of accounts receivable, we will want to know if they are uniformly distributed among multiple debtors or if they are dependent on one large customer. Being dependent on one significant customer is a sure sign to those conducting due diligence procedures to make inquiries of the customer to find out when payment can be reasonably expected, if there is any potential litigation over the amount of the account receivable, or even if the customer is in a financial position to liquidate its debt. An account receivable on the balance sheet is no automatic assurance of its payment.

Related questions, often not easy to determine, concern to what extent a certain percentage of accounts receivable is not going to be collected. In those companies with multiple objects for sale, and revenues dependent on thousands of items being sold, the first question will be if a certain quantity of the accounts receivable will ever be collected; the second question is if the target company is accounting for this eventuality in its accounts.

Historical experience may be of some value to those conducting due diligence procedures, but the most accurate conclusion will be based on a detailed examination of the individual accounts of the debtors. This may not always be possible or even practical; then, of course, estimates will have to be made in accordance with acceptable accounting principles. Of great utility and importance will be the records of the target company, such as aging schedules, average time for collection, and whether accounts receivable are uniformly dispersed among many debtors or whether we are dealing with a company serving a restricted customer base.

7.3.7 Fixed assets

Frequently, the fixed assets of a target company present a hopeless combination of facts. The land on which the factory or premises are sitting is undervalued, so much so that were the building removed, the land would be worth more than the entire equity interest of the owners. The building and equipment may be antiquated, barely serviceable. As to why the buildings are not immediately torn down, the explanation is quite simple. Demolishing the fixed assets requires dismissing all the employees, which is probably not legally possible in many jurisdictions.

The balance sheet valuations therefore often present the dilemma of undervalued assets and overvalued equipment. In these situations, the potential buyer should not be lured into increasing the offered price based on informal declarations, probably easily confirmed, that the book values of the fixed assets do not reflect current economic conditions and represent an enormous capital gains for the owner of these assets, that is, the target company.

Carrying the fixed assets at their historical cost may be a serious insult to the existing inflationary pressure, but no one is going to profit from this economic climate due to social legislation. The potential capital gains are unlikely to be ever realized in the medium term. The land only has value when the employees have left. Furthermore, the purchase of the equity interest is in a going economic concern and not in a real estate venture. Arguments therefore as to unrealistic land values, no matter how accurate, have little interest to the average foreign investor in international joint ventures.

Of greater concern, more relevant, and more subject to due diligence procedures is the state of the building and the equipment that forms part of the fixed assets. Here of course management must communicate effectively to its due diligence team what are the requirements for a successful manufacturing process or other activity.

There is physical deterioration, which will only turn up on a physical examination of the plant. There is obsolescence, which will be known by the buyer's engineers, but this requires an inspection of the plant and its equipment. The depreciation rates of the target company and the local prices for replacement have to be obtained to ensure that the depreciation values being carried on the financial statements are realistic. If the rates are low and the replacement cost is high, the value of the balance sheet asset of equipment will be inaccurate.

7.3.8 Physical Inspection of the Site

It would be natural that the negotiating team of the buyer has visited the premises of the seller several times. However, the personnel entrusted with the acquisition may not have the same technical expertise as their colleagues in the engineering department. Marketing executives may understand quite well the origin and purpose of the product they are selling, but the machinery used to manufacture it will surely have many specifications that change frequently.

In those joint ventures involving plants and equipment, it is essential that an on-site inspection be made of the facilities. This should reveal to the production engineers any signs of obsolescence or machinery not suited for the objective of the joint venture. This is related to the valuations given on the balance sheet to the fixed assets. They may be values that have historical accuracy, but the rates of depreciation are not realistic with current technological advances. Depreciation rates of 15 and 20 years permitted in the local jurisdiction will result in equipment being carried on the balance sheet at a higher value than it is worth. Progress will have overtaken its utility.

7.3.9 Liabilities

The company liabilities due diligence procedures seek are not only the obvious loans or other credit arrangements. It would be unusual in the climate of a joint venture for these to be willfully concealed. Rather, many credit agreements, and other forms of financing, contain clauses whereby a change of control in the borrower, or even a sale of an equity interest, gives the lender the right to accelerate the entire debt.

The loan agreements may permit a sale of equity interests but obligate that the new owners be creditworthy, a standard that will be defined in the loan agreement. What was foreseen as a long-term liability is thus converted into an account payable due immediately. Such provisions may not even be known to the borrower, that is, the target company. They are provisions buried in complex legal language in one of the lending agreement clauses.

Financial due diligence procedures will call for a review of any material lending agreement and acceleration clauses will be revealed. If existing, they are a material variation to the financial statements and will have to be resolved prior to closing. Ordinarily, securing the lender's consent prior to a closing is substantially facilitated in contrast to postsale permission.

Falling within the concept of liabilities, but quickly revealed in legal due diligence procedures, are dividends in arrears. When the target company has issued preferred shares carrying the right to annual cumulative dividends when there are after-tax profits, due diligence procedures will determine if they have been paid or, if not, the extent of the accrued liability.

7.3.10 Tax compliance

One of the more precarious areas when forming a joint venture is tax liability. We are not referring to the tax consequences of the transaction, nor to tax litigation, which will be promptly discovered by legal due diligences. What is in question is if the target company owes any taxes for which there have not been made provisions.

Even the best efforts of the target company accountants may not coincide with the opinion of the local tax department, a fact that may be only revealed after the sale. No amount of academic financial due diligence procedures will uncover a reasonable difference of opinion. This can be done only by a visit to the local tax bureau: informal meetings with the local tax authorities and obtaining a well-informed opinion.

In many jurisdictions, it is possible to obtain an official declaration from the local tax authorities that no taxes are owed. This is of limited although useful value since it will not refer to facts the tax authorities may not have yet considered or even seen. Additionally, the time required to receive such a certificate is usually not within the managed limits of patience of the participants.

The preceding discussion is an indication of some of the basic material an auditing team will review, which often raises lively discussions during negotiations in an acquisition but that will augment in details, topics, and complexity in accordance with the circumstances.

Part Four

7.4 Legal due diligence procedures

As previously discussed, there is a significant difference between establishing a joint venture and purchasing an equity interest in an existing company. It is the acquisition that requires thorough due diligence procedures, both financial and legal. Each team of investigators, both lawyers and auditors, has its own procedures and methods of obtaining information based on experience in similar industries and services. However, legal due diligence procedures are not as industry-dependent as financial due diligence procedures; for example, all companies, whatever their activity, need company articles.

Perhaps more so than the financial investigation, legal due diligence procedures tend to be delegated to the buyer's counsel, and unless there are any critical problems to resolve, management is unlikely to think any more about the issue. Of course, with auditors and lawyers conducting due diligence procedures, there is also a duplication of information but used for different purposes.

The buyer's accountants want to know the stated capital, or its equivalent, of the target company for balance sheet purposes; the attorneys want to know who are the owners of the target company that is represented by the capital to ensure all equity interests are identified. This then confirms the accuracy of the percentage interest being purchased.

A certain lack of interest on the part of management toward legal due diligences is understandable. After all, what is the intrigue that can be stimulated by knowing on what page of the local real estate records the plant site is recorded? The same cannot be said when it is discovered that the holder of a bond has the right to convert a portion of his credit into shares of the borrower, our target company.

Such surprises are not likely in the medium and small company joint ventures in which bonds have probably never been issued. But the variety of facts is so great in the commercial world that statistical certainty is of small comfort. Most due diligence procedures after the signing of a joint venture agreement might be characterized as confirming the obvious. Yet, when there is a divergence between what has been represented and the actual facts, the results can be catastrophic.

Furthermore, aside from the discovery of important facts contrary to what has been represented, it is not possible to effectively manage an international joint venture without an understanding of the basic division of powers between the different organs of the target company, any special rights that may have been created by the articles of the company, and what veto power one group may have over another. All these will be revealed by legal due diligence procedures.

The fundamental legal principles that regulate the functioning of a company should be within the general knowledge of the international manager for these issues will be raised frequently during the multiple conferences preceding the signing of the joint venture agreement. They also form a foundation for structuring a joint venture to ensure the protection of minority interests and preserving any management concessions that have been made in the joint venture agreement.

Lawyers traditionally in common-law jurisdictions have a close working relationship with their clients and often participate significantly in negotiations prior to the signing of the joint venture agreement as well as in the discussion of any problems that should arise, without there being necessarily any litigation pending. In such jurisdictions, lawyers are not sought only when it is necessary to file a complaint in court but rather as advisers to avoid conflict. Invariably, this requires a general knowledge of legal due diligence procedures from the corporate manager in order to appreciate their reason and to form an effective part of the team entrusted with the acquisition.

For all of these reasons—an awareness of possible problems, a better understanding of the mechanisms of corporate life, an appreciation of the issues that must be reviewed by counsel, the expectation to be an active participant in the analysis of practical problems, the necessary foundation to be able to understand how power will be divided among the various organs of the company—legal due diligence procedures merit a short review. This will substantially complement the comprehension of the international manager concerning international joint ventures.

7.4.1 Review of corporate charter, by-laws, and all amendments

Not all jurisdictions have the same documentary requirements for companies. But all jurisdictions will have legislation that indicates the document that gives origin to the company and what this document must contain. Within the contents of what may seem as an excessively long instrument written in a technical language can be garnered the basic structure of any company. This may be summarized as follows:

- name of the company
- capital of the company
- owners of the company
- how the ownership is represented
- transference of ownership
- management
- meeting of the owners
- division of power between management and owners

- voting
- profit distribution
- termination

Much of the complexity of company charters is a development of these themes. There is, of course, a variety of subject matter that may be inserted into the corporate charter in conformity with the experience and foresight of counsel. Nevertheless, the broad categories just listed constitute a reasonable approximation of the skeleton of the corporate entity. From most of these categories will come the troublesome problems managers must confront.

But the corporate charter is more than just a recitation of who has power to delegate what responsibilities. Owners and management should give particular attention to the division of power as defined in the enabling documents. Management will want to especially understand

- the subject matters exclusively within the jurisdiction of the managerial organs, such as the board of directors
- the limitations imposed on management by other sources, such as the shareholders' agreement or the articles of the company
- the topics confided by law or the articles of the company to the shareholders
- what veto power the shareholders have over the judgment of the managers
- the source of this veto power and if it is impregnable to attack

Existing documents colliding with the objectives of the incoming partner will be disclosed during legal due diligence procedures. Proposed amendments can be made an obligation by the joint venture agreement. This is a topic to which we will devote considerable attention in Chapter Eight. Within the separation of powers established by the company articles will lie the solution to a productive ownership and effective management.

7.4.2 Minutes of the Company

In many civil-law countries, by-laws are not used as they are in common-law countries. They do not exist. The articles of the company will establish on whom authority is conferred for any particular topic and the need for any witnesses to attest to signatures. Corporate authority will also emanate from nominations originating with the board of directors.

Particularly in civil-law countries, the authority to represent a corporate entity is surrounded with many formalities, including authentication of signatures by a notarial seal that is founded on a reading of the enabling resolutions passed by the board of directors. When by-laws are used, it is necessary that they be examined to understand in detail how corporate authority is exercised: by whom and subject to what procedures.

However, even if by-laws do not exist, there are the minutes of the meetings of the board of directors, which is an obligatory record book for all companies. When there are minutes, they provide an invaluable source of information as to the internal history of the target company, revealing a wide variety of information that could not be easily found, if ever:

- references to important contracts
- possible litigation
- contemplated purchases
- forecasts of sales
- reports submitted to the board of directors
- possible labor disputes
- expansion plans
- accounting concerns
- expected profits

The extent of the review of the corporate minutes will be conditioned by the importance of the acquisition and the time permitted. At the very least, however, a simple chronological list should be compiled to ensure all minutes are present, even if not read.

7.4.3 CORPORATE EXISTENCE

There is no failure more absurd than finding subsequent to the joint venture agreement that the target company lacks licenses required by legislation, or has failed to register its amended corporate charter, or that it is operating a factory in a green zone area. No matter this has been going on for years. The laxity of one generation of technocrats is easily and speedily replaced by the zealousness of their descendants. One of the first requirements of legal due diligence procedures, therefore, will be to ensure that the company is operating with all necessary licenses.

Equally important is that the target company has been registered at the relevant commercial conservatory. This is the equivalent of a certificate of good standing. Whether companies are formed before a notary in a civil-law country or by an attorney in a common-law jurisdiction, the articles have to be registered and filed with the commercial conservatory.

It may happen that this is not done. There is a failure to register because of some technical data missing. The absence of the registration may go unnoticed; remedying it may be deemed unnecessary. Although the failure to register may not have serious consequences, invariably when a new partner is on the verge of making the purchase, the final notarial act becomes impossible because the notary will not execute the deed of purchase without a certificate from the commercial conservatory stating who the current partners are.

As soon as possible, therefore, managers should request their legal advisors to provide them with the registration certificates. This will avoid last minute delays that become dramatic showdowns between the new partners as the time for closing approaches.

7.4.4 VERIFICATION OF CAPITAL

The joint venture agreement will state what is the capital of the target company and how much of this capital is being sold. The sale of an equity interest carries with it voting rights. Two assumptions are often made that can lead to false expectations. The first is that the stated capital is the issued capital. In many jurisdictions, it is possible to form a company with 1,000 as capital but only issue 750 in shares. The other 250 are reserved for further emissions. This avoids having to comply with multiple legislative requirements concerning augments of capital, such as publication of notices in the local newspaper. Consequently, instead of forming a company with 750 and then later augmenting the capital to 1,000, a company is formed with 1,000 but only 750 are sold. Buying 375 of 750 will constitute 50 percent of the issued shares, but if the other 250 are issued later to another party, the 50 percent is reduced to 37.5 percent (375 out of 1,000 and not 750).

The second assumption, which may have more serious consequences than the first, is that all voting power is equal and is related to percentage ownership. It is if nothing further is done to alter this general rule. But the basic principle of one share, one vote can be altered easily, either by charter provision or private agreement, so that a party with a minority interest can have a veto power on a variety of issues.

This may be conferred easily in the articles, which establish an 80 percent voting majority for mergers; or it may be a result of the law, which instead of requiring 80 percent demands only 75 percent. In either case, a partner with 51 percent cannot muster sufficient votes by mere ownership.

Counsel will therefore examine carefully the law and documents to determine what is the capital, has it all been issued, are there other legal instruments that may be converted to capital, is the voting power synonymous with capital ownership, and how has this been altered. Ownership and management power will be related directly to these questions. A simple schedule should be prepared for the review of management, which indicates

- verification of issued capital
- confirmation if there exist any legal instruments that can be converted to capital, for example, convertible bonds and stock options
- schedule of shares by rights or any special privileges
- list of all owners, that is, shareholders or equivalent, to ensure all capital is represented and identified

The last requirement would seem to have little practical use for medium and smaller companies. Yet, in fact, the contrary is more often the rule. Oftentimes, smaller companies have issued fractional interests to employees through the years to maintain their interest. Such employees may have been retired at the time of the acquisition. The potential buyer wishes to acquire all the outstanding equity except for shares remaining with another major owner. Not being able to identify these fragmented equity interests requires compliance with statutory notices and multiple delays on issues requiring a general meeting of all owners or other matters for which the law demands notice be sent to all owners.

7.4.5 Sale of Equity Interest

The sale of a partial interest in a company may obligate proof that the other equity interests have no objection, and this may include the company. In some situations, particularly with private limited liability companies, total restrictions on the sale of equity interests are permitted and the company's approval is required. Consequently, in addition to ensuring the legality of the company's existence, its completed registration at the commercial registry, we will want also to have the certainty the sale is possible, that there are no legal impediments to the acquisition.

This will further require a review of existing legal documents affecting the joint venture company such as the shareholders' agreement and the joint venture agreement. The articles of the company may have express provisions concerning transfers. But there may be other clauses forming part of private agreements that have direct bearing on the acquisition and these have to be examined carefully.

7.4.6 LIST OF ALL DIRECTORS AND TERM OF OFFICE

As soon as the acquisition is completed, or simultaneously with the legal acts involved, there normally will be a change in the top management of the company. This will usually require resignations of some of the current directors or others with superior management functions. In small companies, knowing the identity of those entrusted with these functions should not present any problems.

However, when purchases are made in companies forming part of larger corporate groups, oftentimes the identity of all the directors may not be known completely. The managers present at the operating company level will be identified easily. But distant nominees whose names have been selected for purposes of the corporate organization, perhaps directors at the home office responsible for a particular global area, will escape local knowledge easily. They are probably honorific appointments with no intent of having practical effects.

Requiring a detailed list of all directors not only serves the more humble task of being complete, it also avoids litigation or embarrassing situations. It may happen that a director called on to resign does not want to terminate his tenure. He may have a small equity position. His management functions are well remunerated. He has not been consulted on the sale or if he has, there was nothing he could do about it anyway, except refuse to cooperate, which includes not voluntarily terminating his tenure of office.

Due diligence procedures will ferret out this possible dilemma as the joint venture agreement will call for appointments of the new partners or their nominees. This can only be accomplished by knowing how many vacancies will have to be filled and who are occupying them at the moment.

7.4.7 CONTRACTS WITH DIRECTORS AND/OR EMPLOYEES

Prior to the acquisition, we need to identity carefully any possible problems in the transition from one management to another. Part of this will be to be aware of any contracts existing with directors and/or employees. Even with directors staying on, there are no assurances that their presence will be pertinent in the near future. In companies of all sizes, this may be a serious problem.

In smaller companies, profits are often taken out through consultancy contracts, which may attract a lower tax rate. It is also a means of giving employment to a family member. In larger companies, operating managers are often hired by the local company so that their salary remuneration is divided between the local company and the home office. Whether we are dealing with directors or shareholders, future conflict will be avoided by knowing previously those contractual relationships and their terms. The joint venture agreement will have listed these potential contracts or will have warranted there are none. Full disclosure therefore should be possible.

7.4.8 REAL ESTATE

Counsel will review many areas that necessitate careful confirmation but that ordinarily will not require a great deal of attention by new management, at least as to the verification process. Ownership of assets must be proved and shown to be free from any encumbrances or litigation. Although leases are not real estate assets in theory, they are considered along with an examination of title belonging to realty. They have to be reviewed to ensure that they are still in existence and that they are not subject to termination because of the planned acquisition. Such an event would be unusual. In acquisitions involving considerable fixed assets, legal due diligence procedures are a painstaking process requiring examination of official real estate records.

The sale of an equity interest is not an assignment of a lease. The purchase of an interest in a company is not the purchase of one of its assets, in this case, a lease. In fact, equity interests are sold to avoid having to assign a lease, which may require the consent of the lessor, and this will be given only with a demand for higher rents. However, one of the functions of counsel will be to examine all significant leases to ensure the acquisition has no effect on their validity.

7.4.9 REVIEW OF ALL MATERIAL SUPPLY AND MANUFACTURING CONTRACTS

Often the business of the target company is dependent on a few supply or manufacturing contracts. This is particularly true in enterprises that sell to large discount houses or other large, wholesale operations. Whether the important contract is to supply or to sell, a target company whose reliance on a limited amount of purchases or sales is clear obligates the purchaser to confirm that these contracts are in full force and vigor. This can be done by a letter of confirmation, a telephone call, or a visit to the entity in question.

7.4.10 REVIEW OF TRANSFERS OF TECHNOLOGY, TRADE SECRETS, AND KNOW-HOW

Even more precarious in acquisitions are the royalty and other intellectual property contracts, which may form an important part of the assets of the target company. The danger here is that the relevant contracts may have a termination clause should any part of the ownership of the target company pass to a competitor. Defining what is a possible competitor is not always as clear as it should be. The relevant contract may go further and require approval of the licensor to the transfer of equity.

These possible restrictions are not an attempt to restrict the movement of capital but rather to prevent the exploitation of the technology being conveyed to others without compensation. By being an owner of a licensee, the joint venture company will naturally acquire the knowledge that is licensed and it is natural that it is passed on to the equity owners.

Similar to supply contracts, the validity of intellectual property licenses may be conditioned on control of the licensee not changing beyond a certain percentage. This would be more likely in transfers of know-how or trade secrets in which what is being transmitted is an oral tradition, not protected in writing because when it is reduced to writing, its exploitation by others would be obtained easily.

7.4.11 ENVIRONMENTAL ISSUES

The depth of this legal review will be commensurate with the activity of the target company. Clearly, an industrial plant site will obligate considerable review of existing laws to determine compliance, whereas a marketing company may require only confirmation of zoning ordinances. When dealing with factories or other industrial output units, the only information that can be safely relied on will be from the ministries or other governmental bodies having jurisdiction over industry, waste, and environmental control. Just determining the identity of the relevant authorities is a difficult task but it has to be done. Oftentimes, a visit to the ministry with the largest jurisdiction, for example, the ministry of industry, will provide a reliable beginning. With a definitive schedule of the competent authorities and a visit to these authorities, compliance can be determined with satisfaction.

7.4.12 Study and review of all litigation records

Pending litigation is easy to detect. Included in this material are administrative procedures, arbitration, and any procedure to which the target company is a party or has been notified to appear. This information can be obtained from counsel to the target company. More difficult to ascertain is litigation that has not surfaced formally, for example, that has no complaint filed in court.

Habitually, litigation is preceded by a letter or a demand. The various departments of the target company have to be consulted to determine if any vexatious communications have been received. Normally, counsel to a potential litigant will address any letter to management. But individuals, asserting claims on their own behalf before consulting an attorney, often send demands to a department head. If the target company is fairly well organized, there should be a file or database for letters received and a notation as to their objective.

Failing this, but being done with a certain sophistication so as not to offend potential partners, is a direct question to the various department managers as to any knowledge of possible complaint, not only from former employees but also customers and suppliers. In very large companies, there is a practical limitation to this inquiry. In smaller businesses, any third-party dissatisfaction of importance is generally known.

Whether existing or potential, the consequences of litigation should never be assumed to be without merit. No matter how unreasonable the claim appears, its defense is a time-consuming process and usually expensive. The worst results should be anticipated always and the appropriate reserves set up or deducted from the purchase price. What seems improbable or a claim founded on palpably untrue facts may be seen in another light by those called to judge.

There is no more erratic course than the route of a lawsuit. Not all roads lead to Rome. Many an attorney has found himself, with his beleaguered client, in the midst of a copse. The joint venture agreement will certainly contain warranties against any pending litigation or known facts that may give rise to litigation.

7.4.13 RESULTS OF INVESTIGATION

By the irony of logic, or, if you prefer, poetic justice, those who conduct due diligence procedures but fail to do them well may find themselves subject for breach of professional responsibility to their clients. Such a possibility naturally raises the question: What should be the results of the investigation? Do counsel, and the auditors, deliver their conclusions item by item in detail to the client, or in the form of a summary, or just a letter stating there have been no breaches of the joint venture agreement and due diligence procedures have not revealed any matters that would materially affect the proposed transaction? Practice varies and the manager must indicate his preference.

Although there are no written rules on this issue, the requirements of professional responsibility would point to all documentation being retained well beyond the closing date. It would be prudent to have such records available until the law forecloses any reasonable possibility of action arising from the transaction, what is referred to as the statute of limitations having expired. This phrase means that certain time periods have elapsed so that claims cannot be raised in court.

Good practice should obligate further action. The advisors should have their conclusions summarized and kept in a manual. Any serious due diligence procedures should culminate in a specification handbook, which, if needed, can be consulted as one would any manual. The working documents should be passed to digital form and stored for the ultimate use of the client. One might argue that even more is required.

Perhaps the material should be delivered also to the client for further safekeeping and use. There is a generalized mental attitude among professionals that the work product is theirs. As with other objects for which payment has been tendered, this seems contrary to the theory of payment and delivery. However, for the moment, the practice is not uniform between clients and those whom they have hired. Of course, the matter can be resolved easily in the initial terms of retainer. The client can simply confirm that the results of due diligence procedures will be delivered in the form the client wishes for its permanent use.

7.4.14 LEGAL DUE DILIGENCE: CHECKLIST FOR MANAGERS

Financial due diligence procedures are probably more conceptual in nature than legal due diligence procedures, seeking to uncover the theoretical basis behind the figures as reported. With legal due diligence procedures, we can prepare a schedule of topics because we are seeking objective evidence. Does something exist or does it not?

In practice, there is often some overlapping between the work of auditors and lawyers. Our list repeats the preceding material and indicates other areas that can serve as a general checklist between the corporate manager and counsel leading to a fuller understanding of its relevancy for the joint venture. The corporate manager will want to know the results of what counsel will eventually review:

- corporate charter
- minutes
- corporate licenses
- operating license
- determination of capital of company
- amount of shares issued
- equity instruments in the hands of third parties
- option rights
- foreign capital authorizations
- consent to sale
- list of shareholders
- list of directors
- contracts among directors, officers, and company
- consultancy agreements
- employee benefit plans
- list of real estate
- list of major equipment
- supply contracts
- technology licenses
- environmental compliance
- known litigation

With the completion of legal due diligence procedures, we approximate the final transaction. We must, most likely, suggest important changes to the existing articles if we are dealing with an acquisition or, if in formation, ensure the joint venture structure protects the minority interests. This is the subject matter of Chapter Eight.

8

HOW TO PROTECT OWNERSHIP RIGHTS AND MANAGEMENT FUNCTIONS: CUSTOMIZING THE INTERNATIONAL JOINT VENTURE

PART ONE

8.1 THE NATURE OF THE PROBLEM: OWNERSHIP RIGHTS AND COMPANY STRUCTURE

Ownership means the exercise of rights and not just owning a percentage of equity. The latter is how ownership is recognized in the law. One of the rights of ownership is management, which requires an active role with influence as to decisions and objectives. Titles without practical consequences are useless. All of these pragmatic outcomes will depend to a great extent on the internal legal structure of the joint venture and how it functions. The particular organization of a company is effectuated through the company articles, which define multiple aspects of how votes are heard and counted. The company articles are the rules affecting the collective voice of the company parliament.

One primary concern in this chapter is on the realties of ownership and the effectiveness of authority. Ownership rights are closely dependent on the division of authority in a company between the managers and the owners. To be an owner means you can exercise power, have influence, issue instructions, take decisions, and implement ideas.

Ownership without authority is only an investment. The exercise of authority is manifested by who has the right to utilize it. Authority is not automatically allocated among the various partners as soon as a joint venture comes into existence. It is contingent on legislative mandates and company articles. The more authority is diffused between the partners, the more we can expect that the joint venture will reflect the collaborative efforts of all.

With a sensible division of authority, we will ensure no one group dominates the joint venture, imposing its will without regard for the interests of others. The legal support of unity by a sensible division of authority, therefore, is a mandatory object of examination to understand how ownership and management rights are performed in practice.

There is a governing board. There are shareholders. There may be a workers' advisory board. There are operating managers. There may be a management committee. There are department heads. There may be a fiscal council. Each of these organs will have a predominant or minor management role to play. Basically, we are concerned about the apportionment of authority between management and the owners.

The former are represented through a board of directors, or other management group, and the latter express themselves through a general assembly. The two poles of authority in any company therefore are a management organ and a gathering of owners, which has various names, such as a shareholders' meeting or a partners' meeting, all of which are generically described as a general assembly.

In large public corporations, the communications distance between these two groups is large, with almost insurmountable barriers erected between management and owners. It is the nature of quoted public corporations that management's judgment, provided it is not abused or betrays the owners, can be altered rarely after the fact. On the other hand, management functions in the everyman joint venture, with its restricted nucleus of owners, are more susceptible of being diluted, supervised, monitored, and even shackled by its owners. It is all a question of customizing the particular joint venture in accordance with the commercial philosophy of its owners.

What influence each group may exercise on the other will depend to some extent on the law of the jurisdiction. Generally, the hegemony of the board of directors and the powers of the general assembly are the principal concerns of the founding partners. However, in many jurisdictions, and dependent on the company form, some organs, such as the fiscal council, will have legislative authority to supervise company accounts, which cannot be altered by the company articles. Restrictions on the powers of the fiscal council would permit the public safety function of such councils to be diluted.

Equally, as a reflection of the social policies of a particular country, workers' councils or labor representation may be conceded a voice in management on vital issues affecting these entities, such as a decision to dismiss a significant percentage of workers. Being a direct consequence of legislative action, such councils do not depend on the intent of the owners for their functions.

But we have other concerns. In part, this chapter is also about material rarely discussed in boardrooms. This is the strategy required to conduct a successful combat, which in the context of international joint ventures means preventing the conflict from surfacing, in other words, not initiating hostilities, but preventing the other party from doing so. One of the themes of this book is that conflict usually takes place only when it is possible, when the obligation to compromise no longer exists. Most businessmen do not initiate hostilities when there is little to be gained except expenditures.

The impetus of collaboration that led to the formation of the joint venture must be clearly supported by a company structure that enforces the sense of unity. This can be achieved by company clauses intended to secure the rights of minority owners. When the rights of the minority must be respected, cooperation is the only sensible approach available to the participants. In a joint venture, harmony means that the rights of the minority will be valued and given representation. The minority will have certain veto rights. Its influence in management will not be illusory. Its voice in the general assembly will have effect, not a whistling in the wind recorded into the resolution book to gather dust without further regard for its contents. Consensus between partners cannot be founded only on an emotional respect of one for the other. Such an attitude is commendable. But when cooperation is a legal necessity, respect will lose its dependency and become a necessity.

A company structure, therefore, is not merely a document for recitation of capital, but rather the final definition of the relationship of the owners of equity to each other and what will be the rules of working together. All the articles of a company can contribute to formulating a harmonious balance between the various interests of all partners, at times in natural conflict, other times in perfect harmony. All want success; not everyone agrees how to obtain it. All want profit; not everyone concurs how it should be utilized.

A well-conceived company pattern will weave its way through the multitude of possible areas of antagonism, inserting company articles that hinder the outbreak of frictions and lay a sensible foundation for their peaceful resolution. These principles converge and are expressed through a reasonable, not extreme, protection given to minority owners who must be consulted on a range of selected issues.

Collaboration, in other words, must be aggressively underpinned and made an obligatory route. Meaningful ownership and productive management are intimately dependent on inherent corporate mechanisms that induce, if not compel, the parties toward cooperation and resolution of friction because they are forced to confer with one another. The more authority is divided and conditioned, the greater the protection given to owners no matter what their equity participation, the more readily each party will enjoy the fruits of ownership, because obligatory cooperation avoids the destructive effects of discord.

Another concern we have is simple enough. Ultimately, the most sensible assurance of effective ownership will be dependent on the owners having to be present for any action to be taken. General assemblies conducted in distant lands without the presence of a substantial majority of the ownership capital invariably result in one group imposing its will. Without the presence of all, the active partners invariably interpret this as a sign of disinterest or else an opportunity to manage the joint venture for their own gain.

Collaboration and cooperation will receive respectable support from the legal concept of quorum, that is, what percentage of capital must be present before there can be any effective general assembly action. This concept of the required presence of a defined ownership percentage before any action can be realized can be extended also to the board of directors.

Consequently, the two most important repositories of power in a company, the board of directors and the general assembly, can have their voting results conditioned on the presence of a platform of equity percentage. Nothing can be done unless a defined percentage of capital is present and prepared to vote. This is an invulnerable method for protecting minority interests.

The realization of an effective international joint venture has these broad avenues:

- *General Assembly Power:* Designing a company structure that divides authority so that the board of directors cannot act without consultation to the owners on a selected list of topics. This requires an agreement on what issues require such a special treatment. The more powers the gen-

eral assembly of owners have on critical issues, the less fear there will
be of arbitrary action by a management committee dominated at any
one moment by a group hostile to minority owners.

- *Supermajority Vote Requirements:* Compromise exists when the need
  for collaboration is mandatory, when no one group can merely outvote
  and relegate to silence the pretensions of other groups. Minority voting
  rights must receive special attention. This can be easily achieved by
  requiring supermajority votes on a range of preferred items. We are not
  intending or counseling the entire elimination of management authority
  from the social organ that normally exercises it. We are advocating a
  partial removal dependent on the importance of the material.

- *Management Board Composition:* A further essential control is over the
  composition of the board of directors. No matter what powers the board
  possesses, the more representative it is of all interests, the more harmonious for all will be its decisions. Thus, the minority interest must be
  legally assured of representation on the supreme management organ.
  Just as we will review methods of protecting minority ownership rights,
  we will also suggest methods for consecrating management functions
  by the minority.

- *Management Board Voting System:* The right to have representation on
  a board of directors does not automatically mean the representation will
  have any influence. A minority board member outvoted on every issue
  might as well not sit on the board. His presence will only result in a
  continual series of articulated dissent recorded in the minutes book. To
  avoid such a useless result, there must be established rules for voting
  that turn the minority member of the board into an effective vote without whose concurrence certain acts cannot be approved. The board of
  directors must also be subject to a qualified majority requirement when
  it comes to voting. Of course, it cannot be on all topics, only those of
  extreme importance to all partners and when possible serious conflict
  can be anticipated.

- *Dismissal Rights Over the Board of Directors:* Although the board of
  directors should act independently, practical control can be achieved by
  a company clause as to rights of dismissal over the board. Without the
  right of dismissal, there is no effective remedy against independent-
  thinking directors whose fidelity to the company supersedes loyalty to
  the principal that elected them. Although nominees normally follow the
  philosophies of their principals, the law does demand of managers impartial, unfettered business judgment. Thus, the principles of the law
  may conflict with the commercial interests of any one partner and not

find the expected support from its nominee. Revocation of the mandate is the only remedy for a faithful performance of laudatory moral objectives.

- *Quorum:* Safeguarding ownership rights and management function will be buttressed by requiring a minimum presence of capital in the board of directors and any general assembly for valid voting to begin and be counted. A definition of a valid quorum is required to protect the minority interest. Quorum rights apply to general assemblies and meetings of the board of directors.

All of the subjects overlap in their consequences and the frontiers between one and the other theme are not distinct. But they all assist in shoring up the rights of the minority and making it difficult for the terms of the joint venture and shareholders' agreement to be breached. This is probably an opportune moment to state what many students and even entrepreneurs do not contemplate.

There is no effective barrier preventing a person from purposely transgressing a contract when such is the intent. Legal documents dissuade and provide a foundation for seeking recourse to a court of law, and the awarding of damages. Nevertheless, there are people who will break agreements, knowing they are doing so, but calculating that the remedy the law provides will arrive too late. All this reaffirms that there exists no legal document that may not be cast aside.

The more there is a duplication of mechanisms to support previously negotiated terms, the less likely a breach becomes. For this reason, legal documents are often repetitious. Redundancy in the law is a literary scandal but usually purposeful. The attentive readers will therefore note a duplication of legal ideas, consequences reinforced through alternate methods, all designed to make it difficult to circumvent the intent of the parties as formulated at the initiation of the joint venture.

8.1.1 THE NATURAL DIVISION OF AUTHORITY IN COMPANIES

The vast majority of international joint ventures result in the joint venture vehicle being a company or a consortium, the classic division between an equity and a contractual joint venture. The use of the word *company* is not intended to be precise but used to suggest the adoption of a legal form in which there is a division between capital, that is, owners, and management.

Companies are the natural choice of entrepreneurs for conducting business. A company form normally confers limited liability to the owners and entrepreneurs rarely wish to expose themselves individually to liability in a foreign jurisdiction. Since the universal share corporation is frequently the specific legal form chosen, our discussion will normally present the material as if this were the joint venture vehicle. However, practically all companies face the same broad legal issues as to division of authority no matter what their specific form, and it is authority that is our principal concern.

When there is commercial legislation authorizing the establishment of companies, there will be found laws and decrees that define the division of authority between owners and management. Under common-law theory, such as in the United States or UK, management is conferred on an independent group, for example, a board of directors, that manages and supervises the company, exercising independent judgment and bearing a relationship of trust to the company. In common-law countries, the board of directors have substantial powers and are not required to seek approval from the owners on many issues.

Some jurisdictions also require members of the board of directors to be shareholders. This is known as having qualifying shares. It is not a universal obligation, and in those jurisdictions where it exists, one share should suffice. Thus, for the foreign investor who wishes to appoint key personnel to a board of directors, this fact is easily accomplished. It is best, if possible, to avoid nominating executives to the board of directors.

When permitted, a more satisfactory solution is to have a corporate entity designated as a board member represented by an individual, which may be the foreign executive. The practical reason for this is that a named individual, who resigns one day because he has changed his employment, requires a substitute nomination and perhaps legal formalities such as the convoking of a general assembly. With a corporate entity as a board member, the representation of this entity can be changed by a simple power of attorney, a much simpler procedure than convoking a general assembly. As indicated, not all jurisdictions accept a corporate entity as a board member.

The acts of the board of directors must be for the benefit of the company, which means for the benefit of the owners. At the end of the accounting year, the board makes a report to the owners, at a general assembly, as to the year's results and makes recommendations as to the application of funds. The owners, usually shareholders when dealing with a stock corporation, indicate their assent or dissent. This is normally done by approving the report of the board of directors. There may be a question-and-answer period, a dialogue between the shareholders and the board of directors. In small companies, in which there are few shareholders, the meeting of the general assembly is normally relaxed, an informal gathering, necessary to comply with legislation, since the majority of the directors and the shareholders may be the same persons.

On the continent, such as in the member countries of the European Union where civil law is predominant, the applicable legislation follows more or less the same scheme but also usually requires the managers to submit to the general assembly more critical questions for their approval. In civil-law countries, the authority of the board of directors is more limited in its scope than in common-law jurisdictions but it still is, nevertheless, considerable.

A typical article in civil-law legislation regulating companies would be that augments of capital of the company must be first submitted to the general assembly for its approval. Therefore, one of the significant differences between the major legal systems of the world is in the common-law tradition that the board of directors has, a priori, substantial powers, whereas in the other, the civil law, the law imposes the need to consult the owners on various strategic issues. The board of directors in common-law jurisdictions is bound more by principles of impartiality and reasonableness and less by items requiring shareholder approval. In civil-law countries, the board of directors is also restrained by principles of trust, but a large range of topics requires the approval of the general assembly of shareholders.

There are even more extreme cases if we make an analysis of the various legal systems in the world. It may even be, as, for example, in Central America, that in a particular jurisdiction, the general assembly is supreme. All matters that are not routine must be submitted to it for its approval. Thus, the variety of division of authority is indeed significant.

However, for the moment, this important difference need not be a deterrent to our general analysis because we are describing a natural division of authority between ownership and management. This division of authority can have additional requirements superimposed on it. Where the civil law states specific items must be submitted to the general assembly of owners, this list can be expanded.

If the common law only requires the board of directors to seek approval on a few narrow issues, such as dividends or applications of funds, we can still curtail the broad powers of the board of directors through the introduction of voting requirements on the board of directors or by inserting company articles that refer to the general assembly for approval of various items. This is particularly true in the closely held corporation, which means a limited amount of shareholders. Once we approach the large publicly subscribed share corporation, or a private corporation but with an exceedingly large shareholder base, the ability to curtail the powers of the board of directors is limited to matters less important. But this limitation is of no serious consequences since our study is not with the public corporation.

We will thus modify the powers of the board of directors through the introduction of particular company articles that in effect draw a circle around sensitive material and then ensure that within this corral all participants must be heard.

Hence, no matter what the jurisdiction, company law is, among other things, about the division of power between two groups: management and owners. The proper curtailment and apportionment of this division will ensure that there is effective minority ownership and the enthronement of minority management control when this has been conceded in the joint venture or shareholders' agreement.

How this modification is created thus is one of the more dramatic aspects of international joint ventures. Without an understanding of how this division works in practice and how it can be altered, the international entrepreneur will be merely lulled into a false sense of security by lengthy documents.

Therefore, even if the division of authority in a company is fixed, it may be easily modified as there are many techniques for diluting the power of one group over another. The traditional division of authority, or corporate governance, can be systemized for purposes of analysis:

- The board of directors, or other management designation dependent on the jurisdiction, is usually the supreme voice. But all legal company forms, whether imposed by law or selected by company articles, must indicate what is the supreme management entity.
- After the board of directors, the shareholders will be the repository of all powers of management. The general assembly of owners elects the board of directors. Similar to a federation in which states grant powers to a central government, so in a company, the owners grant, without having to declare anything, broad powers of management to those they elect. In theory, the extent and limits of these powers are defined by the local legislation and are applied by the law. We may think of this as the natural consequences of silence.
- With the small private corporation, there is substantial flexibility in most jurisdictions that permits the general assembly to alter the consequences of legislation and to obligate the board of directors to seeks its approval on a broad variety of matters. By conditioning the scope of the

powers granted to the board of directors, there is a partial list of conceded powers delegated back to the owners.

- The shareholders concede powers to the board of directors who in turn entrust some of their powers to operating managers or department heads. The precise entity to whom the board of directors may commission powers is very variable, ranging from a general director to a department supervisor, but one important principle is constant. The board of directors cannot deputize more powers then it has by law or is given by the general assembly of owners. Equally important is that the company articles may control what powers are delegated by the board of directors.

We are thus confronted with a further possibility in controlling the degree of authority that, once moored to the wharf of ownership, begins to drift away imperceptibly. If substantial control cannot be achieved over the board of directors, it is still possible to decree in the company articles that the board cannot delegate various items without the consent of the general assembly.

This will lessen operational decisions on important issues conducted contrary to the wishes of a minority interest. The obligation of an impartial business judgment is imposed on a director by law. An operational manager deriving powers from the board is a harder target for an alleged breach of fiduciary duty. The details swamp the principles. The larger the joint venture, the more difficult it is to know who implemented what decision on the operational level. Even if the board of directors has substantial authority, a tight rein on its delegation of powers is prudent. A director has to respond and clarify to a minority owner the reasons for any important facet of joint venture activity.

In summary, the normal chain of management in a company is

- shareholders delegate powers to and elect the
- board of directors who choose and entrust various powers to
- operating managers whose
- powers can never exceed those of the board of directors; thus,
- operational powers are derived from the original source, which is the general assembly; consequently
- the delegation of powers from the board of directors to working managers can be controlled and made subject to the approval of the general assembly

Therefore, there is considerable scope for customizing management to the will of the parties.

Another viewpoint is possible, a restatement that is repetitious, but that reinforces our understanding as it concentrates on operational details. We can also say that

- shareholders grant powers to
- a board of directors, which
- may be broad or limited but
- if there is no company article defining the powers of the general assembly, then
- the law will probably confer substantial, almost unlimited powers on this management organ and
- once these powers are delegated to others, the general assembly loses control;
- the general assembly thus has two routes to contain authority in others: on powers given to the board of directors and on the ease, or lack of it, that these powers can be given to others

8.1.2 MANAGEMENT MODELS: BOARD OF DIRECTORS, GENERAL DIRECTOR, AND OPERATIONAL MANAGER

Businessmen are usually familiar with the functions of a board of directors of share corporations. In many jurisdictions, the board of directors, besides being the supreme management organ, has effective control over the daily decisions being made. The board is a working board, one with real management powers. There are also other models.

There are jurisdictions where the board of directors does not have an active role, but instead there is designated a general director, or management committee, that is responsible for the day-to-day decisions of the company, what we would normally think of as operational management. In these jurisdictions, the board of directors is an honorary board, supervising significant issues but removed from the daily preoccupations of commerce.

Rather, it is the general director who will interface with the public. It is the general director who is the spokesman for the company. If not an individual, in some jurisdictions, there is supervision by a management committee with broad departmental functions. No matter what the variations, the essence is the same. An individual or a group manages subject to the overall power of the board of directors. There is no other possibility. The only immutable quality of management is that the law requires an entity to represent the company. The limits of this representation are open to debate.

Nevertheless, in those jurisdictions that permit variations to the governance of the company even though there is a board of directors, there is still an important control by the board of directors. Although the board may not be actively engaged in the day-to-day problems of company life, whoever is, whether an individual or a committee, receives the right to act subject to the powers conferred by the board of directors. The board of directors controls the reins of management.

The powers delegated to another person may be large or restricted. But nothing is altered because there is a general director. The ultimate authority still remains with the board of directors and who controls the board of directors controls the company. Equally, who can restrict the powers of the board of directors can limit the powers of the operational managers, which are performed through a management committee.

With other forms of companies, or as a result of the jurisdiction of the joint venture company, a different management theory may be in use in contrast to the usual board of directors. In Europe, there is the widely used private limited liability company that is frequently managed by one individual entitled by the local law as the *manager.*

This manager has broad powers that are derived from the mandate conferred by the owners. This mandate can be limited or of very broad scope. However, unlike the ordinary share corporation, private limited liability companies also often provide that the *owners* will be the *managers.* If there is more than one owner, then all have the right of management authority. Later, these powers are delegated to actual executives, the working managers.

Similar to corporations, the powers these managers receive are contained in the legal instrument establishing their authority, which is usually a power of attorney. The powers granted may be ample or limited. But in the private limited liability company, where all owners may exercise management authority, it is simple to control the delegation of these powers. In this respect, the college of owners is similar to the groups of shareholders, in which the consent of many is required for certain delegations of power.

Thus, the two more common forms of joint ventures, the shareholder company and the private limited liability company, partake in the same mechanism. More control over the daily operations is achieved by constraints on the board of directors.

Concerning general partnerships and consortiums, the individual members of each will be able to represent the company, whereas in limited partnerships, there will be one general partner. This general rule can be altered to some degree by an agreement between the members of the general partnership or consortium. Management powers in all these company forms can be delegated, in part or whole, to a management committee whose powers will be defined in the enabling act.

With this knowledge, owners, particularly minority owners, have a route to safeguard their position: redistribute and supervise the source of management so that the minority right must be heard on selected issues and the operational management of the company is not unrestricted. We can now conceptualize two avenues of altering how management power will be constrained:

1. Alter the powers of management conferred by law on the supreme management group through the introduction of company articles. The fewer the items on which management can act without supervision, the more control the shareholders have over their own company. A reasonable balance must be struck between hindering completely the board of directors from managing and restricting on a selected, highly important schedule of items.
2. Supervise the granting of powers from the supreme management organ. This means limiting the conditions under which they can be transferred from the supreme management organ to an operational committee or general director. This will prevent unpleasant surprises or unauthorized acts from taking place at the operational level of management.

PART TWO

8.2 THE POWERS OF THE GENERAL ASSEMBLY

In all those legal forms and jurisdictions where permitted, and this will certainly include the closely held corporation and the private limited liability company, the owners should reserve substantial powers over the following topics. This can be done through the articles of the company, which define when the general assembly must be consulted by the board of directors and when its approval is to be secured. The items are as follows:

Amendment of articles or by-laws

The articles of the company or its by-laws are sacred. Once a partial acquisition has been made or the joint venture company is formed, there should not be permitted any alterations to the articles or the by-laws without the consent of the general assembly.

There is nothing more disheartening than having the articles of the company provide for supermajority voting on a range of issues to protect the minority interests but the board of directors, controlled by the majority, subsequently amend the articles and remove the supermajority provisions. This may be unjust but it is not illegal and can be prevented only by a suitable company article.

Augments of capital and issue of shares

The ability to authorize augments of capital, or approve a new issue of shares, means that other parties will become partners or that one partner, with more recourse to funds, can increase its equity position.

Even if all partners have a right of preference, proportionally, in any authorized augment of capital, this is of little practical value to a partner who has not the cash available for the subscription. A company with a capital of $10,000,000 may have two partners and the capital is divided 60/40. If there is an increase of capital to $20,000,000, all subscribed by the 60 percent partner, the final result is now 80/20 (16,000,000/ 20,000,000).

In jurisdictions that require a 70 percent majority vote on major issues, the platform has been exceeded and the once hindered majority partner becomes sovereign. It is quite usual to have company articles seek authorization from the general assembly for any augments of capital and similar issues.

Dividend policy

Serious arguments are often initiated by divergent views on the application of net operating income. Sometimes, a part of the profit is transferred to retained earnings to be thereafter used for corporate purposes such as investment in equipment or other capital expenditures. With small, private, closely held joint venture companies, it is prudent for the application of profit to be distributed in accordance with the votes of the general assembly and not be within the discretion of the board of directors. Customarily, the board of directors makes recommendations as to the allocation of the profit. Ordinarily, the recommendations of the board of directors are followed, particularly in public corporations where their recommendations cannot be easily vetoed without court action.

However, in order not to fall prey to the distribution of authority mandated by the local legislation, which may confer on the board of directors unfettered judgment concerning the destiny of profit, this is a topic to be reviewed and the necessary insertions put into the company articles. There are limits to the use of the company articles.

The destination of the operating profit should be within the discretion and directions of the general assembly and this certainly can be stipulated in the company articles. Profits are to be distributed in accordance with the decision of the general assembly. In this fashion, whatever special rights minority owners have been able to secure as to the exercise of their voting power can be implemented in the deliberation over the use of profit after taxes.

However, a more subtle problem lies behind the destiny of the profits. How will profits be determined in the first place? This is an accounting concept and it involves a substantial element of discretion relating to capital expenditures, working capital needs, retirement of debt, establishment of reserves, and other items.

This problem cannot be resolved through a company article that defines the application of profit as this is a matter that varies from year to year. The issue is not what to do with profit but how will we know it exists. A formulation in general terms is not practical. It requires above all accounting concepts and then multiple details, formulas, examples, and financial ratios. The determination of the profit is, as already discussed elsewhere, a subject for the shareholders' agreement.

Consequently, the use of profit prior to its distribution implies a two-step legal process:

1. The shareholders' agreement defining as best as possible budgets and uses of profit
2. The articles of the company subjecting the distribution of profit to the determination of the general assembly.

Sale of assets

Less certain is the proper legal source to impose restraints on the board of directors as to its power to sell assets above a certain value. The objective is clear enough. This prevents the production facilities of the joint venture company being sold. One might wonder what sensible entrepreneur would take such a drastic step. In fact, the imagination of an aggressive majority owner against a recalcitrant minority interest knows few boundaries.

Reported cases are a roll call of the vindictive nature of owners. It is not a step that actually has to be taken. The threat of doing it may be sufficient to silence the demands of the minority. Once hostility becomes acknowledged, owners of majority interests will go to extreme lengths to impose their will such as selling off all the assets to a third company, controlled by the majority, for an illusory price, preferring to pay lawyers for their lengthy efforts rather than distributing profits to undesirable partners.

In theory, it is possible to obligate the board of directors to seek approval from the general assembly as to the sale of any major asset. A monetary threshold can be indicated. However, this is not very satisfactory since the threshold would have to be monitored each year so as not to become unrealistic. Additionally, there would be problems of valuation as to any particular asset.

A more practical approach is to utilize either the joint venture or shareholders' agreement in which the limits of authority on the sale of assets can be agreed to. It is not an entirely satisfactory resolution. We have merely transposed to a private agreement the problems that surround the insertion of these ideas in the articles. The most complete solution will be representation on the board of directors. Still, the ideas can be ventilated in a private agreement that serves as a source of interpretation. This use should not be underestimated. Among reasonable partners with a sincere disagreement, an interpretative source is beneficial and at times convincing.

Mergers, formation of subsidiaries, and other alliances

As might be expected, the act of merger is so pervasive in its effects that most jurisdictions require the approval of the general assembly before it can be effectuated. Besides mergers, we can include such serious events as the formation of subsidiaries, significant capital participations in other companies, and any form of alliance involving a capital commitment whose platform has been previously established. The proper place for requiring such approval is in the company articles.

Even if it is known that the local law obligates general assembly approval for mergers, it is unlikely an extension would be made automatically to the formation of subsidiaries and the other examples given.

Consequently, a broad recitation in the company articles elaborating on this theme will prevent devious acts whose only true purpose is either to decapitalize the joint venture or subjugate vocal minority interests.

With no obstacles to a merger, a board of directors conniving with the majority owners can approve the formation of another company with different classes of shares and then merge the joint venture company into the new company with the minority group receiving a class of shares with less rights.

Dissolution and liquidation

Termination of a joint venture company is not what is contemplated by dissolution and liquidation, although this certainly ends the joint venture. In joint ventures, termination is a voluntary act, a mutual attitude by the partners to put an end to their collaboration and proceed to the legal acts known as dissolution and liquidation. We will revert to termination as a general topic in Chapter Nine.

For the moment, our concentration will be on the simpler topic of the board of directors having the power to decide to dissolve the company by the appropriate legal procedures and then proceed to liquidate, or sell, the assets. Such a grave legal act should be reserved for the general assembly. The articles of the company can stipulate that such a decision must be approved by the general assembly.

Bankruptcy initiatives

Potentially less grave in its consequences, but often abused, is the process of a corporate reorganization. This is initiated by the decision of the board of directors to voluntarily put the company into bankruptcy. This process has the legitimate purpose and objective of preventing creditors from suing the company and thus allowing the company to attempt to refinance its debts or otherwise extract itself from a difficult economic situation.

Such a procedure has different names depending on the jurisdiction, such as corporate reorganization, economic recuperation, and economic viability, but the finality is to ward off creditors and allow time for conceiving new solutions to recurring debt problems. This procedure is normally accompanied by the nomination of a referee or trustee by the court who will review the proposed commercial objectives of the company in distress and it is hoped recommend to the court the solutions presented by the bankrupt debtor.

Unfortunately, a review of court literature will reveal many instances when a majority interest deliberately puts the joint venture company into a voluntary reorganization with the undeclared purpose of ruining the minority interest investment or otherwise profiting from the reorganization. This is achieved by convincing the court-appointed referee to recommend financial conditions that a minority interest cannot meet or that may be prejudicial to the minority interest. The misuse of a beneficial law can be prevented only by withdrawing the power to make this decision from the board of directors and remit it to the general assembly for its approval.

Amendment of the joint venture or shareholders' agreement

Whenever possible, the power of amending the joint venture agreement, or any agreement to which the joint venture company is a partner, and that affects in significant degree and detail the relationships between the partners, should always be left to the general assembly. This requirement finds direct expression in a company article. Otherwise, important rights negotiated and incorporated into the joint venture or shareholders' agreement can be altered.

If the board of directors has the power to alter any of the important agreements, then the only refuge of a minority owner is to what extent the voting in the board of directors can be controlled. It is easier to control the voting in the general assembly because each equity owner speaks for himself, without reserve, and subject only to restrictions on voting established in the company articles. Naturally, this admonition is confined to those agreements to which the joint venture company is a party.

The joint venture or shareholders' agreement will be the result of much negotiation and contains the vital, paramount clauses that define how the parties intended the joint venture company should function. These are not documents that should admit of review by anyone other than the original parties to these agreements.

These agreements should not be subject to alteration by a board of directors. They should require the approval of the general assembly since these agreements reflect the interests of the owners of the capital. This inflexible attitude is not modified by the alleged independence of the board of directors, which operates for the benefit of the company.

It is precisely this independence that causes our intractable position, no matter that some members have been elected by a minority partner. If the instructions of the minority partner are not followed by its nominees, the acts of the board remain valid. Even if the enabling act constituting the board of directors requires a specified majority of votes for a particular item, this does not constitute a control over any one member. The members of the board of directors are independent and obligated to render impartial judicious decisions. Although as a practical matter nominees usually follow the orientation of their principals, there can be lapses.

This short list of items that might appear in company articles and that represents a roll call of those rights over which the owners reserve the right to pronounce serves as a reminder of the basic principle being repeated in various facets throughout this book. Management is authority. Authority is not a vague inherent right to command, but rests on the delegation of powers. We readily recognize that the power to command should not be abused. What is often not articulated is that the grant of power can be reckless, negligent, without thought as to its consequences. Prudent management resides in wise delegation and a cautious retention of veto capacity.

Part Three

8.3 Supermajority vote requirements

The closely held private company, what is frequently denominated as the *closed corporation,* requires a controlled division of powers due to the rationale of its existence: pooled resources among partners who need collaboration to commercially succeed. But if we admit the need for the controlled division of authority, it obviously can be only for the protection of the minority interests. The majority needs no protection, except from its own enthusiasm, which if not tethered may lead the joint venture vehicle on a collision course. It is useful to review the various methods for safeguarding minority interests.

Qualified or supermajority voting

The results of voting can be controlled by the use of mechanisms referred to as a *qualified majority,* a *supermajority,* a *casting vote,* a *tie-breaking vote,* or even the *chairman's vote.* Some of these designations have more applicability when referring to a board of directors. For a general assembly, the appropriate language is a qualified or supermajority vote. We mean that majority voting by the simple counting of the nominal value of the shares is not sufficient. Something more is required.

What is intended is to stipulate either that no voting will be considered as conferring a majority vote unless a certain percentage is reached or that, when there is a deadlock, a particular vote will be decisive. The deadlock issue is more relevant to problems of termination or dispute resolution and will be reviewed accordingly in the next chapter. Our present concern is to ensure that important items cannot be resolved without the casting vote of a minority interest, the qualified or supermajority provision.

The local law may require a specified majority of votes on a particular item: for example, 75 percent of the votes in the general assembly must approve an augment of capital. This percentage can be altered by the company articles. Consequently, the strategy of the minority owner is quite clear. First, the parties must agree on what items must be referred to the general assembly for its approval. This remittance should not be left to the dictates of the local law. It may be insufficient.

The more items required to be heard by the general assembly, the more effective will be the influence of the minority partners. Although the local law may require a qualified majority vote on any particular issue unless the parties to the joint venture understand thoroughly the implications of the local legislation, this is an area that should be addressed by the articles of the company. In other words, it is not convenient to leave the material to be decided by the application of the general law.

Once a suitable agenda has been settled in the joint venture agreement to be incorporated into the company articles, the minority partners must then ensure that their voting power is sufficient to be a needed element in the decision-making process of the general assembly. As discussed, this may be done by altering the threshold percentage required, what we have denominated the *qualified* or *supermajority* voting level.

If the local law requires 75 percent of the capital to pronounce on any major issues, a minority interest with 22 percent of the capital of the joint venture company is in trouble. The qualified majority percentage needed to protect its interests adequately on any important topic will be 26 percent. Either the company articles raise the threshold to 79 percent, and 22 percent of the capital is then sufficient to block any action, or the negotiations toward the formation of the joint venture must have an equity position of at least 26 percent as a key objective!

The objective may be stated almost as a formula. First, determine what the local legislation requires as a threshold to be able to act without the consent of the other partners. Then strive to raise this threshold so that without a minority vote, the threshold cannot be reached. The items to which this can apply can be negotiated in the joint venture agreement and then inserted into the articles of the company.

If this is not possible, the joint venture should not be undertaken without having the necessary equity position, which in our example will be 26 percent.

Special voting rights created by the company articles

Another approach to protecting the minority interests is by conferring on them voting rights that augment the effectiveness of their numerical strength or curtail the voting power of the majority. We reviewed these mechanisms in Chapter Five but their repetition is again relevant. Except for the last suggestion, which limits the voting strength of the majority owner, none of the mechanisms is as effective as establishing a qualified majority of votes.

The methods previously discussed in Chapter Four are more effective for ensuring the election of one or more members to the board of directors. They can be used for general assembly voting, but, normally, the manner of counting their total amount will fall short of influencing the decision-making process in the general assembly.

Either the law or the company articles may provide that a specified number of shares may vote in a bloc with the designation of a nominee for this purpose. This is usually a low percentage and is hence not going to have any significant effect on outvoting a bloc constituting a high majority of votes, for example, anything above 51 percent.

Cumulative voting is another method especially designed to ensure election of one or more members to the board of directors. It will not prevent a strong majority from dominating the general assembly on important issues. Plural votes approximate more closely the concept of a qualified majority voting requirement, but not all jurisdictions permit this method. For those that will allow such a provision, a special class of shares will be needed. The right of plural voting cannot be personalized but rather must be attributable to the quality of the shares, which in our case means a class of shares. Unfortunately, besides not being recognized in many jurisdictions, the concept of plural voting is linked with shares and not easily transposed to other legal forms in which there are no shares.

The most likely candidate to be used when it proves impossible to negotiate a qualified majority vote requirement is a limitation on the counting of votes of the majority. Some jurisdictions permit restricting the votes of a class of shares to, for example, 50 percent of the votes and thus this is a method to force a stalemate or prevent any action being taken. Once again, the right of limiting votes must be attributed to a class of shares and we must further ensure that the local jurisdictions recognize this limitation.

In summary, once there has been an agreement on the division of authority between the board of directors and the general assembly, the safest route for protection of minority rights will be the insertion of a qualified majority vote on those items reserved to the general assembly.

PART FOUR

8.4 MANAGEMENT BOARD COMPOSITION

The combined effect of using a qualified majority vote requirement and ensuring an effective representation on the board of directors will confer considerable influence on minority owners. There are two major legal approaches to consolidating a minority interest on the board of directors:

1. through the company articles
2. by the joint venture or shareholders' agreement

Before examining these proposals, it is worth emphasizing now that we are not seeking mere representation on the board of directors or other management committee. We want effective representation, which requires further legal steps. In other words, we will devise a legal method to ensure board of director representation and then we must rely on another legal document or company article to confer a certain influence on the representation. The precise degree will have to be negotiated.

The first sensible step will be to indicate in the company articles how many members will constitute the board of directors or its equivalent if we are not dealing with a share corporation. We then next wish to ensure that the minority interest will have a specified number of the members.

Ordinarily, the number of directors will be indicated in either the joint venture or shareholder's agreement with company articles drafted or amended in harmony with these agreements. It is material over which negotiations have been held and a compromise reached. With the number of members agreed to, the safest legal method is to create a class of shares and attribute to each class how many members of the board of directors the particular class will have the right to elect.

However, dependent on the jurisdiction, the specific joint venture, and the method used to enter into the joint venture, it may be necessary to resort to cumulative voting, plural voting, or even a limitation on the votes of the majority. None of these routes is as secure as conferring the right to nominate a specified number of directors on a class of shares.

Often the company articles merely recite how many members the board of directors will have and the private agreements, such as the shareholders' agreement, will indicate how many members each share or group of shares will have the right to elect. This also is not the safest route to ensuring election of nominees to the board of directors.

Such a right is contained in a private agreement. If the majority owner repudiates the agreement by voting contrary to its provisions in a general assembly, thus electing, for example, the entire board, the minority owner must resort to a court of law to enforce, if possible, the shareholders' agreement. This is not always an effective alternative, and by the time a remedy is granted, the passage of time may have made a favorable judgment of little practical use.

In all cases, the establishment of a class of shares will be legally impregnable to any attack because the rights attached to any class, that is, the right to elect a specified number of members to the board of directors, are recited in company articles and cannot be vitiated by the majority owner. There is no need to rely on a private agreement. The minority rights form part of the constitution of the company. Therefore, elaborate clauses in a private agreement for the election of members to a board by a minority interest should not cloud the vision of those wanting to enforce such rights: The surest route to efficacy will be by the dictates of the company articles, which, it is hoped, are clear in their draftsmanship and unequivocal in their application.

8.4.1 MANAGEMENT BOARD VOTING SYSTEM

Once the legal right to elect one or more members to a board of directors is secured through the creation of a class of shares, the next paramount question is, How does the presence of a minority representation on the board translate into an effective vote? The response is that now there are again two possible methods that certainly can be used together:

1. the company articles can recite how the voting will take place on the board of directors
2. reliance on a private agreement, such as the joint venture, shareholders', or board of directors' agreement, that dictates the method of counting votes

In the company articles, it is a simple enough matter to recite that the decisions taken in the board of directors will be by majority voting. It is also possible to establish a percentage requirement that ensures that the minority owner will have a possible veto right. If there are five members on the board of directors and a 40 percent minority owner has elected two members, company articles requiring four members to vote unanimously on any specified issue obviously grant to the minority owner complete veto power over the decision-making process on the chosen items.

Another alternative to requiring a percentage tally is for the company articles to state that decisions taken by the board of directors to be valid must include the approval of at least the director nominated by class X. When we are not confronting a share corporation, the same principle can be applied to the director nominated by partner B or partner C.

A further possibility is to have a board composed of an equal number of members and give a qualifying vote to one group in the case of a deadlock. This is not entirely satisfactory, since in fairness there would have to be a rotation of this veto, which means a rotation of who has the qualifying vote. When matters begin to disintegrate between partners, the stratagem will translate into bringing up for vote the proper item when the right chairman is in office.

Finally, the entire problem can be treated in the private agreements, such as the joint venture or shareholders' agreement. However, although breach of such agreements may give one partner a right of action against another, it is a complex affair, and most likely any remedy will be provided too late. The private nature of agreements cannot replace the public efficiency of company articles. Putting some items in the articles of the company and leaving others for application by private agreements is a workable though not entirely adequate solution, further provided that there is no contradiction between the articles of the company and the private agreements.

Relying entirely on the use of private agreements for establishing the system of counting and weighing votes on the management level is not a satisfactory platform. Being private agreements, they do not affect third parties. The decisions of the board of directors even in violation of the agreements will be valid. The only recourse to an offended partner will be a court of law. The litigation is long and expensive. This is not a practical course of action.

The use of private agreements is always a fallback position in which the declared purpose of the parties has a substantial moral and eventual legal influence. It is not a complete substitute for the efficiency of the company articles.

Part Five

8.5 Dismissal Rights over the Board of Directors

If various material must be left stipulated only in private agreements, and understanding now the possible infirmities that are inherent in all legal documents, support to private agreements must be derived from other sources. There may be no choice in the matter due to the circumstances of the acquisition.

In this respect, the functioning of assemblies in companies has relevance. Ordinarily, the general assembly of a company meets once a year. This is the usual rule for most legal forms. Management is elected and the following year management submits its report as to its annual governance. Normally, management can convoke a general assembly any time, following certain procedures, denominated a special general assembly, and this is the usual process for public corporations.

Special assemblies have this nomenclature because it is not intended that a company will have more than one general assembly a year. The unexpected convocation of a general assembly is thus a special event, one that interrupts the daily occurrence of corporate events. With such a powerful right residing with the minority owners, it is to be expected management decisions will proceed with due care.

It is also the rule for small privately held companies, but here we can tolerate and even encourage more recourse to the use of special general assemblies being convoked when matters are not functioning as they should. In face of the legal difficulties of transposing to company articles the multiple details of private agreements, a minority interest must prepare itself for the board of directors not conforming to the contents of these agreements which are surely of knowledge to the members.

The most persuasive method to obligate adherence will be the awareness by all parties that the minority interest can call a special general assembly and dismiss the entire board of directors or a good part of it without cause. If cause is made the basis, the dismissal right is illusory. Cause is difficult to prove and will probably not exist except as being a decision contrary to the terms of the joint venture or shareholders' agreement. This is exactly what we want if the right of dismissal is entirely discretionary, not dependent on any objective standard such as good cause. A simple method to ensure private agreements is implemented. But the right must be without cause; otherwise, the interpretation of these private agreements becomes polemic.

Will the minority partners abuse this weapon? Will its existence become a nuisance and disruptive effect on the joint venture? Why would other partners accept this if they will not concede special rights in the articles of the company? The answer is that with various alternatives presented to partners, but all based on the declared right of seeking protection from an abusive majority, we will hope one of the alternatives will appear more reasonable than another. Variety of choice is often productive.

The percentage of what ownership interest is necessary to exercise this power and the possible number of dismissals will have to be negotiated. This will not undo any decisions taken in contradiction to the private agreements. It is, however, a powerful deterrent and moreover, it is effective affirmative action. The average results of democracy are beneficial.

Calling special general assemblies, requiring new elections, and advising the other parties that such elections are necessary because of failure to adhere to agreements in existence are disruptive to the governance of any company and will be seen moreover as laying the foundation for a lawsuit. The procedures for a minority owner to convoke a special general assembly are easily articulated in the company articles.

The right of dismissal of the entire board of directors is not often conceded to minority owners. Its potential use is seen as so threatening that owners with substantial majority interests are unlikely to sanction such a provision. It is, however, a prudent judicious defense designed to prevent breach of agreements laboriously negotiated.

PART SIX

8.6 QUORUM

Quorum rights are the last great refuge of the minority owner. From the principles of quorum rights is derived a protective mantle that the majority cannot remove. Quorum rights are consecrated in the company articles and hence inviolate unless there have been gaps of logic and the majority can amend the articles. At the risk of oversimplification and repetition, we will construct a short organization chart in the typical company to aid in our analysis:

- The board of directors, or other management organ, decides and implements. Usually, the owners, convened at a general assembly, approve a narrow range of issues that may be only confined to approving the financial accounts. In the small closely held company, more authority and the right to veto should reside with the general assembly.

- The company articles will divide authority between management and the owners, requiring the board of directors to seek approval on a variety of issues.
- Before the general assembly or management board can take any decision, the company articles may impose on either body a requirement of a minimum amount of votes regarding a particular topic, for example, a merger with another company. This is frequently denominated a qualified or supermajority vote requirement.
- Besides the matters set forth in the company articles requiring a supermajority vote, there will be established a system for counting and weighing votes at the management level. This system can be enshrined in the articles or private agreements. Probably a mixture will be necessary.
- To ensure that all members of the board of directors conform to these agreements, the minority interest will have the right to convoke a special general assembly and dismiss the entire board. This is not usually a power granted in international joint ventures, but it is a reasonable right and should be thought of as preventive legal action.

The outline just listed is dependent on an essential fact, what might be characterized as the Achilles' heel of company life. All parties must be present to vote. This requirement of *presence* is characterized by the law as a *quorum* obligation and has two facets:

1. the quorum necessary for constituting a board of directors or general assembly
2. the votes present and necessary for valid voting to take place

Quorum rights thus raise two questions:

1. What percentage of capital must be present for any meeting to be validly constituted?
2. Once the meeting is properly constituted, are there any requirements for valid voting?

The latter is not coincident with a qualified majority requirement as we will see shortly.

When conflict threatens to undermine the functioning of an international joint venture, frequently one partner is tempted to bypass serious differences by convoking a board meeting or a general assembly where critical issues are presented for resolution. Meetings validly convoked may actually occur without one or more partners even knowing they took place.

This unfortunate result may be because the company articles do not require more than a public announcement in a local newspaper, followed by a registered letter sent to all partners. This all seems sensible enough except very often people do not receive the letters intended for them; other personnel intervene, sign the necessary postal receipt, and if one of the partners is a multinational corporation, the letter can wander easily through a few departments. Although rare, it cannot be ruled out that the general assembly occurs before the receipt of the notice.

As to public announcements in a local newspaper, far from the main office of the multinational, their publicity aspect have few practical consequences to a partner located in another country. Such laws were not promulgated with the problems of joint ventures foremost in the minds of the legislators. The only method for ensuring that meetings do not occur without the presence of all partners, or at least a significant majority, is by the use of the legal concept of a quorum. When we speak of quorums, we are referring to meetings.

Every meeting has two aspects: (1) how many people must be present before we can say a meeting is properly convened and (2) how many votes must be counted to ensure a valid result. These are different concepts. The first, technically described as the quorum necessary for a valid constituent meeting, will be higher than what is required for voting. If the equity ownership is divided 40 percent–40 percent–20 percent, it would be reasonable to require that no meeting will be properly convened unless there is present at least 80 percent of the capital.

This ensures that both owners with strong equity interests (40 percent–40 percent) must be present before any decisions can be taken. We can understand this. Having only 60 percent of the capital present and being able to take decisions with even a lower percentage might be seen by the 40 percent owner as too strong a risk. In our example, a quorum requirement of 80 percent is the percentage needed to constitute a valid meeting and is referred to as the *constituent quorum*.

However, once a valid meeting is in course, and dependent on the issue before the gathering, it may not be necessary from the viewpoint of the owners that there be the same high percentage of votes cast nor is it necessary that there be any specific quantity of votes on any issue. If 80 percent of the capital ownership appears and 40 percent abstains from voting on an issue, requiring an 80 percent percentage of votes to be cast means that no voting can take place. The *voting quorum*, as it is designated, thus establishes a platform that is less elevated than the constituent quorum.

It is also common for company articles to state that for a valid general assembly to be constituted, there must be present, for example, 75 percent of the capital on the first convocation, and then state that for the second convocation, any capital present will be sufficient to validate the general assembly. The purpose is to formulate a method so that a general assembly can take place. This is language found in many company articles. However, it is not obligatory and it is a bad idea for international joint ventures. It permits meetings to take place without the participation of a predefined number of shareholders. This can be completely altered as already discussed.

The owners can decide when forming the company that without a specified percentage of capital, there has not been formed a proper general assembly. From the viewpoint of the minority owner, his interests are more than adequately protected, for without his percentage, there can be no general assembly. For the majority owner, this is a serious impediment and one that may preclude the functioning of the company. Once again, we see the need for commercial common sense to prevail.

The same logic applies to the board of directors once it is duly convened. What will be the amount of votes present to have a duly convened board of directors? A simple majority? A supermajority? The more the presence requirement approximates the percentage required for a valid assembly, the more the minority interest is protected and the more hampered is the majority owner.

Returning to our example, 80 percent as a quorum requirement for forming a valid board of directors may be reasonable. Once the meeting is properly constituted, the other final issue is how many votes must be present to be able to take a valid vote count. However, it is hoped that the voting system has been established either in the articles or a private agreement to ensure some protection to the minority interests.

The congruence between qualified majority voting in the general assembly and the board of directors is now evident as to the quorum requirements in both organs. In both cases, we are seeking to:

- ensure a high representation before any legal act can take place, in the general assembly or board of directors
- condition the results of the voting in both instances

Part Seven

8.7 Customizing the international joint venture

Through the complex tapestry of international joint ventures, a general pattern should be discernible by now. An effective international joint venture is not erected on the silent pillars of the law. There is no one format that is the correct design, the natural order of our montage. The law favors the expression of intent. The noiseless catacomb of the law must be broken by the voice of the participants. Important rights to the participants should be the subject of articulation in the company articles. Forming part of the constitution of the company they are inviolate, easily enforceable by a court, putting all parties on notice as to their contents.

We cannot expect that veto rights, supermajority voting requirements, and high quorum percentages for a valid constituted general assembly or board of directors will be easily conceded. The possession of these rights often will be fiercely contested by the other partners. Arguments will be advanced that collaboration means just that and not the right of any one person or class of shares to have such a powerful veto. It appears reasonable and yet what is the purpose of any national constitution but to protect the minority against the majority?

If goodwill were to prevail always, there would be few reasons for the extensive legislation existing on such a multitude of topics. The village town meeting, the municipal assembly, and the national parliament are typical examples of institutions to promote social peace and progress. Yet the abuses continue. For a sensible, workable social contract, there must be a restricted base of inviolate rights that cannot be subject to the will of the majority.

Our first objective is to secure these fundamental rights in the articles of the company. This will be done by voting rights that are made subject to specific rules in the general assembly and on the board of directors. The concept of a qualified majority vote on a selected range of topics is formidable insurance as a protection to minority interests. Both in the general assembly and on the board of directors, matters of vital importance will require a high percentage of consensus.

Failing this, it is to be expected some material will be of a private nature or too vague to be transposed to the articles. The joint venture or shareholders' agreement can regulate what cannot be inserted into the company articles. It is not the best solution but the design and future of the joint venture are defined, contours are specified, the goodwill of the average entrepreneur will give voluntary support to the ideas.

In all cases, with or without special voting rights, no voting will be permitted unless a specified amount of capital is present and valid voting may be further conditioned on either a percentage of votes cast or the presence of a class of shares. This will ensure there are no significant decisions taken without the presence of most of the partners.

The availability of all these varied techniques invariably means that legal relationships can be structured along exceedingly complex relationships. A certain caution must be exercised with the natural volition of wanting to define and describe all possible situations. The complexity will degenerate into a hopeless morass of legal entanglement if restraint is not used.

Simplicity is a great virtue in commercial and legal relationships. It will be better to confer veto rights by percentages with no classifications invoked rather than by a detailed list of topics in company articles. This will avoid recourse to interpretation, which is often subject to divergent understanding. This is not always possible. With reason, the majority partner can argue the veto right is too broad.

Everyone grasps a veto, and when conceded, it should be by broad categories, but well-defined, a difficult drafting task. Having a veto right over *accounting* issues will raise questions not easily resolved. A veto right over a *merger* is more definite. When veto rights become overused and the joint venture is not able to function properly, it is time to think of exit.

9

DISPUTE RESOLUTION AND TERMINATION

PART ONE

9.1 INTRODUCTION TO DISPUTE RESOLUTION

When parties to a joint venture disagree, the first divergences may be modest with little immediate impact. Unfortunately, minor lingering differences slowly but resolutely incite general dissatisfaction. This may eventually lead to the end of the collaboration and the possible termination of the original joint venture. The joint venture company may continue although without any of the former partners. Everyone sells out. Or, perhaps, only dissatisfied partners sell. On the other hand, the termination may be complete and all agree to extinguish the joint venture through a dissolution of the joint venture company and a liquidation of its assets.

Disagreements between partners, although normal, thus can have serious consequences and the final result may not be foreseen immediately, particularly when the earliest signs of discord are on operational issues. It is sufficient they appear and are not quickly resolved. Consequently, it is beneficial to have mechanisms in the joint venture documentation that permit an early consideration of differences of opinion and, if necessary, procedures indicating how disruptive differences of opinion will be resolved.

This route, from contention to a firm repudiation of the joint venture requiring a formal arbitration or court judgment, is known as *dispute resolution*. It is the process of suggestions for avoiding conflict to indicating how the parties will resolve what has become a litigious situation. We can construct a list of this sequence, from the more innocuous to the most grave.

Arbitration and litigation are often thought of as the two basic choices to be made when deciding how disputes will be resolved between partners. Yet these two concepts are but two alternatives out of many. In fact, dispute resolution is to establish procedures it is hoped that will not lead to litigation. Dispute resolution is to offer alternatives to litigation with the express purpose of convincing the parties that there is a practical compromise to be reached for the benefit of all.

Some of the techniques to be discussed are quite informal. These are purposeful, partner-friendly mechanisms, creating an atmosphere that builds on consensus, even removing the conflict from one level of management to another. Other suggestions are formal, so that the parties will be finally bound by the decision. But even when a formal decision is necessary, the option is not merely arbitration versus litigation but rather what is the nature of the conflict and what system of resolution is best suited to the facts. Litigation should be the last resort. Once litigation is commenced, it is extremely difficult to ever regain the functioning of the joint venture.

Constructing a list that follows the degree of consequences, dispute resolution is divided into the following categories:

- *Conciliation.* This is the creation of informal, internal company mechanisms.
- *Mediation.* This process voluntarily refers the dispute to an outside third party but without the formal structure of an arbitration nor is it intended to be binding. The parties participate, an attempt is made to find a common ground, there is less stress on legal rights and a search for the common good. There is an attempt to sway the parties by the logic and impartiality of the mediator, who can see the merit to all sides. Mediation in the everyman international joint ventures is not yet in frequent use.
- *Adjudication.* This is a process either chosen by the parties or, less frequently, made obligatory by the local legislation. It results in a binding decision unless the parties elect to go to arbitration or litigation within a specified period. It differs from mediation as the decision is advisory if rejected. There is less participation by the parties. In fact, there may be none.

- *Arbitration.* This is a process either chosen by the parties or made obligatory by local legislation. Under normal circumstances, it is a final decision, or award as the result is technically called.
- *Litigation.* This is recourse to a court of law.

Many parties to a joint venture agreement do not sit down and develop a hierarchy of dispute resolution. During negotiations, possible friction leading to conflict may not be in the forefront of items for discussion. At the end of many conferences, when the issue of possible differences comes into focus, the parties quickly choose either arbitration or litigation. Nor is there any law that requires the succession of events to take place as just indicated, even if the parties have stipulated an orderly process of dispute resolution in documentation.

Subsequent to the formation of the joint venture, the first serious event of disunity that occurs causes one party immediately to go to a court of law, for example, alleging a basic right has been invaded. A typical complaint is that the general assembly did not validly count the votes to the serious prejudice of one of the partners. It is necessary to seek immediate relief from a court to prevent irreparable harm. Circumstances catapult the parties into one of the categories of dispute resolution.

Consequently, the preceding order of legal concepts is not arranged so that one phase must precede the other. Rather it is a schedule with three purposes in mind:

1. to suggest a natural progression for resolving differences which tends toward harmonizing any partnership differences, preserving the joint venture
2. to permit a general discussion of all categories to reveal their characteristics
3. to point out critical issues raised by some, specifically adjudication, arbitration, and litigation

The differences between these categories are not only the seriousness of their consequences. When disagreements arise, some methods for their resolution are more advantageous than others. Even when the dissension is permanent, all the parties may benefit from one choice over another.

9.1.1 CONCILIATION

Every effort should be made to establish mechanisms within the joint venture structure to refer disputes between partners or managers to a higher level of decision where they can be negotiated. This can be done quite simply by the parties agreeing that if the management of the joint venture cannot agree on an important issue, resulting in a deadlock with no action being possible, then the issue will be resolved to the respective board of directors of each partner. Such an administrative procedure need not be confined to differences at the management level of the joint venture. It can be applicable at any level of operations and for any issue.

Particularly after an acquisition, in which there is an entry of new personnel, there is often introduced a new management philosophy. It is natural that there may be reasonable differences of opinion between the former and the newly arrived operating managers. Clashes arise. New methods must be learned. When conflict surfaces, it should not be allowed to simmer, erupting eventually into irreconcilable dissension.

The joint venture agreement should have an informal, but clear procedure to follow, whereby differences of opinion are permitted to be articulated in writing and referred for hearing and decision within the corporate structure. It happens frequently enough that friction at floor level eventually creates divisions within the management due to the familiar psychological tendency to "take sides" in a conflict. The disagreements divide along equity interests and allegiance to the "home" company.

Various simple methods can be used to informally resolve differences. At the board of directors' level, if an impasse develops, there can be an agreement that the vote of the chairman of the board will be decisive, that is, count for more than one vote. This requires the chairman to be changed at least once a year. If the chairman of one group abuses this power, the next chairman will probably retaliate. To some extent, this provides a check on unfair decisions, but it is far from a perfect system.

Another possibility when there is a deadlock is to refer an important issue to a third party not beholden to any one group. This method also has its imperfections as matters cannot be continually referred to other parties and therefore have to be confined to the occasional crucial items creating the deadlock. Very likely the third party will have to undergo a total immersion in the affairs of the company, which is very time-consuming and not conducive to efficient management.

The most satisfactory routine is to have unresolved issues referred to the respective management boards of each partner. Most joint ventures are formed by companies that therefore are subject to their own system of management. For those situations in which an individual forms or is part of a joint venture, this alternative is not viable.

When other management hierarchies do exist, a simple written statement of the problem followed by a mandatory period of review by each management board with a further obligation to meet and attempt to find a solution in good faith produces very satisfactory results in a substantial majority of cases. Written recommendations will follow. Many conflicts arise merely because of personality issues at the operating level. What is seen as critical and crucial at the operating level becomes a minor divergence when presented to boards geographically far removed from the joint venture and a sensible solution is found rapidly.

The issues referred to conciliation within the company may be broad and virtually without limit. Restraint on abuse will operate because the local management is not going to be anxious to continually demonstrate its inability to resolve problems. The possibility of conciliation is an escape valve for the frequent managerial tensions that arise during a joint venture involving different cultures and diverse corporate management philosophies.

The use of conciliation will not be the appropriate subject of company articles. Such procedures are best defined and settled in the private agreements affecting the joint venture company and its participants. Being informal, unstructured, to be encouraged, and not subject to special rules suggest that private agreements are the ideal repository of such ideas.

9.1.2 Introduction to mediation

It would be preferable to utilize a different term other than *mediation* for the process to be described. More accurate descriptions are *third-party recommendations* or *third-party advice.* But the term *mediation* is canonized in commercial practice and more confusion only will be created by insisting on introducing new terminology. Mediation is clearly not negotiation although this designation is sometimes used. Negotiation is a broad term that incorporates so many situations and objectives that its use as a term for resolving differences is not apt.

In the international joint venture context, mediation does not have the same meaning as it does in the alternate dispute resolution process that exists in many countries. In some jurisdictions, a form of mediation is obligatory, imposed by the legal system before recourse can be had to a court of law, for example, in a family law dispute. Some nations may require parties before utilizing the court process to engage in mandatory mediation, for example, in a labor dispute action. This is denominated mediation but not the mediation presently under discussion. This is not the mediation applicable to international joint ventures.

Mediation for our purposes is the intervention of a third party, whether individual or group, selected voluntarily by the parties to the joint venture to give an advisory opinion on a potential conflict. It is not a process forming part of a court action nor is it a process imposed by the legislation of a particular country. We are reviewing the search for a just solution desired by the parties from their own initiatives. It is seeking recourse to third parties for their impartial expert opinion relating to a company and its partners.

Although the words are easily confused semantically, mediation is also not arbitration. Arbitration results in a binding obligatory resolution of a conflict. Mediation and arbitration have little in common other than third-party impartiality. Referring matters to a mediator is really only asking for an advisory opinion. Mediation is a nonbinding step prior to arbitration or litigation. Its utility is that the mediator is seen, and with reason, as a neutral participant whose logical analysis will serve as a beacon as to what may be the final outcome if recourse is left to arbitration or litigation.

It removes the psychological barrier that is created when partners stop even hearing what the reasons of the other party are. The advisory opinion pronounced by the mediator may bring a rude awakening. This same opinion may point out the obvious, which one party would not even consider due to its initial source, that is, the other partner.

An advisory opinion also has a further substantial benefit. It may serve the purpose of a cooling-off period. Intractable positions founded on a narrow view of the facts may soften when the opinion of another dispassionate person is heard.

An additional reason why mediation confers a benefit is that the parties will normally make a complete presentation, even though summarized and in an informal setting, similar to what they would do in arbitration or litigation. They are forced to articulate their reasons and the facts supporting them. The very process of reducing to writing what is seen as the critical divergences and their consequences may assist in putting the conflict in a more reasonable light.

It will assist in pointing out inconsistencies. It is a trial rehearsal and as such there is still time to reflect and adopt another position. Mediation is intended to follow the informal atmosphere of discussions between the different boards of directors who represent the joint venture partners but this time a third opinion is sought, not for its binding effect, but for a concerned, well-balanced, prudent judgment on what appears to be a sensible solution.

Mediation cannot be used with the same frequency as conciliation. It has to be confined to issues that threaten the continued viability of the joint venture. Otherwise, the joint venture will be expending available commercial resources in human resources occupied continually with the issues of mediation. Wisely, the mediation process, as with conciliation, should have been foreseen in the joint venture documentation, although certainly it can be chosen at any stage of conflict. However, similar to all procedures, various issues must be considered when choosing mediation.

9.1.3 ISSUES RELATING TO MEDIATION

As indicated, the process of mediation should be foreseen in the joint venture documentation. The parties early in the discussion stages of joint venture documentation must make some decisions regarding

- mediation as a condition to further action such as arbitration or litigation
- the topics to be mediated
- the selection of mediators
- exchange of information and confidentiality of the mediation process
- the process
- enforceability

Mediation as a condition to further action

The parties at the formation stage of the joint venture may appreciate the value of mediation. It is a desirable alternative. It should help to resolve issues before positions become rigid and discussion nonproductive. As part of the conciliation procedures established by the joint venture documents, there can be the obligation that, on failure for the diverse management boards to reach a conclusion, the respective boards will choose a mediator to hear and make recommendations.

If the topic reviewed in conciliation is of critical importance to the joint venture, it is possible the joint venture documentation has a clause that will obligate the parties to further invoke mediation. However, having an obligation to mediate following a collapse of conciliation appears to be creating an overload of contentious bureaucracy. If conciliation falters, either the parties will accept that the problem is one of many items that must be set aside or one party will feel sufficiently aggrieved so that more serious alternatives are considered. Therefore, we suggest mediation should not be obligatory following a failure of conciliation. It should be optional, a suggestion from the founding partners.

However, if there are no conciliation procedures, we may ask: Should mediation be compulsive, a necessary step prior to one of the parties moving to a more serious phase of disagreement? Conciliation is informal and contained within the company. Mediation requires the intervention of other parties.

This decision involves various philosophical inquiries about the nature of people. Although mediation can be a contractual obligation, instructing people to mediate when they do not wish to do so, this alternative appears counterproductive. We can arrive at the ridiculous phase in which one party goes to court to compel mediation that is supposed to be a voluntary goodwill process. The mediation stage, if ordered by a court, becomes a hollow procedure with the result already known: rejection of the advisory opinion omitted by the recalcitrant party.

Time will be consumed with the parties merely trying to gather information so as to obtain an advantage for a formal court process. Therefore, the joint venture documentation can contain references to conciliation and even mediation, but both processes will be more fruitful in their effect if left to the inclination of the parties. The uses of conciliation and mediation should be entirely voluntary, a broad sweeping phrase in the joint venture agreement inviting the parties to adopt nonlitigious methods prior to a formal procedure, making suggestions as to the steps to be followed.

The topics to be mediated

Mediation is a modest admission that the joint venture is beginning to dysfunction. A broad clause in the private agreements often imposes on the board of directors instructions to seek a solution in good faith on critical issues, and when faced with an impasse, refers the matter to mediation.

It is not a good idea to be too specific. What will be mediated varies from joint venture to joint venture. When the parties show themselves willing to incorporate mediation provisions into their documentation, the topics subject to mediation will be similar to those whose importance merits minority interest protection but that cannot be set forth in the company articles. Thus, issues of budgets, salaries, personnel appointments, research-and-development projects, marketing ideas, and of course interpretation of the joint venture documentation on expansive topics are all relevant matters for mediation.

The precise list can be purposefully vague, for example, all matters affecting the commercial interpretation of the joint venture and its documentation or confined to a schedule prepared by counsel in consultation with the clients. Lack of details in a mediation clause will encourage the parties to voluntarily seek its use. The presence in documentation of the foresight of the founding partners is very persuasive and frequently the corporate boards of the partners insist with each other in adhering to the conditions, binding or not, in the joint venture documentation.

The selection of mediators

The mediator may be an individual or a board of selected experts. There also exist professional mediation boards. If one does not exist in the jurisdiction, it is not difficult to create a board. It is an ad hoc recourse whose objective is to obtain a preliminary nonbinding opinion.

The process of mediation has become a profession. It is possible in some countries for an individual to obtain a certificate of mediation as evidence of possessing the necessary knowledge of a competent mediator. Many bar associations have mediation boards or committees that can organize a mediation process. Retired judges and lawyers are often selected to serve as mediators. However, no matter how august the surroundings of mediation, the basic characteristic of mediation does not change: the issuance of an advisory opinion.

Exchange of information and confidentiality of the mediation process

Once mediation has been selected, the questions of information and confidentiality are forefront. Mediation may fail. A party may consent to mediation merely with the hope of obtaining information. One party does not want to consent to a declaration of dividends. Is a possible sale of an equity interest being concealed? Does the party wish to augment the cash reserves of the joint venture so that a sale of equity becomes more attractive? These are questions that may develop during the mediation process.

Once mediation is chosen, a few elementary precautions will enhance the value of mediation by containing the process within well-defined parameters. If mediation is conducted discerningly, it will be used again. A simple agenda of what the parties will and will not do within mediation is helpful. There should be an agreement that the mediation process is not an information-gathering opportunity but limited to the deadlock in question.

It should be stipulated between the parties that if one does not want to furnish information, it does not have to be given. The parties and the mediator should agree that the mediation process is not a wide-ranging investigation into the motives of each participant. In short, mediation should not have any compulsory aspects to it. It should be a user-friendly procedure in which the parties are genuinely interested in hearing the opinion of a third party.

The information to be provided should be contained to the issue at hand, with the parties free to provide whatever details they wish. This observation will perhaps appear naïve. But its recommendation is not made predicated on the presumed wholesome nature of people to reveal honestly all the facts. This suggestion derives from a realization that mediation, if to be successful, can be neither inquisitorial nor threatening. A participant believing himself ultimately intimidated will become reluctant to continue with the mediation and it will worsen the partnership environment. The scope of information provided therefore should be narrowly confined to the disagreement at hand.

It should be made clear in the mediation process that information given is confidential and private. Such a stipulation will probably have little effect between the parties because should litigation arise, parties are beholden to respond to the inquiries of the court.

However, regarding third parties, the mediator and all parties must agree that no information will be divulged unless so ordered to do so by a court. In the end, this may not be a significant restriction, but at least it prevents all participants, including the mediator, from assuming that the information disclosed becomes a matter of public record.

Within the area of joint ventures, mediation is not imposed on the parties by a judge or the legislation. Naturally, there will be joint ventures with public entities or when a sovereign state is one of the partners. In these circumstances, the process of mediation will be defined and the freedom of the partners as to the procedures to be chosen will be limited. But in the everyman joint venture involving private parties, there will be significant latitude as to the procedural aspects of mediation.

The mediation process

The hallmark of litigation is an adversary setting. There pervades the idea that someone did something wrong. It is the most early of human emotions to be felt and carries forward with substantial force into the adult stage, revealing itself in many courtroom dramas. The objective of mediation is significantly different from litigation. It cannot succeed in an adversarial spirit. One might as well not elect this option.

Furthermore, litigation often does not seek a sensible solution. By this is not meant that judges do not emit reasonable sentences. They do, under the most difficult of circumstances. But the function of a judge is to interpret the law as enacted by the legislature or developed through decades of decisions by other judges, what is known as the doctrine of precedents.

Unlike litigation, or the adversarial process, the true merit of mediation lies in its ability to have a third party suggest a sensible compromise that the parties did not consider or to show the wisdom of a middle road advocated by one of the partners. Fault finding is not appropriate in a mediation process.

If this point of view is correct, the traditional concepts of due process need not be present in mediation. One of the elements of due process is the right to be heard and hear the others. But in mediation, we are not concerned about the truth of anyone's statements, or inconsistencies in positions, promises broken, or misrepresentations made. Although the latter are condemnable, their absence will not lead to an alternate just solution of the problem. They may provide reasons for an unfavorable sentence by a judge, but mediation seeks to avoid advancing toward the adversarial stage. Mediation is concerned less with justice and more with commercial compromise.

All the usual legal appurtenances to a trial need not find their counterpart in mediation nor should they. There is excluded cross-examination and substituted informal meetings with the mediation board. The mediators may consult with the parties without the presence of the other parties. There may or may not be hearings. Cross-examination has no function in mediation. In short, the more informal and less structured is the process, the more viable becomes the acceptance of the final advisory opinion. The mediation board selected to hear and advise will have its recommended procedures, which are usually subject to alteration with the consent of all parties.

Enforceability of mediation

When we speak of enforceability, we are only referring to the obligation to mediate. We already know the results are advisory. If the agreement to mediate is breached a day before procedures are to begin, there lies a claim for damages. However, the damages are more difficult to prove, being intangible, subject to argument and debate. Requesting a court to enforce mediation in the hope the other party will come to reason also appears a vague solution, similar to requiring a painter to produce an eloquent canvas. Without the will, the result is likely to be dismal.

In the everyman joint venture, the obligatory nature of mediation seems inappropriate and at variance with the purpose of such a procedure. The strength of mediation as an alternative to traditional forms of litigation lies in its informality and conviction of the parties that the joint venture should continue to function, but there is an honest difference of opinion on an issue. However, the possibility of mediation will not cure situations in which differences and impasses have become insuperable or a contest of wills has set in to the detriment of the functioning of the joint venture. This requires adjudication, arbitration, or litigation.

Mediation clause

Similar to a clause to attempt to conciliate differences, mediation should not be imposed on the parties by the company articles. Perhaps such a mandate could be inserted in the company articles although the standard to be used as a reference will defy most efforts of draftsmanship. Even assuming the articulation problem is surpassed, inscribing mediation in the company articles does not avoid the main problem: You cannot compel people to have a constructive, nonviolent dialogue.

Consequently, mediation as an alternative step prior to litigation will find its best use in the private agreements between shareholders or in the joint venture agreement.

9.1.4 ADJUDICATION

Adjudication is the process whereby an expert or a board hears and determines a controversy. It differs from mediation in that the decision becomes binding and enforceable unless the parties seek recourse within a specified period of time to either arbitration or a court of law. It is only advisory when one of the parties says "No." When the parties to adjudication accept the results by not taking any steps to the contrary, the decision is subject to enforcement in the jurisdiction of the adjudicators. If the parties do not wish to accept the decision, either party will have a determined period of time to file for arbitration or plead a case in court.

Adjudication can be optional, a method adopted by the parties to the joint venture. However, in some jurisdictions, adjudication is statutory and forms part of an obligatory process in specific contracts. In the UK, a construction consortium joint venture would have to submit to adjudication in the event of a dispute. Statutory adjudication is not sufficiently dispersed in enough jurisdictions to pervade the average joint venture, and for those specific activities in which it is part of the commercial process, such as a public bid, local counsel will provide the details. Nevertheless, voluntary adjudication can be chosen for any joint venture. Why would any parties choose this method? What advantages, if any, does it offer?

Adjudication can offer various concrete benefits: speed, impartiality, expert knowledge, and willing compliance. It therefore will be more readily elected by those multinationals with substantial international joint venture experience than the everyman joint venture.

When there is statutory adjudication, the adjudicator(s) have broad powers of investigation. They can conduct their own inquiries. There is no necessity for formal hearings. There is no requirement of a due process, in which all parties are heard. The adjudicator can make visits to any locale and inspect works in progress. The adjudicator can request the production of documents.

The adjudicator may speak to the parties separately, or none, or only a selected group. There is permitted a wide discretion with no formal procedural. All of these possibilities can be incorporated in voluntary adjudication through proper documentation. Perhaps this will seem inconsistent with notions of *fair play and justice,* but the emphasis on adjudication is on speed and expert resolution and not on courtroom pleadings. It would not be unreasonable for the adjudication process to be restricted to a maximum of 30 days. The lack of due process, or an opportunity for all to be heard, should be seen not as a lack of due process but as its temporary suspension.

Once the decision is rendered, the parties have a brief period to consider whether it will be accepted. All accept the final result. If not, then either arbitration or litigation will be elected, dependent on what the relevant joint venture documentation states. With the introduction of adjudication as a mechanism of dispute resolution, therefore, we encounter a legal problem that is common to adjudication, arbitration, and litigation: the expectation of enforcement. Whatever system of dispute resolution we use, we usually believe that with the final decision or sentence there will be compliance.

This is not so. Neither enforcement, nor compliance, nor even acceptance of a decision or sentence can be taken for granted. Oftentimes, the losing party not only refuses to accept the final award or court sentence, but attacks it when enforcement is sought. The problem of implementing a decision awarded by a nonjudicial entity is frequently encountered in arbitration. This material is best developed within this topic.

9.1.5 Arbitration

Arbitration is often seen as a panacea to the formalities, bureaucracy, and mysteries of litigation in which documents abound and common sense disappears. If the latter is an exaggeration, the former is an overstatement. Arbitration will not make any complex issue more simple. Today, arbitration also has its procedures and order of presentation of evidence. But before examining some technical aspects, a broad question must be addressed. When does one use arbitration and when does one resort to litigation? Here some policy considerations are relevant. In this section, we will consider the appropriateness of arbitration.

If the joint venture involves a substantial majority held by a well-capitalized multinational, every effort should be made by the minority to utilize arbitration. Litigation conducted by a multinational or against one will eventually bankrupt the minority interest. Litigation is a useless alternative for a modest investor unless the principle of the dispute overrides financial considerations. This can happen and there are, fortunately, situations in which counsel will undertake to represent a party on a contingent-fee basis. Yet there are still considerable expenses without reference to fees.

Once litigation surfaces, large corporations refer the issue to their counsel and the matter is more or less put aside by the corporate executives. The dispute becomes a matter for the lawyers. A significant multinational is not going to invest scores of hours of management personnel on litigation involving a joint venture unless it is headline material. Consequently, for the minority interest, litigation will produce modest interest from the majority owner, few results, substantial expenses, and probably little compensation. The battle is waged, the weary warrior is grateful for a glass of water at the end of the day, and will not ask for champagne.

Arbitration is also a preferred method when the joint venture involves a technical operation, one that may invoke questions of an engineering nature. Computer joint ventures are a good example. Referring disputes concerning a computer joint venture to a court of law is to call on a body of learned men who will have to hear much scientific evidence not ordinarily within their everyday experience.

Of course, if the material is well-presented, it will be understood. What a man creates, others can understand. But this will take time. Arbitration is a good solution when it can be anticipated that technical disputes will arise. The arbitration tribunal will surely elect to hear and determine individuals with the necessary background.

Arbitration is also an attractive alternative when all parties are of modest capital means or when the cultural differences are substantial so that one legal system is not easily understood by another. Arbitration is simpler because normally the process excludes various aspects of litigation that can be expensive, such as taking the oral testimony of witnesses prior to or during the evidence phase. It is well suited to the everyman joint venture.

As to significant cultural differences, it is sensible for parties from different cultures to choose a forum that is impartial and without predisposed inclinations to one party from a sense of national identity. The law is not always impartially administrated. It is folly to think it is. A judge from an emerging economy jurisdiction may have a subjective opinion as to the nature of a multinational or as to the economic system of the foreign investor. Profit may not be the prime cultural objective for a particular jurisdiction. Whatever are our personal opinions, we can all agree that the subjective aspect was not contemplated when the joint venture was formed. Arbitration thus permits a forum concerned with only facts.

In addition to acute differences of culture existing, a sovereign state may be a partner. This raises the question as to how one partner can exercise rights against an entity that normally enjoys immunity from litigation. One alternative is to have the sovereign state waive its immunity for any questions arising out of the joint venture. This will be facilitated through recourse to arbitration with the sovereign state acknowledging it has waived its immunity. If the arbitration forum is carefully chosen, this waiver will be held valid.

This situation is to be contrasted with a general waiver in the joint venture documentation that if invoked in litigation before a tribunal will have its recognition dependent on the law of the jurisdiction, which cannot be known at the formation stage. In these circumstances, selecting arbitration permits eliminating doubts as to the effectiveness of a waiver of immunity.

Should arbitration be selected, a number of important decisions will have to be made simultaneously:

- The site of the arbitration. There are many arbitration authorities in different parts of the world. Probably most entrepreneurs have heard of the International Chamber of Commerce in Paris or the American Arbitration Association in New York. But there are many others, in Stockholm, London, Lisbon, and undoubtedly the other major jurisdictions of the world have their local arbitration boards that can be utilized. These are often administered by the industrial or commercial associations operating in the capital of any jurisdiction. The first decision to be taken then is where to have the arbitration.

- The place of the arbitration should above all be made dependent on whether the forum—the jurisdiction—is a sovereign that has ratified a treaty, such as the New York Convention, which will thus render enforcement probable. Conducting arbitration in a forum that is not a member to any arbitration enforcement treaty is probably delaying the one step arbitration was intended to avoid: litigation. Losing parties invariably seek to avoid an unfavorable arbitration decision, and without a treaty to support the winning claimant, a complex lawsuit will emerge in the home jurisdiction of the losing party. Arbitration treaties confine the possible defenses of the losing party to a narrow range of possibilities, such as fraud or lack of due process.

- Once the location of the arbitration has been decided, the next primary consideration will be what is the applicable law. Imagine a French contractor has a joint venture with an Italian partner who is performing services in Morocco. The parties agree to arbitrate their differences in New York. What law will the New York arbitration board apply? Some lawyers would argue that this is the classic case in which the *lex mercatoria* must apply, that general body of commercial law embraced by most industrialized countries. Other attorneys would argue there is no "*lex mercatoria*" and the parties must make an election. The topic of choice of law is complex and cannot be confined to a summary discussion. However, there is a practical parameter that can be indicated. Common sense dictates choosing as the applicable law what can be interpreted and proved with the least effort and represents a sensible compromise for all the parties. Asking the New York arbitrators to apply Moroccan law, although not an insurmountable task, is certainly complicating the issue. It will be easier to obtain expert testimony on French or Italian law. Ultimately, the choice of law will be made by counsel in consultation with the clients and the practical options.

- The language of the proceedings will be equally fundamental. No one would choose an arbitration in a locale where neither party spoke or understood the language. How would the procedures even be initiated? Nor is it fair that only one party understand the procedures. When the obligation of arbitration is decided, it should indicate an arbitration board in which all the parties will understand the language. If this cannot be done, then probably arbitration is not a sensible option. It will never be implemented.

- Once arbitration is decided, the parties must then agree that the arbitration will be final. It is useless to go through protracted arbitration procedures only to find that one party will not comply and appeals to a court of law to overturn the decision or else modify it. Fortunately, there exist legal techniques for ensuring any arbitration decision will be final and this basically requires legal language indicating this objective. The arbitration must be expressed as being final and without further appeal to any court of law except on a narrow range of issues such as the illegal composition of the board or improper arbitration procedures. This is a highly technical area in which counsel will provide the necessary drafting language.

- The last technical choice is whether the parties wish the arbitrators to use the principles of equity, fair play, and common sense or else attempt to apply what is seen as the law of the contract or joint venture. Once again, unless the parties agree that arbitration will be based on a common-sense approach, there seems little reason to invoke the aid of the arbitration board. If interpretation of the law is needed, the tribunal is the proper site because of its long history of impartiality, learnedness, and experience in resolving complex questions of law.

These are some of the broad issues that must be considered when contemplating arbitration as a dispute resolution method. There are naturally many items that are the object of an arbitration agreement, but they are within the province of counsel and raise various legal issues that must be resolved by an understanding of the law of the joint venture. We can describe briefly some of them but with the restricted objective of only raising topics the joint venture partners will want to discuss with counsel:

- How many arbitrators will be necessary and how they will be chosen are pertinent inquiries.
- The issues to be arbitrated. We can see that the parties may want to separate certain topics from others and agree that in one category arbitration will apply and not in another. This seems sensible except any party not wanting to arbitrate will immediately contest the classification. Thus, a policy decision has to be made in face of the joint venture facts and the parties involved.
- When a dispute arises, it is not convenient to have the joint venture unable to function. This refers to legal problems known as *interim relief.* These are questions of possible injunctions or judicial relief designed to preserve the status quo. As a practical matter, it is best not to allow arbitration procedures interrupt the commercial activity involved, unless the relief is needed *in extremis,* that is, it is a critical issue to be

settled immediately being necessary to avoid irreparable harm. Unfortunately, this can be done only by a court of law.

- Litigation usually means the right to compel the other party to reveal and produce various documents, a process known technically as *discovery procedures*. In an arbitration procedure, the parties must decide beforehand to what extent discovery procedures will be permitted.
- The ultimate relief that the parties may expect. It may not be damages. If it is likely other remedies will be sought, such as compelling one party to complete the petrochemical plant contracted, counsel will have to advise if this is a realistic objective in an arbitration hearing.
- Whether the identity of the parties precludes an arbitration ever coming to realization. When one of the parties to the joint venture is a sovereign state, it will be natural that the other partners will think of arbitration elsewhere, in another forum, where any political pressures cannot be brought to bear on the arbitrators. All parties must consider whether arbitration outside the jurisdiction of the sovereign state is a realistic alternative. What if they refuse to appear? The choice of the appropriate forum may reduce this risk. With a sovereign state as one of the joint venture parties, it may be advisable to invoke, if possible, the forum of the International Centre for Settlement of Investment Disputes in Washington, D.C. Thus, we can see that the selection of forum chosen must be made with careful consideration. Technical legal considerations will be determinant. A forum should never be elected simply because it is well known or seems familiar.

9.1.6 TRIBUNAL

In spite of a great deal of skepticism regarding judicial systems, they constitute one of the great monuments of human thought, a tribute to mankind's relentless search for justice. When should recourse to a court of law be preferred over arbitration? Many attorneys believe arbitration produces few results unless the subject matter is technical and a panel of experts is necessary. Their reasoning is arbitration has become sufficiently sophisticated so that it is no less bureaucratic than litigation with a considerable special disadvantage.

Besides having to arbitrate an issue, there must be foreseen the real possibility that the arbitration procedures will result in litigation. Were they valid? Was a serious error committed? Did the arbitration board act within its competence? Did the arbitrators negligently fail to consider material evidence? One trial is replaced by two trials.

Other legal commentators argue that for general questions of fact and law, the solemnity of a courtroom has no substitute. The procedures developed over decades of litigation and judicial review have produced a system that ferrets out facts substantially well and the application of the law is invariably made with impartiality. Arbitration or litigation? It is not a simple choice. Probably the more diverse and different the cultures of the partners, the more suitable is arbitration. But so many variables must be considered that firm conviction is not to be trusted.

When litigation is considered as the preferred method, chauvinism regarding a judicial system is not sensible. It is unlikely that one legal system is superior to another. The overwhelming majority of judicial systems are staffed by highly competent, well-trained jurists. If the parties to a joint venture decide they do not want arbitration, obviously recourse to a court of law is the only alternative. This raises two fundamental problems:

1. What will be the site of the lawsuit, the competent jurisdiction to hear and determine?
2. What will be the applicable law?

The answers are uncertain because they are dependent on so many facts. Yet it is possible to offer some guidelines.

Let us return to our example of the French and Italian joint venture partners operating in Morocco. The joint venture agreement could conceivably provide that the competent jurisdiction will be the New York courts that will apply the law of France. Here we can see multiple problems. How will the New York court obtain jurisdiction over the parties if the parties do not voluntarily submit to its jurisdiction? How will the law of France be proved? How will the judgment of the court be enforced? Do the jurisdictions of the partners have treaties with the United States that render enforcement in France or Italy probable without too many legal procedures? What if the law of France is offensive on public policy on a particular issue in New York but not in Italy? Justly, comparative private international law has been characterized as an intellectual maze that has no comparison.

It is frequent that joint venture agreements refer disputes to another jurisdiction, other than where the joint venture is operating, and also call for the application of a law that is not the local law of the jurisdiction. Again returning to our example, the French and Italian partners could agree that the applicable law was the law of the State of New York. Perhaps there will be reasons that justify this technique. However, in many cases, it appears this is introducing an unnecessary complexity into an already difficult process, litigation, and creating a situation prone to error, to wit, neither the French nor the Italian partner understand sufficiently the law of New York.

Having the French or Italian partners make assumptions as to the law of New York is a serious responsibility. Enforcing the judgments of another jurisdiction is not automatic. There is no way to obtain a judgment in New York, file it in France, and then execute on it with nothing further to do. An action has to be commenced in France on the judgment, which, if less lengthy and more confined to the issue of a fair trial in New York, is still, in spite of its reduced scope, another lawsuit.

These thoughts lead to a tentative conclusion. In the usual case concerning international joint ventures, it would be rare that there was involved a jurisdiction whose legal system was suspect. Of course, it can happen but it certainly is not a common occurrence.

No one would feel the slightest hesitation in having a case decided in France and Italy whose jurisprudence have made notable contributions to the legal systems all over the world including the Anglo-Saxon. This suggests that the forum and the applicable law of the joint venture should be the jurisdiction in which it is operating for a variety of good reasons:

- the parties are present in the jurisdiction through the vehicle of the joint venture
- the operative facts take place in the local jurisdiction
- the witnesses will be there
- the law will be applied by those who understand it: the local courts
- enforcement is facilitated

The resolution of the problem can be viewed in another way. Good reasons should be invoked as to why the local forum is not suitable. If they exist, there are alternatives, such as arbitration. Adding further complexity to the dispute resolution process by requiring recourse to a law other than that of the national forum should require clear well-founded explanations. The practical solution to resolution of disputes in an international joint venture is either to utilize the local legal system or seek to choose a forum for arbitration that offers the most guarantees of enforcement.

Naturally, this will not always be viable. Nor can there be any assurances that a promise to arbitrate will not be repudiated and one of the partners initiates a lawsuit. Legal documents cannot avoid actions apparently in contradiction to their objective.

Of course, the dispute resolution process in all its varied aspects may be unsuccessful. Differences cannot be resolved. Whether by agreement or ultimately through litigation, the joint venture has reached its conclusion. This naturally raises questions concerning termination.

Part Two

9.2 Termination

We have briefly alluded to the problems of termination in Chapter Five, when considering the typical topics that form part of the joint venture agreement. As might be expected, there is concealed within the expression *termination* a wide variety of facts and legal concepts. We will use this expression in a vernacular sense as it facilitates reading and conforms to general business understanding.

Termination means the joint venture is over. It has ended. Perhaps it was by voluntary dissolution, the parties agreeing there was no reason to continue. Or the joint venture was only managing to survive, limping along and the capital of the joint venture has been considerably reduced. Many jurisdictions do not permit a company to continue when its capital has been diluted. Either the partners reinforce the capital or the company must be dissolved. The latter was chosen. The partners want to close down the joint venture company.

The termination may have occurred when one of the partners to a contractual joint venture breached one of the terms of the agreement, resulting in a violation of the agreement that gives rise to the end of the collaboration. One partner sues the other, seeking to put an end to the joint venture. The partner in a consortium who declared it knew how to build a petrochemical plant but has demonstrate dearly it lacks the necessary knowledge to do so. There is no point in continuing and incurring substantial liabilities to the client.

When we speak of termination, we are not referring to any cause that the parties have already foreseen and stipulated how, if a particular event occurs, they will proceed. Possible causes for termination can be delineated. But this is often not the case.

The documents, including the articles of company, may state nothing more than what will be the applicable law if there are any disputes. There may be no agreed-on procedures if a conflict arises. The joint venture documents may not define what constitutes cause for termination. The attorneys who have been responsible for the preparation of the legal documents know well that it is not necessary to state what constitutes a breach and cause for termination. When a breach occurs, its consequences will be immediately legally recognized.

Many advisors to international joint ventures advocate not specifying or detailing material about termination and allowing events to condition how the parties will react and conduct themselves. The alleged virtue to this method is the evolution of the joint venture proceeds according to its inner logic with uncertainty as to what each party will do, impelling the parties toward finding compromises and solutions. Deregulation fosters legal market solutions.

Critics of this approach basically believe that the more collaboration is enforced, the more the logic developed will be toward fruitful compromises. Nevertheless, even not having any specific clauses on dispute does not preclude the right of a party to seek recourse to a court of law. Consequently, silence in drafting is really invoking the aid of the national court system as the only alternative.

The declared point of view of your author is that the more the parties are directed toward mechanisms within a nonadversary setting, such as conciliation proceedings, the more likely a solution will arise that provides for the continuation of the joint venture. The apparent propensity of the human being toward unrelenting legal warfare can be channeled into cantankerous bickering that dissipates with the comforting thought of a healthy profit-and-loss statement. A moot trial in the form of conciliation or mediation often brings a more reflective attitude.

With or without a clear itemized list of termination causes, there looms a subjacent attitude ready to be formulated. When we realize the frequent and various ways in which a termination will arise and the high percentage of conflict that does emerge from all commercial relationships, a preliminary question should be addressed. Assuming the joint venture will result in a conflict between partners that cannot be resolved, what would be a satisfactory solution? Does one partner view himself as a potential seller or buyer? Many joint ventures end in just that situation. One partner buys out the other. It is therefore helpful for each partner to make an early decision, without any reason for termination existing or contemplated, whether he will be a seller or a buyer for a very important reason: restrictions on the transfer of shares, a topic already discussed, but now we can see its practical application.

The restrictions on transfers of joint venture interests can be structured to facilitate or not a sale. If a majority partner knows during the formation stage that he prefers to own the entire capital of the joint venture company in case of conflict, then, if possible, a total restriction on transfers will contribute to that solution. A minority partner wanting to exit will have to sell his interests to the other partner. What needs to be established is the price formula.

If total restrictions are not possible, then other conditions can be inserted in the company articles, such as that a sale cannot be made to a potential competitor, that the potential new partner must have a certain solid reputation in the industry, or that the sale is only possible, having passed all other criteria, if the new purchaser will agree to the terms of the existing joint venture agreement and shareholders' agreement. The more conditions inserted, the more narrow is the range of potential buyers.

On the other hand, if a participant knows he would prefer to exit from the joint venture rather than be a purchaser, then clearly the less impediments, the more easily a new purchaser will be found. In such a situation, this party will strive for only one restriction: having found a buyer, solicited or not, then the other partners will be given notice and have a period of time to agree to the sale or purchase the interests themselves. Since the other partners will not have interference in the setting of the price, their only option being to agree or purchase, the seller has more flexibility in structuring a price on the terms he deems favorable.

To arrive at some tentative conclusions and suggestions in this entire area of termination and dispute resolution, we will develop the following methodology as to contractual and equity joint ventures:

- the reasons for termination
- posttermination issues
- the termination process

9.2.1 TERMINATION BY FAILURE OF A PRECLOSING CONDITION

A contractual or equity joint venture will be preceded by a joint venture agreement. The joint venture agreement may never be consummated. This translates into a closing never taking place. The prospective joint venture is interrupted. The reasons for this are varied, ranging from failure to obtain needed foreign investment licenses to one party not being able to fund his participation.

Whether the failure to realize the joint venture will be a breach or a contingency that does not impute liability will depend on the drafting terms of the joint venture agreement. Clearly, if a party in a joint venture agreement has promised to perform a certain act prior to the formation of the joint venture, such as making a loan to the joint venture, there may well be liability.

In Chapter Five, we covered much material that should be the subject of thought when preparing a joint venture agreement. The principle should be clear. A joint venture agreement will fail to materialize and the terms of this agreement will indicate what future course of action is possible, if any, between the parties, for cancellation of the joint venture agreement without liability or litigation.

9.2.2 TERMINATION BECAUSE THE TERM OF THE JOINT VENTURE IS COMPLETED

Applicable to both contractual and equity joint ventures is a predefined period, after which the joint venture is terminated by mutual consent. In a contractual joint venture, this will be quite common, and may not be a date but an event, for example, the completion of the project. With equity joint ventures, such a clause providing for automatic dissolution and liquidation would be highly unusual. In theory, it is possible.

It may be thought of as mutual consent given in anticipation of the event. Such a company article is a rarity in practice. Not many entrepreneurs will go through the bureaucratic process of forming a company only to agree to its dissolution. If it is a near date, a company is probably not needed. If it is a future date, in the distant horizon, the present commitment may be obviously a lack of business judgment. Future facts are difficult to predict. Parties wishing to have a joint venture for a specific period, perhaps as an experimental phase, are better counseled to adopt the contractual form of joint venture.

9.2.3 CONTRACTUAL JOINT VENTURE: REASONS FOR TERMINATION

The contractual joint venture, being a legal structure not normally intended to endure indefinitely, often conditions more of the personal attributes of a partner as cause for a termination. Common reasons for terminating a contractual joint venture are

- the term of the venture has expired
- failure to obtain a certain performance or net operating income stipulated in the agreement, or any other condition
- bankruptcy procedures against a partner

- any action that puts into cause the financial credibility of the partner such as a public declaration of debt
- failure to comply with the terms of the contractual joint venture (which may create a wide range of responsibilities for each party)
- change in control of the partner if it has a company form
- a broad category known as *force majeure,* which means acts not attributable to any foreseeable act at the time of the joint venture agreement, such as an act of war or earthquake that destroys the plant
- *deadlock issues,* that is, the failure of management to act because of a lack of voting power on a range of selected items

There is clearly a close affinity between the joint venture agreement and the contractual joint venture so that breach of any of the terms of the joint venture agreement may serve as justification for terminating the contractual joint venture which followed it. Merely incorporating by reference all the terms of the joint venture agreement, or any other agreement, into the contractual joint venture will provide all parties with a range of topics and issues that, if not duly performed, will permit a termination of the contractual joint venture.

The use of incorporating other agreements into the contractual joint venture does not find its counterpart easily in equity joint ventures. Company articles do not permit automatic dissolution because of breach of an agreement signed between the original partners. Such a company article would preclude as a practical matter third parties from dealing with the company. Dissolution requires a general assembly. Once a general assembly is convoked, an entire different set of rules becomes applicable, an area we have already developed. Extracontractual obligations seem perfectly normal in a contractual joint venture. Such a reference in an equity joint venture is not customary.

In a contractual joint venture, the parties may go even further than mere legal infractions. There can be created restrictions on general moral behavior that, dependent on the operating jurisdiction, may be perfectly reasonable. As companies act through individuals, this is an attempt by the contractual joint venture company to supervise and fiscalize the acts of key employees in a foreign jurisdiction. The contractual joint venture may contain clauses that cause automatic expulsion of one member if a management committee decides there has been improper moral conduct by one of the partners acting through a representative, that is, an employee.

An even more tenuous standard can be stipulated whereby if the other partners believe the acts of a partner cause the contractual joint venture's public image to suffer, then the agreement will be terminated or other provisions established that may obligate one partner withdrawing from the contractual joint venture.

A substantial number of various standards of personal conduct are possible in a contractual joint venture as the method for terminating the joint venture or expelling a member is more simple than in an equity joint venture.

9.2.4 EQUITY JOINT VENTURE: REASONS FOR TERMINATION

Far more restricted are the reasons that can lead to the termination of an equity joint venture. The partnership form has more ease of termination similar to the contractual joint venture. However, corporations and similar company structures present difficult procedural problems to resolve. Shareholders in a closely held private company may not want as a partner a member whose interest has been attached by a creditor or has become included in the assets of the bankrupt partner. This would result in the equity joint venture having a new partner.

Nevertheless, a dissolution is dependent on the votes of the partners and how the voting is counted may either require the active vote of the bankrupt partner or else the percentage of votes required is low, which created a risk for the other partners when the joint venture was formed. Causing the company to be automatically put into dissolution for any reason, including the bankruptcy of a partner, is also not a practical solution, without considering the legal difficulties that make generalizations suspect.

The same observations can be made about any standard of conduct or event that the partners believe affects the intimate collaboration that had been foreseen in the beginning of the joint venture. The difficulty in implementing the standards adopted so as to effectuate a dissolution increases as the criteria leave objective standards and enter into moral considerations.

For these reasons, a workable compromise is not to turn to dissolution as a method of controlling other partners, but rather utilize techniques that compel an infringing partner to sell his interests. In other words, similar to bonds and the right of redemption, the company has a right to require a transfer back to the company of the interest in question, whether it be a share or other form of equity interest.

The precise legal mechanism, and its legal characterization, will vary from jurisdiction to jurisdiction and with differing degrees of application. One jurisdiction may exclude attaching creditors from this possibility. Against them, the share cannot be obligatorily returned to the company. In some jurisdictions, the transfer back will be characterized as a redemption only applicable to a class of shares. In other jurisdictions, it will be classified as an amortized purchase and standards will be promulgated as to effects on capital and procedural requirements.

With so many possible jurisdictions to consider, we can only discuss general principles. However, it can be asserted that most jurisdictions do allow the articles of a company to obligate an equity interest to be sold back to the issuer, that is, the company. The most common and least controversial is on the death of an individual partner. The joint venture company does not want to have to deal with heirs, and on the demise of a founding partner, his estate must give up the equity interest. What needs to be established, however, will be the causes of redemption or amortization and its price.

PART THREE

9.3 CONTRACTUAL AND EQUITY JOINT VENTURES: ISSUES TO BE CONSIDERED ON TERMINATION

The reasons causing termination are varied. In all cases, a number of questions become highly relevant and there are many. When the termination of the joint venture takes place in a nonlitigious ambiance, it is extremely helpful to have guidelines affecting the postventure conduct of the parties. When litigation is the dominant atmosphere, these guidelines will be a restraint on the parties, a potential barrier to further, future aggressive acts. Typical issues are

- the conduct of parties post-termination, usually concentrated in the topic of no competition
- the continuation of the joint venture
- the continuation of ancillary contracts such as technology licenses
- the liability of a partner on a guarantee and its discharge

9.3.1 POST-TERMINATION RESTRAINTS ON COMMERCIAL CONDUCT

No matter how the termination takes place or for what reason, the parties during the phase of the joint venture agreement should determine what commercial freedom, or lack of it, the parties will have when the joint venture comes to an end, with or without goodwill. This is important because, particularly when there is litigation, the parties are not likely to feel constrained by general principles of good faith or implied conditions against partners competing with one another.

Thus the original parties must consider what market freedom they wish if they are no longer partners. Perhaps this will be dependent on the continued existence of the company if one of the partners continues to operate it. But this alternative should be articulated and its consequences expressed in the joint venture agreement. Competition, or the lack of it, possible territories, products, and distributors are all usual items of commerce and should be regulated prior to the happening of the event.

It might be thought that the smaller local partner would be fearful of having a former multinational partner continue to operate in its jurisdiction. But in fact the balance of power is often equal, for although the local partner may have less financial resources, it will often have more local market knowledge. Therefore, for all former partners, the large capital corporations and the small family companies, there is every advantage in defining future conduct.

9.3.2 TERMINATION: CONTINUATION OF THE JOINT VENTURE

A further recurrent subject, irrespective of the termination, is whether there will be contemplated the continuation of the joint venture by one or more partners. With pending litigation, this is an item to be negotiated and it is difficult to see how, admitting there may be a contested dispute, the parties can foresee this situation in the joint venture agreement.

Of course, in theory, it can be considered, but it is not the most opportune of topics during the negotiations phase. Nevertheless, the continuation of the business is certainly relevant in a termination on mutual consent, or when there is a term, or when events take place leading to a natural end of the joint venture through the demise of one or more of the founders. The company has the right to purchase from the estate the equity interests of the former partner(s), but the deceased partner may have lent the family name with its substantial market value to the company.

Consequently, thoughts about what will be the future of the joint venture company in the event of a termination; how the investment will be returned to its founders; how prices will be calculated; how payment will be made, whether all at once, or in installments, are proper concerns and the more they can be agreed to prior to the happening of the event the more smoothly will be the transition to a different phase: the continuation of the business with new partners.

Naturally, the continuation of the business is related to the subject of noncompetition because it would be senseless to permit the joint venture to continue, payment to be made, and another partner to start a competing line of commerce. A further concern will be issues of competition law, for unrestricted restraints on the commercial activity of third parties will normally be stricken down as anticompetitive and an unreasonable restraint on commerce. Such issues have to be conditioned by the ambit of the local laws.

9.3.3 TERMINATION: CONTINUATION OF CONTRACTUAL OBLIGATIONS

Many joint ventures involve multiple contracts between the joint venture company and one of its partners. Although difficult to implement, controversy between partners should not be allowed to influence the proper functioning of the joint venture. This is an acceptable principle to affirm, but the realities are often one disgruntled partner will attempt to exercise pressure to obtain an objective by threatening to disrupt contractual relations.

A typical example would be a partner who is furnishing technological assistance to the joint venture agreement. Threatening to terminate the assistance, whether for valid reasons or not, will certainly create a difficult situation for the joint venture and probably influence the behavior of the other partners. When termination is tumbling toward litigation, there is nothing to be done except follow the clauses in any collateral agreements, such as the technology assistance agreement, which may buttress the legal obligation of assistance.

Thus, it is prudent to insert in any collateral agreement that differences, whether in litigation or not, derived from other relationships will not affect the performance of the contract under consideration. This will not desist a determined angry partner from claiming breach of the assistance agreement as a further weapon, but it is a legal warning that repudiation of any collateral agreements not substantiated will imply a serious claim for damages.

When termination takes place in a friendly milieu, there should be provisions in the joint venture agreement that clearly call for the continuation of the validity of relevant contracts after the departure of a partner(s). This might seem to be a natural legal consequence because if partner A has a contract with joint venture company B, the withdrawal of partner A should not appear to cause any alteration of the original contractual relationships. However, it must be remembered, many contracts contain clauses conditioning their validity on the management or ownership composition of one of the parties, and therefore rather than having to rely on common-sense interpretations, a clear expression of what will occur will be decisive.

9.3.4 TERMINATION: EXISTING LIABILITIES OF THE WITHDRAWING PARTNER

Especially in a mutual consent environment, the withdrawal of a partner, or the amortization of any equity interest, must be accompanied by the elimination of any liability of the former partner toward a third party concerning guarantees given or loans to be repaid.

In a negotiated withdrawal of one partner, these contingencies would be surely raised. Thus, in a litigious withdrawal, there is less risk if these topics were not regulated. But precisely when the termination comes about without dispute, such as with the demise of a partner, the estate will not want any continued exposure on guarantees given by the former partner, and the lack of mechanisms concerning this situation will cause distressful situations.

This is easily resolved through the mechanisms of the joint venture agreement or even in the company articles, which will recite how any repurchase of an equity interest will take place. The value to be paid will surely include payment of any guarantees still existing. It will be an affirmative obligation on the part of the buyer.

9.3.5 CONTRACTUAL AND EQUITY JOINT VENTURES: TERMINATION ISSUES

The joint venture agreement, the contractual joint venture, the shareholders' agreement, and the articles of the company will provide for different circumstances when termination occurs. The joint venture and shareholders' agreement may provide for termination when there is management deadlock. The contractual joint venture agreement may provide for termination if one partner is declared bankrupt. The articles of the company may provide for dissolution surely by mutual consent or when the capital of the company has been substantially depleted. When the joint venture has come to an end, practical considerations concerning the disposition of the assets become paramount.

If the relevant decisions are not taken early, either in the joint venture agreement or in the company articles, neither litigation nor a negotiated solution will easily resolve the various complex questions. A sample list would include the following topics, which find appropriate treatment in the joint venture agreement:

- If the joint venture company, albeit with a different composition, is to continue, what partners will have the right of purchase? There are five partners and all agree the collaboration is not fruitful, but one wishes, alone, to continue with the joint venture company. What is the price formula and method of payment?

- If a sale of the joint venture company is contemplated to a third party, will it be as a company or by assets? If sold as a going concern, it will realize a better price, but the present partners will be considered about continuing liability for acts during their regency.
- Are there any restrictions to whom it can be sold? If one partner is a multinational, he will not want the business sold to a competitor.
- What if one partner wants part of the business but not the whole? Or just the assets?
- During the life of the joint venture company, perhaps there were developed patents or other technological advances that have value. Who will be the patent owners?

This short list of practical considerations should convincingly display the various problems that are best resolved during the formation stage of the joint venture. Delaying the decision will only complicate the termination process. When the various possibilities on termination cannot be determined early in the formation stage of the joint venture, then at least there should be in place satisfactory mechanisms for dispute resolution. Termination is often caused by unresolved disputes that accumulate like cataracts as soon as the partners lose their commercial vision. Dispute resolution and satisfactory mechanisms concerning same are fundamental to a proper functioning joint venture.

With all documents executed, due diligence procedures completed, and the preclosing conditions properly consummated, it is time to realize the initial and now imminent objective of the participants: the closing.

10

THE CLOSING PROCESS

10.1 OVERALL VIEW OF THE CLOSING PROCESS

For the entrepreneur, the closing is often considered complete after the company is formed or the acquisition is consummated. At other times, the expression *closing* refers to the payments made. The meaning of the word *closing* is not always precise. However, from an analytical viewpoint, the closing is not finished until all steps prior and subsequent to the formation of the joint venture are realized.

The closing process, therefore, may be defined as the chronological enactment of all conditions expressed in the joint venture agreement relating to the formation or realization of the joint venture and the confirmation of all warranties. The closing is not one act but a series of events that leads to satisfaction of all contractual obligations. If there has been careful draftsmanship, the closing is a reflection of the joint venture documentation. Some of the steps occur more or less simultaneously. Each joint venture will have its individual stamp. However, the general outlines are as follows:

- all investment approvals granted as to the import of capital
- all government consents obtained such as from antitrust authorities or other regulatory bodies
- all necessary operating licenses obtained
- zoning and environmental compliance
- all legal formalities completed in preparation of the constitution of the company or the purchase of the equity interest

- due diligence procedures have been completed to the extent possible
- a certificate from the seller has been delivered to the buyer confirming that all the representations and warranties contained in the joint venture agreement are true and correct as of the date of closing.
- delivery of all actualized financial and legal information, for example, the balance sheet dated a few days prior to date of closing.
- adjustments to the purchase price may be necessary in an acquisition as a result of due diligence procedures revealing more accurately the details of the assets and liabilities of the target company
- counsel to the seller confirms there are no known impediments to the realization of the legal acts being undertaken
- all necessary contracts are signed; all necessary consents to assignments of any contracts are produced
- if we are dealing with an acquisition, written approval of the sale from other equity owners will be evidenced
- capital contributions or payments are made
- legal formalities are performed, such as forming the company before the notary or transfer of shares, as well as other posterior requirements such as publication of the articles in the local newspaper and official gazette
- there is normally convened a general assembly and the election of the board of directors or other management organ is completed
- there may be further due diligence procedures as to warranties extending into a period subsequent to the purchase, for example, promised cash flow for a period of three years

Although these events are probably self-explanatory, some brief comments are in order.

Investment approvals

There can be no closing without the necessary licenses relating to the import of foreign capital, which may be within the competence of the central bank or a ministry of the foreign government. The existence of licenses for import of foreign capital is critical for purposes of exporting currency to the home jurisdiction of the foreign investor. This caveat applies as to forming companies and acquisitions.

In some jurisdictions, approval of the capital investment is with one ministry and any foreign exchange transactions are with another ministry. It may be that in a particular jurisdiction, acquisitions can be made without a license provided the amount of equity purchased does not exceed a specified percentage. However, caution must be used with this criterion since not having government approval to any acquisition may make difficult exports of capital. Although there has been substantial progress made globally in liberalizing foreign exchange markets and permitting free movement of capital, even in countries adopting such unrestricted attitudes, registration may be necessary merely for statistical purposes.

Government consents

Whether forming a company or acquiring an equity interest, prior governmental approval may be required. The most obvious examples are when the proposed transaction may raise questions of antitrust law inasmuch as the acquisition may result in controlling a particular industry. Additionally, certain industries or services require the approval of the appropriate governmental authority. Telecommunications and banking are two obvious categories. Early in negotiations, the issue of what governmental approvals are necessary should be discussed so as to condition the realization of the joint venture on the required permissions being granted.

Operating licenses

The joint venture company most likely will need to be in possession of a variety of licenses if it is engaged in any of the primary industries. Even if the activity is a service company, most jurisdictions require licenses to do a business and the extent and nature of these are dependent on the local authorities.

Zoning and environmental compliance

Of course, where the company will be physically located obligates compliance with the zoning ordinances. Due to the nature of the activity, there may be a wide range of environmental laws requiring either licenses or inspection by the competent authorities.

All legal formalities

If a company is to be formed, beyond the drafting of the articles of the company, it may be necessary to make a deposit of the capital, or a part of it, in a bank. This is a fairly frequent jurisdictional requirement. With the purchase of shares, very little formalities are involved although it is prudent to verify, with counsel, the incidence of any stamp taxes that may become due, or even local stock exchange requirements.

Due diligence procedures

The results of the due diligence procedures must be known. There can be no closing without having the information. It will not be unusual for the material gathered during due diligence procedures to raise questions as to compliance with the joint venture agreement. With joint ventures involving significant amounts of capital and a complex commercial organization, variations from the strict letter of the joint venture agreement are natural. Rather than insist on absolute conformity with the language of the joint venture agreement, the parties should try to encounter a sensible compromise. This will be preferable to a repudiation of the joint venture agreement and litigation.

Certificates

Concerning acquisitions, it is indispensable that a certificate from the seller has been delivered to the buyer confirming that all the representations and warranties contained in the joint venture agreement are true and correct as of the date of closing and any exceptions to such a statement must be detailed. In other words, the buyer wants an affirmative statement as to the terms of the contract being intact and any exceptions to this state of affairs must be set forth as in a schedule. This is the purpose for the extensive recitation of warranties in the joint venture agreement. The seller must come forth and confirm their veracity shortly before the closing or else, voluntarily, denounce any material differences. This will lead either to a renegotiation of the terms of the joint venture or a breach of the joint venture agreement.

Financial and legal information

Part of the due diligence procedures will be obtaining substantial, detailed financial and legal information. The precise nature of what is to be sought has been significantly covered in Chapter Seven when reviewing the general aspects of due diligence procedures.

The results of the financial and legal due diligence procedures are of paramount importance necessitating a profound analysis so as to understand their implications. Unlike legal aspects, the financial details of a target company are a dynamic process that can change from day to day. Of course, from one moment to the next, a major lawsuit may be initiated against the target company a few days prior to the closing. But this is unusual.

What is more customary is that the active aspects of financial details will change. For this reason, it is imperative that financial statements be those of a recent date, in this case, as near as possible to the closing event. As to the legal aspects, for example, ensuring there are no mortgages on the real estate owned by the target company, the same orientation is judicious. Everything is in flux. There is constant change. Nothing can be assumed because it was true three weeks ago.

Adjustments

There may be last-minute changes to the joint venture documentation due to discrepancies in the forecasts. This has relevance to acquisitions when the purchase price may be based on a determined financial ratio or net cash flow. The final determination will only be known shortly before the closing. Such adjustments are natural and a constant feature of joint ventures involving acquisitions.

Opinion of counsel

It is a regular feature of international joint ventures for counsel to the seller in an acquisition to issue a letter confirming there are no known obstacles to the transaction foreseen. The purpose of such a letter is to ensure that the internal corporate regulations of the target company have been satisfied.

The attorney for the purchaser will want the assurance from his colleague that the transaction as stipulated is a legal reality. If shares are being transferred, the opinion letter will state

- that the seller is the sole owner
- that the seller has legal capacity to make the sale
- what is the capital of the company
- what interest the shares represent that are being sold
- whether the transfer will confer the percentage interest being bought
- the shares are not subject to any known encumbrances

A typical opinion letter contains a wide range of topics whose objective is to satisfy the purchaser and his counsel that the asset purchased is the asset described in the joint venture agreement and under the conditions therein expressed. In short, the broad message of the opinion letter from the seller's counsel is that there are no known impediments to the transaction contemplated.

We are not referring only to the consent of the other owners as to the equity interest being sold. This naturally would be covered within the terms of the opinion letter. In any event, separate confirmation of this consent will be prudently acquired.

Complementary contracts

It is usual that the average everyman joint venture, as an integral part, has various contracts with third parties and less frequently, the partners. Often, the objective of the joint venture is to ensure the existence or continuity of such contracts. Indeed, one of the more sensitive areas of competition law in various jurisdictions is when suppliers form joint ventures with wholesalers or retailers. Each stands to benefit as each receives the desired necessary complement to its business.

Whatever have been the contracts stipulated by the joint venture agreement, their execution is fundamental to the success of the joint venture and the signing of same prior to or simultaneously with the closing is as crucial as the closing itself. Securing the validity of such contracts is as important as the tender of the purchase price or the contribution to capital.

If the contracts are already in existence, perhaps one partner intends to transfer a technology license it has to the joint venture company, then the necessary consents to assignments of any contracts must form part of the preclosing documentation. It must never be assumed that the law of the particular jurisdiction permits assignments of contracts without the consent of the other signatories.

Even if the law does permit assignments as a matter of law, when the contract is silent on this issue, it is still sensible to obtain the written approval to the transfer from the original licensor or contract party. This will confirm the contract is valid and there are no alleged breaches that will emerge after the transfer. While the local law may permit assignments, independent of the other's consent, if the contract has no regulating clause, this is no guarantee the contract, vital to the success of the joint venture company, is in vigor.

Transfer of interests to third parties

If we are dealing with an acquisition, written approval of the sale from other equity owners must be obtained when there are restrictions on transfers in the articles of the target company. When the transfer must be done before a public official, then production of such a written consent is a requirement for the deed. If the articles are silent, then the general law will prevail and most likely transfers are permitted without further formalities.

However, similar to assignments of contracts, proceeding on assumptions or even uncontested conclusions as to the consequences of the law does not prevent others from disagreeing. Moreover, the articles of a company will not have any relevance on private contracts.

Although a private contract cannot affect transactions with bona fide purchasers having no knowledge, it is most disagreeable to purchase an equity interest and then be confronted with litigation that claims a right of preference. Since the ordinary everyman joint venture is going to be a closely held company, there is surely going to be necessary collaboration on a day-to-day basis between all owners of equity. This alone merits a potential purchaser from requesting confirmation that the intended purchase is in conformity with the articles of the company nor violates any private agreement.

Capital contributions

With the formation of a company, the law may require prior deposits of part of the capital in a bank or other institution. Whether such a requirement exists cannot detract from what is surely fundamental to the success of the joint venture company. At formation, if subscription is intended to be for all the authorized capital, then the capital should be in existence at a local bank ready to be drawn on by the joint venture company as soon as it comes into existence. Concerning an acquisition, less stress on this aspect is needed since it is usual for a seller to request payment prior to a transfer of interests.

But of course cash may not be the only contribution to the capital. As we have indicated elsewhere, other tangible goods may be used, such as equipment, and then we have the intangible rights, such as copyrights or patents. Since the variety of tangible and intangible goods is enormous, we can conclude with only a general caution: Whatever will be the contribution, its transfer to the joint venture company must be an accomplished fact whose legal confirmation will be the responsibility of counsel.

Legal formalities

What is generally considered the closing is the gathering of the partners at the offices of the official where the company will be formed. A general euphoria exists as months of negotiations and the drafting of documents will culminate in either the formation of a company or the transfer of an equity interest. Among the flurry of papers and the usual requests from the notary for proof of various facts, including the identity of the parties, there begins to be felt the growing drama of the commercial adventure soon to become a reality. Of course, the formal act of the formation of the company is but one of a series of further legal formalities that will be necessary.

The articles of company must be registered at the commercial conservatory. The articles of the company must be published. Notices may be required to various governmental departments.

With the formation of the company, the participants naturally focus on the commercial efforts now required and tend to relegate to the background the bureaucratic requirements attendant on the formation of a company. The administrative tasks may be delegated to a company employee and not given to counsel as part of his responsibilities. Many times, a legal problem arises in posterior years when there has been a lapse of some formality, for example, failure to file confirmation of the registration of the company with the central bank. The issue will surface when the request is made to transfer funds out of the local jurisdiction. As soon as the company is formed, the coordination of all further legal formalities should be established and a checklist drawn up so as to ensure full compliance.

Election of officers

The reigning spirit of launching a new enterprise reaches its climax with the election of a board of directors and the nomination of officers. A company cannot function without its legal representatives. This is normally accomplished by the partners adjourning to the company headquarters and constituting an informal general assembly with the election of the board of directors or other management organ. When all capital is represented, there is no need for formal convocations or other formalities. It will be sufficient if the results of the election and the presence of all capital are duly noted in the minutes of the company. This latter requirement will be achieved by having already purchased the necessary minute book at a local stationery store and having it stamped by any required governmental department, such as the ministry of commerce or ministry of finance.

Posterior due diligence procedures

With the completion of the cycle of negotiations and formations, the joint venture company comes into existence. In acquisitions, due to the joint venture documentation, there may be further due diligence procedures because of warranties extending into a period subsequent to the purchase, for example, promised cash flow for a period of three years. When dealing with closely held companies and when the seller may be an individual, the efficacy of the warranties is directly proportional to the integrity of the seller and his whereabouts.

Although apparently a minor detail, the joint venture documentation will have indicated the location of his legal residence. This will be indispensable should legal procedures arise because of a failure of postclosing warranties. It is also circumspect to have as many details concerning the personal facts of the seller as possible without creating a sinister atmosphere of distrust. Such information will have been gathered prior to the formalities of the acquisition.

10.2 CONCLUSION

The process to the formation of an international joint venture is lengthy and complex. The closing represents the realization of enormous effort and cooperation among executives and professionals with considerable competence and knowledge. As with other events in life, there may appear a sudden, generalized lethargy after the formation of the company. There was so much preparation to do and now it has all been completed. To continue with the analogy, such spirits will improve. The future will demand the complete absorption of the founders. The international joint venture has been born.

SELECT BIBLIOGRAPHY

American Bar Association. *Globalization of Capital, Financial and Commercial Markets, Section of International Law and Practice*. Chicago: Section of International Law and Practice, 1995.

American Bar Association. *How to Conduct a Cross-Border Merger and Acquisition/Financing Due Diligence in Multiple Jurisdictions (Including Working with Foreign Counsel)*. Chicago: Section of International Law and Practice, 1995.

American Bar Association. *How to Draft an International Joint Venture Agreement*. Chicago: Section of International Law and Practice, 1993.

American Bar Association. *How to Negotiate an International Joint Venture*. Chicago: Section of International Law and Practice, 1996.

American Bar Association. *How to Structure and Document Cross-Border Privately Negotiated Mergers and Acquisitions*. Chicago: Section of International Law and Practice, 1995.

American Bar Association. *International Joint Ventures, A Practical Approach to Working with Foreign Investors in the U.S. and Abroad*, David N. Goldsweig and Roger H. Cummings, eds. Chicago: Section of International Law and Practice, 1990.

American Bar Association. *Negotiating and Structuring International Commercial Transactions,* Shelly P. Battram and David N. Goldsweig, eds. Chicago: Section of International Law and Practice, 1991.

Antunes, José Manuel Oliveira, and José Antonio Costa Manso. *Relacoes Internacionais e Transferencia de Tecnologia*. Coimbra, Portugal: Almedina, 1993.

Auerbach, Alan J. *Mergers and Acquisitions*. Chicago: University of Chicago Press, 1988.

Barbi, Celso Filho. *Acordo de Acionistas*. Belo Horizonte, Brazil: Del Rey Editora, 1993.

Bellamy, Christopher, and Graham Child. *Common Market Law of Competition*, 4th ed., Vivien Rose, ed. London: Sweet and Maxwell, 1993.

BenDaniel, David J., and Arthur H. Rosenbloom. *International M & A, Joint Ventures and Beyond, Doing the Deal*. New York: John Wiley and Sons, 1998.

Byttebier, K., and A. Verroken. *Structuring International Co-operation between Enterprises*. London, England, and Norwell, MA: Graham and Trotman/Martin Nijhoff, 1995.

Coelho, Eduardo de Melo Lucas. *Direito de Voto dos Accionistas*. Lisbon, Portugal: Rei dos Livros, 1987.

Compton, Charles T. "Changing U.S. View of Joint Ventures." *International Business Lawyer* 26, no. 3 (1998): 97–144.

Fine, Frank L. *Mergers and Joint Ventures in Europe*, 2nd ed. London: Kluwer Law International, 1994.

Fridson, Martin S. *Financial Statement Analysis*, 2nd ed., University ed. New York: John Wiley and Sons, 1996.

International Bar Association. *Due Diligence, Disclosures and Warranties in the Corporate Acquisitions Practice*. London: Graham and Trotman, 1988.

Korah, Valentine. *An Introductory Guide to EC Competition Law and Practice*, 5th ed. London: Sweet and Maxwell, 1994.

Maeijer, J. M. M., and K. Geens. *Defensive Measures Against Hostile Takeovers in the Common Market*. Dordrecht, The Netherlands: Martinus Nijhoff, 1990.

O'Neal, F. Hodge, and Robert B. Thompson. *O'Neal's Oppression of Minority Shareholders*, 2nd ed. Eagan, MN: West Group, 1998.

Practising Law Institute (Chair, Joseph McLaughlin). *Conducting Due Diligence*. New York, 1998.

Practising Law Institute (Chair, Alfred J. Ross, Jr.). *International Joint Ventures*. New York, 1998.

Steadman, Graham, and Janet Jones. *Shareholders' Agreements*. London: Longman Group, 1989.

Ventura, Raul. *Estudos Varios sobre Sociedades Anonimas*. Coimbra, Portugal: Almedina, 1992.

Walmsley, John. *Handbook of International Joint Ventures*. London: Graham and Trotman, 1982.

Whalley, Michael, and Thomas Heyman, eds. *International Business Acquisitions, Major Legal Issues and Due Diligence*. London: Kluwer Law International, 1996.

Wolf, Ronald Charles. *A Guide to International Joint Ventures with Sample Clauses*, 2nd ed. London: Kluwer Law International, 1999.

INDEX

ABOUT THE AUTHOR

Ronald Charles Wolf is an American attorney with forty-three years of law experience. For the past thirty years he has been based in Portugal, where he has advised a wide variety of transnational corporations wishing to do business there. In addition, he is the author of numerous books and articles on the subjects of mergers, acquisitions, and international joint ventures, including the much-acclaimed *A Guide to International Joint Ventures* (1995, 1999).